GALLINAZO:
AN EARLY CULTURAL TRADITION ON THE PERUVIAN NORTH COAST

UCLA COTSEN INSTITUTE OF ARCHAEOLOGY PRESS
MONOGRAPHS
CONTRIBUTIONS IN FIELD RESEARCH AND CURRENT ISSUES IN ARCHAEOLOGICAL METHOD AND THEORY

Monograph 66 *Gallinazo: An Early Cultural Tradition on the Peruvian North Coast*, Jean-François Millaire (ed.), with Magali Morlion

Monograph 65 *Settlement and Subsistence in Early Formative Soconusco: El Varal and the Problem of Inter-Site Assemblage Variation*, Richard Lesure (ed.)

Monograph 64 *The South American Camelids*, Duccio Bonavia

Monograph 63 *Andean Civilization: A Tribute to Michael E. Moseley*, Joyce Marcus and Patrick Ryan Williams (eds.)

Monograph 62 *Excavations at Cerro Azul, Peru: The Architecture and Pottery*, Joyce Marcus

Monograph 61 *Chavín: Art, Architecture and Culture*, William J Conklin and Jeffrey Quilter (eds.)

Monograph 60 *Rethinking Mycenaean Palaces II: Revised and Expanded Second Edition*, Michael L. Galaty and William A. Parkinson (eds.)

Monograph 59 *Moche Tombs at Dos Cabezas*, Christopher B. Donnan

Monograph 58 *Moche Fineline Painting From San José de Moro*, Donna McClelland, Donald McClelland, and Christopher B. Donnan

Monograph 57 *Kasapata and the Archaic Period of the Cuzco Valley*, Brian S. Bauer (ed.)

Monograph 56 *Berenike 1999/2000*, Steven E. Sidebotham and Willeke Wendrich (eds.)

Monograph 55 *Roman Footprints at Berenike: Archaeobotanical Evidence of Subsistence and Trade in the Eastern Desert of Egypt*, René T. J. Cappers

Monograph 54 *Advances in Titicaca Basin Archaeology 1*, Charles Stanish, Amanda B. Cohen, and Mark S. Aldenderfer

Monograph 53 *Us and Them: Archaeology and Ethnicity in the Andes*, Richard Martin Reycraft

Monograph 52 *Archaeological Research on the Islands of the Sun and Moon, Lake Titicaca, Bolivia: Final Results from the Proyecto Tiksi Kjarka*, Charles Stanish and Brian S. Bauer (eds.)

Monograph 51 *Maya Zooarchaeology: New Directions in Theory and Method*, Kitty F. Emery (ed.)

Monograph 50 *Settlement Archaeology and Political Economy at Tres Zapotes, Veracruz, Mexico*, Christopher A. Pool (ed.)

Monograph 49 *Perspectives on Ancient Maya Rural Complexity*, Gyles Iannone and Samuel V. Connell (eds.)

Monograph 48 *Yeki bud, yeki nabud: Essays on the Archaeology of Iran in Honor of William M. Sumner*, Naomi F. Miller and Kamyar Abdi (eds.)

Monograph 47 *Archaeology in the Borderlands: Investigation in Caucasia and Beyond*, Adam T. Smith and Karen S. Rubinson (eds.)

Monograph 46 *Domestic Ritual in Ancient Mesoamerica*, Patricia Plunket (ed.)

Monograph 45 *Pathways to Prismatic Blades*, Kenneth Hirth and Bradford Andrews (eds.)

Monograph 44 *Ceramic Production and Circulation in the Greater Southwest*, Donna M. Glowacki and Hector Neff (eds.)

Monograph 43 *Pottery of Postclassic Cholula, Mexico*, Geoffrey McCafferty

Monograph 42 *Pompeian Households: An Analysis of the Material Culture*, Penelope M. Allison

Monograph 41 *Rethinking Mycenaean Palaces: New Interpretations of an Old Idea*, Michael L. Galaty and William A. Parkinson (eds.)

Monograph 40 *Prehistory of Agriculture: New Experimental and Ethnographic Approaches*, Patricia C. Anderson (ed.)

Monograph 39 *Recent Advances in the Archaeology of the Northern Andes: In Memory of Gerardo Reichel-Dolmatoff*, Augusto Oyuela-Caycedo and J. Scott Raymond (eds.)

Monograph 38 *Approaches to the Historical Archaeology of Mexico, Central and South America*, Janine Gasco, Greg Charles Smith, and Patricia Fournier-Garcia

Monograph 37 *Hawaiian Adze Production and Distribution: Implications for the Development of Chiefdoms*, Barbara Lass

Monograph 36 *New Light on Old Art: Recent Advances in Hunter-Gatherer Rock Art Research*, D. W. Whitley and L. L. Loendorf (eds.)

Monograph 35 *Pottery of Prehistoric Honduras: Regional Classification and Analysis*, J. S. Henderson and M. Beaudry-Corbett

Monograph 34 *Settlement Archaeology of Cerro de las Mesas, Veracruz, Mexico*, Barbara Stark (ed.)

Monograph 33 *Girikihaciyan: A Halafian Site in Southeastern Turkey*, P. J. Watson and S. LeBlanc

Monograph 32 *Western Pomo Prehistory: Excavations at Albion Head, Nightbirds' Retreat and Three Chop Village, Mendocino County, California*, Thomas N. Layton

Monograph 31 *Investigaciones Arqueológicos de la Costa Sur de Guatemala*, David S. Whitley and Marilyn P. Beaudry (eds.)

Monograph 30 *Archaeology of the Three Springs Valley, California: A Study in Functional Cultural History*, Brian D. Dillon and Matthew A. Boxt

Monograph 29 *Obsidian Dates IV: A Compendium of Obsidian Hydration Readings from the UCLA Obsidian Hydration Laboratory*, Clement W. Meighan and Janet L. Scalise (eds.)

Monograph 28 *Archaeological Field Research in the Upper Mantaro, Peru, 1982–1983: Investigations of Inka Expansion and Exchange*, Timothy Earle et al. (eds.)

Monograph 27 *Andean Archaeology: Papers in Memory of Clifford Evans*, Ramiro Matos M., Solveig Turpin, and Herbert Eling, Jr. (eds.)

Monograph 26 *Excavations at Mission San Antonio 1976–1978*, Robert L. Hoover and Julio J. Costello (eds.)

Monograph 25 *Prehistoric Production and Exchange in the Aegean and Eastern Mediterranean*, A. Bernard Knapp and Tamara Stech (eds.)

Monograph 24 *Pots and Potters: Current Approaches in Ceramic Archaeology*, Prudence Rice

Monograph 23 *Pictographs and Petroglyphs of the Oregon Country, Part 2*, J. Malcolm Loring and Louise Loring

Monograph 22 *The Archaeology of Two Northern California Sites*, Delmer E. Sanburg, F. K. Mulligan, Joseph Chartkoff, and Kerry Chartkoff

Monograph 21 *Pictographs and Petroglyphs of the Oregon Country, Part 1*, J. Malcolm Loring and Louise Loring

Monograph 20 *Messages from the Past: Studies in California Rock Art*, Clement W. Meighan (ed.)

Monograph 19 *Prehistoric Indian Rock Art: Issues and Concerns*, JoAnne Van Tilburg and Clement W. Meighan (eds.)

Monograph 18 *Studies in Cypriote Archaeology*, Jane C. Biers and David Soren

Monograph 17 *Excavations in Northern Belize, Central America*, Raymond Sidrys

Monograph 16 *Obsidian Dates III: A Compendium of Obsidian Hydration Determinations Made at the UCLA Obsidian Hydration Laboratory*, Clement Meighan and Glenn Russell

Monograph 15 *Inland Chumash Archaeological Investigations*, David S. Whitley, E. L. McCann, and C. W. Clewlow, Jr. (eds.)

Monograph 14 *Papers in Cycladic Prehistory*, Jack L. Davis and John F. Cherry (eds.)

Monograph 13 *Archaeological Investigations at the Ring Brothers Site Complex, Thousand Oaks, California*, C. W. Clewlow, Jr., David S. Whitley and Ellen L. McCann (eds.)

Monograph 12 *The Running Springs Ranch Site: Archaeological Investigations at VEN-65 and VEN-261*, Jack Prichett and Allen McIntyre

Monograph 11 *The Archaeology of Oak Park, Ventura County, California*, C. William Clewlow, Jr. and David S. Whitley (eds.)

Monograph 10 *Rock Art of East Mexico and Central America: An Annotated Bibliography*, Matthias Strecker

Monograph 9 *The Late Minoan I Destruction of Crete: Metal Groups and Stratigraphic Considerations*, Hara Georgiou

Monograph 8 *Papers on the Economy and Architecture of the Ancient Maya*, Raymond Sidrys

Monograph 7 *History and Prehistory at Grass Valley, Nevada*, C. W. Clewlow, Jr., Helen F. Wells, and Richard Ambro (eds.)

Monograph 6 *Obsidian Dates II: A Compendium of Obsidian Hydration Determinations Made at the UCLA Obsidian Hydration Laboratory*, C. W. Meighan and P. I. Vanderhoeven (eds.)

Monograph 5 *The Archaeology of Oak Park, Ventura County, California*, C. W. Clewlow, Jr., Allen Pastron, and Helen F. Wells (eds.)

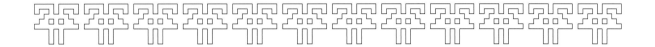

GALLINAZO:
AN EARLY CULTURAL TRADITION
ON THE PERUVIAN NORTH COAST

EDITED BY

JEAN-FRANÇOIS MILLAIRE
WITH MAGALI MORLION

COTSEN INSTITUTE OF ARCHAEOLOGY PRESS
UNIVERSITY OF CALIFORNIA, LOS ANGELES
2009

THE COTSEN INSTITUTE OF ARCHAEOLOGY PRESS is the publishing unit of the Cotsen Institute of Archaeology at UCLA. The Cotsen Institute is a premier research organization dedicated to the creation, dissemination, and conservation of archaeological knowledge and heritage. It is home to both the Interdepartmental Archaeology Graduate Program and the UCLA/ Getty Master's Program in the Conservation of Archaeological and Ethnographic Materials. The Cotsen Institute provides a forum for innovative faculty research, graduate education, and public programs at UCLA in an effort to positively impact the academic, local and global communities. Established in 1973, the Cotsen Institute is at the forefront of archaeological research, education, conservation and publication and is an active contributor to interdisciplinary research at UCLA.

The Cotsen Institute Press specializes in producing high-quality academic volumes in several different series, including Monographs, World Heritage and Monuments, Cotsen Advanced Seminars, and Ideas, Debates and Perspectives. The Press is committed to making the fruits of archaeological research accessible to professionals, scholars, students, and the general public. We are able to do this through the generosity of Lloyd E. Cotsen, longtime Institute volunteer and benefactor, who has provided an endowment that allows us to subsidize our publishing program and produce superb volumes at an affordable price. Publishing in nine different series, our award-winning archaeological publications receive critical acclaim in both the academic and popular communities.

This book is set in Janson Text
Editing, production, and cover design by Leyba Associates, Santa Fe, New Mexico
Index by Robert and Cynthia Swanson

Library of Congress Cataloging-in-Publication Data

Gallinazo : an early cultural tradition on the Peruvian north coast / edited by Jean-Francois Millaire with Magali Morlion. — 1st ed.
        p. cm. — (Monograph ; 66)
    Papers from a roundtable held in Trujillo, Peru in August 2005.
    Includes bibliographical references and index.
    ISBN 978-1-931745-74-1 (trade cloth : alk. paper) —
    ISBN 978-1-931745-75-8 (trade paper : alk. paper)
1. Indians of South America—Peru—Pacific Coast—Antiquities—Congresses. 2. Indian pottery—Peru—Pacific Coast—Congresses. 3. Pottery, Prehistoric—Peru—Pacific Coast—Congresses. 4. Mochica pottery—Congresses. 5. Excavations (Archaeology)—Peru—Pacific Coast—Congresses. 6. Indians of South America—Peru—Pacific Coast—Ethnic identity—Congresses. 7. Social archaeology—Peru—Pacific Coast—Congresses. 8. Ethnoarchaeology—Peru—Pacific Coast—Congresses. 9. Pacific Coast (Peru)—Antiquities—Congresses. I. Millaire, Jean-François. II. Morlion, Magali. III. Series.

F3429.1.P22G35 2009
986.6'301—dc22

                                                        2009028988

Cover photo: Gallinazo face-neck jar, courtesy of Museo Larco, Lima, Peru, ML016251.

CONTENTS

LIST OF ILLUSTRATIONS

LIST OF TABLES

To the memory of Bruce G. Trigger and his fascination with the past.

ABOUT THE EDITORS

Jean-François Millaire is Assistant Professor at The University of Western Ontario and Research Associate at the American Museum of Natural History. His work focuses on early statecraft in the Andean region, and touches on issues of identity, mobility, and cultural history. He is the author of *Moche Burial Patterns: An Investigation into Prehispanic Social Structure* (2002) and has recently initiated a long-term field program at the Gallinazo Group site in the Virú Valley, Peru.

Magali Morlion is an archaeologist who has collaborated with Jean-François Millaire on numerous excavations in Peru and is currently Research Associate in the Virú Polity Project. She was Assistant Editor for the *Guide to Documentary Sources for Andean Studies 1530–1900*, edited by Joanne Pillsbury (2008). Her research interests include pre-Hispanic household rituals and textile technology.

CONTRIBUTORS

Christopher J. Attarian
Baker College of Owosso

Richard A. Busch
Department of Anthropology
University of Denver

Luis Jaime Castillo Butters
Departamento de Humanidades
Pontificia Universidad Católica del Perú

Claude Chapdelaine
Département d'anthropologie
Université de Montréal

Martín del Carpio Perla
Proyecto Arqueológico San José de Moro
Pontificia Universidad Católica del Perú

Christopher B. Donnan
Department of Anthropology
University of California at Los Angeles

Régulo G. Franco Jordán
Fundación Augusto N. Wiese

Gérard Gagné
Département d'anthropologie
Université de Montréal

Catherine M. Gaither
Department of Sociology, Anthropology and
Behavioral Science
Metropolitan State College of Denver

César A. Gálvez Mora
Instituto Nacional de Cultura – La Libertad

Nadia Gamarra Carranza
Proyecto Arqueológico Huaca de la Luna
Universidad Nacional de Trujillo

Jorge Gamboa
Proyecto Valle del Santa
Université de Montréal

Henry Gayoso Rullier
Proyecto Arqueológico Huaca de la Luna
Universidad Nacional de Trujillo

Peter Kaulicke
Departamento de Humanidades
Pontificia Universidad Católica del Perú

Jonathan D. Kent
Department of Sociology, Anthropology and
Behavioral Science
Metropolitan State College of Denver

Krzysztof Makowski
Departamento de Humanidades
Pontificia Universidad Católica del Perú

Jean-François Millaire
Department of Anthropology
The University of Western Ontario

Víctor Pimentel
Proyecto Valle del Santa
Université de Montréal

Teresa Rosales Tham
Facultad de Ciencias Sociales
Universidad Nacional de Trujillo

Richard C. Sutter
Department of Anthropology
Indiana University–Purdue University Fort
Wayne

Santiago Uceda Castillo
Facultad de Ciencias Sociales
Universidad Nacional de Trujillo

Víctor Vásquez Sánchez
Facultad de Ciencias Sociales
Universidad Nacional de Trujillo

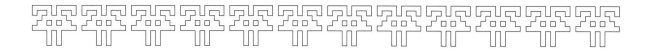

ACKNOWLEDGMENTS

The project of organizing a roundtable on Gallinazo was born in Lima while talking to colleagues at Dumbarton Oaks' conference on Moche political organization, hosted by the Museo Rafael Larco Herrera and the Pontificia Universidad Católica del Perú. I am therefore indebted to Jeffrey Quilter, Andrés Álvarez Calderón de Larco, and Luis Jaime Castillo for inviting me to take part in that stimulating event. In Montreal, the project of revisiting north-coast cultural history was received with great enthusiasm by the faculty and staff of the Department of Anthropology at McGill University, and I would like to thank Rose Marie Stano and John Galaty for their support. My deepest gratitude also goes to the late Bruce G. Trigger, whose excitement at seeing me revisiting north-coast cultural history was (and is) a constant encouragement.

The roundtable was organized while I was a Fellow in Pre-Columbian studies at Dumbarton Oaks, and I wish to thank Jeffrey Quilter, Joanne Pillsbury, Juan Antonio Murro, and Bridget Gazzo for their counsel. The meeting was held at the Hotel Libertador in Trujillo, thanks to the financial support of the Barrick Gold Corporation, Monterrico Metals Plc., Gittennes Exploration Inc., and the Faculty of Arts at McGill University. The success of this gathering was largely due to the professionalism of Edith Márquez Bustamante, Guadalupe Quispe Ihue, and Ruth Pacheco Ortiz.

I am grateful to all of those who took part in this meeting. My warmest thanks go to those who have contributed to the present volume: Christopher Attarian, Richard Busch, Luis Jaime Castillo, Claude Chapdelaine, Martín del Carpio, Christopher Donnan, Régulo Franco, Gérard Gagné, Catherine Gaither, César Gálvez, Nadia Gamarra, Jorge Gamboa, Henry Gayoso, Peter Kaulicke, Jonathan Kent, Krzysztof Makowski, Víctor Pimentel, Teresa Rosales, Richard Sutter, Santiago Uceda, and Víctor Vásquez. Thanks to Delia Aponte, Brian Billman, James Kenworthy, Adriana Maguiña, Delicia Regalado, Jennifer Ringberg, and Lucy Salazar for presenting in Trujillo— although they could not submit written versions of their papers.

I also wish to thank Elizabeth Benson, Richard Burger, and Jeffrey Quilter, who acted as moderators during the meeting. As always, I am also grateful to Patricia Quilcate and Estuardo La Torre for their hospitality and their help. Finally, I would like to thank Claude Chapdelaine and Christopher Donnan for encouraging me to organize this event and to act as the editor of the present volume.

The present work was prepared over a period of three years with the financial support of the Fonds Québécois de Recherche sur la Société et la Culture, the Social Sciences and Humanities Research Council of Canada, Dumbarton Oaks Research Library and Collection, and The University of Western Ontario. I am also grateful for the editorial input of the staff at the Cotsen Institute of Archaeology Press and at Leyba Associates.

This volume was edited in collaboration with Magali Morlion, whose editorial skills, patience, meticulousness, and dedication to the project were vital in making sure it saw the light—safe and sound. *Pour cette raison et pour son infaillible soutien, je tiens à lui dire merci; seuls elle et moi savons combien son appui m'a été précieux.*

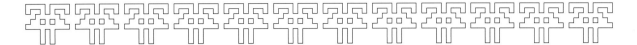

CHAPTER 1

GALLINAZO AND THE
TRADICIÓN NORCOSTEÑA

Jean-François Millaire

The roundtable on Gallinazo held in Trujillo in August 2005 was a natural follow-on from the Lima conference on Moche political organization held the previous year by Dumbarton Oaks, the Museo Rafael Larco Herrera, and the Pontificia Universidad Católica del Perú. Indeed, after this gathering it was clear to most participants that any further discussion of Moche geopolitics, social organization, and history was impaired by our lack of understanding of the wider cultural framework in which Moche art and architecture developed approximately 2,000 years ago (Figure 1.1). This does not diminish the few existing publications that focus on Vicús, Salinar, and Gallinazo. The group's realization simply highlighted the fact that vast sections of Peru's north-coast cultural history were until then neglected as a result of our fascination with Moche art and architecture.

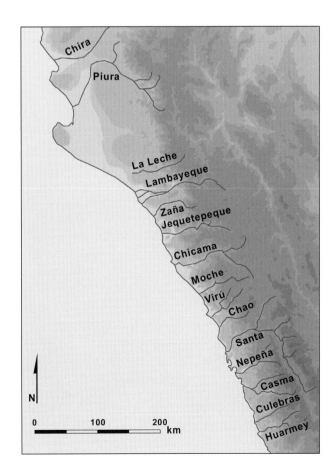

FIGURE 1.1. Map of the north coast of Peru.

1

In this introductory chapter, my intention is to set the stage by briefly presenting the research paradigm in which a majority of scholars have worked over the last 80 years (a paradigm in which ceramics held the status of cultural marker *par excellence*) and by describing an emerging model for understanding this region's rich cultural history. According to this model, the north coast was home to a number of culturally related societies that lived in similar environments, evolved within comparable settlement systems, shared analogous political and social structures, and produced material culture that emphasized their common cultural origin. The ceramic expression of this shared culture is what Andeanists have conventionally recognized as *Gallinazo* ceramics (Figure 1.2).

Instead of a marker of political affiliation (as it has traditionally been described), utilitarian ceramics of Gallinazo style are herein described as the product of a shared artistic tradition: the *tradición norcosteña*. In this context, Vicús (Figure 1.3), Moche (Figure 1.4), and Virú (Figure 1.5) ceramics

FIGURE 1.2. Gallinazo face-neck jar from Castillo de Tomaval. *Illustration courtesy of Museo Larco, Lima, Peru, ML018016.*

FIGURE 1.3. Vicús ceramic vessel. *Illustration courtesy of Museo Larco, Lima, Peru, ML004435.*

FIGURE 1.4. Moche stirrup-spout bottle.
Illustration courtesy of Museo Larco, Lima, Peru, ML002335.

FIGURE 1.5. Virú (Gallinazo Negative) ceramic vessel. *Illustration courtesy of Museo Larco, Lima, Peru, ML018888.*

represent fine wares produced by individual polities to emphasize their distinctiveness in relation to other ethnically related neighboring groups. This new model obviously emphasizes the complexity of north-coast cultural history, and more accurately depicts the rich cultural mosaic that characterized this area prior to the arrival of Spanish troops in 1532.

AN ENDURING PARADIGM

Students of Andean studies have traditionally been presented with a survey of north-coast archaeology that features the emergence of the Moche during the Early Intermediate period, an early civilization believed to have flourished amid a cultural landscape consisting of "lesser-developed societies." In the last half century, a substantial amount of work has therefore been directed toward identifying what was unique to the Moche (i.e., what this people possessed that others lacked).

Sustaining this scenario was the strong belief that the Moche represented a distinct society that defined itself in relation to other coastal groups. In this context, societies that did not produce Moche-style ceramics were presented as earlier residents or as competing factions hardly worth studying. This enduring paradigm originated from the seminal work of Rafael Larco Hoyle and Wendell Bennett on the phenomenon they respectively called the "Virú" and "Gallinazo" culture.

In 1933, Larco Hoyle recognized a previously undefined archaeological culture while conducting excavations in the Moche Valley, a culture he named "Cultura negativa" on the basis of the negative-resist decorated ceramics he had found (Larco Hoyle 1945:1). Later, while conducting excavations at the site of Castillo de Tomaval in the Virú Valley (Figures 1.6, 1.7), this pioneer of Andean archaeology found burials that contained vessels decorated with negative painting (Figure 1.8), which he characterized (following a commonplace tradition of naming archaeological units according to the location where they were first identified or had flourished) as the quintessential attribute of the "Virú" culture. At Castillo de Tomaval, Larco Hoyle found those burials to be stratigraphically lower (and hence earlier) than graves furnished with Moche-style artifacts (Larco Hoyle 1945). From then on, Virú and Moche were presented as two successive phases in the local cultural sequence. Implicit was the idea that the Virú culture had developed in this area until the Moche flourished, triggering Virú decline.

Research conducted by Bennett largely confirmed Larco Hoyle's work (Bennett 1939, 1950). In 1936, this scholar undertook work on a cluster of platforms in the lower Virú Valley: a settlement he named the Gallinazo Group (Figures 1.6, 1.9). Excavations led to the identification of several types of ceramic vessels, two of which became quintessential features of Gallinazo materiality: fine negative-resist ceramics referred to as Gallinazo Negative ware (the negative-resist decorated ceramics identified by Larco Hoyle) and utilitarian containers decorated with incisions and appliqué (respectively named Castillo Incised and Castillo Modeled wares, which could collectively be simply referred to as Castillo Decorated ceramics; Figure 1.10).

Notwithstanding the quality of Bennett's publications, they actually marked the beginning of 80 years of misunderstanding, a phenomenon Christopher Donnan argues resulted in a "Gallinazo illusion" (see Chapter 2). Indeed, the inclusion of utilitarian wares as defining features of the Gallinazo culture (Larco Hoyle's Cultura virú) led to the treatment of these containers as physical evidence of the presence, spread, and decline of an ancient people who may never have existed in such an incarnation.

Bennett's work was only the beginning of a very fertile period of research in Virú. During the 1930s and 1940s, several archaeologists undertook fieldwork as part of the Virú Valley Project. From this program, one study stood out: Gordon Willey's (1953) *Prehistoric Settlement Patterns*. It revolutionized the field, giving birth to regional analysis in archaeology. Extensive surveys led Willey to document several settlements that featured both Gallinazo Negative and Castillo Decorated wares. In this and other publications, the Gallinazo and Moche cultures came to be presented as two distinct societies that had successively occupied the coast. This was possibly the result of what Garth Bawden defines as "the traditional need for archaeologists to equate art styles with distinct human groups, and to order them in neat evolutionary sequences" (Bawden 2004:121).

In this context, archaeologists believed that the development of Gallinazo society had been abruptly interrupted by the Moche military conquest of the coast during the first centuries of the present era. Willey and colleagues argued that Moche war leaders had challenged the Gallinazo political system by taking control of local administrative centers (Willey 1953). This was particularly evident in the sudden increase of Moche-like artifacts in settlements that featured Gallinazo Negative or Castillo Decorated ceramics. Moche society was thus presented as a polity that had grown into a multi-valley state after having conquered ethnic "Gallinazo" populations, a thesis still widely accepted today.

During the following decades, research everywhere along the littoral continually seemed to confirm this paradigm. Indeed, most Moche settlements (villages or cities where Moche art and architecture had flourished) also feature utilitarian Gallinazo-style ceramics, especially the typical Gallinazo face-neck jar (Figure 1.11). These vessels were typically interpreted as the remnants of an early Gallinazo occupation predating the establishment of a single Moche state, or as the development of two (northern and southern) or more autonomous Moche states.

Noteworthy in this light is Heidy Fogel's (1993) study of Gallinazo-style ceramics from

FIGURE 1.6. Satellite view of Virú Valley. *Illustration courtesy of NASA Landsat Program 2000, Landsat ETM+ scene ELP009R066_7T20000602, SLC-Off, USGS, Sioux Falls.*

FIGURE 1.7. Castillo de Tomaval.

FIGURE 1.8. Virú face-neck jar from Castillo de Tomaval.
Illustration courtesy of Museo Larco, Lima, Peru, ML010467.

FIGURE 1.9. The Gallinazo Group.

FIGURE 1.10. Castillo Decorated face-neck jar.
Illustration courtesy of Museo Larco, Lima, Peru, ML016110.

archaeological contexts in the Virú and neighboring valleys, an investigation she was sadly never able to pursue further. Fogel argued that after having consolidated their power in the Virú Valley, Gallinazo leaders had extended their control over other oases, therein constructing the first multi-valley state in the Andean region, a thesis that found very little support in subsequent years.

Not everyone had conducted research with this paradigm in mind, however. As early as 1957, Heinrich Ubbelohde-Doering expressed doubts on the idea that Gallinazo and Moche represented distinct cultural entities (Ubbelohde-Doering 1957). While conducting fieldwork at the site of Pacatnamú, Ubbelohde-Doering uncovered burials that contained fine Moche vessels as well as utilitarian ceramics of Gallinazo style, suggesting that the two archaeological cultures were contemporaneous and possibly more closely related than was generally thought. Similarly, Peter Kaulicke (1992) raised the fundamental possibility that the Vicús, Salinar, Gallinazo, and Moche cultures actually represented divergent stylistic manifestations of largely contemporaneous north-coast peoples. Finally, in a key article, Izumi Shimada and Adriana Maguiña offered new insights into the position of Gallinazo within north-coast cultural history (Shimada and Maguiña 1994).

FIGURE 1.11. Gallinazo face-neck jar. *Illustration courtesy of Museo Larco, Lima, Peru, ML016251.*

Criticizing the currently accepted model, they presented evidence indicating that Gallinazo and Moche communities were not successive occupants of the coastal environment but had lived side by side, competing for the same resources throughout the Early Intermediate period. Even more important was their insight that the duration of this cohabitation between the producers and users of Moche- and Gallinazo-style ceramics differed from one valley to another. Even though it is now clear that some of their conclusions were incorrect, this article nevertheless marked a turning point in Gallinazo studies.

These authors and other scholars (e.g., Castillo 2001; Bawden 2004) encouraged archaeologists to answer a fundamental question: How closely related were the producers and users of Gallinazo- and Moche-style ceramics found within the same site or valley? Were they ethnically distinct peoples fighting for control of land and people (as was recently the case with the Tutsis and Hutus in Rwanda)? Did they represent linguistically distinct formations evolving in parallel (as is somehow the case of Francophones and Anglophones in Canada today)? Could it be that they were actually part of the same political entities? Such questions clearly called for a major reevaluation of the nature of Gallinazo and Moche archaeological cultures, as well as a reflection on the usefulness of ceramics as a source of evidence for reconstructing north-coast cultural history.

NEW WORK IN VIRÚ

The types of questions previously cited were central to recent investigations conducted in the Virú Valley, first at the site of Huancaco by Steve Bourget and later at Huaca Santa Clara by Jean-

François Millaire in collaboration with Estuardo LaTorre and Jeisen Navarro. Huaca Santa Clara is a settlement that was believed by members of the Virú Valley Project to have functioned as a Gallinazo civic center until it fell under Moche rule (Willey 1953). It therefore represented a perfect locus for testing the currently accepted scenario of a Moche conquest of the coast in about the fourth century of the present era.

Huaca Santa Clara is located in the middle valley, south of the Virú River. The site consists of a series of adobe platforms, built on the flanks of a small hill that dominates the landscape near the present-day village of Virú (Figure 1.12). The discovery of residences near the hilltop, accessible only through a complex system of baffled entrances, and the presence of a system of large-scale storage facilities for agricultural products together confirm that the settlement functioned as a local administrative center (Figure 1.13; Millaire 2004a). Throughout the excavation process, quantities of utilitarian ceramics of Gallinazo style (Castillo Incised and Modeled types) were uncovered (Figure 1.14), as well as typical Gallinazo Negative containers (Figure 1.15). A radiocarbon dating program—which included dates taken from deep stratified deposits as well as from rooms located near the present surface of the site—revealed that the site was occupied between approximately 10 B.C. and A.D. 670 (see Chapter 9).

Excavations at Huaca Santa Clara failed to produce evidence that the area had fallen under the direct control of Moche war leaders. Indeed, we found no trace of the massive destruction associated with military conquest, nor did we see any decline or alteration of the local material culture, a phenomenon that would inevitably have accompanied such a major sociopolitical change. Toward the end of the Early Intermediate period, however, Moche stylistic influence became prominent throughout the valley in the form of ceramics of Huancaco style (Willey 1953; Bourget 2004).

This ceramic type—previously described as a Moche fine ware that had traveled south with conquering troops—is essentially a Moche-like ware probably produced in Virú by Virú ceramists (Bourget 2004). If there was political change, the present evidence seems to suggest that it happened with the concord of local leaders. In this context, the emergence of the Huancaco style might represent an example of what Bawden defines as an "ideological adjustment" to the

FIGURE 1.12. Huaca Santa Clara on Cerro Cementerio.

0   25   50   100 m

FIGURE 1.13. Archaeological plan of Huaca Santa Clara.

spread of the Moche phenomenon (Bawden 1995) or as the material result of the "art of Moche politics" (Bawden 2004).

These results led me to argue that the region was likely never conquered by a multi-valley Moche state, although the region was certainly affected by endemic competition between dominant city-states (Millaire 2004a). I also posited that north-coast communities likely lived in city-state–like polities, scattered over the territory to take full advantage of resources. Although some valleys may have hosted only one regional polity, other areas were apparently more fragmented politically. Finally, I argued that the littoral would have hosted not two ethnically distinct social for-

mations, but several polities of common cultural origin.

Thus, the presence of Moche-style material culture along the littoral could be interpreted as the result of the hegemonic policy of a confederation of Moche city-states (e.g., an alliance between Huacas de Moche and the El Brujo Complex). The situation was different from one valley to another, however, as is clear from the work of Claude Chapdelaine and his team in the Santa Valley (see Chapter 11).

In addition to gathering a wealth of data on the Virú polity, our field research produced results that led us to investigate wider issues of north-coast cultural history. One such issue had to do

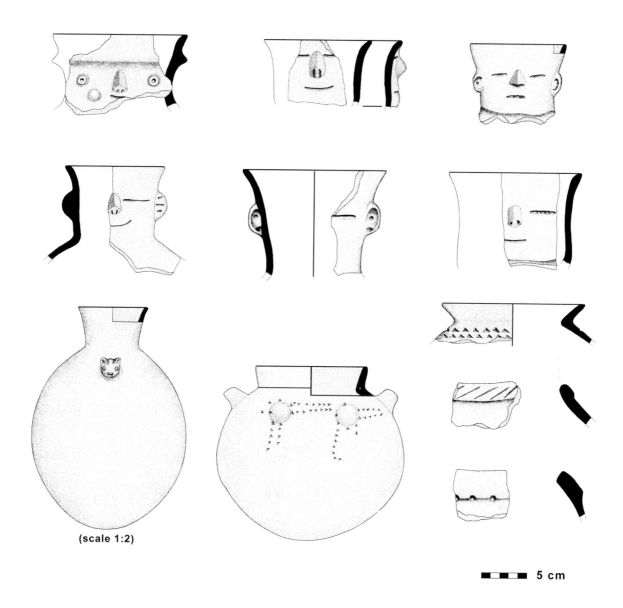

(scale 1:2)

5 cm

FIGURE 1.14. Utilitarian ceramics of Gallinazo style (Castillo Incised and Modeled types) from Huaca Santa Clara.

with the types of ceramics represented in the 8,000 or so sherds recovered from surface collection and excavations at Huaca Santa Clara and their relative value as sociocultural markers. During the analysis process, it became increasingly clear that Castillo Modeled, Castillo Incised, and Castillo Plain pottery—known to have been produced over extremely long periods (Ford 1949:Figs. 4, 5)—featured containers that were structurally and stylistically similar to the domestic pottery produced elsewhere along the north coast throughout the Early Intermediate period.

I therefore started to feel increasingly uncomfortable with studies in which utilitarian ceramic *types* were used as evidence for the development, spread, and decline of some form of Gallinazo *political entity*. I also came to doubt arguments in which these types of containers were presented as sociopolitical markers, in the way archaeologists typically use corporate-style ceramics to identify polities whose "life histories" are relatively well defined in time and space. Furthermore, I started to distrust any publication that mentioned the presence of a "Gallinazo occupation" on a site and

FIGURE 1.15. Gallinazo Negative (Virú)
face-neck jar from Huaca Santa Clara.

felt that it was time for north-coast specialists to sit down around a table and discuss this vast archaeological misunderstanding.

TWO MISTAKES

If a meeting's achievement is measured by how profoundly it changes the way people see the evidence, I can candidly say that the roundtable was a success. It marked a turning point for those of us who work in valleys where ceramics of Gallinazo style are found. At this gathering, we identified flaws in the way we had treated this archaeological culture, and contributors presented critical evidence that will inevitably lead us to rewrite entire aspects of north-coast cultural history.

As I pointed out to the contributors when inviting them to submit written contributions to this book, I believe we have made two important mistakes in studying what is commonly known as Gallinazo ceramics. First, following the seminal work of Bennett, we have compounded two ceramic ensembles under the label "Gallinazo": utilitarian incised and appliquéd pottery (Castillo Decorated) and Gallinazo Negative fine ware.

Incised and appliquéd pottery (the typical Gallinazo face-neck jars) are found in every valley of the Peruvian north coast, from Casma to Piura and in certain regions throughout the sequence where sufficient research has been done (Shimada and Maguiña 1994; see also Chapter 7). Gallinazo Negative, on the other hand, is essentially a corporate style, the production of which was largely restricted to Virú.

The first category of pottery (incised and appliquéd pottery) corresponds to what most archaeologists recognize as the typical Gallinazo artifact, and it appears to represent a pottery style associated with a pan–north-coast cultural tradition distinct from the corporate styles produced by the various political entities that ruled over this vast and diverse territory, whether those were multi-valley states, valley-wide states, or city-state systems (Quilter 2002; Bawden 2004; Millaire 2004a). Henceforth, when using the term "Gallinazo" I believe we should be referring to the relatively coarse incised and appliquéd pottery found along the northern littoral of Peru in association with a variety of corporate styles.

The second category of pottery, Gallinazo Negative, corresponds to a fine-ware ceramic produced for leaders of the polity that ruled over the Virú Valley throughout the Early Intermediate period—a political entity I identify as the "Virú polity" in recognition of Larco Hoyle's seminal work in this area. Most Virú vessels would have been used locally, but it is likely that some entered the inter-polity exchange system. Needless to say, the northern Andes boasted other types of ceramics featuring negative-painted designs.

This highlights our second mistake: we have come to talk about the producers and users of Gallinazo incised and appliquéd pottery in terms of a human group distinct from the producers and users of Vicús, Salinar, Moche, and Virú ceramics. One of the most important contributions of this book is to present a number of contextually documented cases in which ceramics of Gallinazo and Vicús, Moche, or Virú style were likely used by the same individuals, raising strong doubts about the enduring paradigm within which a majority of scholars have been conducting research.

The fact that Gallinazo incised and appliquéd ceramics are found in association with fine-ware vessels of various corporate styles within different coastal oases is, of course, leading scholars to critically reexamine north-coast cultural history. For example, in this volume Christopher Donnan analyzes the co-occurrence of ceramics of Gallinazo and Moche styles in the Jequetepeque Valley, whereas Martín del Carpio reexamines ceramics recovered during years of research at San José de Moro and Pacatnamú.

Régulo Franco and César Gálvez undertake a similar exercise with material from the El Brujo Complex, and Santiago Uceda, Henry Gayoso, and Nadia Gamarra review evidence from Huacas de Moche. Interestingly, without having agreed to do so beforehand, they all found that the producers and users of Moche fine ware were also consumers of Gallinazo-style utilitarian ware.

The other contributions to this book explore specific aspects of the relation between so-called "Gallinazo" groups and other archaeological cultures (Richard Sutter; Jonathan Kent, Teresa Rosales, Víctor Vásquez, Richard Busch, and Catherine Gaither; Claude Chapdelaine, Víctor Pimentel, and Jorge Gamboa; and Gérard Gagné) or undertake a more theoretical reflection on the nature of Gallinazo materiality (Krzysztof Makowski; Christopher Attarian; Luis Jaime Castillo; and Peter Kaulicke).

From this, a new model seems to emerge. Gallinazo, rather than being an early cultural phenomenon or a distinct society, seems to represent a norcosteño popular substrate within which a number of political entities developed. This scenario helps to explain the presence in the same archaeological contexts of ceramics of Gallinazo style and corporate wares as well as the widespread distribution and time depth that characterizes the production of Gallinazo-style ceramics. As such, during the Early Intermediate period the north coast would have hosted not two opposing political formations (as was once thought), but several polities that shared a common ethnic identity (Bawden 1995, 2004).

Also clear is the fact that all of those polities were part of a unique cultural entity we could define as the tradición norcosteña. This does not minimize the existence of cultural diversity along the littoral. Rather, it highlights the presence of a broader tradition within which diversity existed and provides archaeologists with a framework for discussing the nature of the relations among Vicús, Salinar, Moche, and Virú polities.

This new way of presenting north-coast geopolitics might represent the birth of a new paradigm (Kuhn 1962): a set of assumptions, concepts, and practices that constitutes a way of viewing reality, guiding scholars in developing research problems, conducting fieldwork, and structuring their results. If this new model is correct, the task is huge: we need to revise the chronologies that were made on the basis of the identification of utilitarian Gallinazo-style pottery and, of course, rewrite most settlement pattern studies in which utilitarian Gallinazo-style pottery was used as a chronological and ethnic marker.

GALLINAZO AND THE *TRADICIÓN NORCOSTEÑA*

There are several areas of study for which close comparisons between north-coast archaeological cultures could help define the nature of this tradición norcosteña while providing opportunities to document what was unique to individual city-states, polities, and regional confederations. For example, a close examination of the settlement patterns of producers of Gallinazo-style ceramics would certainly shed light on shared land exploitation principles while highlighting regionally specific patterns.

Was the Gallinazo de Santa settlement system identical to that developed by pre-Moche occupants of the Chicama Valley? How distinct were north-coast settlement hierarchies compared to those of oases located farther south? Whatever the questions that guide future research, scholars will inevitably have to review most settlement pattern studies in which Gallinazo was understood to represent an early ethnic group distinct from the Moche.

The same is true for architecture, whether domestic or civic. Based on the use of mold-made adobes, Early Intermediate–period civic buildings gained the monumentality that would characterize Andean architecture until the Spanish conquest. In this context, tiered platforms were built in strategic locations in relation to agricultural land and water canals, a pattern strongly suggesting elite control over people and resources. A detailed architectural study of mound building along the littoral would certainly lead to the identification of regionally specific building techniques, such as the use of river cobbles at the El Brujo Complex or the widespread use of the chamber-infill technique in Virú.

The same study would certainly also highlight the fact that platform mounds built under the auspices of Vicús, Salinar, Moche, and Virú leaders followed similar architectural canons anchored in local tradition. It would also unequivocally demonstrate that cane-marked adobes (or stairways) are not ethnic markers and were used for the construction of buildings associated with Vicús, Salinar, Moche, and Virú material culture (compare Chapter 11).

Mortuary practices represent yet another area in which our collective fascination with the Moche has tended to obscure the similarities that undoubtedly existed between the various polities that occupied the north coast throughout the Early Intermediate period. Again, this will inevitably lead scholars to revise Moche burial pattern studies that only took into consideration graves that featured Moche-style ceramics, while dismissing others (which lacked such materials) on the grounds that they were most likely "early contexts" (Donnan 1995; Millaire 2002). Gérard Gagné's study (see Chapter 12) of human remains associated with Gallinazo de Santa material culture reveals how the local community shared a large part of its mortuary practice with populations that had already embraced Moche stylistic expression (Millaire 2004b), giving us a taste of how stimulating research will become once scholars move beyond the old paradigms.

A study of funerary practices should take into account the rich information conveyed by textiles from burial contexts. At Huaca Santa Clara, we were lucky to work in an environment in which preservation was excellent. Throughout the excavation process, more than 700 textile fragments were recovered from superficial levels, living areas, and storage units. Until now, relatively few textiles were available for defining the Virú textile style. As discussed elsewhere in this volume (see Chapter 9), the most salient characteristic of elaborate Gallinazo fabrics was the use of undyed cotton in plain weaves and the use of camelid hair dyed in bright colors for creating elaborate designs on slit tapestries and fabrics with supplemental wefts.

What is striking with this collection is not Virú artistic and technical idiosyncrasy, however, but the fact that these textiles belong to a wider north-coast textile tradition (Conklin 1978). On the basis of the techniques used, the internal structure of the fabrics, and the motifs represented, our collection is typically norcosteña. Virú textiles are very close stylistically to those produced by weavers from Huacas de Moche, Pacatnamú, and Sipán to the north and from El Castillo to the south.

This has led me to argue that all of these textiles were manifestly the product of a tradition drawing its technical skills and artistic tastes from a common cultural background. Of course, the fact that these contemporaneous groups shared what appears to have been the same textile technology and wore clothes adorned with extremely similar designs should serve as a cautionary note to archaeologists exploring the concept of ethnicity using fine-ware ceramics as their sole source of information.

The list of areas where Early Intermediate–period polities could be compared and contrasted is clearly too long to be covered here. Nevertheless, it is worth mentioning that strong similarities are already apparent in terms of subsistence, cooking tools, food preparation methods, storage systems, and metallurgy (Bawden 1995:260). On the basis of present evidence, it is therefore clear that Vicús, Salinar, Moche, and Virú societies were closely related and probably periodically engaged in social, economic, and political interactions throughout the Early Intermediate period (see Chapter 13). It is likely that neighboring polities shared a common ethnic identity as well as parts of their belief systems and ritual practices.

However, what clearly differentiated Vicús, Salinar, Moche, and Virú polities was their respective fine-ware ceramics. According to Bawden, the birth of Moche ideological symbolism marked the development of a new political ideology that constituted "innovation in regional tradition" (Bawden 2004:122). Considering the new evidence presented in the following chapters, Bawden's insight that Moche was the expression of a new political discourse that emerged and developed from an early cultural tradition of the Peruvian north coast seems very attractive.

Nonetheless, I would question the idea that Moche symbolism need have been the expression of a *political* ideology. Could it not simply be the expression of a messianic religious discourse local leaders were ready to adopt because it served their interests? This would help to explain why in some areas local leaders seem to have adopted Moche art and attributes while the population continued to produce, use, and discard utilitarian Gallinazo-style containers. If this were the case, this new discourse could well have traveled along the littoral without recourse to armies, combats, population displacements, and massive killings. Nevertheless, what is clear is that Moche discourse—whether political, religious, or both—did not spread uniformly along the littoral. It probably followed its jagged terrain, contoured its desert areas, and crossed its rivers, being accepted, rejected, transformed, tailored, and selectively incorporated to fit local needs.

In looking at the future, it seems clear that if we wish to understand the complex cultural history of the Peruvian north coast, we must set out to reanalyze the material culture of communities who produced, used, and discarded utilitarian ceramics of Gallinazo style, indiscriminately of the fine ware used. Only then will it be possible to talk about the complex geopolitical history of the north coast and to elucidate some of the key events that have marked the road of Andean civilization.

REFERENCES

Bawden, Garth
  1995 The Structural Paradox: Moche Culture as Political Ideology. *Latin American Antiquity* 6(3):255–273.
  2004 The Art of Moche Politics. In *Andean Archaeology*, Helaine Silverman (ed.), pp. 116–129. Oxford: Blackwell Publishing.

Bennett, Wendell C.
  1939 *Archaeology of the North Coast of Peru: An Account of Exploration and Excavation in Viru and Lambayeque Valleys.* Anthropological Papers of the American Museum of Natural History Vol. 37, Pt. 1. New York: The American Museum of Natural History.

  1950 *The Gallinazo Group: Viru Valley, Peru.* Yale University Publications in Anthropology 43. New Haven: Yale University Press.

Bourget, Steve
  2004 Cultural Affiliation during the Early Intermediate Period: The Huancaco Case, Virú Valley. In *New Perspectives on the Moche Political Organization*, Jeffrey Quilter, Luis Jaime Castillo, and Joanne Pillsbury (eds.), manuscript accepted for publication. Washington, D.C.: Dumbarton Oaks Research Library and Collection.

Castillo, Luis Jaime
  2001 The Last of the Mochicas: A View from the Jequetepeque Valley. In *Moche Art and Archaeology in Ancient Peru*, Joanne Pillsbury (ed.), pp. 307–332. Washington, D.C.: National Gallery of Art and Yale University Press.

Conklin, William J.
  1978 Estructura de los tejidos moche. In *Tecnología andina*, Rogger Ravines (ed.), pp. 299–332. Lima: Instituto de Estudios Peruanos.

Donnan, Christopher B.
  1995 Moche Funerary Practice. In *Tombs for the Living: Andean Mortuary Practices*, Tom D. Dillehay (ed.), pp. 111–159. Washington, D.C.: Dumbarton Oaks Research Library and Collection.

Fogel, Heidy
  1993 Settlements in Time: A Study of Social and Political Development during the Gallinazo Occupation of the North Coast of Perú [sic]. Unpublished Ph.D. dissertation, Yale University, New Haven.

Ford, James A.
  1949 Cultural Dating of Prehistoric Sites in Virú Valley, Peru. In *Surface Survey of the Virú Valley, Peru*, James A. Ford and Gordon R. Willey (eds.), pp. 29–87. Anthropological Papers of the American Museum of Natural History Vol. 43, Pt. 1. New York: The American Museum of Natural History.

Kaulicke, Peter
  1992 Moche, Vicús Moche y el Mochica Temprano. *Bulletin de l'Institut Français d'Études Andines* 21(3):853–903.

Kuhn, Thomas S.
  1962 *The Structure of Scientific Revolutions.* Chicago: University of Chicago Press.

Larco Hoyle, Rafael
  1945 *La cultura virú.* Buenos Aires: Sociedad Geográfica Americana.

Millaire, Jean-François
  2002 *Moche Burial Patterns: An Investigation into Prehispanic Social Structure.* BAR International Series 1066. Oxford: BAR.
  2004a Moche Political Expansionism as Viewed from Virú: Recent Archaeological Work in

the Close Periphery of a Hegemonic City-State System. In *New Perspectives on the Moche Political Organization*, Jeffrey Quilter, Luis Jaime Castillo, and Joanne Pillsbury (eds.), manuscript accepted for publication. Washington, D.C.: Dumbarton Oaks Research Library and Collection.

2004b The Manipulation of Human Remains in Moche Society: Delayed Burials, Grave Reopening, and Secondary Offerings of Human Bones on the Peruvian North Coast. *Latin American Antiquity* 15(4):371–388.

Quilter, Jeffrey
2002 Moche Politics, Religion, and Warfare. *Journal of World Prehistory* 16(2):145–195.

Shimada, Izumi, and Adriana Maguiña
1994 Nueva visión sobre la cultura gallinazo y su relación con la cultura moche. In *Moche: Pro-puestas y perspectivas*, Santiago Uceda and Elías Mujica (eds.), pp. 31–58. Travaux de l'Institut Français d'Études Andines 79. Lima: Universidad Nacional de La Libertad and Instituto Francés de Estudios Andinos.

Ubbelohde-Doering, Heinrich
1957 *Der Gallinazo-Stil und die Chronologie der alt-peruanischen Frühkulturen*. Bayerische Akademie der Wissenschaften. Philosophisch-Historische Klasse, Sitzungberichte 9. Munich: C. H. Beck.

Willey, Gordon R.
1953 *Prehistoric Settlement Patterns in the Virú Valley, Perú* [sic]. Smithsonian Institution, Bureau of American Ethnology Bulletin 155. Washington, D.C.: Government Printing Office.

CHAPTER 2

THE GALLINAZO ILLUSION

Christopher B. Donnan

Archaeologists working on the north coast of Peru have made a serious mistake in identifying Gallinazo ceramics. This has misled us to believe that Gallinazo culture was extremely widespread, from the Piura Valley in the north to the Casma Valley in the south (Figure 2.1). This, however, is an illusion. Gallinazo-style ceramics and Gallinazo culture have a very limited geographical distribution. It is imperative that we reassess the evidence for the presence of Gallinazo in light of current archaeological evidence.

In 1939, Wendell Bennett (1939) excavated a cluster of archaeological sites in the lower Virú Valley that he called the Gallinazo Group (Figure 2.1). He published a brief report about his excavation that same year, and in 1950 published a monograph titled *The Gallinazo Group: Viru Valley, Peru* (Bennett 1950). In his monograph, he provided a description of the architecture he had uncovered and demonstrated that the adobes used were distinctly cane marked.

In addition, Bennett provided a well-illustrated description of the associated ceramics. These included fine ware and domestic ware. The fine ware, which he called Gallinazo Negative, was essentially what Rafael Larco Hoyle had been calling "Virú" in his publications (1945, 1946a, 1946b, 1948). This ware is characterized by a range of vessel forms, including stirrup-spout bottles, spout-and-bridge bottles, and double-chambered whistling bottles. The vessels were often modeled to depict animals, people, or architecture. They were then carefully burnished and fired in an oxidizing atmosphere to create an orange color. Finally, they were decorated with a negative (resist) application of organic black pigment that left them with a black-and-orange color scheme (Figure 2.2).

The domestic ware Bennett found at the Gallinazo Group had a coarser temper than the fine ware, and was unburnished. Although many of the vessels were undecorated, some had simple modeling (generally on their necks or upper chambers) portraying the faces of humans, birds, and animals. These faces were often elaborated with appliqué and incision to depict eyes and mouths, or to add simple lines and dots on the cheeks (Figure 2.3a–i). Figurines from Bennett's excavations were similar to the domestic ware in

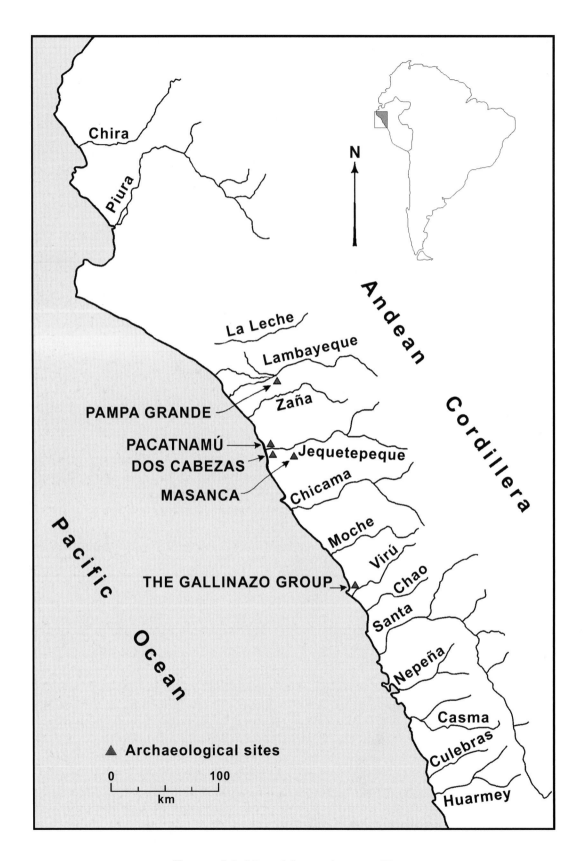

FIGURE 2.1. Map of the north coast of Peru.

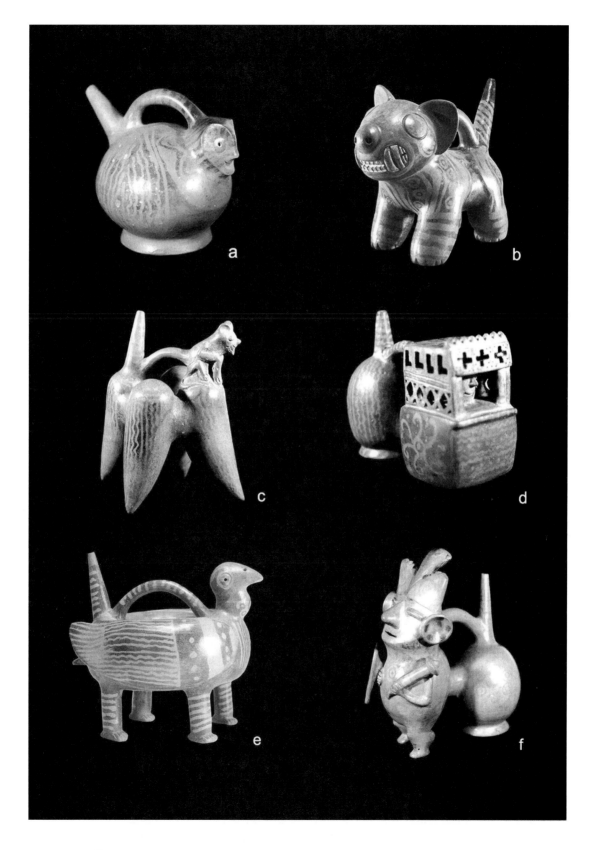

FIGURE 2.2. Fine-ware ceramics of the type identified as Gallinazo Negative
by Bennett, and as Virú by Larco Hoyle.

being unburnished and having faces elaborated with appliqué and incision (Figure 2.3j–k).

The importance of Bennett's publications cannot be overstated. They provided the first information about the domestic ware and figurines associated with Gallinazo Negative fine ware (what Larco Hoyle called Virú style) and led archaeologists to think that the decorated domestic wares and the figurines were distinctive and reliable identifiers of the Gallinazo ceramic tradi-

tion. Moreover, they led archaeologists to identify the presence of Gallinazo culture wherever these domestic ware ceramics were found. This was the beginning of the "Gallinazo illusion."

In 1952, Strong and Evans published their study of the Formative and Florescent epochs in the Virú Valley (Strong and Evans 1952), which included a discussion and illustration of ceramics similar to those reported by Bennett from the Gallinazo Group. This only reinforced the idea

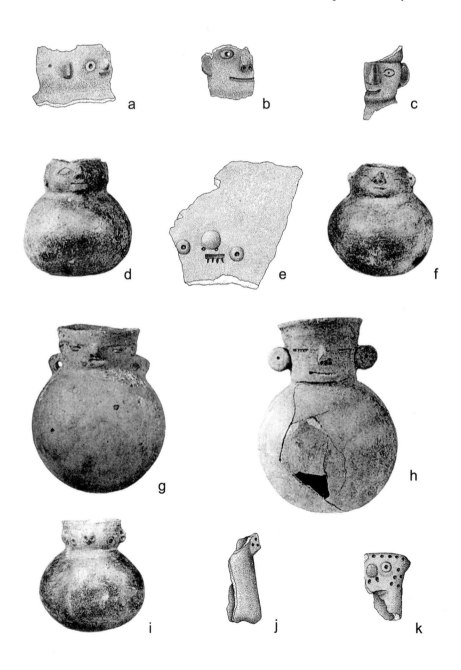

FIGURE 2.3. Domestic ware excavated by Bennett at the Gallinazo Group in the Virú Valley.
Illustration after Bennett (1950).

that Gallinazo Negative fine ware *and* the domestic ware elaborated with appliqué and incision were hallmarks of Gallinazo ceramics, and that either one could be used to identify the presence of Gallinazo culture.

In 1938 through 1939, and 1957, Ubbelohde-Doering excavated at Pacatnamú, a site at the delta of the Jequetepeque River (Figures 2.1, 2.4). Although he did not find any Gallinazo Negative fine ware, he found some domestic ceramics with appliqué and incision similar to that published by Bennett. He thought these ceramics were evidence of a Gallinazo occupation, and noted that they were at least in part contemporary with the Moche-style ceramics he also found at the site. In 1957, Ubbelohde-Doering published an article suggesting that the association of these two styles resulted from the intrusion of Moche people at Pacatnamú, a site previously occupied by Gallinazo people.

Since 1957, archaeologists working at various sites on the north coast (myself included) have found domestic ceramics and figurines with appliquéd and incised decor similar to that published by Bennett. We simply assumed that they indicated a Gallinazo occupation. In many sites, we found them associated with Moche ceramics, leading us to believe that those sites must have been occupied by both Moche and Gallinazo people.

In 1994, Izumi Shimada and Adriana Maguiña published a seminal article (Shimada and Maguiña 1994) tracing the association of Gallinazo- and Moche-style ceramics at sites along the north coast of Peru. They suggested that Gallinazo style did not simply precede Moche style but continued as late as Moche V (currently thought to date between A.D. 650 and 800), and that Gallinazo and Moche were two distinct polities that coexisted for centuries. It should be noted, however, that they were using

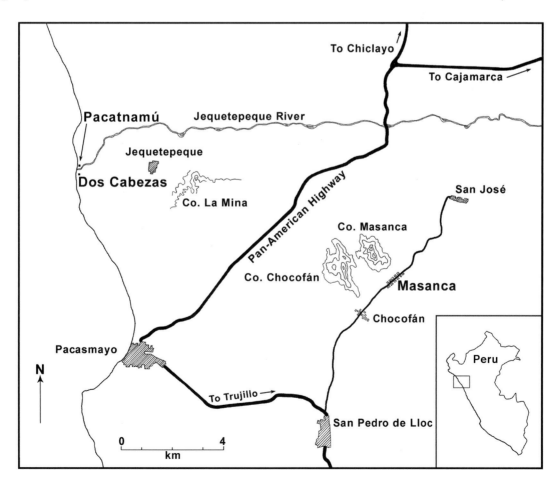

FIGURE 2.4. Map of the lower Jequetepeque Valley.

domestic ceramics with decor similar to that published by Bennett to identify Gallinazo culture—not Gallinazo Negative fine ware (Figure 2.5).

I directed an excavation at Pacatnamú between 1983 and 1987. Like Ubbelohde-Doering, we found no Gallinazo Negative fine ware at the site but did find domestic ware with decor similar to that published by Bennett from the Gallinazo Group (Figure 2.6). It was consistently associated with Moche ceramics (Figure 2.7). In addition, we excavated three burials at Pacatnamú that had this

type of domestic ware in direct association with Moche ceramics (Donnan and McClelland 1997: 65, 105, 108).

In 1994, we began excavating the site of Dos Cabezas, located across the river from Pacatnamú at the delta of the Jequetepeque River (Figure 2.4). Over a period of eight field seasons, we found hundreds of ceramic fragments and many complete vessels of domestic ceramics with decor similar to that published by Bennett from the Gallinazo Group (Figure 2.8). We also found fig-

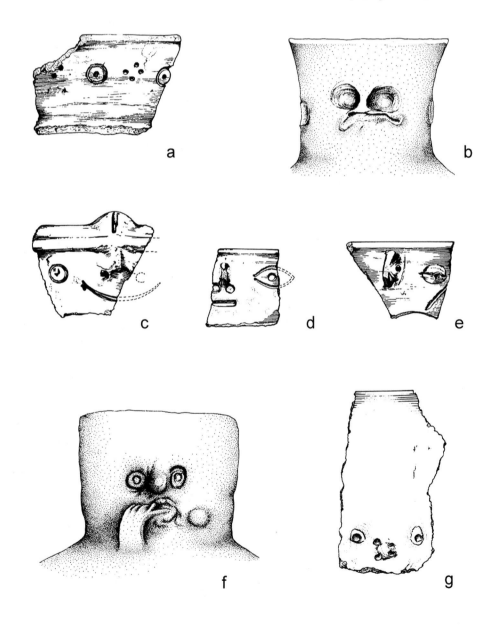

FIGURE 2.5. Domestic ware found at various sites in the Lambayeque Valley.
Illustration after Shimada and Maguiña (1994).

FIGURE 2.6. Domestic ware from Pacatnamú.

FIGURE 2.7. Moche ceramics from Pacatnamú.

FIGURE 2.8. Domestic ware from Dos Cabezas.

urines similar to those Bennett reported (Figure 2.9), but the domestic ware and figurines were consistently associated with Moche ceramics (Figure 2.10), not with Gallinazo Negative fine ware. One Moche tomb even contained one vessel of this domestic ware associated with 12 Moche vessels (Donnan 2001, 2003).

Domestic ware with decor similar to that published by Bennett from the Gallinazo Group has also been found in burials at the site of Masanca, located farther inland in the Jequetepeque Valley (Figure 2.11). In all instances, however, the ware was associated with Moche ceram-

ics (Figure 2.12). Not a single sherd of Gallinazo Negative fine ware has been found at the site (Donnan 2006).

It might be suggested that the domestic ceramics with decor similar to that published by Bennett from the Gallinazo Group were being used by Gallinazo people living at the sites of Pacatnamú, Dos Cabezas, and Masanca while Moche people were using the Moche-style ceramics. There are, however, problems with this scenario. First, the decorated domestic ware and Moche-style ceramics are repeatedly found in direct association with each other in midden

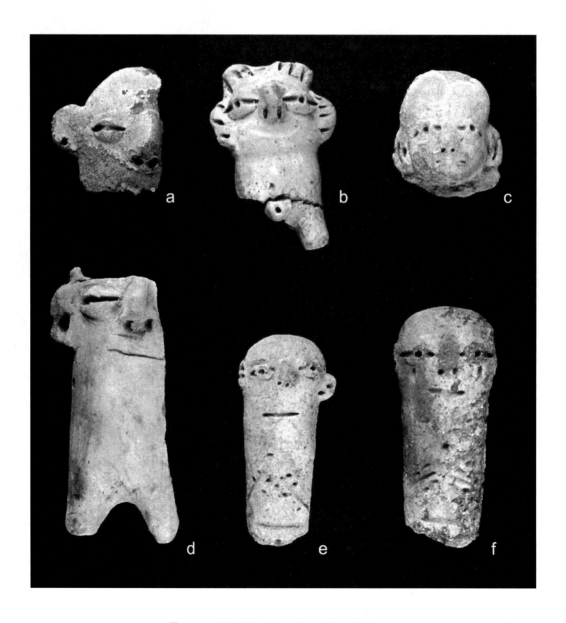

FIGURE 2.9. Figurines from Dos Cabezas.

FIGURE 2.10. Moche ceramics from Dos Cabezas.

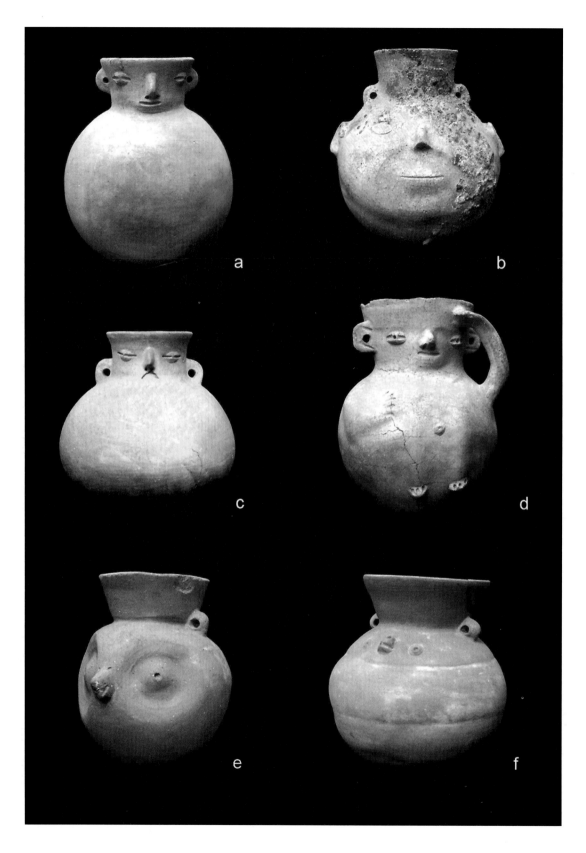

FIGURE 2.11. Domestic ware from Masanca.

FIGURE 2.12. Moche ceramics from Masanca.

deposits, on house floors, and even in burials—something that would not occur if the two types of ceramics belonged to two separate cultural groups. Moreover, if the Moche people were not using the domestic ware, they would have had no domestic ware at all—no cooking *ollas*, no large jars for preparing *chicha*, no storage jars, and so on. Conversely, the Gallinazo people would have had no fine-ware ceramics for ritual purposes.

The repeated association of incised and appliquéd domestic ware and Moche ceramics at Pacatnamú, Dos Cabezas, and Masanca clearly indicates that what has been thought of as Gallinazo domestic ware is not Gallinazo. It is simply the common domestic pottery widely used on the north coast of Peru from about 200 B.C. until A.D. 800.

During that time, distinct styles of fine ware were in use at different locations and in different time periods. One of these was Gallinazo-style fine ware (Gallinazo Negative), and another was Moche-style fine ware. The fine-ware styles appear to have been associated with distinct polities (perhaps as a means of expressing their identity) and are much more restricted in time and space than the common domestic pottery. Using domestic pottery with decor similar to that published by Bennett as an indicator of Gallinazo culture is the source of the Gallinazo illusion.

An analogy can be drawn to clarify this argument. In about A.D. 900, paddle stamping began to be used to decorate domestic pottery on the north coast of Peru. Paddle-stamped domestic pottery was first associated with Lambayeque-style fine ware, but soon it also became commonly associated with Chimú-style fine ware. When the Inca conquered the north coast, the domestic ware continued to be paddle stamped but was then associated with a fine ware we identify as Chimú-Inca. The Inca were subsequently conquered by the Spanish, which ushered in a style of fine-ware ceramics we identify as Colonial period. Meanwhile, the common domestic ware continued to be paddle stamped.

On the north coast of Peru today, paddle-stamped domestic pottery is still being produced, continuing a tradition of domestic pottery decoration that has been ongoing for more than a thousand years! Clearly, it would be very misleading to identify the presence of Lambayeque, Chimú, Chimú-Inca, or Colonial-period occupations on the basis of paddle-stamped domestic pottery. Yet, we have been identifying the presence of Gallinazo on the basis of domestic pottery with decor similar to that published by Bennett—features that characterize the common domestic pottery used on the north coast throughout the Early Intermediate period. Like paddle-stamped domestic pottery, the domestic pottery published by Bennett had a duration of more than a thousand years and was associated with various styles of fine ware—including Gallinazo and Moche fine ware.

There is one other observation that can help clarify the Gallinazo illusion. If in 1939 Bennett had excavated Dos Cabezas rather than the Gallinazo Group, he would have identified domestic-ware ceramics with incised and appliquéd decor as Moche. Subsequently, whenever similar ceramics were found, they would have been identified as Moche—not as Gallinazo. Then, if someone today were to excavate the Gallinazo Group for the first time, they might be perplexed to find that the fine ware is a distinctive negative-painted non-Moche style (Gallinazo Negative) associated with "Moche" domestic ware—like that found at Dos Cabezas. This might lead them to speculate that there was a colony of Moche people living side by side with Gallinazo people in the lower Virú Valley!

Our mistake in using incised and appliquéd domestic ware as an identifier of Gallinazo has led to a variety of conclusions about the cultural history of the north coast we now need to address. In 1993, Heidy Fogel completed a study of Gallinazo on the north coast of Peru based on her identification of numerous archaeological sites where Gallinazo ceramics had been found. She concluded, among other things, that Gallinazo was the first state-level society to develop on the north coast and that its widespread distribution and control emanated from the Virú Valley (Fogel 1993:257–258).

Unfortunately, nearly all of Fogel's "Gallinazo" sites were identified by the presence of domestic ceramics with decor similar to that published by Bennett from the Gallinazo Group (very few of the sites had Gallinazo Negative fine ware). Because the sites lacking Gallinazo Negative fine ware could just as well be Moche as Gallinazo, her arguments about how and when a state level of complexity developed on the north coast cannot be supported.

In 1988, David Wilson published his extensive study of the Santa Valley (Wilson 1988), where he identified numerous Gallinazo settlements and ranked them in size and importance. He suggested that the valley had a large Gallinazo occupation and that it was subsequently colonized by Moche people from the Moche Valley. It should be noted, however, that Wilson seldom identified Gallinazo sites on the basis of Gallinazo Negative fine ware (the sites were typically identified on the basis of domestic ceramics with decor similar to that published by Bennett from the Gallinazo Group). Because many, if not most, of the sites Wilson identified as Gallinazo may be Moche, his estimates of the Gallinazo population, its distribution in the valley, and its organization are unsupportable.

Similarly, Shimada's identification of a Gallinazo presence at the Moche site of Pampa Grande in the upper Lambayeque Valley (Figure 2.1) is based entirely on the presence of domestic ceramics with decor similar to that published by Bennett from the Gallinazo Group (Shimada 1994). No Gallinazo Negative fine-ware ceramics have ever been reported from Pampa Grande. Therefore, Shimada's suggestion that there was a colony of Gallinazo people living alongside the Moche people at Pampa Grande cannot be supported.

There are many other instances of archaeologists being misled by the Gallinazo illusion. In some instances, this has simply resulted in sites being identified as having had a Gallinazo occupation, whereas in other instances it has been the basis of major reconstructions of the role played by the Gallinazo in the cultural history of the north coast.

I wish to make clear that I do not claim to be wiser than my colleagues. On the contrary, I too was fooled by the Gallinazo illusion. Like most

archaeologists working on the north coast of Peru, I learned that the presence of Gallinazo was identifiable by Gallinazo Negative fine ware as well as by domestic ceramics with decor similar to that published by Bennett from the Gallinazo Group. I also learned that cane-marked adobes were an indicator of Gallinazo.

Years ago, when I first visited Dos Cabezas, I noted that most of the monumental structures were built with cane-marked adobes and that the surface of the site had fragments of domestic ceramics with decor similar to that published by Bennett from the Gallinazo Group. Thus, for many years I regarded Dos Cabezas as a Gallinazo site. Even when I began excavating there in 1994, I thought that it was essentially a Gallinazo site but that it might have a small Moche component. I could not have been more wrong. It is a huge and very important Moche site.

When Jean-François Millaire invited me to participate in the 2005 roundtable on Gallinazo, I decided to present a talk on the association of "Gallinazo" domestic ware and Moche fine ware I had excavated at Pacatnamú, Dos Cabezas, and Masanca. I wanted to demonstrate that the domestic ceramics with decor similar to that published by Bennett from the Gallinazo Group were neither Gallinazo nor Moche but were simply the common domestic ware being used widely on the north coast during the Early Intermediate period.

Listening to the presentations given by others at the roundtable, I became increasingly convinced that we had all been using false criteria to identify the presence of Gallinazo on the north coast—that we had been misled by the Gallinazo illusion. After the roundtable, in corresponding with Millaire about my thoughts on the Gallinazo illusion, he stated, "If this new interpretation is right, the task is huge. We will need to revise the chronologies that were made on the basis of 'Gallinazo' incised and appliquéd pottery and, of course, rewrite most settlement pattern studies in which 'Gallinazo' incised and appliquéd pottery is usually used as a chronological and ethnic marker."

I agree with his assessment. However, I would add that we must also dismiss the studies that have attempted to assess the role of "Gallinazo" in the cultural development of the north coast. The task is indeed huge, but it will be immensely rewarding. It will bring about a much more accurate reconstruction of the remarkable cultural history of northern Peru. Let us begin.

REFERENCES

Bennett, Wendell C.
  1939 *Archaeology of the North Coast of Peru: An Account of Exploration and Excavation in Viru and Lambayeque Valleys.* Anthropological Papers of the American Museum of Natural History Vol. 37, Pt. 1. New York: The American Museum of Natural History.
  1950 *The Gallinazo Group: Viru Valley, Peru.* Yale University Publications in Anthropology 43. New Haven: Yale University Press.

Donnan, Christopher B.
  2001 Moche Burials Uncovered. *National Geographic* 199(3):58–73.
  2003 Tumbas con entierros en miniatura: Un nuevo tipo funerario moche. In *Moche: Hacia el fin del milenio*, Santiago Uceda and Elías Mujica (eds.), vol. 1, pp. 43–78. Lima: Universidad Nacional de Trujillo and Fondo Editorial, Pontificia Universidad Católica del Perú.
  2006 A Moche Cemetery at Masanca, Jequetepeque Valley, Peru. *Ñawpa Pacha* 28: 151–193.

Donnan, Christopher B., and Donna McClelland
  1997 Moche Burials at Pacatnamu. In *The Pacatnamu Papers*, Volume 2: *The Moche Occupation*, Christopher B. Donnan and Guillermo A. Cock (eds.), pp. 17–187. Los Angeles: Fowler Museum of Cultural History, University of California.

Fogel, Heidy
  1993 Settlements in Time: A Study of Social and Political Development during the Gallinazo Occupation of the North Coast of Perú [sic]. Unpublished Ph.D. dissertation, Yale University, New Haven.

Larco Hoyle, Rafael
  1945 *La cultura virú.* Buenos Aires: Sociedad Geográfica Americana.
  1946a A Cultural Sequence from the North Coast of Perú [sic]. In *Handbook of South American Indians*, Volume 2: *The Andean Civilizations*, Julian H. Steward (ed.), pp. 149–175. Smithsonian Institution, Bureau of American Ethnology Bulletin 143. Washington, D.C.: Government Printing Office.
  1946b La cultura viru. *Revista geográfica americana* (Buenos Aires) 25(115):209–222.
  1948 *Cronología arqueológica del norte del Perú.* Buenos Aires: Sociedad Geográfica Americana.

Shimada, Izumi
  1994 *Pampa Grande and the Mochica Culture.* Austin: University of Texas Press.

Shimada, Izumi, and Adriana Maguiña
  1994 Nueva visión sobre la cultura gallinazo y su relación con la cultura moche. In *Moche: Propuestas y perspectivas*, Santiago Uceda and Elías Mujica (eds.), pp. 31–58. Travaux de l'Institut Français d'Études Andines 79. Lima: Universidad Nacional de La Libertad and Instituto Francés de Estudios Andinos.

Strong, William D., and Clifford Evans
  1952 *Cultural Stratigraphy in the Virú Valley, Northern Peru: The Formative and Florescent Epochs.* New York: Columbia University Press.

Ubbelohde-Doering, Heinrich
  1957 *Der Gallinazo-Stil und die Chronologie der altperuanischen Frühkulturen.* Bayerische Akademie der Wissenschaften. Philosophisch-Historische Klasse, Sitzungsberichte 9. Munich: C. H. Beck.

Wilson, David J.
  1988 *Prehispanic Settlement Patterns in the Lower Santa Valley, Peru: A Regional Perspective on the Origins and Development of Complex North Coast Society.* Washington, D.C.: Smithsonian Institution Press.

CHAPTER 3

VIRÚ–MOCHE RELATIONS:
Technological Identity, Stylistic Preferences, and the Ethnic Identity of Ceramic Manufacturers and Users
Krzysztof Makowski

This chapter[1] is intended to demonstrate that the present debate surrounding the cultural and political phenomena associated with the production of ceramics of Virú, Gallinazo, and Suchimancillo styles goes on without overcoming the limitations and biases inherent in the first studies produced on this subject toward the middle of the last century. Indeed, scholars have not accepted Rafael Larco Hoyle's (1945) definition of the Virú culture, nor his proposed stylistic sequence for Virú ceramics (Larco Hoyle 1948)—a typology of containers from burial contexts (decorated with white-on-red paint, negative paint, or modeled appliqué).

Instead, the term "Gallinazo" introduced by Wendell C. Bennett (1939, 1950) and James A. Ford's chronology (Ford 1949; Ford and Willey 1949) was adopted by north-coast specialists. The two chronologies (Larco Hoyle's and Ford's) have little in common in terms of methodology. To Larco Hoyle (1945), the term "Virú" describes a regional culture native to the Virú Valley whose artisans produced a distinct type of funerary ceramic strongly influenced by the Moche style. Ford (1949) essentially defines the term "Gallinazo" as a segment of time in his seriation of Virú Valley ceramics, essentially based on the technological evolution of containers.

Within Ford's classification, a ceramic ware can include pieces of different styles (e.g., Virú and Santa-Recuay) if they are produced with a similar paste and feature a similar finish. Conversely, two fragments of a single container can be classified as two distinct ceramic wares when one is decorated and the other is not. Moreover, the sample analyzed by Ford includes numerous fragments from domestic contexts (and ritual ceramics are underrepresented). As a result, the term "Gallinazo" (like the term "Huancaco") was coined with strictly chronological meaning and was only meant to describe the prehistory of the Virú Valley. It therefore lacked any ethnic connotation and only referred to a segment in an abundant matrix of ceramic ware.

Despite this, starting with Gordon Willey's (1953) influential publication on settlement patterns, scholars have started to use the compound term "Virú-Gallinazo" to describe a style and a specific regional culture—and by extension a specific ethnic group in conflict with the Moche. Thanks to fieldwork conducted since the 1960s, the ceramic traits originally associated with the Virú Valley's "Gallinazo" were identified in various contexts between Huarmey and Piura. Interestingly, those traits were generally found on utilitarian pottery directly associated with ceremonial Moche ceramics. Those contextually documented ceramic associations were identified within a territory that essentially corresponds to the area of diffusion of the Moche style. This makes it essential to reconsider the relation between Gallinazo and Virú phenomena, on the one hand, and between the Gallinazo and Moche, on the other.

While doing so, it seems important to respect the original substance of the concepts introduced by the successive scholars. The term "Gallinazo" corresponds to a technological and formal domestic ceramic tradition widely spread among the populations that also used fine Virú-style ceramics in funerary contexts. The latter were gradually substituted by Moche-style containers as their users accepted inclusion in the Moche political entity. The technological and formal variability observable among Gallinazo-style ceramics is potentially a reflection of the ethnic identity of the producers and users of the containers.

In contrast, the term "Moche" refers to the stylistic and functional (formal and iconographic) characteristic of ceremonial ceramics produced in specialized workshops. Those workshops existed due to the new technological and formal possibilities brought about by political integration: one or several emerging territorial states that shared similar ideological principles, including origin myths, ritual, and so forth (see Chapter 9). Unlike the Gallinazo style, the Moche style therefore needs to be understood as a political phenomenon—possibly supra-ethnic but at least supra-local.

This distinction is important because it is well known that ethnic frontiers do not necessarily coincide with political borders. The presence or absence of Moche artifacts in Gallinazo contexts is likely due to changing political conjuncture, and to whether or not local communities had access to the production of specialized work-

shops—a phenomenon clearly related to local political conditions. This chapter reviews the early research on those north-coast cultures and then focuses on new evidence available on the chronological position of Early Intermediate–period ceramics. The chapter concludes with a discussion of the important concepts of ethnicity and material culture.

EARLY RESEARCH ON THE VIRÚ-GALLINAZO AND MOCHE CULTURES

Wendell Bennett (1939) was the first scholar who showed (from test pits in the Gallinazo Group in the Virú Valley) that one could indeed posit the presence of a regional culture characterized by a particular ceramic style, which he named "Gallinazo." A high percentage of ceramic materials lacked decoration (70.83%), even though the sample came from domestic and ceremonial contexts as well as from burials (Bennett 1939:71). The remaining percentage showed evident connections with Moche (Early Chimú) and Recuay styles, and to a lesser extent with Epigonal–Middle Horizon 2–3 styles. The discovery of a fragment of a Recuay-style tapestry directly associated with a Moche I–style bottle (Bennett 1939: burial 5A-a, 57, 66; Fig. 15a) inside the burial of an individual seated in flexed position provided additional support for the previously mentioned connection.

After the Second World War, Rafael Larco Hoyle published a brief study (1945) wherein he introduced the concept of the "Virú culture." His conclusions were somewhat contradictory in nature. On the one hand, Larco Hoyle showed with solid arguments that the Moche and Virú cultural styles were fully coeval. He thus perceived only two phases: one we call "Auge" (apogee)—which would be contemporary with Moche—and a decadent one, which would have survived up to the Middle Horizon (Larco Hoyle 1945:1).

The recurrence of Virú spout-and-bridge bottles with Moche I sculptural forms and other Virú-Moche hybrid bottles (Larco Hoyle 1945:9), as well as stirrup-spout bottles imitating Moche forms, gave solid support to this chronology. On the other hand, Larco was convinced that the style defined from a series of stirrup-spout and spout-and-bridge bottles—as well as face-neck jars or jars with sculpted appliqué on the shoulders—corresponded to a people who had not undergone a major expansion, adding that scholars have to note this people's "admirable spirit of independence shown in upholding their religion, their customs, and their art despite the domination of other peoples" (Larco Hoyle 1945:1).

Three years later, Larco Hoyle modified his ideas in his influential *Cronología arqueológica del norte del Perú* (1948). Under the influence of the discussions he had with the members of the Virú Valley Project (Willey 1946), Larco Hoyle placed all forms of Virú ceramics lacking a connection with the Moche style in the final phase of the Formative period. He still believed that the Virú style survived the onslaught of the Moche culture, but only in the first phase of Moche development. According to Larco Hoyle, the origins of the Moche style lay in the creative fusion of the experience of Cupisnique and Salinar potters. He also considered the Virú style from Chicama (wherein the Virú and Salinar traditions blended) coeval with the rise of Moche style at the beginning of his Auge period.

Ford and Willey (1949) and Strong and Evans (1952) acknowledged that Larco Hoyle's Virú-style pieces could be included in the phases they called Gallinazo, whereas the Moche III, Moche IV, and Moche V vessels fell in their Huancaco phase. The methodologic and conceptual differences between these two positions are enormous, however. The American scholars classified the sherds from surveys and test pits excavated using arbitrary levels, emphasizing the color and texture of the ware as well as the characteristics of the surface finishing. They then compared the sherds with complete pieces, particularly specimens in the Larco Hoyle collection. The classificatory groups (taxa) were then subjected to a double analysis: site and excavated-level recurrence and statistical analysis of the number of fragments corresponding to each collection unit. The results were then processed with a frequency seriation.

We must bear in mind that just like other segments in the sequence in Ford's seriation, the Gallinazo and Huancaco phases do not hold a necessary and direct relation with cultural changes (such as stylistic and iconographic variations) or with relevant modifications in mortuary behavior—and much less with craniometrical evidence. Furthermore, the seriation made following these criteria gives rise to a picture exhibiting a marked technological continuity. Phases are simply defined as periods wherein certain classificatory units are numerically well represented and the recurrence of others is rising or falling.

In the case of the Gallinazo phase, the segment of the seriated sequence was defined as the period of decline of Puerto Moorin White-on-Red ceramics and the appearance of other taxa, such as the scarcely represented Virú Plain and Tomaval Plain taxons (Strong and Evans 1952: 260–326). This period was also marked by the rise of other taxa (which appear during the Late Puerto Moorin phase), such as Huacapongo Polished Plain, Sarraque Cream, Gloria Polished Plain, Castillo Plain, Queneto Polished Plain, Valle Plain, Gallinazo Negative, Carmelo Negative, and Castillo Modeled ceramics.

Castillo Modeled is a taxon defined by the decoration technique. As such, it gathers fragments featuring various pastes and finishes: 61.2% are typical of the Castillo Plain, 19.6% of the Sarraque Cream, 6.19% of the Carmelo Negative, and 6.19% of the Huacapongo Polished Plain. Finally, this period was marked by the recurrence of the scantly represented Gallinazo Broad-Line Incised and Castillo Incised taxa. These two taxa comprise many plain wares: 83.4% of the sherds are Castillo Plain, 11.8% are Huacapongo Polished Plain, 1.47% are Gloria Polished Plain, 1.47% are Sarraque Cream, 1.1% are Puerto Moorin Incised Red, and 0.735% are Queneto Plain.

In this seriated sequence, Strong and Evans have corrected the mistake made by Ford (1949), who had initially inverted the Gallinazo-Huancaco sequence. Once the correction had been made, it was clear that the origin of all recurring classificatory units in the Gallinazo period lay in the final Puerto Moorin segments and that all retained their popularity throughout the Huancaco period—at least to the same extent as in the corresponding sequence for the second half of the Gallinazo period. The end of the Gallinazo period was defined by the significant presence of decorated ceramics in the Moche style (known as Huancaco Red-and-White, Huancaco Red-White-and-Black, Huancaco Polished Black) and by Virú Plain ceramics.

The disproportion between the recurrence of utilitarian shapes and possibly ceremonial ones with figurative decorations and/or fine finishing is remarkable. In the Huancaco period, the bottles, flaring vases (*floreros*), dippers (*cancheros*), and small and midsize decorated jars are as frequent (or even more common) than utilitarian and non-decorated shapes, whereas in the previous Gallinazo period they simply comprise a small share (of about 10%).

Willey's pioneering study (1953) of the settlement patterns in the Virú Valley with Ford's chronology in hand was the final and decisive step in the development of the hypothesis regarding the relations between the Gallinazo and Huancaco periods and between the Virú and Moche styles. Comparing the complexity of public works in both periods with those of the Puerto Moorin period, Willey concluded:

> The complex irrigation systems, extending from the canal intakes high in the Upper Huacapongo down to the coast, could have functioned only under a closely coordinated management. The mammoth building projects of this same Late Gallinazo Period also demanded a strong, centralized government or a tightly knit and amazingly smooth-running confederacy. . . . The first large population centers in the Valley date from the Gallinazo Period. . . . Such sites were urban concentrations, although they differ in lack of plan from the urban centers of the late periods of Perú [sic], such as Chanchan. . . . Settlement organization and architectural types remain much the same in the Huancaco Period as they did in the Late Gallinazo phase. The unusually large site of Huancaco, which has the appearance of an impressive Pyramid Mound joined to a palace complex, is the most probable "capital" for a unified Valley command during the period. This unified Valley command was probably in the hands of Mochica war leaders. Their presence and control is implied in the art style of the Huancaco

Period which is pure Mochica. . . . In the decorated grave pottery of the Huancaco Period, the old Gallinazo styles have been completely replaced by the Mochica ware; and at some of the Gallinazo Castillo Fortifications Mochica ceramics are found overlying those of the Gallinazo Period. (Willey 1953:396–397)

More than half a century ago, three different ways of interpreting the relations between Virú-Gallinazo and Moche-Mochica were therefore introduced in the literature. These three positions differed but had in common the idea that ceramics are a sure indicator of ethnic identity.

- *Larco Hoyle:* Virú = ethnic aspect (rivals and subjects of the Moche)

- *Ford and Strong and Evans:* Gallinazo = temporal aspect (an antecedent of the Moche)

- *Willey:* Gallinazo = political aspect of the state or confederacy of macro-chiefdoms, rivaling and finally subjugated by the people of the neighboring Moche Valley

These three ways of understanding the Virú-Gallinazo relations with Moche-Huancaco left an imprint on the discussion of this issue that has lasted to the present day. The proposal advanced by Ford and by Strong and Evans was strengthened by the finds made by the Chan Chan–Moche Valley Project headed by Michael Moseley and Carol Mackey.

Theresa Topic (1977:51–128, 138) recorded a Gallinazo occupation below levels with Moche ceramics at a considerable depth (3.05–5.60 m) to the north and west of the area extending between the Huaca del Sol and Huaca de la Luna (see Chapter 7). It must be stressed that at Huacas de Moche, mortuary contexts containing Virú-Gallinazo ceramics also have Moche I and Moche II pieces as well as hybrid Gallinazo-Moche–style vessels (Topic 1977:128–132). Thus, the sequence proposed by Larco Hoyle in 1948 (Salinar, Virú-Gallinazo, Virú-Gallinazo/Orange Mochica/ Mochica I, Mochica II–V) was apparently confirmed by the stratigraphic data from systematic excavations.

The surveys of the lower Santa and Casma Valleys undertaken by David J. Wilson (1988) likewise strengthened with new data the scenario posited by the members of the Virú Valley Project. Wilson not only used Willey's site-recording methodology and typological criteria, but followed Ford's and Strong and Evans's chronologies. There is a substantial methodologic difference between these procedures, however. Wilson (1988:66–72) did not find it convenient to develop his own frequency seriation, from which a local chronology could be posited for each of the valleys surveyed. Nor did he seek stratigraphic support for his proposal.

Wilson's chronology is based on the comparison of materials from sites he believed had a single component in Santa and Casma, and from the drawings and photographs with which Ford and Strong and Evans had illustrated their chronologies for the Virú Valley. The formal typology and some characteristics of the finishing therefore take on decisive weight as diagnostic variables. For instance, the Early Suchimancillo period (Virú-Gallinazo) was defined by 6 types of bowls, 11 types of jars, sculpted animal faces modeled on the shoulders of the jugs, white-and-orange/redware decorations, and kaolinite ware.

Decorated bowls with burnished lines from the Vinzos (Puerto Moorin–Salinar) period were still in use during the Early Suchimancillo period. The index of formal/stylistic connection with the highlands was particularly high, at 65%. In Wilson's Late Suchimancillo period (Wilson 1988: 67–68), the following are diagnostic: 5 types of bowls, 11 types of jars, triangles with incised dots on the edges of the jars, a wide white-on-red band, human and animal faces, and kaolinite ware. In this case, the index of formal/stylistic connection with the highlands falls to 30%.

As in the chronology of the Virú Valley Project, the Vinzos and Suchimancillo periods are essentially characterized by the forms and scant decorations of plain utilitarian vessels—with shapes facilitating the storage, cooking, and pouring of liquids and solids. The subsequent period, Guadalupito (Huancaco-Mochica IV–V), is instead characterized by fine ceramic forms and decorations with a clear ceremonial role, which likewise comprise some utilitarian shapes such as small and midsize vessels: one type of bowl, three types of jars, flaring vases, figurative and geometric white-on-red and red-on-white decorations,

portrait vessels, depictions of the fanged Moche deity, and spouts characteristic of Moche bottles. Also diagnostic of this period are perfect oxidizing firing (shown by the brick-red color) and the use of molds. Wilson notes that:

> while there are similarities with respect to colors used in decoration (e.g., white, cream, and red) and design features . . . , there is also substantial variability in the number and types of specific motifs present in the assemblages of each of the valleys. Among other things this suggests that ceramics were produced locally for the most part during this period, even though potters clearly followed Moche canons rather closely. (Wilson 1988:69)

From the inferred population density, the presumed area cultivated with maize, and the complexity and size of the settlements, Wilson (1988:296–345) infers that it was only in the Guadalupito period that the Santa Valley was incorporated into a multi-valley state whose capital was located in the Moche Valley. However, the Suchimancillo period was also characterized by a complex settlement pattern with four ranked tiers, as well as by an irrigation network. The proposal is based on the history of local and regional ceramic styles, as well as on iconographic evidence, particularly combat scenes and images of individuals dressed as warriors seated atop stepped structures.

Wilson interprets these depictions as testimony that a central authority dressed as a warrior from the Moche Valley was able to wage wars of conquest and subdue neighboring peoples. Wilson likewise uses the argument advanced by Alfred Kroeber (1944:126) regarding the small number of basic forms that characterized the Moche style in contrast with remarkable local variability. Strangely, Wilson does not realize that these basic forms are related to small and midsize vessels used to serve and handle liquids and that those vessels could hardly have been used as substitutes for the pots and jars so typical of Suchimancillo ceramics (and which are rare in Moche samples).

In two successive studies, Heidy Fogel (1987, 1993) reviewed the Virú-Gallinazo materials from systematic excavations and surveys made in the

Virú, Moche, and Santa Valleys. The starting point was a critical review of Bennett's stratigraphic test pits using the field documentation and an analysis of the ceramic materials (Fogel 1987). Fogel managed to define three successive phases: Early, Middle, and Late Gallinazo.

The sequence posited by Fogel has two weaknesses. First, her Early Gallinazo phase was defined from a very small number of fragments and an even smaller number of diagnostic characteristics. The lowest levels bearing Early Gallinazo ceramics have structures built with ball adobe bricks, *tapia* (puddled adobe), and cane-marked adobe bricks. The architecture of the superimposed levels with Middle and Late Gallinazo ceramics has walls built solely with cane-marked adobe bricks. This early phase was defined based on three subtypes of small and midsize jars with a straight flaring neck, a non-diagnostic grating bowl, a thickened rim from a neckless pot, and a fragment from a pedestal base that is also non-diagnostic. The poor diagnostic nature of this sample precludes a convincing comparison with materials from other valleys.

Another problem lies in the fact that Fogel made no systematic study of Gallinazo-associated materials—particularly of Recuay and Early Moche styles—in collections from the Moche, Virú, and Santa Valleys. Fogel also did not take into account the radiocarbon dates associated with these styles. Despite abundant evidence to the contrary, Fogel (1993:164–165) was convinced that Larco Hoyle's Moche I developed at the end of her Late Gallinazo phase.[2]

Fogel also raised the possibility that the Moche I and Moche II phases were part of what she called the transitional Gallinazo-Moche style and should therefore not be considered autonomous phases (Fogel 1993:237). This agrees with her main thesis, which states that a strong and expansive political center with the potential to subdue the neighboring valleys arose in Virú during the Middle Gallinazo phase. The presumed evidence for a conquest of the Moche Valley comes from cemeteries and settlements (Fogel 1993:204–209).

During the late 1980s, the first project of systematic excavations with several parallel lines of research in the upper Piura Valley took place under the direction of Jean Guffroy, Peter Kaulicke, and Krzysztof Makowski. I personally (Guffroy, Kaulicke, and Makowski 1989:123) intended to elucidate the relations between the multiple styles, local and potentially foreign, present in this valley in the Early Intermediate period. This was done through excavations at the sites of Cerro Vicús and Pampa Juárez.

These sites are adjacent to looted cemeteries that contained burials featuring ceramics of Early Moche and Virú-Gallinazo styles. Along with a group of students, Makowski (Murro 1990; Eléspuru 1993; Amaro 1994; Makowski et al. 1994) also began a systematic registry and analysis of the ceramic pieces in these same styles using collections recovered by Guzmán Ladrón de Guevara and José Casafranca in their excavations, as well as pieces with unknown provenience in public and private collections (Makowski, Amaro, and Eléspuru 1994).

The results concur with data from excavations undertaken on Vicús and Moche-Gallinazo monumental architecture (Kaulicke 1991, 1992). Diagnostic Virú-Gallinazo features, such as tapia walls and the typical pottery with close parallels in the Virú and Jequetepeque Valleys, appear in the stratigraphic levels superimposed over levels with Vicús-Vicús architecture and ceramics dating to the earliest developmental phase of the latter style. The diagnostic fragments of Moche-style bottles and dippers are directly associated with the Virú-Gallinazo materials in primary contexts and in unaltered occupation levels. It must be emphasized that the Vicús style developed coevally with the Moche and Virú-Gallinazo styles throughout the Early Intermediate period, as evidenced by their direct association (Makowski et al. 1994; Makowski 2004:52–55).

Based on these data, I developed the following interpretive proposal (Makowski 1994b, 1998, 2004): a major change took place in the occupational sequence of the upper Piura Valley between the Vicús-Vicús (Kaulicke's [1991] Tamarindo A) and Early Vicús-Moche (A.D. 200–500; Kaulicke's [1991] Tamarindo B and C1) phases. Some populations appeared that manufactured and used the largely utilitarian Virú-Gallinazo pottery, as well as fine ceremonial wares in the Orange Mochica and Mochica I and Mochica II styles—

along with some variants of Larco Hoyle's phase III. These populations subdued the local populace, and Moche-style constructions and cemeteries (such as those of Loma Negra and Huaca de las Cruces) were established in the midst of Vicús buildings and burials.

In 1994, Izumi Shimada and Adriana Maguiña posited a different interpretation of the relations between Virú-Gallinazo and Moche (Shimada and Maguiña 1994). They convincingly showed that the two styles are coeval and are present in the same contexts, from the initial sequence of the Moche culture to its latest phases. For them, each of these styles corresponds to an ethnic group that coexisted in the large expanse where the Moche culture developed. The Virú-Gallinazo style would therefore likewise correspond to a population subdued by elites that used Moche fine wares.

NEW EVIDENCE ON NORTH-COAST CHRONOLOGY

A major reanalysis of north-coast chronology is now urgent in light of new evidence amassed in the last 10 years, and these modifications will likewise impinge to a great extent upon the problem posed by the relations between Moche-Huancaco and Virú-Gallinazo phenomena. It is clear that the morphologic features of the Moche I and Moche II stirrup spouts may be considered fully coeval with those of Moche III. There is likewise no solid evidence to support the presence of a phase II in terms of occupational and cultural development.

This seems proven by the stratified contexts of the Huaca de la Luna (Kaulicke 1992; Fogel 1993), Huaca el Brujo (Franco, Gálvez, and Vásquez 2003:157–158), and Huancaco (Bourget 2003) and by burial assemblages with reliable radiocarbon dates, such as those from Dos Cabezas (Donnan 2003) and Pacatnamú (Ubbelohde-Doering 1966:23–24). Although it can be claimed that some relatively archaic stylistic features in the morphology of vessels and in fine-line paintings with Moche I and Moche II spouts are associated with the very origins of the Moche style (Donnan and McClelland 1999), it is no less true that the presence of these same features does not

suffice to ascribe a piece to the initial phases of the chronological sequence.

The radiocarbon dates suggest that Moche I and Moche II features were popular between A.D. 200 and 600, and that Moche IV and Moche V features occurred between A.D. 400 and 800 (Makowski, Amaro, and Eléspuru 1994). Moche III can be coeval with either period. For this reason, it seems more accurate to divide the Moche sequence into two major periods (A.D. 200–500 and 500–800) rather than three.

The data from two major Moche ceremonial and urban centers in the Moche and Chicama Valleys—as well as the results of the Upper Piura, Sipán, and Dos Cabezas projects—fully support this conclusion. It is worth noting that during the first period, Virú-Gallinazo ceramic materials are not only always associated with Moche materials, accounting for 80% to 90% of each sample recorded in systematic excavations. The percentages are the opposite in burial contexts, particularly in those of the high Moche elite (Donnan 2003).

Recent evidence has led to a reconsideration of Willey's influential proposals (1953). Steve Bourget (2003) has collected data showing that Huancaco (Virú's presumed Moche capital city and the eponymous site of this phase, whose major architectural component was abandoned in the sixth or seventh century A.D. according to three calibrated radiocarbon dates) does not have a direct relation with the culture of the Moche Valley. The only stylistically Moche vessel is a phase I bottle similar to the one recorded by Bennett (1939:Fig. 15) in burial n° 5 from the Gallinazo Group. As regards construction systems and organization of space, the architecture of the palace is similar to that found in the Moche and Chicama Valleys. This architecture is divided into plazas and roofed areas laid out in three ascending levels, with a system of restricted entrance and adorned with wall paintings.

It must be emphasized that the present evidence from Huaca de la Cruz also does not necessarily support the proposals made by Strong and Evans (1952:192–203) and Willey (1953) regarding the military expansion of the Moche state during phases III and IV, which would have entailed the implementation of an efficient system of territorial control over the lower and middle valley. Juan Mogrovejo (1995:42–55) correctly notes that Bennett (1939:31–32, 34, 50) and Strong and Evans (1952:192–203) recorded direct associations between Moche I and Moche II ceramics and Gallinazo-style pottery. The most revealing case is that of Bennett's (1939:Fig. 7a) burial G11 A, which held in the same chamber bottles and jars with the formal and decorative characteristics that recur in Larco Hoyle's (1948) phases I and II and to a lesser extent in his phase III.

The excavations made by Krzysztof Makowski and Milosz Giersz in the Culebras Valley, on the southern frontier of the Moche area (Giersz and Przadka 2003), provide additional data for a revision of the influential chronology posited by the Virú Valley Project. During the 2003 and 2004 seasons, we excavated an elite Moche residential and ceremonial compound at Quillapampa. Quillapampa lies on the road from Pañamarca (in Nepeña) to Huarmey, and offers visual control of a large expanse of the Culebras Valley. The structure of orthogonal layout is distributed along several successive and ascending terraces over a sandy knoll that rises over the valley at a strategic location. The retaining walls are of stone, and the buildings atop the terraces are of wattle and daub. The roofs were adorned with ceramic clubs. A labyrinthine access system leading to the top was partially exposed during the excavations.

A chamber constructed of plain parallelepiped adobe bricks was erected during the enlargement of the building (Figure 3.1). Its contents were completely disturbed by looters, but part of a rich assemblage was recovered: ornaments of gilded copper and abundant fine Moche III ceramics (Figure 3.2). The profiles of the unit where the chamber was found produced good data on the chronological sequence. The chamber was associated with the second of three successive floors that extend over the large rectangular rooms on the summit. The structure and the first floor were associated with Gallinazo White-on-Red and Gallinazo Negative sherds (Figure 3.3), as well as with Moche Red-on-Cream sherds. Below the structure, which apparently dates to the end of the Early Moche period (A.D. 200–500), there was a level of wattle-and-daub architecture related to late Early Horizon ceramics (decorated with dotted circles and triangles filled with incisions).

The Moche and Virú-Gallinazo ceramics from Quillapampa are similar to those associated with the first architectural phases of Huaca Cao Viejo and the ceremonial buildings of Huaca de la Luna (see Chapters 6 and 7). The specific characteristics of the ware and the slip in most of the pieces suggest that these specimens were manufactured locally, however. The presence of an elite residence of this size with chamber burials shows that a people fully identified with the Moche culture (its rites and iconography) were in control of the route from Nepeña to Huarmey since the earliest phases. There certainly is a need for a reassessment of the role the manufacture of ceremonial ceramics had in the political life of the Early Intermediate period.

The results attained by our research in Piura, at the other end of the "Moche world," compel us to document this complex problem. The Moche occupation of the Piura River basin was an enclave on the most important route of long-distance trade that crossed the Andes—the road followed by traders of *Conus* sp., *Spondylus* sp., and *Strombus* sp. shells (Hocquenghem 1991; Hoc-

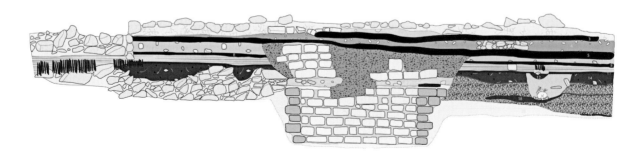

FIGURE 3.1. Moche building made with stone and plain adobe bricks, Quillapampa.

FIGURE 3.2. Fragmented Moche ceramics from burial.

quenghem et al. 1993). During the first centuries of the present era, this area provided access to the Loja region and was under the control of populations culturally connected with the north Andean area. Their elites had direct access to goods and specialists from the Tumaco–La Tolita area.

The warrior populations in Piura are associated with Virú-Gallinazo ceramics (predominant in domestic contexts) and with Moche I, Moche II, and Moche III ceramics—which are particularly common in the tombs of rulers (e.g., at Loma Negra) but on average do not seem to comprise more than 10% of the total number of fragments or pieces found. These warrior populations seem to have followed the route along Olmos, the piedmont, and the upper-middle basin of the Piura Valley. Their arrival is related to the abandonment of the alleged Vicús ceremonial center at Loma Valverde.

The stratigraphic superposition of the vestiges, the coexistence of Vicús and Moche monumental architecture, and the stylistic dialogue that existed between Vicús and Moche-Gallinazo elite potters during the Vicús–Early Moche period all suggest that the southern leaders carried out a policy that included local rulers in political (and religious) life during the first or second century of southern dominance. Later we find that the workshops pro-

ducing Vicús elite ceramics vanished, which brought about a decline in the repertoire of themes and personages and a diffusion of the domestic ceramic forms and techniques known as Sechura (in Lanning's [1963] terminology), which were adapted to ceremonial uses (Amaro 1994; Makowski et al. 1994:299–304, Figs. 206–237; Makowski 2004:53–55).

The excavations and surveys undertaken by the Pontificia Universidad Católica del Perú-Office de la recherche scientifique et technique d'Outre-Mer (PUCP-ORSTOM) Upper Piura Project provided a relatively detailed perspective on the functioning of one of the major centers of power in the upper Piura Valley that lay below the Cerro Vicús, on the left bank of the Piura River. Its core comprised two high platforms raised with plain, unmarked rectangular adobe bricks (with several successive enlargement phases, from Early Vicús-Mochica to well into Late Vicús-Mochica). Fronting these platforms were plazas with evidence of successive reunions that entailed the consumption of beverages and meat in a ritual context.

There is some evidence of possible human and camelid sacrifices (Kaulicke 1991). The surrounding domestic occupation was neither necessarily dense nor permanent, and seems to have been associated with periodic rituals. A similar

FIGURE 3.3. Ceramic fragments from excavation of Moche building (see also Figure 3.1): (*a*) Gallinazo White-on-Red sherds and (*b*) Gallinazo Negative sherds from disturbed fill of burial chamber.

picture is observable to the south of the complex, where the cemeteries of Yécala and Loma Negra extend over more than a square kilometer. An extensive field with workshops associated with dwellings and encampments was recorded at the edge of the cemeteries. Surface finds and excavations revealed the presence of potters' and smiths' kilns (Makowski and Velarde 1998 [1996]). The ceramics associated with these activities are of Gallinazo, Moche, and Vicús styles, as well as some exotic minority traditions from the coast and highlands. This same combination of styles appears in the neighboring cemeteries.

It could be argued that the manufacture of mortuary accoutrements and the ceremonies entailing sacrifices and banquets shared by people of different origins served as a solid, religion-based, political support that enabled southern Moche leaders to establish comfortable relations of ritual kinship. These same relations opened the door to the prized tropical shells, and perhaps to sources of copper in the Sechura desert and of gold from the Quiróz River.

TECHNOLOGICAL IDENTITY OF CERAMICS PRODUCERS

How may a possible ethnic origin be empirically supported without falling into the trap of a circular argument developed from variables of form and style? In the approach taken here, a relatively easy means of exploring this problem is to correlate the technological identity of a producer with his/her ability to reproduce the forms, decorative techniques, and designs that recur in one or several styles.

To this end, a conventional macroscopic ware analysis was used. Iván Amaro and Krzysztof Makowski (Amaro 1994; Makowski 1994b) thus distinguished 19 wares that correspond to the same number of different technological traditions, with the following cultural and stylistic affiliations: five of Moche style, eight in the Vicús style, four of Virú style (Figures 3.4–3.9), and two wares classified as exotic due to their characteristic Ecuadorian influence (from the coast and the highlands, respectively). The wares were distinguished from one another by the choice of clays and temper, the techniques used to prepare the ware and build the vessels, and the firing conditions and preferences used in the finishing.

Iván Ghezzi then analyzed the thin sections with an electron microprobe at Yale University. These same samples were also analyzed by Hector Neff with the laser ablation inductively coupled plasma mass spectrometry (LA-ICP-MS) analytical technique (Speakman and Neff 2005). An attempt was also made to specify the recurrence of mineralogical components in each ware. The electron microprobe yielded results that provided a description of the chemical composition of the ceramic samples in qualitative and quantitative terms ("bulk chemistry analysis") and allowed the minerals to be identified.

Microphotographs of thin sheets were analyzed at the Pontificia Universidad Católica del Perú to complete the petrography analysis with a quantitative mineralogical analysis of clay inclusions (Figures 3.10, 3.11). Rosabella Alvarez-Calderón and Manuel Lizárraga then subjected these sheets to a mineralogical analysis of forms, sizes, densities, and characteristics of the inclusions using imaging software.

Thus far, only 34 thin sections have been analyzed (2 per sample) due to the costs involved. The results agree with those obtained through a traditional macroscopic analysis, however. The Gallinazo wares are quite close to the Moche wares in composition. Except for one case, potters seem to have used the same sources of clay and actually used related techniques to prepare the wares and build the vessels. The macroscopic analysis ascertained that the Gallinazo wares comprise a significant number of Moche forms and designs.

Vicús wares are distant, but the exotic wares of Ecuadorian origin are even more distant (a cluster with six variables). It must be noted, however, that a number of sherds with typical Vicús wares are related with Moche forms. The same conclusion was reached through stylistic comparisons. This concurs with the data derived from burials and ceremonial contexts, where the presence of more than one style in primary sealed contexts is quite frequent.

In general, the networks of ceramic distribution bear no direct relation to the political or ethnic identity of the users, particularly when one analyzes complex societies (Makowski and Vega Centeno 2004). In other words, correspondence among political space, area of diffusion of a ceramic style, and ethnic identity seldom happens. On the other hand, there is no question that the chronological and spatial distributions of ceramic styles follow directly from the organization of the output and distribution of the artifacts. They are likewise an expression of the political, economic, and ideological relations in society.

We must therefore not expect that the mapping of the distribution of styles will always allow us to identify ethnic spaces, or to clearly and accurately delimit the frontiers separating different peoples and states. The technological tradition is a more straightforward and unequivocal index of ethnic identity. When workshops have a well-defined technological tradition, however, they may use their ample repertoire of raw materials and procedures to produce pottery in varied styles.

The hypothetical parallel development of Salinar-Mochica and Early Gallinazo-Virú-Gallinazo as a manifestation of two different ethnic identities (one of them subordinate to the other) can be supported in terms of an abstract stylistic evolution and/or on the basis of some loans or technological continuities in the specialized manufacture of pottery. The latter follows from the identities of the producers, but not necessarily from the users of the vessels. Even so, there are no contextual or occupational data with which to support this.

Virú 1

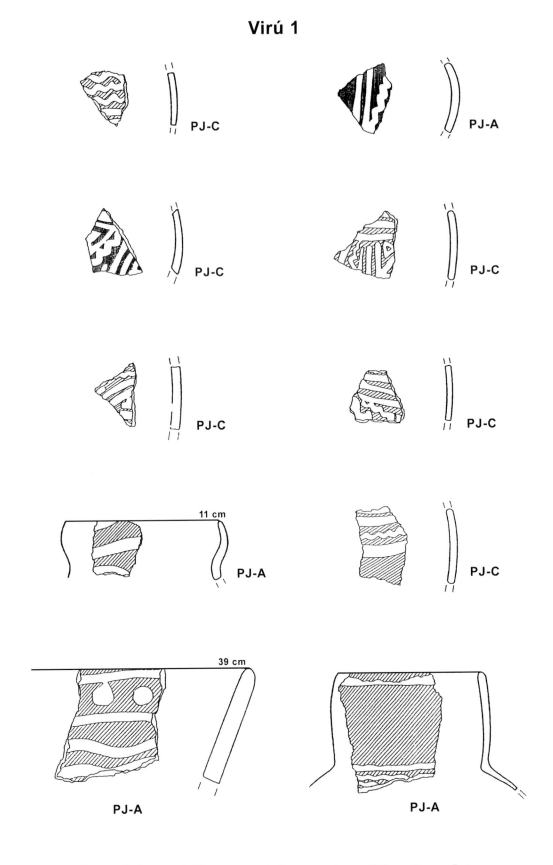

FIGURE 3.4. Virú-Gallinazo ceramic fragments (ware 1) from Pampa Juárez.
Compare with Kaulicke (1994:356, Fig. 10.6, Vicús-Tamarindo C).

Virú 1

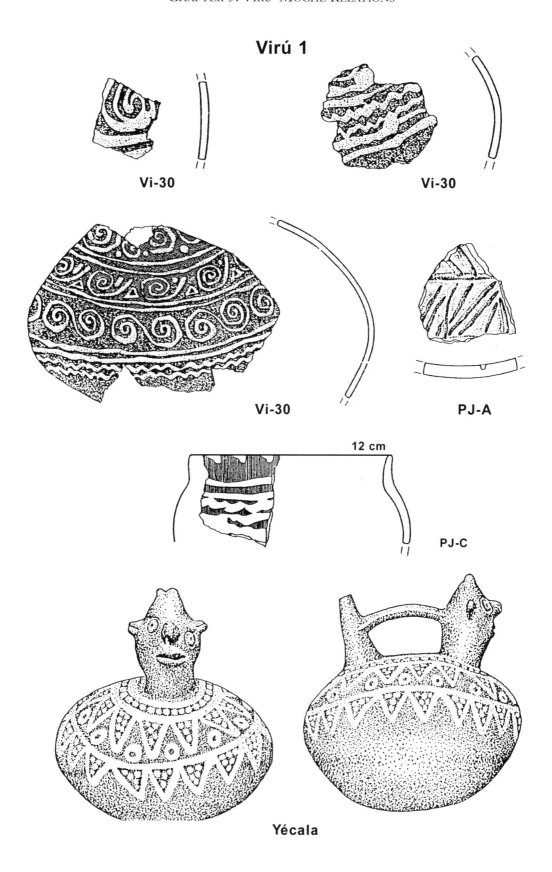

Vi-30

Vi-30

Vi-30

PJ-A

12 cm

PJ-C

Yécala

FIGURE 3.5. Virú-Gallinazo ceramic fragments (ware 1) from Pampa Juárez and Yécala. Compare with Strong and Evans (1952:Figs. 59A, D, N; 60A; 61A, Gallinazo Negative).

Virú 1

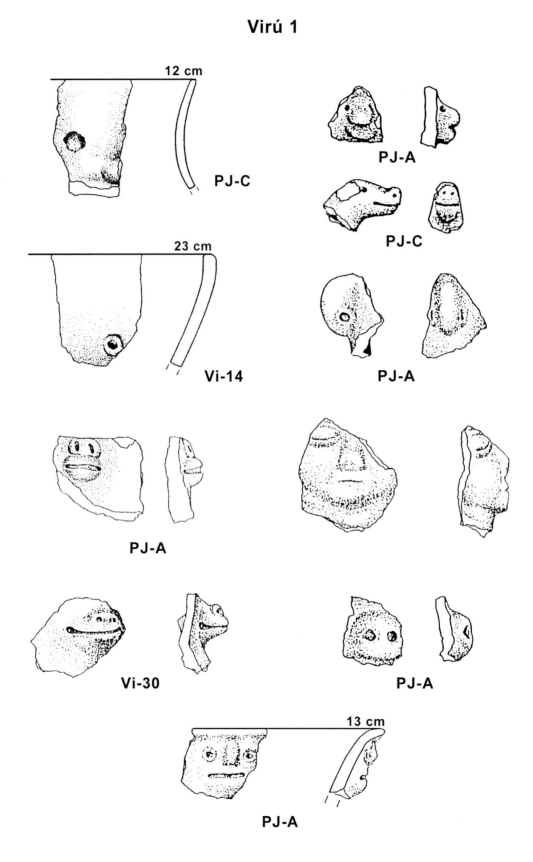

FIGURE 3.6. Virú-Gallinazo ceramic fragments (ware 1) from Pampa Juárez. Compare with Kaulicke (1994:353, Figs. 10.14A–B, Vicús-Tamarindo C1) and Strong and Evans (1952:Figs. 60J, K, O, Castillo Modeled).

Virú 2

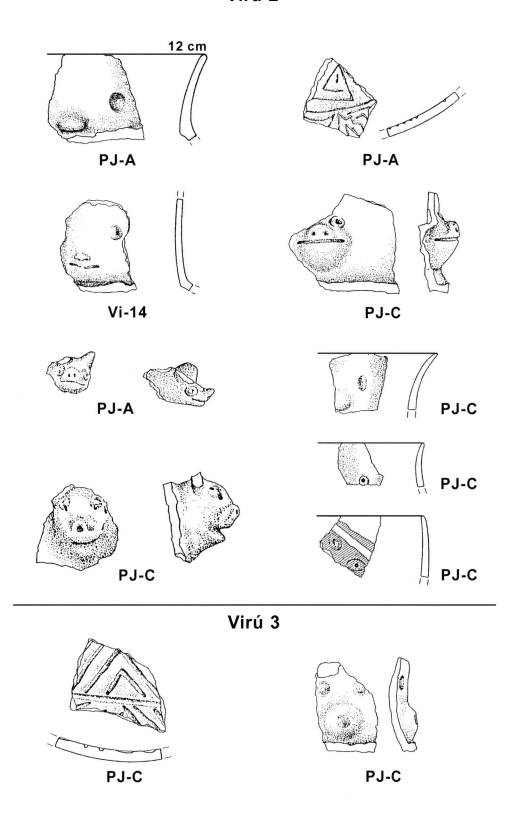

FIGURE 3.7. Virú-Gallinazo ceramic fragments (wares 2 and 3) from Pampa Juárez. Compare with Kaulicke (1994:353, Fig. 10.14D) and Strong and Evans (1952:Figs. 67K, L, Castillo Incised).

Virú 4

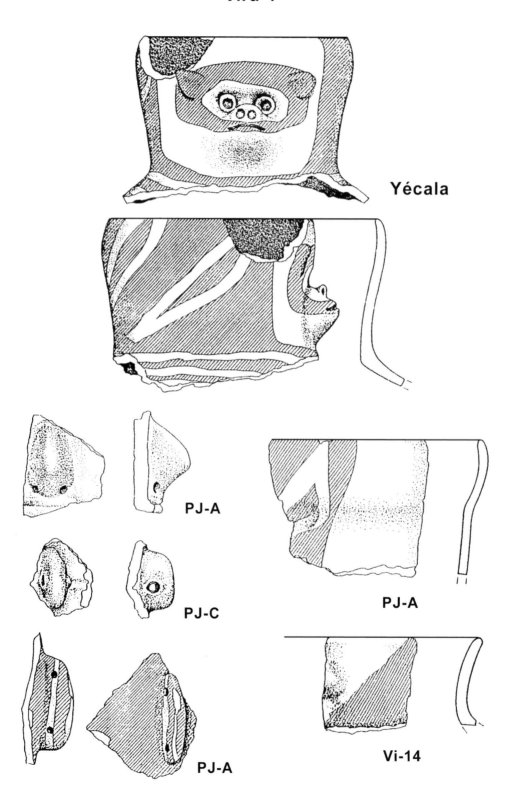

FIGURE 3.8. Virú-Gallinazo ceramic fragments (ware 4) from Pampa Juárez and Yécala.

Virú 4

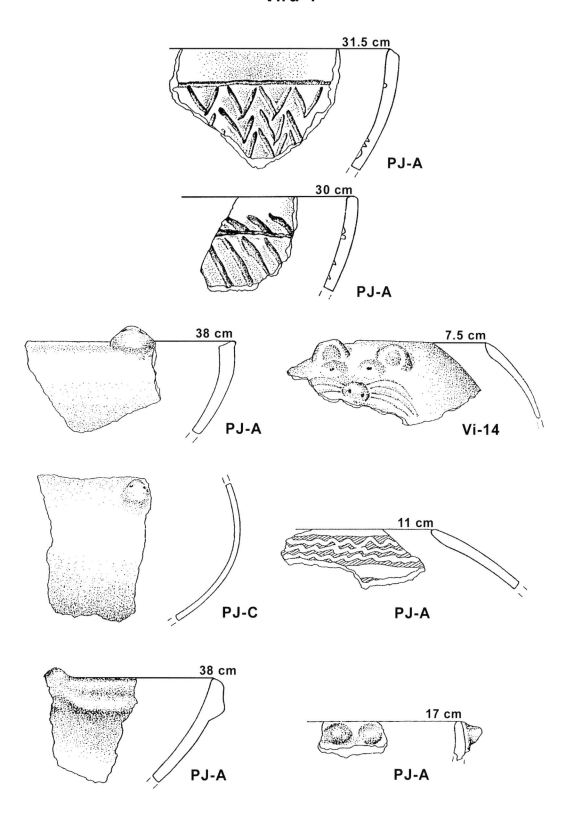

FIGURE 3.9. Virú-Gallinazo bowl and grater bowl fragments (ware 4) from Pampa Juárez.

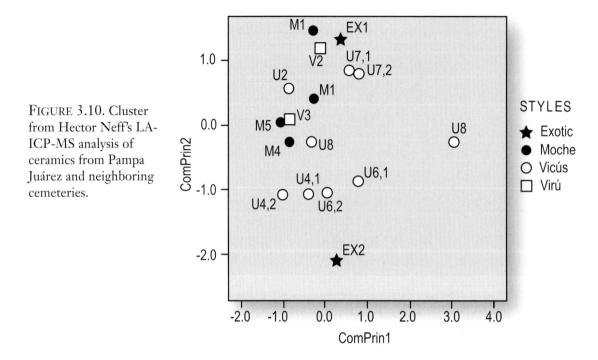

FIGURE 3.10. Cluster from Hector Neff's LA-ICP-MS analysis of ceramics from Pampa Juárez and neighboring cemeteries.

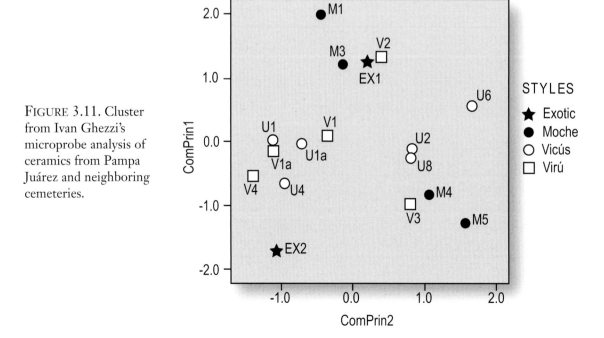

FIGURE 3.11. Cluster from Ivan Ghezzi's microprobe analysis of ceramics from Pampa Juárez and neighboring cemeteries.

Nowhere in the Moche cultural area has it been shown that the users of Virú-Gallinazo utilitarian ceramics had to abandon their ceremonial centers and elite settlements to the users of Moche utilitarian pottery. On the contrary, Virú-Gallinazo ceramics are abundant in all sampling of Early Moche habitational contexts. These samples comprise types functionally related with the cooking and storage of food, as well as with food being served. Only occasionally did the workshops that made storage jars, pots, and grating bowls also produce some ceremonial forms such as bottles and dippers.

The ceramics known as Mochica-Moche instead comprise almost exclusively ceremonial forms: bottles, dippers, flaring bowls (in the south), and small and midsize jars. In the Early Moche period (A.D. 200–500), the workshops that specialized in fine and coarse ceramics also dedicated themselves occasionally to the manufacture of utilitarian forms. In the Late Moche period (A.D. 500–800), a more intensive use of technology in ceramics took place, with the generalized use of molds and the paddle and anvil (as well as large furnaces)—and this had natural repercussions.

Large workshops—such as those of the Huaca de la Luna (Uceda and Armas 1997, 1998) and Cerro Mayal (Russell, Leonard, and Briceño 1998; Russell and Jackson 2001)—satisfied most of the needs of the surrounding populations and imposed a relatively uniform style related to the highly technical Moche tradition. Wherever we find these workshops, the presence of the Gallinazo style decreases substantially, although some Gallinazo characteristics survive, such as faces modeled on vessel necks and designs incised on the insides of grating bowls. Naturally, the first vessels to be discontinued in manufacture were the fine Virú ceremonial vessels. The Virú-Moche transitional style (Larco Hoyle 1945; Fogel 1993) marks the moment such ceremonial vessels vanished.

Burials with Virú-Gallinazo ceramics usually exhibit the characteristics of the matrix or chamber and extended position of the body typically defined as Moche (Larco Hoyle 1945; Millaire 2002), except in cases of possible interaction with the highland Recuay tradition. In addition, no remarkable differences have been noted between Middle and Late Gallinazo and Moche monumental architecture in the Moche, Chicama, Santa, and Virú Valleys (Table 3.1).

TABLE 3.1. Relations between Virú-Gallinazo and Mochica-Moche "culture styles."

VIRÚ-GALLINAZO	MOCHICA-MOCHE
Largely utilitarian pottery (± 90%): large storage jars, cooking vessels with and without a neck, grating bowls, jars, and bowls.	*Occasionally* utilitarian pottery (± 10%): cooking vessels with and without a neck, small and midsize jars, bowls, and plates.
Occasionally ceremonial pottery (± 10%): spout-and-bridge bottles, and dippers.	*Largely* ceremonial pottery (± 90%): stirrup-spout bottles, single-spout and spout-and-bridge bottles, dippers, small and midsize jars, flaring bowls, vases, and dippers.
SHARED BY VIRÚ-GALLINAZO AND MOCHICA-MOCHE	
Chamber and pit burials with skeleton in extended position, lying on the back. Copper objects were placed in the mouth.	
Headdresses with an upright feather and two stepped signs, and types of dress.	
Ceremonial architecture built with cane-marked adobe bricks, sometimes decorated with polychrome murals or relief.	
Agglutinated domestic architecture and elite orthogonal structures.	
Defensive and ceremonial enclosures of the "castle" type.	
A recurring and direct association of diagnostic components for both cultural styles in the same habitational and ceremonial spaces, in the same burial chambers, and in the same cemeteries.	

A comparison of iconography provides more important arguments for a final rejection of the scenario wherein two peoples, the Virú-Gallinazo and the Moche, clashed during the rise of the expansive Moche state. Were this hypothesis correct, one would expect to find a strong differentiation in attire and headpieces during the period of open conflict, as these clashes usually strengthen respective ethnic identities. One would also expect to find images of competing leaders in Moche scenes of combat and human sacrifice (something that does not exist) and would also expect the attributes of the vanquished chiefs to vanish from iconography after the presumed Moche victory.

The helmets, headdresses, and attire that recur in the scant Virú figurative bottles and jars are present in Moche iconography in the early and late periods. Helmets with stepped signs, turbans with a feline head or body, and headdresses with two vertical feathers (Figure 3.12) worn by officials (Makowski 1994a) appear in the various

rituals depicted in Moche iconography and are not preferentially associated with the depiction of neighboring highland peoples.

It is clear that individuals with Virú-style dress and headdress took part in activities—processions, dances, deer hunts, sea lion hunts, nocturnal offerings where coca was consumed, snail collecting, flower throwing, combat, presentation of the cup, and races between naked prisoners—alongside other individuals wearing the attire considered typical of the Moche.[3] These persons have the roles of warrior, attendant, musician, and chief—and nothing indicates that they held a subordinate role.

Moreover, the feline headdress (Morales, Asmat, and Fernández 2000) was closely related to the priestly role. It was worn by the person presiding over the sacrifice ceremony (Kutscher 1983). Furthermore, the recurring attributes of the Virú-style persons previously cited characterize major coastal deities such as the Terrestrial Twin, the

FIGURE 3.12. Reconstruction of the Virú-style headdresses. *Illustration courtesy of Hugo Ikehara.*

Marine Twin, the warrior Owl (or sacrificer), the Bat sacrificer, and the Eagle warrior.[4]

It must be noted that the two twins have a major role in Moche religious ideology and are among the entities whose deeds are most often depicted in detail (Castillo 1989; Bourget 1994). The list of their deeds in the scenes depicted in relief and in fine-line painting suggests that their role was that of the ancestral civilizing heroes of Moche society (Hocquenghem 1987:184–185). The supernatural owls and bats, in turn, appear to be in charge of human sacrifices—as acolytes and epiphanies of the god of the mountains and of the underworld (Makowski 1996).

ETHNICITY AND MATERIAL CULTURE

A review of the history of the research on the relations between the Virú-Gallinazo and the Moche shows the strong influence the traditional *ethos* and culture still exert on north-coast archaeology. In these approaches,

> through the concept of an archaeological culture the past is reconstructed in terms of the distribution of homogeneous cultures whose history unfolds in a coherent linear narrative measured in terms of objectified events, such as contacts, migrations and conquests, with intervals of homogeneous, empty time between them. . . .This kind of temporal framework is what Fabian (1983: 23) identifies as "typological time." (Jones 1996:65, 76, n. 3)

It helps to recall here, per Bruce Trigger (1989: 155–174) and Colin Renfrew (1996:126–128), that this meaning of culture arose in the midst of debates on the origins of Western civilization. The works and perspectives of Gustaf Kossinna and Gordon Childe have exerted a strong influence on the debate. On the other hand, as Siân Jones (1996:64) correctly notes, "the expectations of boundedness, homogeneity and continuity which have been built into ideas concerning culture since the nineteenth century are related to nationalism and the emergence of the nation-state."

Three antecedents have left a deep imprint on the conceptual foundations of the cultural-historical approach previously cited: the typological method of Oscar Montelius, Leo Frobenius's ideas on *Kulturkreise* or cultural areas (Díaz-Andreu 1996:55), and the normative proposals made by Kossinna. The latter believed that the consistency, permanence, and homogeneity of an archaeological culture bear a direct relation to the degree of purity and consistency of the ethos—which is characterized not just by a language, but by a race, religion, assemblage of institutions and mores, and particular creative skill. In sum, according to Kossinna, these outweigh a culture's historical role. For Kossinna, as for Childe, "Prehistory can recognize peoples and marshal them on the stage to take the place of the personal actors who form the historian's troupe" (Childe 1940:2).

Since Childe wrote the previous, some profound changes have taken place in the way problems raised by an ethnic identity are perceived in archaeology and anthropology. For Jones (1996: 66), these began in the 1960s and early 1970s, a period that saw "the proliferation of research into ethnicity, and the use of 'ethnic group' in place of 'tribe' and 'race'," as well as an increasing emphasis that was "placed on the self-identifications of the social actors concerned, the processes involved in the construction of group boundaries, and the interrelationships between socio-cultural groups" (Jones 1996:66).

For Fredrik Barth (1969:10), whose particularly influential and significant contribution marked a veritable turning point in the discussions regarding this issue, the identity of an ethnic group does not follow from a list of similarities and differences established by the researcher, but from "categories of ascription and identification by the actors themselves." This is a subjective "we-feeling" (Francis 1947:397) that may only be broached from an emic perspective rather than an etic one (Renfrew 1996:130).

If this is so, we must conclude with Richard Fardon (1987:176) that rather than discovering a general form of universal difference, archaeologists invented it! However, new paths were opened by the contributions made by structuralism as regards technological identity (the *chaîne opératoire*), mortuary behavior, and the organization of domestic space—as well as by Pierre Bourdieu's post-structuralist theories.

From the perspective of Bourdieu's (1977) theory of practice, "the subjective construction of ethnic identity in the context of social interaction is grounded in the shared subliminal disposition of the habitus which shape, and are shaped, by commonalities of practice" (Jones 1996:68). A shared habitus engenders feelings of identification among people similarly endowed. These feelings are consciously appropriated and given form through existing symbolic resources (Bentley 1987). Identities are not permanent. They are developed in a historical context and modified or replaced with other identities throughout time via a discourse among the social actors within each society and with neighbors. As Jones argues:

> It is at such a discursive level that ethnic categories are produced, reproduced and transformed through the systematic communication of cultural difference with relation to the cultural practices of particular "ethnic others.". . . Hence, configurations of ethnicity, and consequently the styles of material culture involved in the signification and structuring of ethnic relations, may vary in different social contexts and with relation to different forms and scales of social interaction. From an archaeological point of view the likely result is a complex pattern of overlapping material culture distributions relating to the repeated realisation and transformation of ethnicity in different social contexts, rather than discrete monolithic cultural entities. Patterns in the production and consumption of material culture involved in the communication of the "same" ethnic identity may vary qualitatively as well as quantitatively in different contexts. Furthermore, items of material culture which are widely distributed and used in a variety of social and historical contexts may be curated and consumed in different ways and become implicated in the generation and signification of a variety of expressions of ethnicity. . . . The systematization and rationalization of distinctive cultural styles in the process of the recognition, expression, and negotiation of ethnic identity is likely to result in discontinuous, non-random distributions of

material culture of the type suggested by Hodder (1982) and Wiessner (1983). (Jones 1996:69, 72)

The position taken here regarding the relations between the Virú-Gallinazo and Moche "culture styles" concurs with the theoretical positions summarized previously. It is here assumed as a working hypothesis that the identity articulated through the Virú-Gallinazo style can be defined in ethnic terms and was developed through a process of expansion and confrontation with native coastal populations north of the Virú Valley. Also important was the coexistence and constant confrontation with highland neighbors—the users of the culture styles classified as components of the "white-on-red horizon" and its later manifestations (i.e., Cajamarca, Huamachuco, and Recuay).

According to Tamara Dragadze (1980:162) and Colin Renfrew (1996), ethnicity is based on several aspects and factors that potentially coexist and are interrelated. Renfrew (1996:130) posits that ethnicity is based on shared territory or land, on common descent, on a shared language, on a community of customs or culture, on a community of beliefs or religion, on a name or "ethnonym" to express the identity of the group, on self-awareness or self-identity ("an important ingredient of the self-awareness is a perception of the 'otherness' of the others, the outsiders, the barbarians, those who are not 'us'"), and on a shared history or myth of origin.

The persistent Virú-Gallinazo technological identity—perceivable in the manufacturing and finishing techniques of domestic ceramic vessels, in the characteristic repertoire of vessels with forms (e.g., dippers and graters) not used by neighboring peoples, and in associated mortuary customs—allows a comfortable and convincing definition of the Virú-Gallinazo space (a shared territory) and time to be put forward.

This territory was not necessarily contiguous. It is still too early to add textile and metallurgical techniques to the list of potential reflections of ethnic identities, but preliminary research in these fields suggests that these aspects likewise exhibit their own and distinctive characteristics in comparison with those of the neighbors in Vicús, Cajamarca, and Recuay. Interestingly, the idiosyncrasies of the bearers of all of these culture styles seem to have been consolidated at the same time and in the same context (i.e., that of confrontation over control of the coastal valleys in the first and second centuries A.D.).

The range of headdresses and dress, which still awaits a systematic study, suggests that the self-awareness of being different from the rest was articulated through attire—possibly in ceremonial and festive contexts, as well as in the symbols of power wielded. On the other hand, the fact that the gods behaved as ancestors of the coastal warriors and wore Virú-Gallinazo–style attire and headdresses suggests the presence of common origin myths.

In the interpretive scenario here developed, the Virú-Gallinazo culture characterized the warrior people responsible for the conquest of Peru's north coast as far as the Piura Valley during the second century of the present era. It is likewise posited that the ethnic identity of the invaders endured as the axis of political identity of the Moche elites. Even so, the rise and consolidation of powerful territorial states and the subsequent and indispensable negotiation with the conquered Vicús peoples (as well as access to new "foreign" technologies and skilled labor) soon brought about a rapid and profound transformation of the Virú-Gallinazo culture. The latter was gradually replaced by the Moche culture between the second and the sixth centuries A.D.

The elites of different origins who lived peacefully alongside one another within the frontiers of the Moche states had access to ceremonial vessels, textiles, metal ornaments, and weapons manufactured in specialized workshops. To judge by the frequently cosmopolitan characteristics (Makowski 1994b) of ceramics of Moche I, Moche II, and Moche III styles, it can be assumed that the ethnic identities of manufacturers and users were often the same. On the other hand, the negotiations carried out between the native elites and the new Moche elites also left their mark. New ceremonial centers built with the pooled labor of the conquerors and conquered replaced the local spaces where celebrations, ritual combats, and sacrifices were held. The traditional ways in which vessels and dress were made endured longer in the local output meant for domestic use.

In the perspective here adopted, the presence/absence of Virú-Gallinazo or Moche ceramics in a given context is therefore not by itself a reliable index by which to pass judgment on the nature of the relations between the site under study and the Moche states. The recurrence of Moche-style ceramic objects potentially depended on the access local authorities had to specialized artisans skilled in this style, on the functional characteristics of the context (production site, public space, workshop, warehouse, ceremonial space where offerings were made or sacrifices took place, dwelling, and so forth), and on the status/rank of the user. The dress and vessels (bottles, midsize jars, vases, and dippers) used in ceremonies were available to all individuals considered full-fledged members of the coastal Moche society, as long as local specialized output and limited exchange were able to satisfy the demands posed by the valley's population.

ACKNOWLEDGMENTS

The author first wishes to acknowledge the support of CONCYTEC and the Pontificia Universidad Católica del Perú, and its presidents Dr. Salomon Lerner and Ing. Luis Guzmán Barrón Sobrevilla. My thanks also go to the Pontificia Universidad Católica Direction of Investigation Fund and its director Margarita Suárez for scholarships obtained in 1987, 1988, and 2005. My gratitude also goes to Dr. Piotr Bielinski, Dean of the Faculty of Historical Sciences at Warsaw University; to Dr. Mariusz Ziólkowski, Director of the Polish Center of Andean Archaeology, who made possible our research in the Alto Piura and Culebras Valleys; and to our collaborators Iván Amaro, Juan Antonio Murro, Otto Eléspuru, Iván Ghezzi, Rosabella Alvarez-Calderón, Manuel Lizárraga, Milosz Giersz, and Patrycja Przadka.

NOTES

[1] Translated from the Spanish by Javier Flores Espinoza and Jean-François Millaire.

[2] Fogel (1993:164–165) mentions the finds made by Theresa Topic in the test pits below Huaca de la Luna, which yielded evidence of platforms, elongated enclosures, plazas, and burials associated with

Moche I and Moche II pottery. One of the burials in test pit 1 held two Moche I vessels and a hybrid Gallinazo-Moche vessel. The other burial, in test pit 4, only had one Moche III bottle. According to Fogel (1993):

> One could posit that these Moche I and II vessels were intrusive, and that the first two phases of the Moche sequence were extant elsewhere. One could also propose that the Moche I and II phases were actually ceramic forms that were part of a terminal Gallinazo III phase, similar hybrid vessels have been found in the Virú Valley. (Collier 1953 [sic = 1955])

3   Individuals with Virú-style dress and headdress are found in scenes of processions (Hocquenghem 1987:Fig. 46), dances (Hocquenghem 1987:Fig. 96), deer hunts (Kutscher 1983:Figs. 74, 75, 77, 83, 87), sea lion hunts (Hocquenghem 1987:Fig. 121), nocturnal offerings where coca was consumed (Hocquenghem 1987:Figs. 68, 70–72, 74), snail collecting (Bourget 1990), flower throwing (Hocquenghem 1987:Fig. 3), combat (Kutscher 1983:Fig. 111; Hocquenghem 1987:Fig. 147), presentation of the cup (Donnan 1975), and a race between naked prisoners (Kutscher 1983:Fig. 123).

4   For examples of the Terrestrial Twin (a turban with the feline head, torso-with-head, or full body), see Giersz, Makowski, and Przadka (2005:cat. nos. 297, 298, 302, 303, 305–315, 318–320, 322–333, 335–336, 338, 339–342, 345–347) and Lieske (1991: 51–77, deity a-F, Figs. 1–73). For the Marine Twin (a ribbon with two vertical feathers on the forehead), see Giersz, Makowski, and Przadka (2005) and Lieske (1991:31–37, 89, deity a-D, Figs. 15, 19, 23, 25, 26, 29–31). For the Marine Twin with the body of a crab, see Lieske (1991:34, 35, 37, deity a-J, 89, Figs. 1–3), and Giersz, Makowski, and Przadka (2005:cat. nos. 128, 169, 174, and 175). For the warrior Owl (or sacrificer), the Bat sacrificer, and the Eagle warrior (a headdress with two stepped signs and a half-moon feather in the middle), see Hocquenghem (1987:Fig. 3) and Lieske (1991:109–113, deity z-B, Figs. 4, 10, 17, 23; 111, deity z-C, Fig. 11; and 124, deity z-E, Figs. 5–7).

REFERENCES

Amaro, Iván
  1994   Reconstruyendo la identidad de un pueblo. In *Vicús*, Krzysztof Makowski, Christopher B. Donnan, Iván Amaro Bullon, Luis Jaime Castillo, Magdalena Díez Canseco, et al.
  (eds.), pp. 23–81. Colección Arte y Tesoros del Perú. Lima: Banco de Crédito del Perú.

Barth, Fredrik
  1969   Introduction. In *Ethnic Groups and Boundaries: The Social Organization of Culture Difference*, Fredrik Barth (ed.), pp. 9–38. Boston: Little, Brown.

Bennett, Wendell C.
  1939   *Archaeology of the North Coast of Peru: An Account of Exploration and Excavation in Viru and Lambayeque Valleys*. Anthropological Papers of the American Museum of Natural History Vol. 37, Pt. 1. New York: The American Museum of Natural History.
  1950   *The Gallinazo Group: Viru Valley, Peru*. Yale University Publications in Anthropology 43. New Haven: Yale University Press.

Bentley, Carter G.
  1987   Ethnicity and Practice. *Comparative Studies in Society and History* 29(1):24–55.

Bourdieu, Pierre
  1977   *Outline of a Theory of Practice*. Cambridge, UK: Cambridge University Press.

Bourget, Steve
  1990   Los caracoles sagrados en la iconografía moche. *Gaceta arqueológica andina* (Lima) 5 (20):45–58.
  1994   El mar y la muerte en la iconografía moche. In *Moche: Propuestas y perspectivas*, Santiago Uceda and Elías Mujica (eds.), pp. 425–447. Travaux de l'Institut Français d'Études Andines 79. Lima: Universidad Nacional de La Libertad and Instituto Francés de Estudios Andinos.
  2003   Somos diferentes: Dinámica ocupacional del sitio Castillo de Huancaco, valle de Virú. In *Moche: Hacia el final del milenio*, Santiago Uceda and Elías Mujica (eds.), vol. 1, pp. 245–267. Lima: Universidad Nacional de Trujillo and Fondo Editorial, Pontificia Universidad Católica del Perú.

Castillo, Luis Jaime
  1989   *Personajes míticos, escenas y narraciones en la iconografía mochica*. Lima: Fondo Editorial, Pontificia Universidad Católica del Perú.

Childe, Gordon V.
  1940   *Prehistoric Communities of the British Isles*. London: W & R Chambers.

Collier, Donald
  1955   *Cultural Chronology and Change as Reflected in the Ceramics of the Virú Valley, Peru*. Chicago: Chicago Natural History Museum.

Díaz-Andreu, Margarita
  1996   Constructing Identities through Culture: The Past in the Forging of Europe. In *Cultural*

Identity and Archaeology: The Construction of European Communities, Paul Graves-Brown, Siân Jones, and Clive Gamble (eds.), pp. 48–61. London: Routledge.

Donnan, Christopher B.

1975 The Thematic Approach to Moche Iconography. *Journal of Latin American Lore* 1(2): 147–162.

2003 Tumbas con entierros en miniatura: Un nuevo tipo funerario moche. In *Moche: Hacia el final del milenio*, Santiago Uceda and Elías Mujica (eds.), vol. 1, pp. 43–78. Lima: Universidad Nacional de Trujillo and Fondo Editorial, Pontificia Universidad Católica del Perú.

Donnan, Christopher B., and Donna McClelland

1999 *Moche Fineline Painting: Its Evolution and Its Artists*. Los Angeles: UCLA Fowler Museum of Cultural History.

Dragadze, Tamara

1980 The Place of 'Ethnos' Theory in Soviet Anthropology. In *Soviet and Western Anthropology*, Ernest Gellner (ed.), pp. 161–170. London: Duckworth.

Eléspuru, Otto

1993 La cerámica vicús de las tumbas del cementerio de Yécala. Unpublished bachelor's thesis, Pontificia Universidad Católica del Perú, Lima.

Fabian, Johannes

1983 *Time and the Other: How Anthropology Makes Its Object*. New York: Columbia University Press.

Fardon, Richard

1987 "African Ethnogenesis": Limits to the Comparability of Ethnic Phenomena. In *Comparative Anthropology*, Ladislav Holy (ed.), pp. 168–188. Oxford: Basil Blackwell.

Fogel, Heidy

1987 The Gallinazo Occupation of the Viru Valley, Peru. Unpublished master's thesis, Yale University, New Haven.

1993 Settlements in Time: A Study of Social and Political Development during the Gallinazo Occupation of the North Coast of Perú [sic]. Unpublished Ph.D. dissertation, Yale University, New Haven.

Ford, James A

1949 Cultural Dating of Prehistoric Sites in Virú Valley, Peru. In *Surface Survey of the Virú Valley, Peru*, James A. Ford and Gordon R. Willey (eds.), pp. 29–87. Anthropological Papers of the American Museum of Natural History Vol. 43, Pt. 1. New York: The American Museum of Natural History.

Ford, James A., and Gordon R. Willey (editors)

1949 *Surface Survey of the Virú Valley, Peru*. Anthropological Papers of the American Museum of Natural History Vol. 43, Pt. 1. New York: The American Museum of Natural History.

Francis, E. K.

1947 The Nature of the Ethnic Group. *American Journal of Sociology* 52(5):393–400.

Franco, Régulo, César Gálvez, and Segundo Vásquez

2003 Modelos, función y cronología de la Huaca Cao Viejo, Complejo El Brujo. In *Moche: Hacia el final del milenio*, Santiago Uceda and Elías Mujica (eds.), vol. 2, pp. 125–177. Lima: Universidad Nacional de Trujillo and Fondo Editorial, Pontificia Universidad Católica del Perú.

Giersz, Milosz, and Patrycja Przadka

2003 *Sitios arqueológicos de la zona del valle de Culebras*, Volume 1: *Valle bajo*. Warsaw: Sociedad Polaca de Estudios Latinoamericanos, Misión Arqueológica Andina de la Universidad de Varsovia.

Giersz, Milosz, Krysztof Makowski, and Patrycja Przadka

2005 *El mundo sobrenatural mochica: Imágenes escultóricas de las deidades antropomorfas en el Museo Arqueológico Rafael Larco Herrera*. Lima: Universidad de Varsovia and Fondo Editorial, Pontificia Universidad Católica del Perú.

Guffroy, Jean, Peter Kaulicke, and Krzysztof Makowski

1989 La prehistoria del departamento de Piura: Estado de los conocimientos y problemática. *Bulletin de l'Institut Français d'Études Andines* 18(2):117–142.

Hocquenghem, Anne Marie

1987 *Iconografía mochica*. Lima: Fondo Editorial, Pontificia Universidad Católica del Perú.

1991 Frontera entre "áreas culturales" nor y centroandinas en los valles y en la costa del extremo norte peruano. *Bulletin de l'Institut Français d'Études Andines* 20(2):309–348.

Hocquenghem, Anne Marie, Jaime Idrovo, Peter Kaulicke, and Dominique Gomis

1993 Bases de intercambio entre las sociedades norperuanas y surecuatorianas: Una zona de transición entre 1500 A.C. y 600 D.C. *Bulletin de l'Institut Français d'Études Andines* 22(2): 443–466.

Hodder, Ian

1982 *Symbols in Action: Ethnoarchaeological Studies of Material Culture*. Cambridge, UK: Cambridge University Press.

Jones, Siân

1996 Discourses of Identity in the Interpretation of the Past. In *Cultural Identity and Archaeology:*

The Construction of European Communities, Paul Graves-Brown, Siân Jones, and Clive Gamble (eds.), pp. 62–80. London: Routledge.

Kaulicke, Peter

1991 El período intermedio temprano en el Alto Piura: Avances del proyecto arqueológico "Alto Piura" (1987–1990). *Bulletin de l'Institut Français d'Études Andines* 20(2):381–422.

1992 Moche, Vicús Moche y el Mochica Temprano. *Bulletin de l'Institut Français d'Études Andines* 21(3):853–903.

1994 La presencia mochica en el Alto Piura: Problemática y propuestas. In *Moche: Propuestas y perspectivas*, Santiago Uceda and Elías Mujica (eds.), pp. 327–358. Travaux de l'Institut Français d'Études Andines 79. Lima: Universidad Nacional de La Libertad and Instituto Francés de Estudios Andinos.

Kroeber, Alfred

1944 *Peruvian Archeology in 1942*. Viking Fund Publications in Anthropology 4. New York: Viking Fund.

Kutscher, Gerdt

1983 *Nordperuanische Gefässmalereien des Moche-Stils*. Materialen zur Allgemeinen und Vergleichenden Archäologie 18. Munich: C. H. Beck.

Lanning, Edward P.

1963 *A Ceramic Sequence for the Piura and Chira Coast, North Peru*. University of California Publications in American Archaeology and Ethnology Vol. 46, No. 2. Berkeley: University of California Press.

Larco Hoyle, Rafael

1945 *La cultura virú*. Buenos Aires: Sociedad Geográfica Americana.

1948 *Cronología arqueológica del norte del Perú*. Buenos Aires: Sociedad Geográfica Americana.

Lieske, Bärbel

1991 Göttergestalten und Göttergeschichten in den Gefässmalereien der altperuanischen Moche-Kultur. Unpublished Ph.D. dissertation, Freie Universität Berlin, Berlin.

Makowski, Krzysztof

1994a La figura del "oficiante" en la iconografía mochica: ¿Shamán o sacerdote? In *En el nombre del señor: Shamanes, demonios y curanderos del norte del Perú*, Luis Millones and Moisés Lemlij (eds.), pp. 52–101. Biblioteca Peruana de Psicoanálisis. Lima: Australis.

1994b Los señores de Loma Negra. In *Vicús*, Krzysztof Makowski, Christopher B. Donnan, Iván Amaro Bullon, Luis Jaime Castillo, Magdalena Díez Canseco, et al. (eds.), pp. 83–141. Colección Arte y Tesoros del Perú. Lima: Banco de Crédito del Perú.

1996 Los seres radiantes, el águila y el búho: La imagen de la divinidad en la cultura mochica (siglos II–VIII D.C.). In *Imágenes y mitos: Ensayos sobre las artes figurativas en los Andes prehispánicos*, Krzysztof Makowski, Iván Amaro, and Max Hernández (eds.), pp. 13–114. Lima: Fondo Editorial SIDEA and Australis.

1998 Cultura material, etnicidad y la doctrina política del estado en los Andes prehispánicos: El caso mochica. In *Actas del IV Congreso internacional de etnohistoria*, vol. 1, pp. 125–147. Lima: Fondo Editorial, Pontificia Universidad Católica del Perú.

2004 *Enciclopedia temática del Perú*, Volume 9: *Primeras civilizaciones*. Lima: El Comercio.

Makowski, Krzysztof, and Milena Vega Centeno

2004 Estilos regionales en la costa central en el Horizonte Tardío: Una aproximación desde el valle de Lurín. *Bulletin de l'Institut Français d'Études Andines* 33(3):681–714.

Makowski, Krzysztof, and María Inés Velarde

1998 [1996] Taller de Yécala (siglo III/IV D.C.): Observaciones sobre las características y organización de la producción metalúrgica vicús. *Boletín del Museo de Oro* (Bogotá) 41: 99–117.

Makowski, Krzysztof, Iván Amaro, and Otto Eléspuru

1994 Historia de una conquista. In *Vicús*, Krzysztof Makowski, Christopher B. Donnan, Iván Amaro Bullon, Luis Jaime Castillo, Magdalena Díez Canseco, et al. (eds.), pp. 211–281. Colección Arte y Tesoros del Perú. Lima: Banco de Crédito del Perú.

Makowski, Krzysztof, Christopher B. Donnan, Iván Amaro Bullon, Luis Jaime Castillo, Magdalena Díez Canseco, et al. (editors)

1994 *Vicús*. Colección Arte y Tesoros del Perú. Lima: Banco de Crédito del Perú.

Millaire, Jean-François

2002 *Moche Burial Patterns: An Investigation into Prehispanic Social Structure*. BAR International Series 1066. Oxford: BAR.

Mogrovejo, Juan

1995 La evidencia funeraria mochica de Huaca de la Cruz, valle de Virú. Unpublished licentiate thesis, Pontificia Universidad Católica del Perú, Lima.

Morales Gamarra, Ricardo, Miguel Asmat Velarde, and Arabel Fernández López

2000 Atuendo ceremonial moche: Excepcional hallazgo en la Huaca de la Luna. *Iconos* (Lima) 3:49–53.

Murro, Juan Antonio

1990 Cerámica de la colección vicús del museo municipal de Piura: Ensayo de seriación y cronología relativa del estilo. Unpublished licentiate thesis, Pontificia Universidad Católica del Perú, Lima.

Renfrew, Colin
1996 Prehistory and the Identity of Europe: Or, Don't Let's Be Beastly to the Hungarians. In *Cultural Identity and Archaeology: The Construction of European Communities*. Paul Graves-Brown, Siân Jones, and Clive Gamble (eds.), pp. 125–137. London: Routledge.

Russell, Glenn S., and Margaret A. Jackson
2001 Political Economy and Patronage at Cerro Mayal, Peru. In *Moche Art and Archaeology in Ancient Peru*, Joanne Pillsbury (ed.), pp. 159–175. Washington, D.C.: National Gallery of Art and Yale University Press.

Russell, Glenn S., Banks L. Leonard, and Jesús Briceño
1998 The Cerro Mayal Workshop: Addressing Issues of Craft Specialization in Moche Society. In *Andean Ceramics: Technology, Organization, and Approaches*, Izumi Shimada (ed.), pp. 63–89. Philadelphia: University of Pennsylvania Museum of Archaeology and Anthropology.

Shimada, Izumi, and Adriana Maguiña
1994 Nueva visión sobre la cultura gallinazo y su relación con la cultura moche. In *Moche: Propuestas y perspectivas*, Santiago Uceda and Elías Mujica (eds.), pp. 31–58. Travaux de l'Institut Français d'Études Andines 79. Lima: Universidad Nacional de La Libertad and Instituto Francés de Estudios Andinos.

Speakman, Robert J., and Hector Neff
2005 *Laser Ablation ICP-MS in Archaeological Research*. Albuquerque: University of New Mexico Press.

Strong, William D., and Clifford Evans
1952 *Cultural Stratigraphy in the Virú Valley, Northern Peru: The Formative and Florescent Epochs*. New York: Columbia University Press.

Topic, Theresa L.
1977 Excavations at Moche. Unpublished Ph.D. dissertation, Harvard University, Cambridge, Massachusetts.

Trigger, Bruce G.
1989 *A History of Archaeological Thought*. Cambridge, UK: Cambridge University Press.

Ubbelohde-Doering, Heinrich
1966 *Kulturen Alt-Perus: Reisen und archäologische Forschungen in den Anden Südamerikas*. Tübingen: Wasmuth.

Uceda, Santiago, and José Armas
1997 Los talleres alfareros en el centro urbano Moche. In *Investigaciones en la Huaca de la Luna 1995*, Santiago Uceda, Elías Mujica, and Ricardo Morales (eds.), pp. 93–104. Trujillo: Facultad de las Ciencias Sociales, Universidad Nacional de La Libertad.
1998 An Urban Pottery Workshop at the Site of Moche, North Coast of Peru. In *Andean Ceramics: Technology, Organization, and Approaches*, Izumi Shimada (ed.), pp. 91–110. Philadelphia: University of Pennsylvania Museum of Archaeology and Anthropology.

Wiessner, Polly
1983 Style and Social Information in Kalahari San Projectile Points. *American Antiquity* 48(2): 253–276.

Willey, Gordon R.
1946 The Chiclín Conference for Peruvian Archaeology, 1946. *American Antiquity* 12(2): 132–134.
1953 *Prehistoric Settlement Patterns in the Virú Valley, Perú* [sic]. Smithsonian Institution, Bureau of American Ethnology Bulletin 155. Washington, D.C.: Government Printing Office.

Wilson, David J.
1988 *Prehispanic Settlement Patterns in the Lower Santa Valley, Peru: A Regional Perspective on the Origins and Development of Complex North Coast Society*. Washington, D.C.: Smithsonian Institution Press.

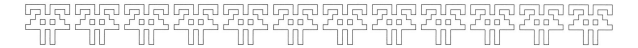

CHAPTER 4

MIDDLE MOCHE AND GALLINAZO CERAMIC STYLES AT SAN JOSÉ DE MORO

Martín del Carpio Perla

In 1936, Wendell C. Bennett carried out excavations at the Gallinazo Group in the Virú Valley, where he documented the "Gallinazo" occupation of this important settlement—a culture originally known as "Cultura virú," following the work of Rafael Larco Hoyle (Larco Hoyle 1945). During the excavation process, Bennett identified various types of ceramics associated with the Gallinazo occupation of the valley (Gallinazo Negative, Castillo Incised, and Castillo Modeled) and recognized the presence of different construction techniques.

Indeed, some walls were made of puddled adobe (*tapia*), whereas others were built with adobes made in a variety of sizes and shapes, the most common being the small cane-molded rectangular adobe. Based on those construction techniques, Bennett divided the occupation of the site into three chronological phases. He argued that the Gallinazo would have occupied the site between A.D. 300 and 700 (Bennett 1950:18), prior to the Moche (Huancaco) occupation in the valley.

A year later, in 1937, Heinrich Ubbelohde-Doering undertook archaeological investigations on the plaza located in front of Huaca 31 at Pacatnamú in the Jequetepeque Valley. In this location, he uncovered a cemetery with graves furnished with ceramic vessels of Gallinazo and Moche styles (Ubbelohde-Doering 1967; G. Hecker and W. Hecker 1983:grave EI and grave MXII). This led him to argue that the Moche style appeared in this region when the settlement was inhabited by a Gallinazo population.

Later on, during the early 1940s, Larco Hoyle undertook excavations in cemeteries on the Cerro Santa Ana in the Chicama Valley (Larco Hoyle 1948). In this location, he uncovered graves that contained ceramic vessels, the style of which he defined as "Gallinazo de Chicama" (a local variant of the Virú ceramic). Other types found he classified as Moche I (Larco Hoyle 1948:25). According to this scholar, the Virú and Gallinazo de Chicama cultures had occupied the coast during a relatively long period—being coeval with Salinar and Moche I and Moche II phases (Larco Hoyle 1948: 22, 25).

From the work of Bennett, Ubbelohde-Doering, and Larco Hoyle, the ceramic styles associated with the Gallinazo phenomenon in different valleys of the north coast were understood as the product of a unique culture whose characteristic features (apart from the ceramic style) included specific construction techniques (Bennett 1950: 64–69) and burial patterns. Funerary contexts consisted principally (although not exclusively) of large burial pits with individuals in extended supine position and few ceramic offerings (Larco Hoyle 1945:2, 25–26; Bennett 1950:108).

Moreover, the previously cited three authors also believed in a partial coexistence of Gallinazo (or Virú) and Moche societies along the littoral (Larco Hoyle 1948:25; Ubbelohde-Doering 1967: 22), or at least in a Moche influence on Gallinazo (Bennett 1950:100), as indicated by the discovery of artifacts of both styles within specific funerary contexts.

Recently, the idea of equating artistic styles and archaeological cultures has been challenged. Ceramic objects traditionally recognized as Galli-nazo (manufactured by a unique ethnic group) are believed to be the domestic ware of a number of distinct societies that occupied the coast during the Early Intermediate period (Makowski 2004: 39; Prieto 2004:41; see also Chapters 2, 7). This chapter focuses on funerary offerings from graves uncovered at San José de Moro, which featured ceramics of Gallinazo and Moche styles (contexts similar to those uncovered by Ubbelohde-Doering and Larco Hoyle). The chapter also attempts to explain the co-occurrence of the two styles within funerary contexts.

GRAVES WITH CERAMICS OF GALLINAZO AND MOCHE STYLES AT SAN JOSÉ DE MORO

San José de Moro is located on the northern margin of the Jequetepeque Valley, on the shores of the seasonal Chamán River, about 20 km from the ocean (Figure 4.1). The San José de Moro cemetery is known to present a long occupational sequence, from the Middle Moche period to the Chimú era (Castillo and Donnan 1994a).

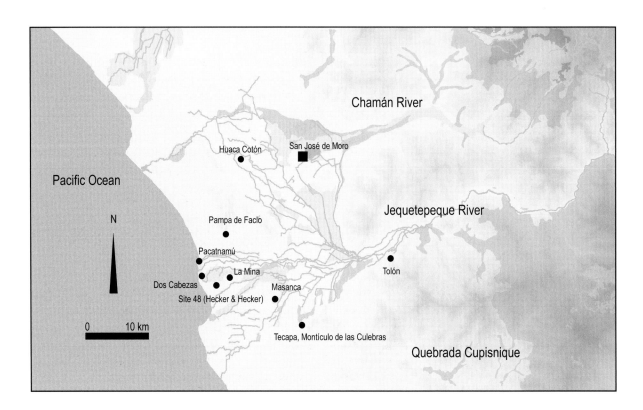

FIGURE 4.1. Map of the Jequetepeque Valley, including sites mentioned in the text.

Excavations conducted as part of the Proyecto Arqueológico San José de Moro in 2000 led to the discovery of two funerary contexts in the deepest occupational levels of the site, both classified as Gallinazo burials (Figure 4.2). Those graves were found within a large area of excavation (area 15–16), where five more burials had been uncovered, some of which contained Moche-style ceramics. This occupational phase—the earliest at San José de Moro—was defined by members of the project as the Middle Moche A (MMA) period (Del Carpio 2008) and dates back to approximately A.D. 500 to 670.

The cemetery was abandoned after this occupational phase, as indicated by the presence of a layer of mud of alluvial origin. The site was reoccupied during a second funerary event. Ten graves from this period were uncovered (Figure 4.3). This occupation is defined as the Middle Moche B (MMB) period, and dates to approximately A.D. 670 to 750. Excavations at San José de Moro led to the identification of a total of 46 graves dating from the MMA period and 17 from the MMB.[1]

Interestingly, ceramics of Gallinazo and Moche styles were uncovered within the graves or in the fill associated with both periods. A few ceramic vessels and thousands of fragments from early occupational layers provide data for defining the presence of the Gallinazo phenomenon in San José de Moro.

Boot-shaped graves were found in levels associated with both periods. All of these graves contained the remains of a single individual, in extended supine position and buried with its head oriented toward the southwest. During the MMA and MMB periods, fragments of copper were placed in the mouth and hands of the dead, whose corpse was subsequently wrapped in a cane tube or placed within a cane coffin tied with ropes.

Differences between the graves of the MMA and MMB periods were also noted, however. During the MMA, gourd containers, camelid remains (usually the skull and legs), and between one and three ceramic vessels were placed in burials. During the MMB, in addition to copper fragments, the dead were only provided with a fragment of a face-neck jar of Moche or Gallinazo style. Moreover, although boot-shaped chambers of both periods were sealed using adobe bricks, during the MMA period those were rather large and flat—made in cane molds using clay from the sterile subsoil. Adobes from the subsequent period were

FIGURE 4.2. Graves M-U844 and M-U845 at San José de Moro.

FIGURE 4.3. Graves M-U824, M-U823, and M-U821 from
the Middle Moche B cemetery at San José de Moro.

smaller and were made with clay soil from the first occupation level (filled with inclusions). Those adobes were also possibly manufactured using wood-plank molds.

A preliminary analysis of the osteologic remains shows that only a small segment of the population was buried in this cemetery. Indeed, osteometric analyses revealed a scarcity of children and teenagers, as well as a small number of females compared to males (Del Carpio 2008). This cemetery was probably designed for the burial of adult males, and this function was apparently maintained during subsequent occupational phases.

It is important to note that a series of taphonomic processes altered the correct anatomic position of the skeletons inside those graves. Bones from the hands, feet, and thoracic cage show some degree of disarticulation, ranging "from minimal shifting of individual bones to the large scale movement of bones and entire body segments" (Nelson 1998:196). Interestingly, a careful analysis of the remains from both periods revealed that the disarticulations resulted from the lowering of the cane tubes and coffins

through the vertical shaft of the graves, with the corpses head-down (Nelson 1998:203).

According to Andrew Nelson, these individuals already would have been in a state of advanced decomposition when buried, although not completely in skeletal form. This seems to indicate that the funerary process of those individuals was long enough for the body to start decomposing prior to the burial ceremony (Nelson 1998).

CERAMIC OFFERINGS

Burials of the MMA phase often comprised white-slipped vessels decorated with purple and orange paint, or black polished vessels: stirrup-spout bottles, medium-size jars with flaring neck, and bottles with small rounded handles (Figure 4.4a–d). Such Moche-style ceramics are typical of the area that stretches between the Jequetepeque Valley and the upper Piura region (Kaulicke 1992, 1998; Castillo and Donnan 1994b; Shimada 1994). Utilitarian jars with signs of use were also often placed by the deceased as funerary offerings (Figure 4.4e–g). These containers have a characteristically pinkish or orange color, and feature either an

FIGURE 4.4. Ceramics of Moche and Gallinazo styles from
the Middle Moche A cemetery at San José de Moro.

everted or slightly convex neck. Some of those
vessels also feature lateral handle-like applications.
These artifacts clearly fall within the repertoire of
what we generally define as the Gallinazo ceramic
style.

One of the most interesting funerary contexts
of the MMA cemetery is grave M-U813 (Figure
4.5). It contained the remains of the eldest person
uncovered in the entire cemetery, who was buried
with a metalworker's toolkit. Inside this grave,
three vessels were found (Figures 4.4a, 4.4f, and
4.9a): two bottles of Moche style and one face-
neck jar of Gallinazo style (Castillo Modeled).

Burials associated with the second occupational phase (MMB) were very distinct in terms
of ceramic offerings. Indeed, only fragments of
Gallinazo- or Moche-style jars were placed at the
feet of the deceased before the body was baled
with a cloth. Because no other sherds from those
broken vessels were found nearby, it could be
argued that the wrapping of the bodies took place
in the attendants' residence, outside the cemetery
of San José de Moro. The ceramics associated with
MMB burials feature fragments of Moche-style
face-neck jars (wrinkled human faces or owls),
fragments of jars with composed neck, or typical

Gallinazo face-neck jars of the Castillo Modeled type (Figure 4.6).

Hence, although there always was a marked preference for funerary offerings of Moche style at San José de Moro, burials also usually contained ceramic vessels (cooking vessels or Castillo Modeled face-neck jars) of Gallinazo style. Incidentally, a study of San José de Moro burial patterns shows nothing to suggest that individuals buried with Gallinazo-style artifacts had received a different treatment in death (Del Carpio 2008).

Indeed, these individuals were not buried with less deference regarding the structure of the grave, the position or orientation of the body, and the treatment of the corpse. Graves containing ceramic vessels of Gallinazo style therefore conform to the characteristics of burials furnished with Moche artifacts only (Donnan 1995; Millaire 2002).

FIGURE 4.5. Grave M-U813 from the Middle Moche A cemetery at San José de Moro.

FIGURE 4.6. Fragments of Moche and Gallinazo face-neck jars from
the Middle Moche B cemetery at San José de Moro.

UTILITARIAN CERAMICS FROM OCCUPATIONAL LEVELS

The complex funerary ceremonies performed in San José de Moro probably required the construction of temporary shelters for the relatives of the deceased and for officiating funerary specialists. Evidence of residential activities was uncovered on the occupation floors of the two successive burial grounds in the form of post holes and hearths. Those were possibly the remains of small shelters used by the mourners during the funerals. Judging from the amount of work needed for the excavation of boot-shaped chambers, it is likely the participants had to live in this location for several days.

A few complete ceramic vessels were found in association with these temporary shelters. These ceramics are in every respect similar to the ceramics of Gallinazo style found within the burials. These vessels featured pinkish or orange paste, and either everted or slightly convex necks. Other containers were taller, had not been used on a hearth, and appear to have served as liquid con-tainers—possibly for water or maize beer. These vessels are characteristic of Gallinazo utilitarian wares found in other settlements in the Jequete-peque Valley and elsewhere along the north coast.

Throughout the excavation process at San José de Moro, thousands of ceramic fragments were also uncovered. These were from utilitarian vessels and corresponded to the Castillo Plain, Castillo Incised, and Castillo Modeled ceramic types as defined by members of the Virú Valley Project (Bennett 1939, 1950; Ford 1949; Strong and Evans 1952; Willey 1953; Collier 1955). Needless to say, these ceramic types represent the quintessential ceramic attributes of the Gallinazo ceramic style (see Chapter 1). It is important to note that neither Gallinazo Negative vessels nor fragments that are punched or have appliqué strips (Bennett 1950:Figs. 18–20, 23a–d) have been uncovered at San José de Moro.

Throughout the occupation of San José de Moro, utilitarian ceramics of Gallinazo style form a coherent ensemble. A careful study nevertheless reveals that the forms evolved through time (Figure 4.7). Indeed, during the MMA period, utilitarian

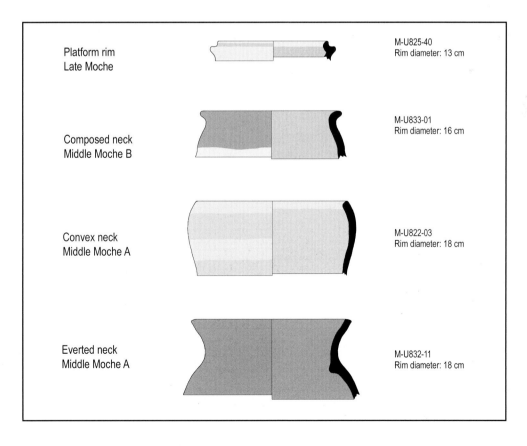

Platform rim
Late Moche

M-U825-40
Rim diameter: 13 cm

Composed neck
Middle Moche B

M-U833-01
Rim diameter: 16 cm

Convex neck
Middle Moche A

M-U822-03
Rim diameter: 18 cm

Everted neck
Middle Moche A

M-U832-11
Rim diameter: 18 cm

FIGURE 4.7. Utilitarian jars of the Middle Moche A, Middle Moche B, and Late Moche phases at San José de Moro.

ware typically featured either everted or slightly convex necks, whereas during the MMB period there was a clear preference for jars with composed necks or typical Gallinazo face-neck jars of the Castillo Modeled type (Figure 4.6). This is a highly significant trend, as it suggests that utilitarian jars with platform rims—typical of the Late Moche occupation of the Jequetepeque Valley—came from jars with composed necks of the MMB period. Elsewhere along the coast, utilitarian jars with an everted or slightly convex neck appear to be produced throughout the Early Intermediate period.

Similarly, face-neck jars from the MMB period are usually taller than those from the previous phase. Tall Castillo Modeled and Moche press-mold face-neck jars may in fact have paved the way for the development of face-neck jars (King of Assyria type of Ubbelohde-Doering 1967:24) typical of the Late Moche occupation of site (Fig-

ure 4.8). These vessels also seem to be exclusive to the Jequetepeque Valley, although similar jars were uncovered at Pampa Grande in the Lambayeque Valley (Shimada 2001:Fig. 5f).

On the basis of the data presented previously, nothing indicates that San José de Moro was occupied by two culturally or politically distinct human groups, each producing its own type of ceramic containers. In fact, in this area, ceramics of Gallinazo and Moche styles were apparently manufactured and used by the same people. The difference between ceramics of both styles essentially lay in their respective function: vessels of Gallinazo styles were mainly used as utilitarian containers and were brought to San José de Moro by those who took part in the extended mortuary ceremonies, whereas ceramics of Moche style were probably manufactured to serve as ritual offering.

FIGURE 4.8. Jar of the King of Assyria type and jar with platform rim from the Late Moche period at San José de Moro.

A MACRO-REGIONAL ENTITY IN JEQUETEPEQUE

It is difficult to make sense of the present evidence from the San José de Moro cemetery as long as it is understood as an isolated phenomenon. Fortunately, several important archaeological sites have been studied comprehensively, some of which show unquestionable evidence of close relations with San José de Moro. Of all archaeological sites excavated in this region, Pacatnamú shows the closest relation to San José de Moro. Research carried out at this site under the direction of Ubbelohde-Doering and later by Christopher Donnan and Guillermo Cock led to the identification of a large number of Moche burials in two distinct cemeteries of the site: along the northern facade of Huaca 31 (Ubbelohde-Doering 1983; G. Hecker and W. Hecker 1983, 1995) and to the northwest of Huaca 45 (Donnan and McClelland 1997).

The burial ground located in front of Huaca 31 presents significant similarities with the earliest cemetery (MMA) at San José de Moro: in the use of boot-shaped chambers, in the orientation and position of the deceased, and in the nature of funerary offerings.[2] Indeed, ceramic vessels uncovered in graves from both sites are extremely similar, including artifacts of Gallinazo and Moche styles that are nearly identical (Figure 4.9). Although Huaca 31 and Huaca 45 cemeteries may have served two distinct communities, it is likely that both belonged to a unique cultural formation.

Absolute dating from Jequetepeque and Lambayeque supports this view, showing that the Moche occupation of the two regions was essentially coeval (Table 4.1). No Early Moche–style ceramic has yet been found at either of these sites (for a description of this ware, see Donnan 2003 and Castillo and Donnan 1994b), and there is no evidence of an earlier "Gallinazo" settlement at Pacatnamú or at San José de Moro. In fact, Gallinazo ceramics are not only coeval with Moche vessels at both sites; they also clearly were produced by a unique social formation.

Farther away from San José de Moro is the site of Sipán, in the Lambayeque Valley, where magnificent graves were rescued from looting (Alva and Donnan 1993; Alva 1998, 2001). Although comparisons can only be tentative, it is important to mention the fact that at least some fine vessels from Sipán—in particular those from the burial of the "Old Lord" (tomb 3; Alva 1998:Plate 270)—are similar to ceramic vessels of Moche style uncovered inside MMA graves at San José de Moro (Del Carpio 2008). Other contexts also contained ceramic containers of Gallinazo style, similar to those found at San José de Moro (Alva 1998:Plate 46).

Based on current evidence, it could therefore be argued that the Jequetepeque and Lambayeque Valleys were home to a macro-regional group from the beginning of the Moche sequence in the region (Middle Moche), although our vision is clearly biased toward funerary contexts. This cultural formation would have occupied the area north of the Jequetepeque River, the surroundings of the Chamán River, and possibly even the Zaña and Lambayeque drainages. Within this zone, the fine ware used in ritual activities (at least during mortuary ceremonies) were MMA ceramics from San José de Moro, Middle Moche vessels from Pacatnamú, and Moche III vessels from Sipán. On the other hand, throughout this area, utilitarian wares were manufactured using what has come to be defined as the Gallinazo ceramic style.

If this assumption is correct, and there existed a macro-regional entity north of the Jequetepeque River, one wonders what was happening south of this natural boundary. On this bank of the Jequetepeque River lie the sites of Tolón, La Mina, Masanca, and Dos Cabezas (Figure 4.1). These sites have yielded fine ceramics of what is generally known as the Early Moche ceramic style (Castillo and Donnan 1994b:164; Narváez 1994; Donnan 2003).

Indeed, although no scientific excavation has yet been carried out at Tolón or La Mina, Donnan uncovered some funerary contexts at Masanca and Dos Cabezas—which contained Early Moche ceramics together with utilitarian containers of Gallinazo style (see Chapter 2) but no objects of Middle Moche style. Interestingly, absolute dates obtained from Dos Cabezas burials suggest that this settlement was essentially coeval with the occupations of Pacatnamú and San José de Moro (if slightly earlier; Table 4.1).

FIGURE 4.9. Ceramic vessels of Gallinazo and Moche styles from San José de Moro and Pacatnamú.
Illustration after Ubbelohde-Doering (1983).

Table 4.1. Absolute and relative dating for the Moche occupation of the Lambayeque and Jequetepeque Valleys.

LAMBAYEQUE VALLEY			
	CONTEXT	RADIOCARBON AGE	CALIBRATED AGE	REFERENCE

	CONTEXT	RADIOCARBON AGE	CALIBRATED AGE	REFERENCE
Sipán	Priest (tomb 2)	1190 ± 80 B.P.	A.D. 680–990	Roque et al. (2002)
	Warrior priest (tomb 1)	—	A.D. 170–350	Alva and Donnan (1993)

	CONTEXT	THERMOLUMINESCENCE AGE	DATE	REFERENCE
Sipán	Priest (tomb 2)	1355 ± 76	A.D. 566–718	Roque et al. (2002)
		1325 ± 62	A.D. 610–734	Roque et al. (2002)
		1282 ± 87	A.D. 628–802	Roque et al. (2002)
		1136 ± 66	A.D. 795–927	Roque et al. (2002)
		1213 ± 68	A.D. 716–852	Roque et al. (2002)

JEQUETEPEQUE VALLEY			
	CONTEXT	RADIOCARBON AGE	CALIBRATED AGE	REFERENCE

	CONTEXT	RADIOCARBON AGE	CALIBRATED AGE	REFERENCE
San José de Moro	Burial M-U413	1400 ± 60 B.P.	A.D. 540–730	Luis Jaime Castillo, personal communication (2005)
Pacatnamú	H45-CM1, burial 20	1260 ± 80 B.P.	A.D. 750	Donnan and McClelland (1997)
	H45-CM1, burial 25	1480 ± 80 B.P.	A.D. 510	Donnan and McClelland (1997)
	H45-CM1, burial 80	1350 ± 80 B.P.	A.D. 600	Donnan and McClelland (1997)
	H31, NW corner (three dates combined)	1465 ± 50–100 B.P.	A.D. 485	Shimada and Maguiña (1994)
Dos Cabezas	Burial 2	1530 ± 60 B.P.	A.D. 410–645	Donnan (2003)
	Burial 2	1580 ± 60 B.P.	A.D. 390–600	Donnan (2003)

QUELCCAYA ICE CAP			
	CONTEXT	EVENT	DATE	REFERENCE

	CONTEXT	EVENT	DATE	REFERENCE
Quelccaya Ice Cap		Drought	A.D. 524–540	Shimada et al. (1991)
		Drought	A.D. 563–594	Shimada et al. (1991)
		El Niño event	A.D. 602–635	Shimada et al. (1991)
		Drought	A.D. 636–645	Shimada et al. (1991)

I would therefore argue that the so-called Early Moche vessels (produced south of the Jequetepeque River) and Middle Moche ceramics (manufactured north of the river) were roughly contemporaneous, and that these traditions of fine ware were mutually exclusive. Fine ceramics from the south show a preference for kaolinite clay, sculptural vessels, and incrustation of stones and shells. The spouts usually correspond to Larco Hoyle's Moche I ceramics. To the north, fine ceramics often feature bottles with squat globular bodies, white slip, and designs made with orange or purple paint.

The spouts usually correspond to Moche III–phase bottles in Larco Hoyle's morpho-stylistic sequence. Indeed, although some ceramic vessels of Early Moche style have been uncovered north of the Jequetepeque River—for example, grave VVII at Pacatnamú (G. Hecker and W. Hecker 1983:Fig. 63.1)—it is likely that those were not manufactured locally but were the products of exchange. On the other hand, it should be emphasized that it is currently impossible to distinguish utilitarian ceramics of Gallinazo styles from settlements located north and south of the Jequetepeque River.

The Gallinazo occupation of the northern Jequetepeque area has somehow been neglected by archaeologists. The small number of objects of Gallinazo style is striking when compared with an abundance between the Chicama and Casma Valleys (W. Hecker and G. Hecker 1990:24; Shimada and Maguiña 1994:40). Although there are tens of Early Horizon settlements in the Jequetepeque area (Ravines 1983; Pimentel 1986; W. Hecker and G. Hecker 1990) and a hundred or so of Moche sites (Dillehay 2001), only seven have yielded ceramics of Gallinazo style: San José de Moro, Huaca Cotón, Pacatnamú, Dos Cabezas, Masanca, the Montículo de las Culebras, Tepeca, and Hecker and Hecker's site 48 (Ubbelohde-Doering 1957; W. Hecker and G. Hecker 1990:24).

This scarcity might simply be a result of north-coast archaeologists' bias toward sites that yielded Moche-style artifacts. Interestingly, the sites that produced ceramics of Gallinazo style also featured ceramics of Moche style. None of those sites presented a superposition of Gallinazo and Moche artifacts. In fact, artifacts of Gallinazo and Moche styles were found within the same contexts and were thus essentially coeval.

This suggests that the Gallinazo style entered the northern Jequetepeque Valley together with Moche artifacts between about A.D. 540 and 730. Based on current evidence, the idea that the Moche invaded the area and conquered a local Gallinazo society needs to be rejected. Rather, it seems likely that Gallinazo vessels simply were the utilitarian ware of those who developed, produced, and discarded fine Moche ceramics.

DISCUSSION

The fact that ceramics of Gallinazo style appear earlier than Moche-style containers along the Peruvian north coast is undeniable, as evidenced by the absolute dating of settlements located between the Chicama and Casma Valleys. This archaeological sequence—largely based on the stylistic evolution of fine ceramic vessels—was mistakenly projected in every area where artifacts of Gallinazo and Moche styles were identified. As a result, the thesis put forward was that a "Gallinazo culture" had occupied a territory the Moche eventually conquered and occupied (Shimada and Maguiña 1994:33).

Based on the data presented here, however, it is clear that the Gallinazo style in the Jequetepeque Valley does not predate the Moche style but that these styles were coeval. The situation north of the Jequetepeque may be somehow similar. Indeed, surveys conducted in these areas seem to suggest the co-occurrence of the two ceramic traditions (Shimada and Maguiña 1994: 40). Here again, the two styles may have been the product of a single social formation. Archaeological sites from La Leche Valley also yielded large quantities of ceramics of Gallinazo style. Incidentally, in some of these sites (such as Huaca La Merced), artifacts of Gallinazo style were found together with Middle Moche ceramics (Shimada and Maguiña 1994:48).

Toward the beginning of the sixth century A.D., during the MMA phase, attendants buried their dead with ceramics of Gallinazo and Moche styles in the San José de Moro cemetery. These artifacts were apparently manufactured to fulfill distinct functions, however. Moche ceramic vessels were essentially used within funerary contexts, whereas Gallinazo artifacts were mainly of utilitarian character, functioning as containers for the storage and preparation of food and drinks to be used throughout the extended mortuary process. At least some of these containers found their way into graves, possibly filled with food or drink of some sort.[3]

San José de Moro was not an isolated phenomenon during the Early Intermediate period. In fact, information available from Pacatnamú and Sipán suggests that Gallinazo and Moche styles coexisted in symbiosis. These settlements, and others that await excavation, must have formed part of a unique cultural formation at the beginning of the Moche period in the region, one in which the population manufactured utilitarian ceramics in the Gallinazo style.

ACKNOWLEDGMENTS

I would like to thank the members of the Proyecto Arqueológico San José de Moro, and especially its director Luis Jaime Castillo Butters. My gratitude also goes to Paloma Manrique de Del Carpio from the Museo Larco, and to Jean-François Millaire and Magali Morlion for the translation of this article and their constructive comments. Without their help this contribution would not have been possible.

NOTES

[1] Both periods were labeled "Middle Moche" based on the association of ceramics of Middle Moche style as defined by Luis Jaime Castillo and Christopher Donnan (1994b).

[2] It should be pointed out, however, that the Pacatnamú graves offer a much better state of preservation than those of San José de Moro, and that at least some funerary contexts are much more complex than those under study (e.g., graves EI, MXI, and MXII).

[3] Regarding food offerings within Early Intermediate–period graves, see Gumerman (1994, 1997) and Donnan (1995).

REFERENCES

Alva, Walter
1998 *Sipán, descubrimiento e investigación*. N.p: Edición del autor.

2001 The Royal Tombs of Sipán: Art and Power in Moche Society. In *Moche Art and Archaeology in Ancient Peru*, Joanne Pillsbury (ed.), pp. 223–245. Washington, D.C.: National Gallery of Art and Yale University Press.

Alva, Walter, and Christopher B. Donnan
1993 *Royal Tombs of Sipán*. Los Angeles: Fowler Museum of Cultural History, University of California.

Bennett, Wendell C.
1939 *Archaeology of the North Coast of Peru: An Account of Exploration and Excavation in Viru and Lambayeque Valleys*. Anthropological Papers of the American Museum of Natural History Vol. 37, Pt. 1. New York: The American Museum of Natural History.
1950 *The Gallinazo Group: Viru Valley, Peru*. Yale University Publications in Anthropology 43. New Haven: Yale University Press.

Castillo, Luis Jaime, and Christopher B. Donnan
1994a La ocupación moche de San José de Moro, Jequetepeque. In *Moche: Propuestas y perspectivas*, Santiago Uceda and Elías Mujica (eds.), pp. 93–146. Travaux de l'Institut Français d'Études Andines 79. Lima: Universidad Nacional de la Libertad and Instituto Francés de Estudios Andinos.
1994b Los Mochica del norte y los Mochica del sur. In *Vicús*, Krzysztof Makowski, Christopher B. Donnan, Iván Amaro Bullon, Luis Jaime Castillo, Magdalena Díez Canseco, et al. (eds.), pp. 143–181. Colección Arte y Tesoros del Perú. Lima: Banco de Crédito del Perú.

Collier, Donald
1955 *Cultural Chronology and Change as Reflected in the Ceramics of the Virú Valley, Peru*. Chicago: Chicago Natural History Museum.

Del Carpio, Martín
2008 La ocupación mochica medio en San José de Moro. In *Arqueología mochica: Nuevos enfoques*, Luis Jaime Castillo Butters, Hélène Bernier, Gregory Lockard, and Julio Rucabado Yong (eds.), pp. 81–104. Lima: Fondo Editorial, Pontificia Universidad Cátolica del Perú and Instituto Francés de Estudios Andinos.

Dillehay, Tom D.
2001 Town and Country in Late Moche Times: A View from Two Northern Valleys. In *Moche Art and Archaeology in Ancient Peru*, Joanne Pillsbury (ed.), pp. 259–283. Washington, D.C.: National Gallery of Art and Yale University Press.

Donnan, Christopher B.
1995 Moche Funerary Practice. In *Tombs for the Living: Andean Mortuary Practices*, Tom D.

Dillehay (ed.), pp. 111–159. Washington, D.C.: Dumbarton Oaks Research Library and Collection.

2003   Tumbas con entierros en miniatura: Un nuevo tipo funerario moche. In *Moche: Hacia el final del milenio*, Santiago Uceda and Elías Mujica (eds.), vol. 1, pp. 43–78. Lima: Universidad Nacional de Trujillo and Fondo Editorial, Pontificia Universidad Católica del Perú.

Donnan, Christopher B., and Donna McClelland
1997   Moche Burials at Pacatnamu. In *The Pacatnamu Papers*, Volume 2: *The Moche Occupation*, Christopher B. Donnan and Guillermo A. Cock (eds.), pp. 17–187. Los Angeles: Fowler Museum of Cultural History, University of California.

Ford, James A.
1949   Cultural Dating of Prehistoric Sites in Virú Valley, Peru. In *Surface Survey of the Virú Valley, Peru*, James A. Ford and Gordon R. Willey (eds.), pp. 29–87. Anthropological Papers of the American Museum of Natural History Vol. 43, Pt. 1. New York: The American Museum of Natural History.

Gumerman, George
1994   Corn for the Dead: The Significance of *Zea mays* in Moche Burial Offerings. In *Corn and Culture in the Prehistoric New World*, Sissel Johannessen and Christine A. Hastorf (eds.), pp. 399–410. Boulder, Colorado: Westview Press.
1997   Botanical Offerings in Moche Burials at Pacatnamu. In *The Pacatnamu Papers*, Volume 2: *The Moche Occupation*, Christopher B. Donnan and Guillermo A. Cock (eds.), pp. 243–249. Los Angeles: Fowler Museum of Cultural History, University of California.

Hecker, Giesela, and Wolfgang Hecker
1983   Gräberbeschreibung. In *Vorspanische Gräber von Pacatnamú, Nordperu*, by Heinrich Ubbelohde-Doering, pp. 39–131. Materialen zur Allgemeinen und Vergleichenden Archäologie 26. Munich: C. H. Beck.
1995   *Die Grabungen von Heinrich Ubbelohde-Doering in Pacatnamu, Norperú: Untersuchungen zu den Huacas 31 und 14 sowie Bestattungen und Fundobjekte*. Berlin: Dietrich Reimer.

Hecker, Wolfgang, and Giesela Hecker
1990   *Ruinas, caminos y sistemas de irrigación prehispánicos en la provincia de Pacasmayo, Perú*. Patrimonio Arqueológico Zona Norte 3. Trujillo: Instituto Departamental de Cultura – La Libertad.

Kaulicke, Peter
1992   Moche, Vicús Moche y el Mochica Temprano. *Bulletin de l'Institut Français d'Études Andines* 21(3):853–903.

1998   Algunas reflexiones sobre la cronología mochica. In *50 años de estudios americanistas en la Universidad de Bonn: Nuevas contribuciones a la arqueología, etnohistoria, etnolingüística y etnográfica de las Americas*, Sabine Dedenbach-Salazar Sáenz (ed.), pp. 105–128. Estudios Americanistas de Bonn 30. Markt Schwaben, Germany: A. Saurwein.

Larco Hoyle, Rafael
1945   *La cultura virú*. Buenos Aires: Sociedad Geográfica Americana.
1948   *Cronología arqueológica del norte del Perú*. Buenos Aires: Sociedad Geográfica Americana.

Makowski, Krzysztof
2004   *Enciclopedia temática del Perú*, Volume 9: *Primeras civilizaciones*. Lima: El Comercio.

Millaire, Jean-François
2002   *Moche Burial Patterns: An Investigation into Prehispanic Social Structure*. BAR International Series 1066. Oxford: BAR.

Narváez, Alfredo
1994   La Mina: Una tumba Moche I en el valle de Jequetepeque. In *Moche: Propuestas y perspectivas*, Santiago Uceda and Elías Mujica (eds.), pp. 59–92. Travaux de l'Institut Français d'Études Andines 79. Lima: Universidad Nacional de La Libertad and Instituto Francés de Estudios Andinos.

Nelson, Andrew
1998   Wandering Bones: Archaeology, Forensic Science and Moche Burial Practices. *International Journal of Osteoarchaeology* 8:192–212.

Pimentel, Víctor
1986   *Felszeichungen im mittleren und unteren Jequetepeque-Tal, Nord-Peru*. Materialien zur Allgemeinen und Vergleichenden Archäologie Band 31. Munich: C. H. Beck.

Prieto, Gabriel
2004   La poza de Huanchaco: Una aldea de pescadores durante el colapso del estado moche, valle de Moche. Unpublished licentiate thesis, Universidad Nacional de Trujillo, Trujillo.

Ravines, Rogger
1983   *Arqueología del valle medio del Jequetepeque*. Materiales para la arqueología del Perú 2. Lima: Proyecto de Rescate Arqueológico Jequetepeque.

Roque, Céline, Emmanuel Vartanian, Pierre Guibert, Max Schvoerer, Daniel Lévine, Walter Alva, and Hogne Jungner
2002   Recherche chronologique sur la culture mochica du Pérou: Datation de la tombe du Prêtre de Sipán par thermoluminescence (TL) et par radiocarbone. *Journal de la Société des Américanistes* 88:227–243.

Shimada, Izumi

1994 Los modelos de la organización sociopolítica de la cultura moche. In *Moche: Propuestas y perspectivas*, Santiago Uceda and Elías Mujica (eds.), pp. 359–387. Travaux de l'Institut Français d'Études Andines 79. Lima: Universidad Nacional de la Libertad and Instituto Francés de Estudios Andinos.

2001 Late Moche Urban Craft Production: A First Approximation. In *Moche Art and Archaeology in Ancient Peru*, Joanne Pillsbury (ed.), pp. 177–205. Washington, D.C.: National Gallery of Art and Yale University Press.

Shimada, Izumi, and Adriana Maguiña

1994 Nueva visión sobre la cultura gallinazo y su relación con la cultura moche. In *Moche: Propuestas y perspectivas*, Santiago Uceda and Elías Mujica (eds.), pp. 31–58. Travaux de l'Institut Français d'Études Andines 79. Lima: Universidad Nacional de La Libertad and Instituto Francés de Estudios Andinos.

Shimada, Izumi, Crystal Barker Schaaf, Lonnie G. Thompson, and Ellen Mosley-Thompson

1991 Cultural Impacts of Severe Droughts in the Prehistoric Andes: Application of a 1,500-Year Ice Core Precipitation Record. *World Archaeology* 22(3):247–270.

Strong, William D., and Clifford Evans

1952 *Cultural Stratigraphy in the Virú Valley, Northern Peru: The Formative and Florescent Epochs*. New York: Columbia University Press.

Ubbelohde-Doering, Heinrich

1957 *Der Gallinazo-Stil und die Chronologie der altperuanischen Frühkulturen*. Bayerische Akademie der Wissenschaften. Philosophisch-Historische Klasse, Sitzungberichte 9. Munich: C. H. Beck.

1967 *On the Royal Highways of the Inca: Archaeological Treasures of Ancient Peru*. New York: Praeger.

1983 *Vorspanische Gräber von Pacatnamú, Nordperu*. Materialien zur Allgemeinen und Vergleichenden Archäologie 26. Munich: C. H. Beck.

Willey, Gordon R.

1953 *Prehistoric Settlement Patterns in the Virú Valley, Perú* [sic]. Smithsonian Institution, Bureau of American Ethnology Bulletin 155. Washington, D.C.: Government Printing Office.

CHAPTER 5

URBANISM AND SOCIAL CHANGE DURING THE GALLINAZO AND MOCHE PERIODS IN THE CHICAMA VALLEY

Christopher J. Attarian

This chapter looks at cultural changes within the Gallinazo culture in the Chicama Valley throughout the Early Intermediate period. During this time, dramatic demographic and cultural changes occurred, possibly related to the rise of the Moche state. To understand this dramatic occurrence, three concepts interrelate: urbanism, community identity, and ethnogenesis. Urbanism is a process in which people come together into a community of unprecedented size and scale. The process of urbanism is likely to have profound effects on cultural systems because many life ways (work, food procurement, exchange, religion, hierarchic authority) are altered in response to changes in population density. Community identity is about distinct identities arising and communities relating to one another. Variations in habitus and style can be useful in differentiating one community from another. Ethnogenesis is a process in which a change in external situation causes a change in community identity. Urbanism can be the stimulus that triggers ethnogenesis. This is what likely occurred in the Chicama Valley circa 200 B.C.

PRE-URBAN SETTLEMENT PATTERNS OF THE CHICAMA VALLEY

Gallinazo culture is recognized to predate (and in some areas, overlap in time with) the stylistic and social developments of the Moche culture. In some regions, particularly in the valleys south of Moche, scholars have claimed that two political groups (one Moche and the other Gallinazo) were interacting contemporaneously with each other. In the Chicama Valley, this does not appear to be the case. Here, settlement data suggests that the Gallinazo were an existing cultural tradition from which (or upon which) a very distinct elite artistic style developed, recognizable as the Moche styles of pottery and architecture.

The settlement pattern in the Chicama Valley prior to urbanization is one of small fortified villages everywhere in the valley (Figure 5.1), with a concentration in the upper regions of the lower valley (Russell 1992). This pattern is similar to the settlement of the Virú (Willey 1953), Moche (Billman 1996), and Santa (Wilson 1988) Valleys. Pottery from these sites includes Castillo Plain,

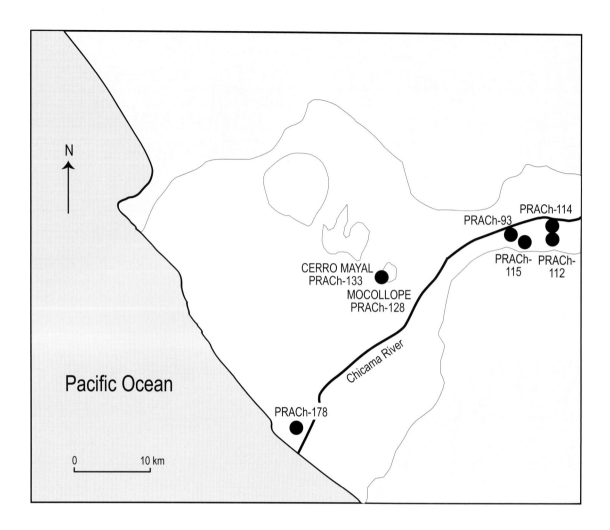

FIGURE 5.1. Chicama Valley (location of relevant sites indicated).

Castillo Incised, and Salinar White-on-Red (Strong and Evans 1952; Leonard and Russell 1992). These types suggest that the sites were occupied toward the beginning of the Early Intermediate period. Interestingly, these sites lack any Moche-style pottery, including the diagnostic orange-paste ware produced at the site of Cerro Mayal and known to be used in domestic contexts (Russell, Leonard, and Briceño 1994). Thus, these sites are considered pre-Moche Gallinazo settlements.

The settlement system is best interpreted as one of independent farming communities located with a priority on village and canal defense. Exactly who the villages were defending against remains a mystery, but others have provided compelling (and competing) theories from other north-coast valleys (Wilson 1988; Billman 1996).

Site Abandonment

At some point prior to the spread of Moche-style pottery, most of the village sites were abandoned and the population at Cerro Mocollope started to expand. Evidence of this abandonment comes from a lack of Moche-style pottery and the absence of stratigraphic evidence, which would suggest a longer period of occupation at the village sites previously cited (Attarian 2003a).

Conversely, at Mocollope a new area of habitation was occupied along the base of the mountain, below the *tapia* fortifications on the ridge. The architecture is shallow, often being a single occupation floor built on sandy soil, with no artifacts within it. This suggests that the expansion was from new settlers to the site. Radiocarbon dates indicate that the expansion took place about

100 B.C., or between 200 B.C. and A.D. 10 (Attarian 2003a).

Migration and Urbanism at Mocollope

The growth of Mocollope and the subsequent changes that led to the rise of the Moche culture can be studied in terms of an emergent urban center. Mocollope is early as an urban center for the Moche culture, but not unique. Studies have identified settlement nucleation and possible urbanism in other valleys that date to the emergence of Moche material culture and, presumably, Moche political power (Wilson 1988; Bawden 1996; Billman 1996).

The development of cities is considered by most scholars a crucial characteristic of complex societies (Childe 1950; Carneiro 1967; Flannery 1972; Wright 1977, 1986; Service 1978; Claessen 1984; Johnson and Earle 1987; Spencer 1990; Blanton et al. 1993). Cities are, however, a cause as well as a result of cultural change. Urban sites form the context in which increased social complexity, craft specialization, and population migration combine to affect culture change and development. The shift in settlement to Mocollope, and possibly to the large complex at El Brujo, contributed to the emergence of political power in Chicama, as seen by the large monumental constructions and the appearance of Moche fineline pottery in the archaeological record.

Correlates of Urbanism at Mocollope

Much has been said about how to define urban versus nonurban sites. Strict taxonomies are useful, but often devolve into bragging matches between regions. A cross-cultural analysis of urban centers (including ancient Greece, Medieval Europe, Mesopotamia, Mexico, and Oaxaca), as well as comparisons with ethnographies from modern industrial cities, reveals four empirical correlates of urban centers: relatively high population density, increase in economic exchange, existence of robust specialized production, and centralized control of exchange and production (Attarian 2003a, 2003b).

Urban sites are relatively high in population by at least one order of magnitude. They are the principal location of specialized craft production, surplus labor mobilization, and most exchange. Urban sites will be the location of managerial power because this is where the majority of economic activities are taking place. The site of Mocollope displays evidence of urbanism. Our data show that the urbanization of Mocollope begins during what is known locally as the Late Gallinazo period, contemporaneous with only the earliest dates associated with Early Moche pottery. Although some of the characteristics of urbanism have not been found associated with the earliest occupation phases, the site develops into the principal center of population, craft, and elite power later in the Early Intermediate period.

Relatively High Population Density

The development of a large population that requires surplus production is a critical part of the definition of the mature city (Rowe 1963; Silverman 1988). Although there is no particular population threshold that defines a city (Blanton 1976: 253), cities are characterized by relatively unprecedented population sizes and densities compared with previous settlements in the area. Concentration of resources and the development of exchange systems encourage settlement by creating access to goods and services. Other reasons, such as mutual defense, can induce smaller groups to aggregate.

Today, the ruins of Mocollope cover an area of 42 hectares (ha). However, the site is surrounded by a modern village and sugarcane fields. Around the monumental core of the site are lower areas (with residential architecture) that extend into the modern village and cane fields. It is likely that the settlement was originally larger, however. One suggestion for the size of Mocollope is the nearby site of Cerro Mayal (a Moche ceramic production center), located about 1 km away.

Previous studies at Cerro Mayal have explored the date of occupation and use of the site, showing it to be a place of attached, full-time ceramic specialization contemporary with the Middle and Late Moche occupation at Mocollope (Russell, Leonard, and Briceño 1994; Attarian 1996). It is possible that the urban center of Mocollope extended from the monumental core at Cerro Mocollope all the way to Cerro Mayal.

Exchange

Changes in exchange systems can have an effect of community identity. As exchange systems move from reciprocity to centralized or profit-motivated systems, the self-sufficiency of communities declines. Interdependency of unrelated groups becomes critical. In addition, economic specialization is encouraged, and this restructures indigenous networks and relationships among groups.

Karl Polanyi (1944) pioneered a systematic view of exchange systems that has influenced the way some Andean scholars have looked at ancient economies (Stanish 1992). Forms of exchange are redistribution, administered trade, price-fixing market exchange, and reciprocity (Polanyi 1944; Stanish 1992; Attarian 2003a:36–41). All of these exchange systems may or may not be functioning to some degree in an emerging urban society. Redistribution, administered trade, and market exchange all encourage nucleation of settlement. In each of these, nodes of exchange arise where the cost of obtaining goods is lower.

Redistribution and administered trade are both centralized systems that require administrative authority to operate and that usually involve centralized distribution and collection. In these cases, the population would tend to nucleate around the administrative centers in order to be closer to distribution points. Market exchange does not need an administration to function but benefits from a system of enforced rules that manage proper conduct among trading parties. Likewise, enforcement is more efficient if trading is conducted in a centralized location, such as the great markets of Tenochtitlán (Brumfiel 1987; Hicks 1987). Often an increase in the amount of exchange is correlated with urbanism.

There is little direct evidence of exchange at Mocollope. Some indication, however, can be inferred from the site of Cerro Mayal. Survey of the Chicama Valley has shown that Cerro Mayal pottery was exchanged throughout the valley. Excavations at Mocollope have revealed a few *Spondylus* shell beads, native to the Ecuadorian coast. Camelid bones have also been found at the site, but it is unknown if camelid herds were maintained at Mocollope or if the animals were brought down from the highlands. Even if a herd of camelids was maintained at Mocollope, the ini-tial stock must have been brought from the highlands.

Specialized Labor, Surplus Labor, and Craft Specialization

Emerging craft specialization may cause changes in community identity. This is clearly evident in the transition from a purely agrarian economy to an economy featuring an urban-specialist component. Craft specialization contributes to ethnogenesis because it presents people with new economic roles in society. Workers who used to farm will become potters, weavers, and metalsmiths in the new economy. Their exchange partners may include people from outside their old village community. The increased interdependence can create a new need to aggregate goods and services (Wolf 1966; Johnson 1982). This also introduces an element of economic competition that may not have existed in the smaller village communities (Childe 1950).

Craft specialization is a crucial component of the economic and social environment of cities (Brumfiel and Earle 1987; Sinopoli 1988; Costin 1991). Often these activities take place in urban centers where labor is plentiful, exchange partners are nearby, and supervision by an elite (in cases of attached specialization) is less expensive for the elite to manage. Nonmarket economies are also affected by craft specialization. Often ruling elites impose specialization on communities to provide a component necessary for administered trade or redistribution (Earle 1987). This is documented for many Andean societies, including the Moche (Patterson 1987; D'Altroy 1992; Attarian 1996; Stanish 1997).

The large ceramic workshop (Cerro Mayal) associated with Mocollope produced ceramic vessels of Moche IV and Moche V styles according to Rafael Larco Hoyle's stylistic sequence (Larco Hoyle 1948), and it was occupied between A.D. 550 and 800 (Russell and Jackson 2001:159). Cerro Mayal dates to about 200 years after urbanization began at Mocollope, yet it is likely that specialized and attached production was emerging during the period of urbanization, as they are well developed during subsequent ceramic phases.

Ritual activities are also an area of specialization in the economy. During the rise of the Moche culture, ritual institutions played an increasingly important role in society. This is seen by the greater labor investment in platform mound constructions and the elaboration of supernatural art. The large pyramidal mounds at Mocollope date to the Moche period. In the case of structure A at Mocollope ("El Palacio"), thick adobe walls divide the interior space into chambers that were painted with larger-than-life Moche warriors. These paintings are similar to ritualistic scenes found on other Moche buildings such as Huaca de la Luna at Huacas de Moche and Huaca Cao Viejo at the El Brujo Complex.

In other urban case studies—for example, the Greek city of Megalopolis (Demand 1990) and Teotihuacán in central Mexico (Millon 1967)—corporate religion played a significant role in structuring the ideology of urban migrants. Moche ideology may have played a similar role in assimilating the various immigrant groups. Imagery in Moche elite art includes scenes of victorious Moche warriors and depictions of rulers and warriors involved in ritual activities. It also includes individuals that appear to be supernatural beings.

Depictions of supernatural beings are rare in Gallinazo art compared with representations of animals, people, and buildings. Moche material culture developed as an elite art style somewhere on the north coast during Moche I and Moche II phases (ca. A.D. 100–300). By the Moche III and Moche IV phases, they became ubiquitous in non-elite contexts, including in the production at Cerro Mayal. Moche artistic themes are seen as reflecting an ideology that starts out as an elite style imposed as part of the new social organization of the emerging Moche state. Gradually, as the process of ethnogenesis creates a new social identity, these images are no longer restricted to the elite but are used by individuals of all status levels.

Centralized Control

The empirical correlate of centralized control is an associated rise in political hierarchy. The control of surplus and the centralization of craft labor create new opportunities for social stratification. Centralized control reflects the emergence of elite groups with proportionately more power over the institutions that generate and control access to wealth.

Creation and control of these institutions (ritual, political, and economic) are located in a central place to optimize efficiency. Henry Wright (1986:358) found that nucleation of population correlates with an increase in social complexity in many cases worldwide. The dependent population will, by necessity, congregate where access to services is easiest. The result is that elites, administrative centers, and the greater population tend to nucleate.

Centralized control is evident at Mocollope in the elaborate elite architecture and in the presence of Gallinazo Negative pottery. The large structures (marked A, C, and E in Figure 5.2) show that a significant amount of labor was invested in these platforms. There is not enough evidence to determine the use of structure E, but structures A and C are analogous to other Moche platform mounds, such as those found at Huacas de Moche and the El Brujo Complex.

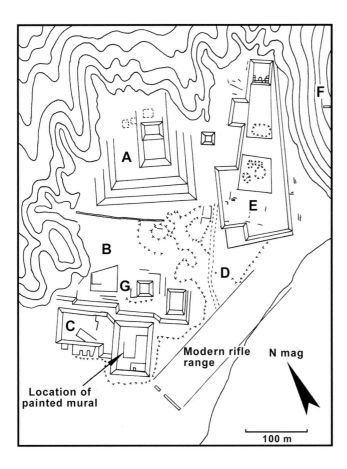

FIGURE 5.2. Mocollope (site 128) map showing urban zones.

Evidence of provisioning the potters at Cerro Mayal suggests that a specialized administration at Mocollope controlled the distribution of food to craft specialists (Attarian 1996; Russell and Jackson 2001). Centralized control developed at Mocollope as the site attracted rural migrants and (as was the case at other urban centers) as the larger population and economic complexity encouraged an increased control of resources and economic systems, such as trade and production.

The previously cited four correlates, which describe the conditions of emerging cities and the conditions that encourage ethnogenesis, were documented through archaeological research at Mocollope. The site was a central node of population nucleation and centralized political control, even before the appearance of Moche fine-line pottery and Moche monumental architecture.

VILLAGE COMMUNITY IDENTITY AND ETHNOGENESIS

Having established that Mocollope was an emerging urban settlement during the Early Intermediate period, we can ask how urbanism causes cultural change. Urbanism involves population resettlement in emerging cities. Arriving migrants face a new economy, new neighbors, and new rules and laws. When we view culture as a product of human interaction with the social and physical environment, culture should change in response to the new situation (Netting 1968, 1977; Rappaport 1968; Harris 1977; Hill 1977).

It has long been thought that ethnic group distinctions would become less pronounced in areas of interaction. The tendency of two groups to become economically interdependent encourages social stability, which is better maintained if the two groups deemphasize differences that could become divisive (Barth 1969). On the other hand, Ian Hodder has demonstrated that in instances of conflicting interest, groups may tend to emphasize their identity in opposition to others (Hodder 1979).

These two studies give us a model for looking at how and when group markers will be deemphasized or emphasized. Ethnogenesis describes the process by which new social identities are created that reflect new and shared conditions (Wolf 1982; Gailey 1987; Roosens 1989; Gregory 1992;

Brumfiel 1994; Grant, Oliver, and James 1996). As groups of people enter a new environment, their previous sense of identity will be challenged and reshaped by the new conditions they must confront to survive.

The leading research on ethnicity has concluded that the concept of ethnic identity and interaction is relevant to small-scale communities (Barth 1969; Cohen 1974; Roosens 1989). Critical points are that identity is self-defined and defined by others in how they perceive the other group (Barth 1969), that identity is born out of interactions that are situation dependent (Cohen 1974), and that cultural values and identity can be observed in cultural forms (Barth 1969; Roosens 1989). All of these authors conceive of ethnicity as operating at the individual level, as well as at the small-community and linguistic group levels. In addition, socially defined interaction is a necessary precondition to the identification of ethnic groups.

Gallinazo villages in the Chicama Valley shared much of their material culture (Bennett 1950; Strong and Evans 1952; Collier 1955). The methodology used here is designed to elucidate variation within the uniformity of Gallinazo culture. In so doing, we can see cultural developments that coincided with the dramatic social changes associated with Moche civilization.

METHODOLOGY

Pottery is a useful medium for examining style because of its plasticity and therefore because of its potential for decoration, regardless of its relevance to function (Sackett 1990). Particular decorations and styles function as communicating devices for group identity and distinction. The intentional use of decoration on ceramics is particularly well documented as a medium for communicating identity to members of other groups (Wheat, Gifford, and Wasley 1958; Washburn 1977; Wobst 1977; Hodder 1979, 1982; Plog 1980; Wiessner 1983, 1984, 1990; Sterner 1989; Braun 1991; van der Leeuw 1991; Brumfiel 1994: 96).

To study dynamic stylistic expression, the Castillo Incised type of decorated pottery—first described by Strong and Evans (1952:316–325)— was selected due to its decorated characteristics and ubiquity (Figure 5.3). Castillo Incised is a domestic pottery type (found at Mocollope in both the pre-urban and urban occupation phases) common to the north coast of Peru during the Early Intermediate period. Castillo Incised pottery is defined by the incision of various small, repeated elements, including small triangles, dots, small circles, dashes, and squares. Sometimes appliquéd strips are attached to the vessel, and these are incised with the same shapes, in addition to diagonal dashes, divots, or dashes that penetrate the entire appliquéd band.

An attribute analysis system was devised to analyze Castillo Incised pottery. By focusing on one variety of decorated pottery, this analysis can exploit differences in the decorations and construct statistical comparisons of variability between assemblages. By using more than one dimension (or attribute) to examine variation, variability can be exposed that is not apparent when using a type-variety analysis. Our analysis found 10 attributes that defined the variation found within the Castillo Incised type. These are:

- Location (of the incised element)
- Number of rows (of elements incised)
- Incised element
- Pattern
- Banded design
- Zone designed
- Space between elements
- Appliqué
- Space between groups
- Number of elements per group or row

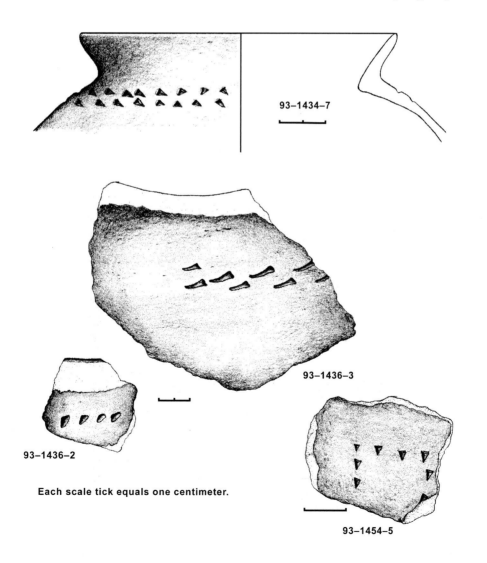

93–1434–7

93–1436–3

93–1436–2

Each scale tick equals one centimeter.

93–1454–5

FIGURE 5.3. Examples of Castillo Incised pottery used for analysis.

The methodology and the full range of attribute variation are fully illustrated by Attarian (2003a). In addition to the village sites shown in Figure 5.1, Mocollope is divided into seven urban zones designated by the letters A through G (Figure 5.2). These zones were defined with the goal of creating units of analysis that are reflective of the architecture believed to be representative of the Gallinazo occupation and of ensuring ceramic assemblages that are adequate for testing. A description of each urban zone and each village site can be found in Attarian (2003a).

Four hundred and seven analyzable Castillo Incised sherds were found from all five rural village sites and the urban center of Mocollope. Many showed unique attributes, and their inclusion would have resulted in statistical noise. After all low-value sherds were removed, the remaining total was 272 sherds. One hundred and thirty-eight of these are from the village sites of PRACh-93, PRACh-112, PRACh-114, PRACh-115, and PRACh-178. One hundred and thirty-four sherds are from the four urban zones of Mocollope (site PRACh-128, urban zones A, B, E, and F). The final distribution is outlined in Table 5.1 (Attarian 2003a:357–361).

TABLE 5.1. Summary of pottery assemblages.

ASSEMBLAGE	NO. OF SHERDS	PERCENT
PRACh-93	79	29.04
PRACh-112	8	2.94
PRACh-114	16	5.88
PRACh-115	14	5.15
PRACh-178	21	7.72
Mocollope Zone A	25	9.19
Mocollope Zone B	70	25.74
Mocollope Zone E	35	12.87
Mocollope Zone F	4	1.47
Total	272	100.00

ANALYSIS AND RESULTS

Our research determined that four possible hypotheses can be generated from the preceding

discussion to explain group interaction with the urban environment (Attarian 2003a, 2003b). They provide a guide for the interpretation of data in a way that is meaningful to the issues of community integration, conservancy, and ethnogenesis that have been raised. These hypotheses have been published and tested previously (Attarian 2003b). Here they are repeated and tested again, with additional data and consideration of more rural sites. Chi-square analysis was used to test whether differences between villages and sectors of the urban site are statistically meaningful (Attarian 2003a).

When considering evidence of changing group identity and expression, emerging differences in wealth between groups need to be accounted for (see hypothesis 2 in Table 5.2). Previous research on the coast of Peru has identified artifact types that co-occur and that require high amounts of labor. These items include metal artifacts such as ornaments, tools, textiles, and beads (Rowe 1946; Murra 1975; Netherly 1977; Gumerman 1991; Lechtman 1997). Copper, silver, and gold were all used by the peoples of the Peruvian north coast. Findings at Mocollope and Gallinazo villages revealed little usable evidence for measuring wealth differences. A larger sample of architecture and intact habitation floors will be needed to discern differences in wealth among communities.

The first set of analyses aimed at determining if individual rural communities had assemblages that were stylistically distinct from one another. If this were not the case, it would be impossible to detect continuity between a particular village and an urban zone in Mocollope. The individual rural sites are significantly different from one another across all of the tested attribute dimensions except "appliqué" (Attarian 2003a:Table 6.5). This conclusion allows us to proceed and test the rural assemblages against the individual urban zone assemblages for continuity or difference.

The second set of analyses was targeted at determining if each urban zone was distinct from the others. The data show that each is distinct from another (Attarian 2003a:Table 6.12). This fact allows us to reject hypothesis 4.

The third round of analysis involved comparing each rural village assemblage to each urban zone. This would tell us if a particular village community maintained its social identity and spa-

TABLE 5.2. Summary of material correlates of each hypothesis.

HYPOTHESIS 1 (H1)	HYPOTHESIS 2 (H2)	HYPOTHESIS 3 (H3)	HYPOTHESIS 4 (H4)
Change due to new and unique social networks and communities.	Change due to differences in wealth and power.	No new communities form. Indigenous communities maintain their identity within the urban environment.	A new but uniform social identity forms.
H1 POTTERY STYLE	**H2 POTTERY STYLE**	**H3 POTTERY STYLE**	**H4 POTTERY STYLE**
New/different styles in distinct areas of the city.	New/different styles, correlated with traditional wealth items.	Same as earlier rural sites. Styles may or may not be spatially segregated.	New/different style, uniform throughout the city.

tial proximity after migrating to Mocollope. The following results were observed: sites PRACh-93, PRACh-112, and PRACh-178 were not statistically similar to any previously defined urban zone. Site PRACh-114 was statistically similar to urban zone E, and site PRACh-115 was statistically similar to urban zone F.

SUMMARY OF RESULTS

There is evidence of the urban zones at Mocollope being stylistically distinct from one another. Therefore, one can conclude that ethnogenesis was not creating a pan-urban shared identity. Rather, Mocollope was a society composed of distinct communities. Analyses show that at least two villages maintained their traditional style of pottery decoration after the population migrated to Mocollope. Statistically similar attribute distributions between villages and urban zones suggest that the migrants maintained their identity through the production of utilitarian wares long after they moved to Mocollope. Hypothesis 3 predicts that the process of ethnogenesis was not causing new communities to form at Mocollope. Rather, in response to the new urban environment, the rural communities maintained their social identity.

The stylistic character of three village assemblages (PRACh-93, PRACh-112, and PRACh-178) could not be identified at Mocollope. For this reason, we can conclude that these three village communities have undergone ethnogenesis and have taken on a new identity at Mocollope.

Because hypothesis 4 was also rejected, we can conclude that hypothesis 1 or 2 best explains the situation. Concerning hypothesis 2, wealth artifacts were too rare to allow for a statistically significant analysis, and thus we are unable to draw a conclusion. In any event, new social interactions brought about by the correlates of urbanism likely created distinct community identities in certain regions of the site of Mocollope.

CONCLUSIONS

Between 200 B.C. and A.D. 200, settlement patterns in the Chicama Valley underwent a shift toward settlement nucleation that included the emergence of an urban site at Mocollope. The new urban environment created conditions, described here as the correlates of urbanism, that promoted changes in community identity. In some cases, the rural populations that migrated to Mocollope underwent the process of ethnogenesis, in which their sense of a cohesive community was lost and a new community identity was formed. The evidence of this new community identity was found in the shared use of stylistic elements in domestic pottery.

The results show positive evidence of ethnogenesis occurring at Mocollope, with variation in the process apparent across the site and for different immigrant groups. Furthermore, the results give insight into the social organization of the Chicama Valley and help explain the social changes that preceded and may have contributed to the rise of Moche style and later to the Moche polity.

Sources of Error

One possible source of error in this analysis is the long period over which these assemblages were deposited. It is possible that the communities in urban zones E and F are more recent arrivals to Mocollope and therefore have not had to endure the influences of the new environment for as long as the communities in urban zones A and B. Given more time, ethnogenesis may have occurred in urban zones E and F.

Another potential source of error is that not all rural village sites are included in the study. There are two possibilities for why this is likely. The survey of the Chicama Valley covered about one-third of the lower valley. Moreover, the survey only covered the southern half of the valley neck—where most Gallinazo villages are located. A more complete survey will likely reveal more villages, and it is possible that some of these communities will match the styles found in urban zones A and B.

The incomplete survey argument also applies to Mocollope. A larger ceramic assemblage from more areas of the site will improve the accuracy of the comparisons. Some areas of the site were not excavated, and it is also likely that there are residential areas of the site that are now destroyed or hopelessly buried under modern construction. These undiscovered areas might contain the communities that match rural villages PRACh-93, PRACh-112, and PRACh-178. Finally, the drawing of the urban zones was done using surface architecture as a guide. In truth, these areas could be redrawn in many different ways. By redrawing the urban zones, the stylistic assemblages also change. This will likely change the results of the comparisons with rural sites.

ACKNOWLEDGMENTS

This research was funded by the UCLA Department of Anthropology, the UCLA Friends of Archaeology, the University Research Expeditions Program (UREP), and a National Science Foundation Grant (award number BCS9908396). This work draws on three distinct archaeological projects. First is the research of Banks Leonard and Glenn Russell from 1989 through 1993. Second is the work that Glenn Russell, Thomas Wake, Rosario Becerra, and Christopher Attarian conducted at the site of Mocollope. Third is the investigation of Gallinazo villages, directed by Kory Tyka Avila and Christopher Attarian. We wish to thank everyone who helped and advised on these projects. This chapter is dedicated to the memory of José Celestino Suárez of Mocollope.

REFERENCES

Attarian, Christopher J.
1996   Plant Foods and Ceramic Production: A Case Study of Mochica Ceramic Production Specialists in the Chicama Valley, Peru. Unpublished master's thesis, University of California, Los Angeles.
2003a Pre-Hispanic Urbanism and Community Expression in the Chicama Valley, Peru. Unpublished Ph.D. dissertation, University of California, Los Angeles.
2003b Cities as a Place of Ethnogenesis: Urban Growth and Centralization in the Chicama Valley, Peru. In *The Social Construction of Ancient Cities*, Monica L. Smith (ed.), pp. 184–211. Washington, D.C.: Smithsonian Institution Press.

Barth, Fredrik
1969   *Ethnic Groups and Boundaries: The Social Organization of Culture Difference*. Boston: Little, Brown.

Bawden, Garth
1996   *The Moche*. Cambridge, Massachusetts: Blackwell.

Bennett, Wendell C.
1950   *The Gallinazo Group: Virú Valley, Peru*. Yale University Publications in Anthropology 43. New Haven: Yale University Press.

Billman, Brian R.
1996   The Evolution of Prehistoric Political Organizations in the Moche Valley, Peru. Unpublished Ph.D. dissertation, University of California, Santa Barbara.

Blanton, Richard E.
1976   Anthropological Studies of Cities. *Annual Review of Anthropology* 5:249–264.

Blanton, Richard E., Stephan A. Kowalewski, Gary M. Feinman, and Laura M. Finsten
1993   *Ancient Mesoamerica: A Comparison of Change in Three Regions*. Cambridge, UK: Cambridge University Press.

Braun, David P.
1991   Why Decorate a Pot? Midwestern Household Pottery, 200 B.C.–A.D. 600. *Journal of Anthropological Archaeology* 10:360–397.

Brumfiel, Elizabeth M.
  1987   Elite and Utilitarian Crafts in the Aztec State. In *Specialization, Exchange, and Complex Societies*, Elizabeth M. Brumfiel and Timothy K. Earle (eds.), pp. 102–118. Cambridge, UK: Cambridge University Press.
  1994   Ethnic Groups and Political Development in Ancient Mexico. In *Factional Competition and Political Development in the New World*, Elizabeth M. Brumfiel and John W. Fox (eds.), pp. 89–102. Cambridge, UK: Cambridge University Press.
Brumfiel, Elizabeth M., and Timothy K. Earle (editors)
  1987   *Specialization, Exchange, and Complex Societies.* Cambridge, UK: Cambridge University Press.
Carneiro, Robert L.
  1967   On the Relationship between Size of Population and Complexity of Social Organization. *Southwestern Journal of Anthropology* 23(3): 234–243.
Childe, V. Gordon
  1950   The Urban Revolution. *The Town Planning Review* 21:3–17.
Claessen, Henri J. M.
  1984   The Internal Dynamics of the Early State. *Current Anthropology* 25(4):365–379.
Cohen, Abner (editor)
  1974   *Urban Ethnicity*. London: Tavistock Publications.
Collier, Donald
  1955   *Cultural Chronology and Change as Reflected in the Ceramics of the Virú Valley, Peru*. Chicago: Chicago Natural History Museum.
Costin, Cathy L.
  1991   Craft Specialization: Issues in Defining, Documenting, and Explaining the Organization of Production. *Archaeological Method and Theory* 3:1–56.
D'Altroy, Terence N.
  1992   *Provincial Power in the Inka Empire*. Washington, D.C.: Smithsonian Institution Press.
Demand, Nancy H.
  1990   *Urban Relocation in Archaic and Classical Greece: Flight and Consolidation*. Norman, Oklahoma: University of Oklahoma Press.
Earle, Timothy K.
  1987   Specialization and the Production of Wealth: Hawaiian Chiefdoms and the Inca Empire. In *Specialization, Exchange, and Complex Societies*, Elizabeth M. Brumfiel and Timothy K. Earle (eds.), pp. 64–75. Cambridge, UK: Cambridge University Press.
Flannery, Kent V.
  1972   The Cultural Evolution of Civilizations. *Annual Review of Ecology and Systematics* 3: 399–426.

Gailey, Christine W.
  1987   Culture Wars: Resistance to State Formation. In *Power Relations and State Formation*, Thomas C. Patterson and Christine W. Gailey (eds.), pp. 35–56. Washington, D.C.: American Anthropological Association.
Grant, David M., Melvin L. Oliver, and Angela D. James
  1996   African Americans: Social and Economic Bifurcation. In *Ethnic Los Angeles*, Roger Waldinger and Mehdi Bozorgmehr (eds.), pp. 379–411. New York: Russell Sage Foundation.
Gregory, Steven
  1992   The Changing Significance of Race and Class in an African-American Community. *American Ethnologist* 19(2):255–274.
Gumerman, George
  1991   Subsistence and Complex Societies: Diet between Diverse Socio-Economic Groups at Pacatnamú, Peru. Unpublished Ph.D. dissertation, University of California, Los Angeles.
Harris, Marvin
  1977   *Cannibals and Kings: The Origins of Cultures.* New York: Random House.
Hicks, Frederic
  1987   First Steps toward a Market-Integrated Economy in Aztec Mexico. In *Early State Dynamics*, Henri J. M. Claessen and Pieter van de Velde (eds.), pp. 91–107. Leiden: E. J. Brill.
Hill, James N.
  1977   Systems Theory and the Explanation of Change. In *Explanation of Prehistoric Change*, James N. Hill (ed.), pp. 59–103. Albuquerque: University of New Mexico Press.
Hodder, Ian
  1979   Economic and Social Stress and Material Culture Patterning. *American Antiquity* 44(3): 446–454.
  1982   *Symbols in Action: Ethnoarchaeological Studies of Material Culture*. Cambridge, UK: Cambridge University Press.
Johnson, Gregory A.
  1982   Organizational Structure and Scalar Stress. In *Theory and Explanation in Archaeology*, Colin Renfrew, Michael J. Rowlands, and Barbara Abbott Segraves (eds.), pp. 389–421. New York: Academic Press.
Johnson, Allen W., and Timothy K. Earle
  1987   *The Evolution of Human Societies: From Foraging Group to Agrarian State*. Stanford, California: Stanford University Press.
Larco Hoyle, Rafael
  1948   *Cronología arqueológica del norte del Perú*. Buenos Aires: Sociedad Geográfica Americana.

Lechtman, Heather
    1997 Copper Artifacts from Moche Burials at
          Pacatnamu. In *The Pacatnamu Papers*, Volume
          2: *The Moche Occupation*. Christopher B. Don-
          nan and Guillermo A. Cock (eds.), pp. 251–
          254. Los Angeles: Fowler Museum of Cultur-
          al History, University of California.
Leonard, Banks L., and Glenn S. Russell
    1992 Informe preliminar: Proyecto de reconoci-
          miento arqueológico del Chicama, resultados
          de la primera temporada de campo, 1989.
          Unpublished report submitted to the Institu-
          to Nacional de Cultura, Lima.
Millon, René
    1967 *Teotihuacán: The Largest City of the Pre-
          Columbian New World*. New York: n. p.
Murra, John V.
    1975 *Formaciones económicas y políticas del mundo
          andino*. Lima: Instituto de Estudios Peruanos.
Netherly, Patricia
    1977 Local Level Lords on the North Coast of
          Peru. Unpublished Ph.D. dissertation, Cor-
          nell University, Ithaca, New York.
Netting, Robert McC.
    1968 *Hill Farmers of Nigeria: Cultural Ecology of the
          Kofyar of the Jos Plateau*. Seattle: University of
          Washington Press.
    1977 *Cultural Ecology*. Menlo Park, California:
          Cummings.
Patterson, Thomas C.
    1987 Tribes, Chiefdoms, and Kingdoms in the Inca
          Empire. In *Power Relations and State Forma-
          tion*, Thomas C. Patterson and Christine W.
          Gailey (eds.), pp. 117–127. Washington, D.C.:
          American Anthropological Association.
Plog, Stephen
    1980 *Stylistic Variation in Prehistoric Ceramics: Design
          Analysis in the American Southwest*. Cambridge,
          UK: Cambridge University Press.
Polanyi, Karl
    1944 *The Great Transformation*. New York: Farrar &
          Rinehart.
Rappaport, Roy A.
    1968 *Pigs for the Ancestors: Ritual in the Ecology of a
          New Guinea People*. New Haven: Yale Univer-
          sity Press.
Roosens, Eugeen
    1989 *Creating Ethnicity: The Process of Ethnogenesis*.
          Newbury Park, California: Sage Publications.
Rowe, John
    1946 Inca Culture at the Time of the Spanish Con-
          quest. In *Handbook of South American Indians*,
          Volume 2: *The Andean Civilizations*, Julian H.
          Steward (ed.), pp. 183–330. Smithsonian Insti-

tution, Bureau of American Ethnology Bul-
          letin 143. Washington, D.C.: Government
          Printing Office.
    1963 Urban Settlements in Ancient Peru. *Ñawpa
          Pacha* 1(1):1–27.
Russell, Glenn S.
    1992 Preceramic through Moche Settlement Pat-
          tern Change in the Chicama Valley, Peru.
          Paper presented at the 55th Annual Meeting
          of the Society for American Archaeology, Las
          Vegas.
Russell, Glenn S., and Margaret A. Jackson
    2001 Political Economy and Patronage at Cerro
          Mayal, Peru. In *Moche Art and Archaeology in
          Ancient Peru*, Joanne Pillsbury (ed.), pp.
          159–175. Washington, D.C.: National Gallery
          of Art and Yale University Press.
Russell, Glenn S., Banks L. Leonard, and Jesús Briceño
    Rosario
    1994 Producción de cerámica moche a gran escala
          en el valle de Chicama, Perú: El taller de
          Cerro Mayal. In *Tecnología y organización de la
          producción de cerámica prehispánica en los Andes*,
          Izumi Shimada (ed.), pp. 201–227. Lima:
          Fondo Editorial, Pontificia Universidad
          Católica del Perú.
Sackett, James R.
    1990 Style and Ethnicity in Archaeology: The Case
          for Isochrestism. In *The Uses of Style in Archae-
          ology*, Margaret W. Conkey and Christine A.
          Hastorf (eds.), pp. 32–43. Cambridge, UK:
          Cambridge University Press.
Service, Elman R.
    1978 Classical and Modern Theories of the Origins
          of Government. In *Origins of the State: The
          Anthropology of Political Evolution*, Ronald
          Cohen and Elman R. Service (eds.), pp. 21–34.
          Philadelphia: Institute for the Study of
          Human Issues.
Silverman, Helaine
    1988 Cahuachi: Non-Urban Cultural Complexity
          on the South Coast of Peru. *Journal of Field
          Archaeology* 15(4):403–430.
Sinopoli, Carla M.
    1988 The Organization of Craft Production at Vij-
          ayanagara, South India. *American Anthropolo-
          gist* 90(3):580–597.
Spencer, Charles S.
    1990 On the Tempo and Mode of State Formation:
          Neoevolutionism Reconsidered. *Journal of
          Anthropological Archaeology* 9:1–30.
Stanish, Charles
    1992 *Ancient Andean Political Economy*. Austin: Uni-
          versity of Texas Press.

1997 Nonmarket Imperialism in the Prehispanic Americas: The Inka Occupation of the Titicaca Basin. *Latin American Antiquity* 8(3): 195–216.

Sterner, Judy
1989 Who is Signalling Whom? Ceramic Style, Ethnicity and Taphonomy among the Sirak Bulahay. *Antiquity* 63(240):451–459.

Strong, William D., and Clifford Evans
1952 *Cultural Stratigraphy in the Virú Valley, Northern Peru: The Formative and Florescent Epochs.* New York: Columbia University Press.

van der Leeuw, S. E.
1991 Variation, Variability, and Explanation in Pottery Studies. In *Ceramic Ethnoarchaeology*, William A. Longacre (ed.), pp. 11–39. Tucson: University of Arizona Press.

Washburn, Dorothy Koster
1977 *A Symmetry Analysis of Upper Gila Area Ceramic Design.* Cambridge, Massachusetts: Peabody Museum of Archaeology and Ethnology, Harvard University.

Wheat, Joe Ben, James C. Gifford, and William W. Wasley
1958 Ceramic Variety, Type Cluster, and Ceramic System in Southwestern Pottery Analysis. *American Antiquity* 24(1):34–47.

Wiessner, Polly
1983 Style and Social Information in Kalahari San Projectile Points. *American Antiquity* 48(2): 253–276.
1984 Reconsidering the Behavioral Basis for Style: A Case Study among the Kalahari San. *Journal of Anthropological Archaeology* 3:190–234.
1990 Is There a Unity to Style? In *The Uses of Style in Archaeology*, Margaret W. Conkey and Christine A. Hastorf (eds.), pp. 105–112. Cambridge, UK: Cambridge University Press.

Willey, Gordon R.
1953 *Prehistoric Settlement Patterns in the Virú Valley, Perú* [sic]. Smithsonian Institution, Bureau of American Ethnology Bulletin 155. Washington, D.C.: Government Printing Office.

Wilson, David J.
1988 *Prehispanic Settlement Patterns in the Lower Santa Valley, Peru: A Regional Perspective on the Origins and Development of Complex North Coast Society.* Washington, D.C.: Smithsonian Institution Press.

Wobst, H. Martin
1977 Stylistic Behavior and Information Exchange. In *For the Director: Research Essays in Honor of James B. Griffin*, Charles E. Cleland (ed.), pp. 317–342. Ann Arbor: Museum of Anthropology, University of Michigan.

Wolf, Eric R.
1966 Kinship, Friendship, and Patron-Client Relations in Complex Societies. In *The Social Anthropology of Complex Societies*, Michael Banton (ed.), pp. 1–22. London: Tavistock Publications.
1982 *Europe and the People without History.* Berkeley: University of California Press.

Wright, Henry T.
1977 Recent Research on the Origin of the State. *Annual Review of Anthropology* 6:379–397.
1986 The Evolution of Civilizations. In *American Archaeology, Past and Future: A Celebration of the Society for American Archaeology, 1935–1985*, David J. Meltzer, Don D. Fowler, and Jeremy A. Sabloff (eds.), pp. 323–365. Washington, D.C.: Society for American Archaeology and Smithsonian Institution Press.

CHAPTER 6

GALLINAZO-STYLE CERAMICS IN EARLY MOCHE CONTEXTS AT THE EL BRUJO COMPLEX, CHICAMA VALLEY

Régulo G. Franco Jordán and César A. Gálvez Mora

Since 1990, the El Brujo Complex (Figure 6.1) —a large pre-Hispanic settlement located in the lower Chicama Valley (Figure 6.2)—has been under investigation thanks to a tripartite agreement among the Fundación Augusto N. Wiese, the Instituto Nacional de Cultura, and the Universidad Nacional de Trujillo. Research has focused on the cultural history of this site between the Preceramic and Colonial periods. Here, our intention is to present data on the presence of artifacts of Gallinazo style in contexts that also feature Early Moche (Moche I) material culture.

The data, which were gathered during recent fieldwork seasons, all come from secure archaeological contexts. The sample of Gallinazo-style ceramics from this site is composed mainly of simple jars decorated with incisions, punctations, and appliqué. The jars are comparable to similar containers uncovered elsewhere in Chicama and in other valleys along the coast.

The earliest information available on the presence of ceramics of Gallinazo style in Chicama came from the work of Rafael Larco Hoyle (1945, 1948), a pioneer of archaeological research on the Gallinazo (Virú) culture. One of Larco Hoyle's contributions was to argue for the coeval nature of Gallinazo and Moche ceramics, at least until the Moche II phase.

Four decades later, Banks Leonard and Glenn Russell undertook survey work in the middle Chicama Valley, establishing a ceramic chronology for the Early Intermediate period in this region (Leonard and Russell 1992). According to this chronology, phase I was characterized by the presence of white-on-red ceramic vessels decorated with incisions, punctations, and appliqué—the typical Gallinazo-style jar (Figure 6.3). The most common shapes are neckless *ollas*, jars with short, funnel-shaped necks, and straight-neck jars with a wide flat rim. Phase II apparently saw the introduction of new ceramic types (which the authors do not describe).

During phase III, Gallinazo Negative ceramic vessels started to appear. Various types of bottles were also being produced, as well as Salinar-like white-on-red jars (Larco Hoyle 1944; 1946: 155–161). The latter differ from phase I jars in

FIGURE 6.1. Aerial photograph of the El Brujo Complex showing location of principal structures.

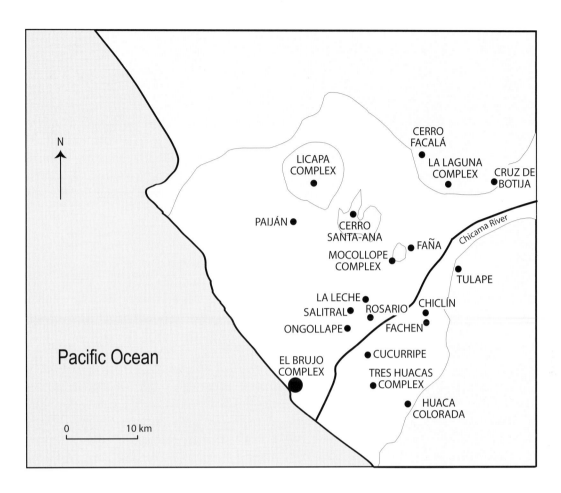

FIGURE 6.2. Map of major pre-Hispanic settlements in the Chicama Valley.

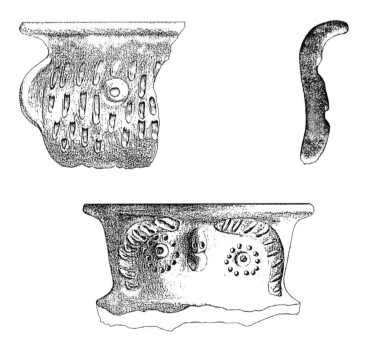

FIGURE 6.3. Ceramics of Gallinazo style from the Chicama Valley.

that the paste and surface treatment are of higher quality and the geometric decoration is stylistically closer to Moche ceramics. According to Leonard and Russell, it is likely that the fine white-on-red ceramic—which they label "Proto Moche Blanco/Rojo Fino"—predates or was coeval with Early Moche vessels (Leonard and Russell 1992: 31–34).

This phase was also marked by major transformations in settlement patterns, which they argue would reflect the first political unification of the lower Chicama Valley by a polity that would have had its capital at Mocollope. However, recent investigations at the El Brujo Complex place doubts on this scenario, suggesting that the political center of this early regional polity was not based at Mocollope but was close to the seashore (Franco, Gálvez, and Vásquez 1994, 1995, 1999, 2001a, 2001b, 2001c, 2003).

The El Brujo Complex

At the El Brujo Complex, Gallinazo-style ceramics were uncovered during excavations conducted on Huaca Cao Viejo, on Montículo I, inside the

Ceremonial Well, and on Huaca El Brujo (Figure 6.1). Huaca Cao Viejo consists of a large adobe platform mound fronted by a large ceremonial plaza (Figure 6.4) and flanked by additional structures to the east and west. These three architectural elements were maintained throughout the seven construction phases documented at the site (A–G). In this sequence, building A corresponds to the most modern structure and building D to the fourth construction phase.

During excavation of the Upper Platform, several Gallinazo-style ceramic vessels were uncovered. Some vessels came from excavations carried out in the inner southwest corner of the Ceremonial Patio of building D, where the remains of a series of individuals were uncovered. Below the floor, which corresponds to the first remodeling of the patio (phase D-1), the remains of a female wrapped inside textiles and reed mats were found (tomb 1/1998). Bowls with a lateral handle (*cancheros*) decorated with white-on-red geometric designs were found as part of the offerings, together with stirrup-spout bottles (Figure 6.5).

The bottles correspond stylistically to Moche I and Gallinazo styles, and some of them feature

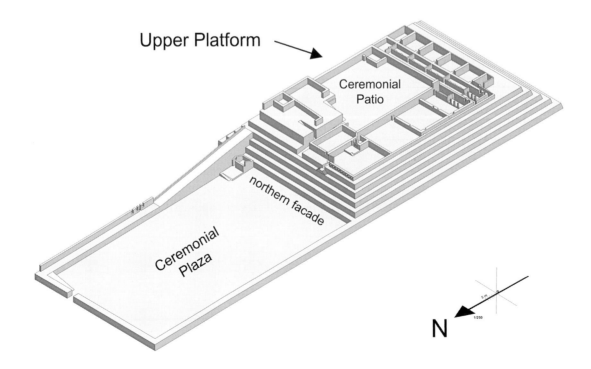

FIGURE 6.4. Isometric reconstruction of Huaca Cao Viejo.

FIGURE 6.5. Stirrup-spout bottles from tomb 1 (1998) in southwest corner
of the Ceremonial Patio of building D at Huaca Cao Viejo.

stirrup-spout handles similar to those of Cupisnique vessels. Black-ware bottles with composite
bodies were also uncovered. In this same sector,
two small Gallinazo-style jars were also found
inside a pit excavated during the construction of
building C (Figure 6.6). One features a funnel-
shaped neck and is decorated with cream-colored
paint and punctations. The other is decorated
with geometric and reticulated designs using fugitive paint.

In the southwest corner of the Upper Platform, two fragments of Gallinazo-style jars were
found inside a fill above a large burial chamber
associated with Moche III and Moche IV ceramics (tomb 2). The first features a human face,
whereas the other is decorated with an animal-
like figure made with incisions, punctations, and
appliqué. Although these Gallinazo-style sherds
were found in a secondary context, we believe
they were associated with primary contexts
removed during the excavation of the burial
chamber, which cut through buildings D and E.

Excavations in the northwest sector of the
Upper Platform led to the discovery of an adult
individual (tomb 1/1999) buried inside a loose
patch of soil (associated with building C), which
also contained a concentration of ceramic fragments of Moche I style. Our analyses reveal that
this was in fact a secondary burial. Indeed, the
remains were moved to this location during one
of the remodeling events associated with the construction of building C on top of building D. This
leads us to believe that the remains and associated
offerings were originally from a disturbed grave
from building D.

Near this burial, fragments of high-quality
sculpted vessels of Moche I style were found in
association with Gallinazo-style ceramics. The
Moche-style ceramics include anthropomorphic
and zoomorphic vessels, as well as figurines,
plates, and bowls with lateral handles (Figure 6.7).
The Gallinazo-style ceramics feature face-neck
jars decorated with incisions, punctations, and
appliqué (Figure 6.8).

FIGURE 6.6. Jars from a pit associated with the construction of building C of Huaca Cao Viejo.

FIGURE 6.7. Moche-style ceramics from the north-west sector of the Upper Platform of Huaca Cao Viejo.

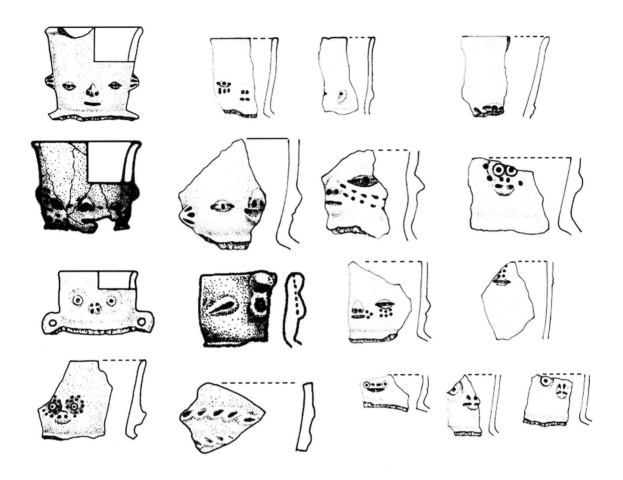

FIGURE 6.8. Gallinazo-style ceramics from the northwest sector
of the Upper Platform of Huaca Cao Viejo.

While conducting excavations in the upper western part of the northern facade of Huaca Cao Viejo, a large quantity of ceramics and human remains were uncovered in spaces hollowed-out inside building C. The ceramics included Gallinazo-style face-neck jars with incised and punctated designs (Figure 6.9), as well as a Moche I stirrup-spout vessel.

Some of the best evidence of the coeval nature of Gallinazo and Early Moche ceramics comes from the Northwest Patio of the Upper Platform, near the northern facade (Figure 6.10). The material is from tomb 3, a grave that contained the remains of a female, accompanied by individuals of lesser status. Early Moche-style vessels were found inside this grave, including stirrup-spout bottles (Figure 6.11a). One is decorated with a scene in which an officiating woman applies her left hand to the chest of a baby girl who is suckling her mother's breast.

Another vessel shows a seated individual with a hemispheric hat. The grave also contained small jars fired in oxidizing atmosphere, painted with geometric motifs using white and black fugitive paint (Figure 6.11b). Morphologically and stylistically, these jars represent an unheard-of variant of Moche ceramic. Small Gallinazo-style jars were also found in this location (Figure 6.11c).

In the fill above this grave, we uncovered a large jar with a semiglobular body and a tall and slightly funnel-shaped neck, decorated with the head of an owl made with fine incisions, low reliefs, and faint cream-colored paint highlights (Figure 6.12). This vessel is similar to other ceramics found inside building C. Four rounded jars and two bowls were found directly above the

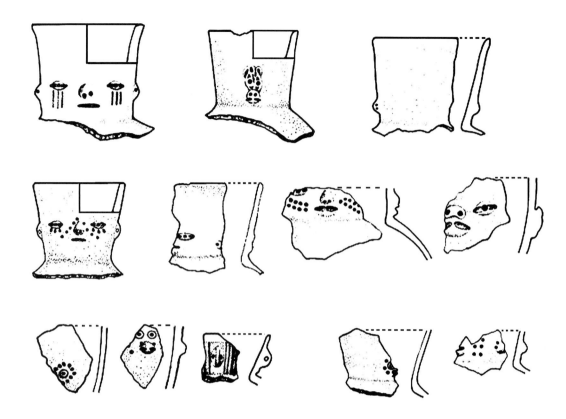

FIGURE 6.9. Gallinazo-style ceramics from the northern facade of Huaca Cao Viejo.

FIGURE 6.10. Northwest Patio, Upper Platform of Huaca Cao Viejo.

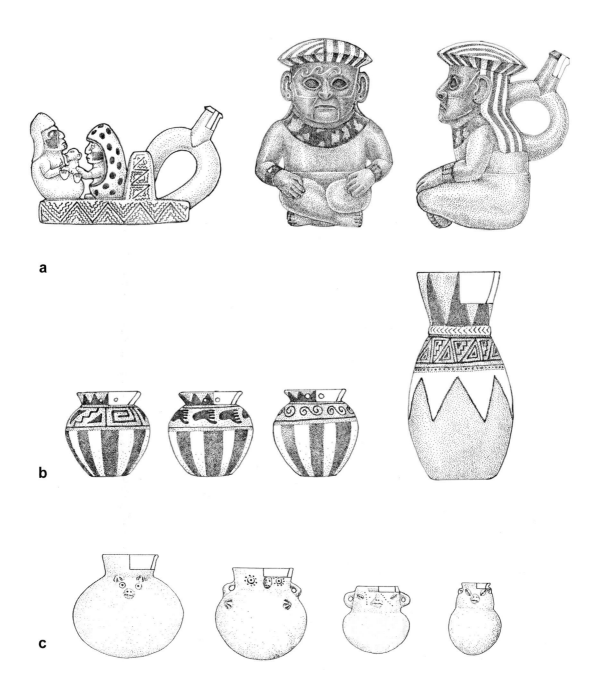

Figure 6.11. Ceramics associated with tomb 3 at Huaca Cao Viejo.

grave inside a hearth used during the mortuary ritual.

Finally, fragments of Gallinazo-style face-neck jars and Early Moche–style ceramics were found together at the foot of the northern facade of Huaca Cao Viejo and in the fill that covers the floor of building D. Similarly, in the lower central part of the western facade of building D, a small enclosure filled with refuse also contained ceramics of Gallinazo and Moche styles. These ceramics included fragments of Moche-style stirrup-spout bottles, *floreros*, and anthropomorphic figures with incised geometric designs. Gallinazo-style ceramics included figurines, face-neck jars

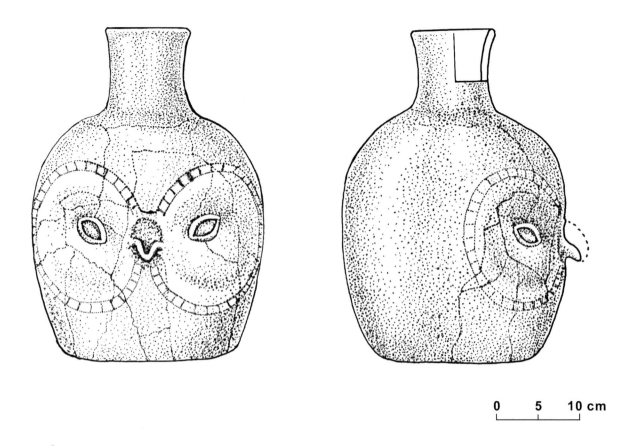

FIGURE 6.12. Ceramic jar from fill above tomb 3 at Huaca Cao Viejo.

with perforated ears, and fragments featuring representations of human faces, mammals, and birds.

Gallinazo-style ceramics were also uncovered in other sectors of the El Brujo Complex. For example, to the northeast of Huaca Cao Viejo lies Montículo I, a small Late Moche building with lateral ramps. Excavations revealed the presence of earlier structures with burials at its base. A Moche storage jar was found nearby, inside of which was discovered a fragment of a Gallinazo-style face-neck jar with tearful eyes.

To the north of Huaca Cao Viejo we uncovered a 12.5-m-deep spiral-shaped well filled with soil, stones, human bones, and a large quantity of Early Moche–style ceramic fragments, including floreros, plates, jars, and figurines (Franco, Gálvez, and Vásquez 1998; Jiménez 2004). Interestingly, Gallinazo-style ceramics decorated with incisions and punctations were also uncovered during the excavation process. These included face-neck jars, figurines, and plates with an annu-lar base decorated with fugitive paint (Franco and Gálvez 2003).

In 1993 and 1994, excavations were undertaken with the objective of understanding the temporal relation between the well and the surrounding structures. This process led to the discovery of a large quantity of ceramics of Gallinazo and Moche styles associated with structures that antedate the construction of the well. The Gallinazo-style fragments came from small jars, plates, storage jars, cancheros, bowls, figurines, and miniature face-neck jars.

Finally, preliminary work conducted inside the trench on the southern facade of Huaca El Brujo (Franco, Gálvez, and Murga 2002) led us to document early construction levels at the base of this platform. In this context, two fragments of Gallinazo-style ceramics were found in association with a single stirrup-spout vessel of Early Moche style. Both Gallinazo-style fragments came from face-neck jars (Figure 6.13).

Figure 6.13. Face-neck jar from Huaca El Brujo.

Beyond the El Brujo Complex

The coeval nature of ceramics of Gallinazo and Early Moche styles is not a phenomenon unique to the El Brujo Complex, as is clear from research conducted elsewhere in the Chicama Valley (Figure 6.2). For example, while doing fieldwork at the site of Cerro Santa Ana (Cerro Constancia), Larco Hoyle uncovered a grave that contained ceramic vessels of Gallinazo (Virú Auge) and Early Moche (Mochica I) styles (Larco Hoyle 1948).

However, Larco Hoyle noted that, unlike Gallinazo Negative ceramics from Virú, the vessels were first covered with a white slip and the treatment of colors was inverted. Moreover, the absence of correspondence between Virú and Chicama vessel shapes led him to argue that the latter were directly derived from the local Salinar tradition, as opposed to being products of import. Larco also noted the important influence of the local Gallinazo (Virú de Chicama) style on the Early Moche ceramic tradition (Larco Hoyle 1948:24–27).

Similarly, excavations inside the Capilla del Señor de la Caña in Chiclín led to the discovery of two burials located only a few meters apart (Ocas 1998; Goycochea 2004). Those graves contained vessels (a bottle, several jars, and a vessel decorated with a modeled face) decorated with incisions and punctations with a well-fired, orange-reddish paste reminiscent of Salinar ceramics. Interestingly, the sample also includes modeled vessels with feline heads, a popular form in Early Moche ceramics. It also features vessels with cubic chambers: decorations consisting of incisions and punctations in the treatment of the modeled figures. Finally, the Museo de Chiclín collections include a series of miniature Gallinazo-style face-neck jars reportedly from the village and from other settlements in the valley.

Gallinazo-style ceramics were also recovered during a surface collection on the hillsides of Cerro Facalá, which is topped by a Moche structure built with adobes produced in cane molds. Interestingly, those adobes are similar to those used during the earliest construction phases recorded at Huaca Cao Viejo. Ceramics from Cerro Facalá are essentially utilitarian in nature, and include jars with convex necks decorated with protuberances and triangular incisions, straight-neck jars decorated with ovoid incisions around the neck, and jars with funnel-shaped necks and thickened rims decorated with parallel lines of triangular incisions. Among other objects, bowls and graters were also found, but there were no face-neck jars (Avila 1997).

The coeval nature of Gallinazo- and Moche-style ceramics was also documented outside the Chicama Valley. In Jequetepeque, for example, in a burial from Dos Cabezas (tomb 2), Christopher Donnan uncovered utilitarian vessels of Gallinazo style, together with Early Moche ceramics (Donnan 2003). Similarly, Heinrich Ubbelohde-Doering (1967:22) reported the discovery of offerings of Moche and Gallinazo styles in graves located near Huaca 31 at Pacatnamú, including face-neck jars of Gallinazo style featuring incisions, punctations, and pinches (Ubbelohde-Doering 1957, 1983; see also Chapter 4).

Likewise, at Santa Rosa de Quirihuac in the Moche Valley, George Gumerman and Jesús Briceño uncovered Gallinazo-style face-neck jars together with Early Moche bottles (Gumerman and Briceño 2003). Those, of course, are only a few instances in which the coeval nature of Gallinazo- and Moche-style ceramics has been documented by north-coast specialists.

DISCUSSION

The evidence previously presented indicates that in the Chicama Valley, utilitarian ceramics of Gallinazo style were being produced without major change until well into Moche times (see Chapter 5). In this context, one could argue that, as a substitute for fine Gallinazo-style vessels, utilitarian forms such as jars were intentionally selected to be used as funerary offerings, together with fine Moche-style ceramics—as illustrated by the burial uncovered on the Northwest Patio of the Upper Platform of Huaca Cao Viejo (tomb 3).

The funerary nature of these utilitarian vessels was suggested by the unusual absence of ware. The reason behind this choice is a theme worth exploring, as this odd association likely alludes to the material expression of the concept of "opposites" related to the cult of the dead—a principle that would later be expressed through the presence of unfired (instead of fired) clay figurines in association with sacrificed males at Huaca de la Luna (Bourget 2001).

The evidence previously presented seems to suggest that the local elites, originally in control of the production of ceramics of Gallinazo style, started to adopt the new ceramic canons we describe as Early Moche. This is evidenced by the presence of vessels of Gallinazo style in association with Early Moche ceramics in different contexts—for example, in graves from the Ceremonial Patio (tomb 1/1998) and from the Northwest Patio (tomb 3). These vessels feature handles clearly reminiscent of Cupisnique material culture, but the treatment of the faces is typical of Gallinazo-style ceramics from Chicama and elsewhere along the coast. This suggests the existence of a transitional stage during which ceramists produced hybrid vessels.

What led the local elites to integrate this new ceramic style is unclear. It can be hypothesized, however, that this was part of a movement to consolidate their prestige and power at the local and regional levels. Nevertheless, the evidence currently available does not allow us to confirm this or other hypotheses, in part because more data are needed from a larger number of settlements, something that is only available for subsequent periods.

ACKNOWLEDGMENTS

We would like to thank the Fundación Augusto N. Wiese, the Instituto Nacional de Cultura, and the team of professionals, technicians, and workmen from the El Brujo Complex for their valuable help throughout the investigation process. Our thanks also go to Dr. Jeffrey Quilter for providing us with information on the material uncovered inside the Ceremonial Well; to archaeologists Juan Vilela, Hugo Ríos, Sandra Sánchez, Carmen Gamarra, Denis Vargas, and Jaime Jiménez; to the conservator Segundo Lozada; and to Carlos Araujo and Edwin Angulo for their help in the elaboration of this chapter. We would also like to thank Jean-François Millaire for his translation from the Spanish. Finally, our gratitude goes to Jorge Cox Denegri for agreeing to let us reanalyze part of the collections from Chiclín.

REFERENCES

Avila Vereau, Kory Tika
  1997 Investigación arqueológica en Cerro Facalá, valle Chicama. Unpublished licentiate thesis, Universidad Nacional de Trujillo, Trujillo.
Bourget, Steve
  2001 Rituals of Sacrifice: Its Practice at Huaca de la Luna and Its Representation in Moche Iconography. In *Moche Art and Archaeology in Ancient Peru*, Joanne Pillsbury (ed.), pp. 89–109. Washington, D.C.: National Gallery of Art and Yale University Press.

Donnan, Christopher B.
  2003 Tumbas con entierros en miniatura: Un nuevo tipo funerario moche. In *Moche: Hacia el final del milenio*, Santiago Uceda and Elías Mujica (eds.), vol. 1, pp. 43–78. Lima: Universidad Nacional de Trujillo and Fondo Editorial, Pontificia Universidad Católica del Perú.
Franco Jordán, Régulo, and César Gálvez Mora
  2003 Un caso de arquitectura mochica subterránea. *Arkinka* 97:88–95.
Franco Jordán, Régulo, César Gálvez Mora, and Antonio Murga Cruz
  2002 La Huaca El Brujo: Arquitectura e iconografía. *Arkinka* 85:86–97.
Franco Jordán, Régulo, César Gálvez Mora, and Segundo Vásquez Sánchez
  1994 Programa arqueológico complejo El Brujo. Informe final, temporada 1994. Unpublished report submitted to the Instituto Nacional de Cultura, Lima.
  1995 Programa arqueológico complejo El Brujo. Informe final, temporada 1995. Unpublished report submitted to the Instituto Nacional de Cultura, Lima.
  1998 Un pozo ceremonial moche en el complejo arqueológico "El Brujo." *Ciencias sociales, revista de la facultad de ciencias sociales* (Trujillo) 5:307–315.
  1999 Programa arqueológico complejo El Brujo. Informe final, temporada 1999. Unpublished report submitted to the Instituto Nacional de Cultura, Lima.
  2001a Desentierro y reenterramiento de una tumba de elite mochica en el complejo El Brujo. *Boletín* [Programa Arqueológico Complejo El Brujo] 2:1–24.
  2001b La Huaca Cao Viejo en el complejo El Brujo: Una contribución al estudio de los Mochicas en el valle de Chicama. *Arqueológicas* (Lima) 25:123–173.
  2001c Arquitectura e iconografía de un edificio mochica temprano en el complejo El Brujo. *Arkinka* 73:92–99.
  2003 Modelos, función y cronología de la Huaca Cao Viejo, complejo El Brujo. In *Moche: Hacia el final del milenio*, Santiago Uceda and Elías Mujica (eds.), vol. 2, pp. 125–177. Lima: Universidad Nacional de Trujillo and Fondo Editorial, Pontificia Universidad Católica del Perú.
Goycochea Larco, José Alberto
  2004 Patrones de enterramiento de la cultura virú en el poblado menor de Chiclín, valle de Chicama. Unpublished licentiate thesis, Universidad Nacional de Trujillo, Trujillo.

Gumerman, George, and Jesús Briceño
   2003   Santa Rosa-Quirihuac y Ciudad de Dios: Asentamientos rurales en la parte media del valle de Moche. In *Moche: Hacia el final del milenio*, Santiago Uceda and Elías Mujica (eds.), vol. 1, pp. 217–243. Lima: Universidad Nacional de Trujillo and Fondo Editorial, Pontificia Universidad Católica del Perú.

Jiménez Saldaña, Jaime L.
   2004   Informe de excavaciones, temporada junio 2004, sector pozo ceremonial, Programa arqueológico complejo El Brujo. Manuscript on file at the Instituto Nacional de Cultura, Lima.

Larco Hoyle, Rafael
   1944   *Cultura salinar: Síntesis monográfica*. Buenos Aires: Sociedad Geográfica Americana.
   1945   *La cultura virú*. Buenos Aires: Sociedad Geográfica Americana.
   1946   A Cultural Sequence from the North Coast of Perú [sic]. In *Handbook of South American Indians*, Volume 2: *The Andean Civilizations*, Julian H. Steward (ed.), pp. 149–175. Smithsonian Institution, Bureau of American Ethnology Bulletin 143. Washington, D.C.: Government Printing Office.

   1948   *Cronología arqueológica del norte del Perú*. Buenos Aires: Sociedad Geográfica Americana.

Leonard, Banks L., and Glenn S. Russell
   1992   Informe preliminar: Proyecto de reconocimiento arqueológico del Chicama, resultados de la primera temporada de campo, 1989. Unpublished report submitted to the Instituto Nacional de Cultura, Lima.

Ocas Cuenca, José
   1998   Registro arqueológico de emergencia en el sitio de Chiclín. Informe técnico. Unpublished report submitted to the Instituto Nacional de Cultura – La Libertad, Trujillo.

Ubbelohde-Doering, Heinrich
   1957   *Der Gallinazo-Stil und die Chronologie der altperuanischen Frühkulturen*. Bayerische Akademie der Wissenschaften. Philosophisch-Historische Klasse, Sitzungsberichte 9. Munich: C. H. Beck.
   1967   *On the Royal Highways of the Inca: Archaeological Treasures of Ancient Peru*. New York: Frederick A. Praeger.
   1983   *Vorspanische Gräber von Pacatnamú, Nordperu*. Materialien zur Allgemeinen und Vergleichenden Archäologie 26. Munich: C. H. Beck.

CHAPTER 7

THE GALLINAZO AT HUACAS DE MOCHE: STYLE OR CULTURE?

Santiago Uceda Castillo, Henry Gayoso Rullier, and Nadia Gamarra Carranza

This chapter documents the Gallinazo presence at the Huacas de Moche Complex in the Moche Valley, focusing on two specific contexts: the urban sector (principally through analysis of ceramics from a deep stratigraphic cut in architectural complex 35) and platform I of Huaca de la Luna. Beforehand, however, a discussion of the key concepts of culture and style will serve to highlight the confusion surrounding the Gallinazo phenomenon.

Indeed, in the past the term "Gallinazo" has been used to identify a population from the Virú Valley and, by extension, to characterize the ceramics it produced. When Gallinazo-style vessels were found elsewhere along the coast, those artifacts were also used by archaeologists to infer a Gallinazo occupation of those distant regions. We argue that the use of the concept of "Gallinazo style" should be restricted to ceramic vessels decorated with negative-resist paint (the Gallinazo Negative and Carmelo Negative ceramic types[1] in the Virú Valley).

CULTURE AND STYLE

To understand the Gallinazo phenomenon, it is first important to distinguish between the concepts of "culture" and "style." Toward the end of the nineteenth century (in his famous work *Primitive Culture*), ethnologist Edward B. Tylor adopted the globalizing concept of *culture*, defining it as "that complex whole which includes knowledge, beliefs, art, morals, law, custom, and other capabilities and habits acquired by man as a member of society" (Tylor 1871:1). Later, Gustaf Kossinna defined the concept of *material culture*, establishing the foundations of what would become the *cultural-historical approach* in archaeology (Trigger 1989:163–167).

Kossinna's ideas emerged in a context of nationalism awakening in Germany, at a time when archaeologists were solicited to study the nation's roots and foster an understanding of how ancient Germans had lived. Leaving aside the evolutionist ideas held until then, Kossinna's work was based on the notion that material culture is a reflection of ethnicity. As such, similarities and differences in material culture were believed to reflect similarities and differences in ethnicity.

Cultures were therefore conceived in terms of geographically and temporally defined complexes with their own material culture. As Bruce Trigger noted, Kossinna argued that "by mapping the distributions of types of artifacts that were characteristic of specific tribal groups, it would be possible to determine where these groups had lived at different periods in prehistory" (Trigger 1989:165). In this context, continuity in material culture was understood as ethnic continuity.

The idea of "archaeological cultures" put forward by Gordon Childe has its roots in the work of Kossinna. Childe set his focus on certain types of remains (such as pots, implements, ornaments, burial rites, housing forms, and so forth) that were consistently found together (Childe 1929). He defined these as *cultural groups*, or simply as *cultures*, assuming that each compound was the material expression of a distinct people (Childe 1936, 1978).

According to Childe, a culture was therefore first and foremost defined as the co-occurrence of a determined number of characteristics in the archaeological record. This notion of culture (defined as the *normative approach*) was based on two axioms: objects are the expression of cultural norms or behaviors, and those norms ultimately define what culture is (Johnson 2000:34). Discussing Childe's approach, Trigger noted:

> He stressed that each culture had to be delineated individually in terms of constituent artifacts and that cultures could not be defined simply by subdividing the ages or epochs of the evolutionary archaeologists either spatially or temporally. Instead the duration and geographical limits of each culture had to be established empirically and individual cultures aligned chronologically by means of stratigraphy, seriations, and synchronisms. (Trigger 1989: 170)

During the 1960s, this normative conception of culture was subject to criticisms from "New Archaeologists," who defined cultures in terms of *systems*, understood as extrasensory forms of human adaptation to environment. Cultures were conceived as systems in which the various components were related to one another to form a functioning organism, analogous to other types of systems in the physical and natural worlds.

Although those critiques had an influence on the way research was conducted—and especially against the idea that one could identify prehistoric human groups through their material culture—the cultural-historical approach nonetheless remained central to how most archaeologists approached *archaeological cultures*. Indeed, the recurring discovery of sets of artifacts in a specified geographical area is still widely used today to identify groups of people who at one time in history shared those features for one reason or another. In this context, north-coast specialists have used the terms "Moche culture" and "Gallinazo culture" to characterize the co-occurrence of a number of features in the archaeological record, which were (at least implicitly) assumed to be the material expression of distinct peoples.

However, Jorge Muelle was probably right in pointing out that the term *style* should be used before the term *culture* when discussing such local complexes (Muelle 1960:15). The concept of *style* covers various realities. According to Alfred Kroeber:

> A style is a strand in a culture or civilization: a coherent, self-consistent way of expressing certain behavior or performing certain kinds of acts. It is also a selective way: there must be alternative choices, though actually they may never be elected. Where compulsion or physical or physiological necessity reign, there is no room for style. (Kroeber 1957:150)

The concept of *style* therefore refers to the form in contrast to the substance, and it implies a certain dose of consistency and coherence (Kroeber 1957). All styles implicitly "accept" a certain level of innovation, however, which is essentially a creative function.

According to Muelle, styles share a number of characteristics (Muelle 1960). Every style represents a specific type of artistic expression, typical of a particular human group. It can characterize a specific people, but also its relation to other societies. It represents taste, preferences, and rejections of certain forms, lines, colors, and compositions. It is also independent of materials and themes, as each style treats subject matter in its own way, using its own support.

A style is also an abstraction (i.e., something that transcends the unit) that goes beyond individual artists. As such, it is never found within a single object. Styles go through processes of formation, evolution, and disintegration: they are born, they develop, and eventually they disappear. Nonetheless, all styles are first and foremost part of continuums and therefore always have antecedents that also had antecedents. In other words, styles are essentially historical phenomena.

During the pre-Hispanic period in the Andean region, there were basically two groups of styles. On the one hand, there were elite styles essentially associated with sumptuous and ritual objects (e.g., Moche fine-line art). On the other hand, there were styles related to the commoners, usually associated with utilitarian or domestic artifacts (e.g., Castillo Incised and Castillo Modeled ceramics). Whereas the evidence suggests that elite styles tended to change and were influenced by sociopolitical developments, utilitarian styles could remain practically unchanged for long periods—at least during the Early Horizon, Early Intermediate period, and Middle Horizon. One mistake was obviously to lump both groups of styles under the label "Gallinazo" and to use Castillo-style ceramics as evidence of a Gallinazo culture.

Gallinazo-style Ceramics along the North Coast

Before discussing the presence of ceramics of Gallinazo style at Huacas de Moche, a few words on the Gallinazo phenomenon along the north coast will help highlight the complex cultural history of this region. As will become clear, archaeologists have traditionally identified as "Gallinazo" two distinct categories of artifacts: elite wares decorated with negative-resist paint (the Gallinazo Negative and Carmelo Negative ceramic types in the Virú Valley) and utilitarian containers decorated with incised and modeled designs (Castillo Incised and Castillo Modeled types). The compounding of these two categories of containers

has obviously had important consequences on our understanding of the region's cultural history.

Rafael Larco Hoyle was the first scholar to formally identify (while conducting excavations in the Moche Valley) Gallinazo Negative ceramics, a ceramic style he named "Cultura negativa" based on the decorated ceramics he uncovered. He also observed that in the Chicama Valley, Gallinazo (which he called "Cultura negativa" and "Virú de Chicama") and Salinar material culture were essentially coeval, and that they were found on top of levels associated with Cupisnique artifacts (Larco Hoyle 1945). Larco Hoyle also argued that in this region, Gallinazo material culture was eventually supplanted by Moche artifacts (see Chapters 5, 6).

A few years later, Wendell Bennett undertook extensive work at the Gallinazo Group in the Virú Valley, where he uncovered large quantities of Gallinazo Negative artifacts together with even larger quantities of utilitarian wares decorated with incisions and appliquéd modeled designs. For the sake of clarity, those ceramics that were classified as Castillo Incised and Castillo Modeled in Virú and that are found in several valleys along the north coast are defined here as Castillo Decorated.

These vessels are rarely polished and are decorated with modeled clay applications or with incisions and excisions. Most vessels present a mix of incised and modeled decorations, however. Bennett classified Gallinazo ceramics and architecture into a tripartite chronology: Gallinazo I, Gallinazo II, and Gallinazo III (Bennett 1939, 1950). He was also responsible for the term "Gallinazo," which he first used to describe the site of the Gallinazo Group and then to identify the archaeological culture that occupied the site, and finally to define the period during which this culture occupied the valley.

Bennett noted that ceramics from funerary contexts were different from utilitarian wares associated with all three Gallinazo subperiods (Bennett 1950:89). As part of the Virú Valley Project, James Ford produced a seriation of ceramics from archaeological contexts, based on variations in the paste and surface treatment of ceramic sherds in time and through space (Ford 1949). Gallinazo-style ceramics (Gallinazo Negative, Carmelo Negative, Castillo Incised, Castillo Modeled, and so on) were classified by Ford within Early, Middle, and Late Gallinazo subphases. William Strong and Clifford Evans tested Ford's seriation in a series of excavations in stratified deposits (Strong and Evans 1952).

Based on the extensive work conducted by members of the Virú Valley Project, archaeologists working in other regions were able to compare local ceramics against the Virú sequence. In doing so, it became clear that the Castillo Decorated type (so popular in Virú) was a pan–northcoast style during the Early Intermediate period. It became equally clear that Gallinazo Negative ceramics (closely associated with Castillo Decorated vessels in Virú) did not have such a wide distribution.

For example, Peter Kaulicke reports a type of ceramic from the Vicús area known as Vicús-Tamarindo C, produced between the third and sixth centuries A.D. Some examples of this type are reminiscent of vessels of Castillo Modeled and Castillo Incised types (Kaulicke 1994:353, Figs. A, B, C, G), whereas others feature designs in negative-resist paint (Kaulicke 1994:347). Some ceramics from the earlier Vicús-Tamarindo B period also feature negative-resist designs.

Farther south, work conducted at Pampa Grande by Kent Day and Izumi Shimada helped to document a "Gallinazo" presence in the Lambayeque Valley. Shimada found that this large settlement was divided into two sectors by a large gully (Shimada 1994, 2001). The northern sector would have hosted a Moche population that occupied residential and administrative architecture. To the south, however, the settlement features agglutinated dwellings, tools associated with agricultural activities, and large quantities of ceramics of Gallinazo style (and only a few Moche artifacts), which led Shimada to argue that the area hosted a "Gallinazo population."

According to Izumi Shimada and Adriana Maguiña, during the Late Moche period a local Gallinazo population was relegated to subordinated positions, living under the control of the Moche, who had established a new sociopolitical order (Shimada and Maguiña 1994:53). However, when Shimada and Maguiña talk about a Gallinazo occupation at Pampa Grande, they essentially refer to individuals who produced and used Castillo Decorated ceramics, utilitarian wares

similar to Castillo Incised and Castillo Modeled ceramics from Virú.

Farther south, in La Leche Valley, Shimada and Maguiña also reported the discovery of fragments of the Castillo Decorated type in settlements such as Cerro Sajino, Cerro Huaringa, Cerro La Calera, Paredones-Huaca Letrada, and Cerro Vichayal (Shimada and Maguiña 1994: Figs. 1.4a, 1.8, 1.9). Again, no Gallinazo Negative vessels were found in this region, with the exception of the site of Huaca La Merced (Batán Grande), where negative-painted ceramics and utilitarian wares of "pure Gallinazo style" were found in the same context mixed with press-mold face-neck jars of Moche III style. These Moche vessels were decorated with typically Moche white-on-red or red-on-cream paint (Shimada and Maguiña 1994: 50).

While working in the Jequetepeque Valley, Wolfgang and Giesela Hecker suggested the existence of a Jequetepeque I style of utilitarian ceramics stylistically close to coeval styles that developed elsewhere, such as the Virú (Gallinazo) and Vicús styles (Hecker and Hecker 1980:294). Work conducted by Luis Jaime Castillo at San José de Moro helped to clarify the nature of the Gallinazo presence in this area. A number of burials with offerings including face-neck (or effigy) jars of Castillo Decorated style were uncovered within the Middle Moche cemetery (see Chapter 4).

Some of these jars feature tear-shaped excisions and other facial traits typical of Gallinazo-style ceramics from other regions (Castillo 2003: Figs. 18.12, 18.14). One of the most common characteristic traits is the presence on the vessel surface of modeled arms, one of which usually touches the character's face (Castillo 2003:Fig. 18.16).[2] These ceramics are evidently stylistically related to Castillo Modeled and Castillo Incised types from the Virú Valley. Incidentally, no Gallinazo Negative vessels have yet been found in the Jequetepeque Valley.

Excavations by Christopher Donnan at Dos Cabezas in the lower Jequetepeque Valley revealed that the site featured ceramics traditionally associated with the Gallinazo, Moche, and Lambayeque cultures. The burial of a very tall man was found inside excavation unit A53 (Donnan and Cock 1999; Donnan 2001, 2003).[3] Two radiocarbon dates were obtained from this grave. When calibrated using two standard deviations, the data suggest that the burial dates to between A.D. 390 and 600 (Donnan 2003:76).

This individual was buried with spectacular offerings, including several ceramics of Moche I style and a typical Castillo Decorated jar (Donnan 2003:Plate 2.3b). This vessel is adorned with small rounded handles at the neck and with the face of an owl stylistically similar to that of the Virú Valley's Castillo Modeled ceramics.

The work of Christopher Attarian has helped to document the Gallinazo occupation of the Chicama Valley (Attarian 2003; see also Chapter 5). Attarian's research indicates that at one point in history, rural populations who produced and used Castillo Decorated ceramics congregated in semi-urban agglomerations such as Mocollope, where they slowly started to produce fine-ware vessels of Moche style while maintaining their own utilitarian ceramic tradition. Similarly, vessels that can be classified as Castillo Decorated ceramics were uncovered at the Huaca Cao Viejo in the El Brujo Complex in association with vessels of Moche style (see Chapter 6).

Farther south, at the site of Santa Rita B in the Chao Valley, a team led by Jonathan Kent reported the co-occurrence of ceramics of Moche style and vessels that clearly feature Castillo Modeled and Castillo Incised attributes (see Chapter 10). In the Santa Valley, work carried out by Christopher Donnan, by David Wilson, and by Claude Chapdelaine and his team also helped document the Gallinazo phenomenon (Donnan 1973; Wilson 1988; see also Chapter 11).

Ceramics of Castillo Decorated style were found throughout the valley, but only a few artifacts decorated with negative-resist paint were uncovered. Finally, it is worth mentioning that Gallinazo-style artifacts housed in the Museo Larco in Lima are reported to have been found in the valleys of Chicama, Virú, Chao, and Santa. (The Museo Larco collections are accessible online.)

According to Theresa Topic, the "Gallinazo" occupation of the Moche Valley mainly focused on the middle area (Topic 1982). Heidy Fogel concurred with this, adding that it occurred mainly during the Middle Gallinazo phase (following

Ford's chronology), although she noted that a few artifacts from Cerro Oreja suggest the existence of an Early Gallinazo occupation (Fogel 1993:98). More recently, in his survey of the Moche Valley, Brian Billman reported that 66 settlements featured a "Gallinazo occupation," emphasizing the importance of two sites: Cerro Oreja and Pampa de la Cruz (Billman 1996).

According to Billman, during the Gallinazo phase the population density of the Moche Valley increased and Cerro Oreja became the principal settlement in the valley (Billman 1999). Work carried out at this site by the Instituto Nacional de Cultura led to the discovery of more than 900 burials, the majority of which were associated with Gallinazo artifacts (see Chapter 8).[4] Castillo Decorated and Gallinazo Negative ceramic vessels were uncovered at Cerro Oreja.

Based on their work in the upper Moche Valley, George Gumerman and Jesús Briceño argued that the Late Gallinazo and Moche I phases correspond to a single temporal period (Gumerman and Briceño 2003:223). Indeed, at the site of Santa Rosa de Quirihuac they uncovered face-neck jars of "Gallinazo style" together with a fragment of a stirrup-spout bottle of Moche I style. Again, those Gallinazo-style ceramics can be classified as Castillo Decorated ceramics because they are identical to Castillo Incised and Castillo Modeled vessels from the Virú Valley.

GALLINAZO-STYLE CERAMICS AT HUACAS DE MOCHE

The Urban Sector

Work carried out in the wide plain located between Huaca del Sol and Huaca de la Luna led to the discovery of a large urban sector (Figures 7.1, 7.2), where multifunctional compounds related to inhabitation, production activities, and storage facilities were documented (Chapdelaine 2001; Uceda 2005). In the early 1970s, Theresa Topic carried out excavations at this site as part of the Chan Chan–Moche Valley Project (Topic 1977, 1982). Based on evidence from two deep exploratory trenches excavated at the foot of Huaca del Sol, strata cuts 1 and 4 (Figure 7.3), Topic was able to document a continuous occupation from

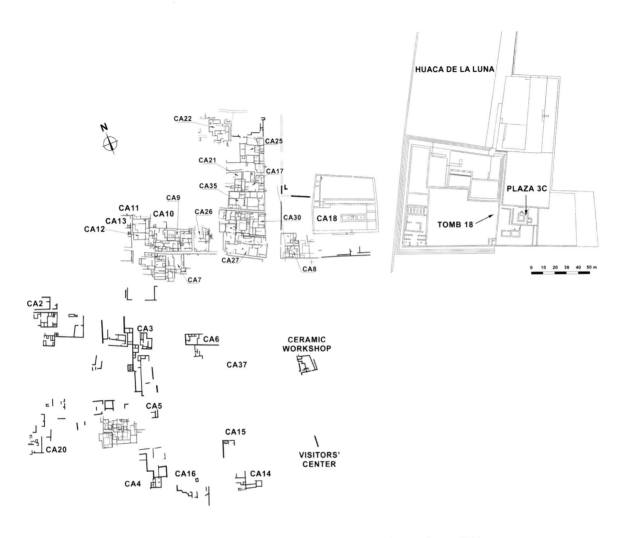

FIGURE 7.1. Plan drawing of the architectural complexes (CA)
excavated in the urban sector at Huacas de Moche.

the Moche I phase to the Moche IV phase (Topic 1977:136).

In the deepest levels, within stratigraphic unit G, the ceramic sample showed the co-occurrence of Moche I ware and vessels decorated with techniques she described as having "Gallinazo antecedents" (Topic 1977:306). Indeed, within stratigraphic units G and F (aside from Moche I and Moche II ceramics), the so-called Drag-Jab (Topic 1977:Figs. 4.1, 4.2)—typical of the Castillo Modeled ceramic type in Virú—represented, respectively, 2.4% and 2.2% of all decorated sherds.

However, ceramics with appliquéd decorations (including vessels with the addition of clay fillets and/or lumps) were found throughout the sequence by Topic (1977:Table 4.38). Punctated clay knobs were apparently more popular during the late occupational phases, whereas punctated fillets were especially common in level G, where they represent 17.8% of all decorated ceramics. Appliquéd braids were more common in contexts associated with Moche III and Moche IV ceramics (levels D and E), but they were also present in earlier levels. Applications of punctated-fillet animals (stylized birds or animal heads), stylistically reminiscent of Castillo Modeled ceramics from the Virú Valley, were found by Topic in equal proportions throughout the sequence (Topic 1977: 309).

According to Topic, when Huacas de Moche was founded, "the residents of the Moche Valley were undergoing a change in ceramics from the Gallinazo tradition to the Moche tradition." She added that "the distinction between these two

FIGURE 7.2. Partial view of architectural complexes 8, 9, 18, 27, 30, 35 and plaza 3 at Huacas de Moche.

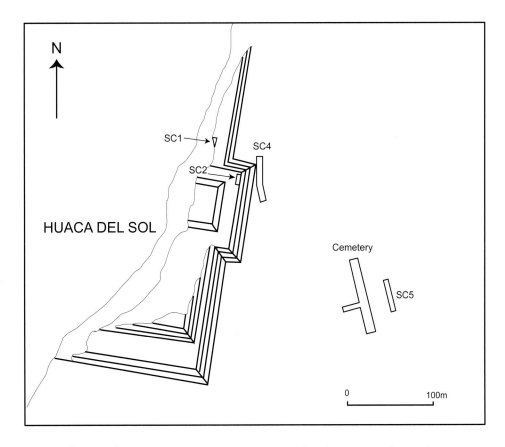

FIGURE 7.3. Plan drawing of the Huaca del Sol at Huacas de Moche, showing the location of strata cuts 1 and 4.

styles of ceramics appears to be less sharp than was once thought." Indeed, she pointed out that "utilitarian wares show considerable continuity from one phase to another, and even the fine wares show some blurring and overlapping of the two styles. . ." (Topic 1977:333).

Large-scale investigations in the urban sector were undertaken in 1994, providing us with a much better understanding of this area of the site. Inside most architectural complexes where archaeological work took place, work focused on the last occupational phase, which featured Moche IV ceramics (Chapdelaine 2001). Later, exploratory trenches helped us document the occupational sequence at the site (e.g., in a deep trench inside architectural complex 35, where several occupation floors were identified).

Architectural complex 35 covers an area of 495 m² (15 m north–south × 33 m east–west) and

is bordered by architectural complexes 17 and 21 to the north, by architectural complex 30 to the south, and by avenue 1 to the east (Figures 7.1, 7.4). Ricardo Tello and other members of the Proyecto Arqueológico Huaca de la Luna excavated a deep trench inside this complex to establish a complete stratigraphic column for the site (Tello et al. 2002, 2004, 2006).

This exploratory trench of 9.8 × 4.6 m × 8 m deep (trench 9) was excavated through the floor of room 35-5 (Figures 7.5, 7.6). Careful analysis revealed the existence of 13 superposed floors. Occupational levels associated with floors 13 through 7 date to the Moche II phase in Larco Hoyle's morpho-stylistic sequence (Larco Hoyle 2001 [1938–1940]), whereas levels associated with floors 6 through 3 date to the Moche III phase (Tello et al. 2003:93–99). The ultimate levels were associated with Moche IV ceramics.

Figure 7.4. General view of architectural complex 35 at Huacas de Moche.

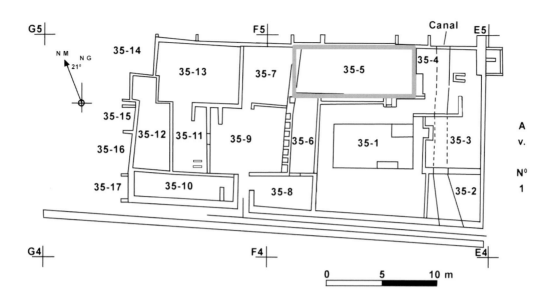

FIGURE 7.5. Plan drawing of architectural complex 35 at Huacas de Moche.

FIGURE 7.6. Stratigraphic cut from trench 9 (looking east),
architectural complex 35 at Huacas de Moche.

Henry Gayoso and Nadia Gamarra studied utilitarian ceramics from this exploratory trench to create a classificatory typology (Gayoso and Gamarra 2005). Results from their analyses showed that domestic ceramics remained practically unchanged throughout the occupational sequence at Huacas de Moche, confirming what Topic had previously argued (Topic 1977). Their analyses therefore demonstrated that Moche utilitarian ceramics are ill suited to the relative dating of Moche settlements, at least in this part of the valley.

When considering decorated fragments from their sample, Gayoso and Gamara found that the most popular decorative elements (53.3% of all decorated fragments) are in fact typical of Virú's Castillo Incised and Castillo Modeled ceramics

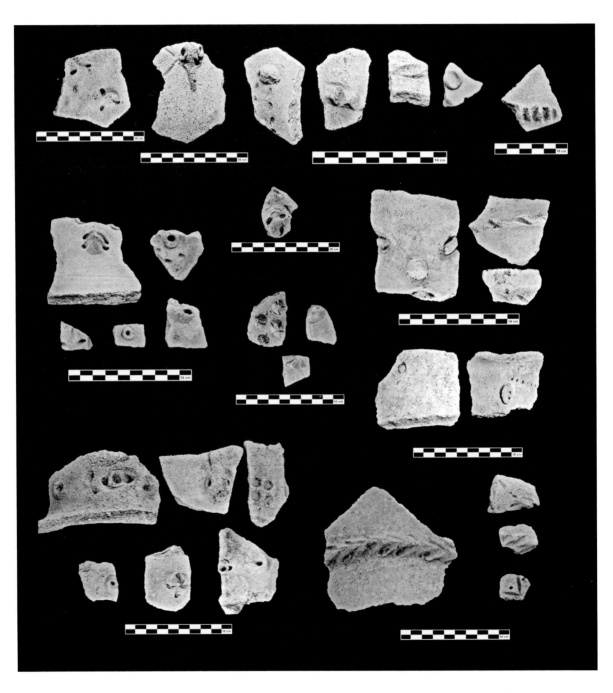

FIGURE 7.7. Decorated utilitarian ceramic fragments from trench 9, architectural complex 35 at Huacas de Moche.

(Figure 7.7) and could therefore correspond to the broadly defined Castillo Decorated style. It is important to note that utilitarian ceramics with this type of decoration were found in similar proportions within every occupation level, which leads Gayoso and Gamarra to argue that there was continuity in the use of this ceramic style.

The evidence previously presented is corroborated by results from excavations carried out in the 36 other archaeological complexes from the urban sector. Indeed, although the presence of ceramics of Gallinazo style was never formally reported by investigators since work began in 1993, it is clear from the various reports and publications available today that utilitarian ceramics with incisions and appliquéd modeled designs (ceramics of Castillo Decorated style) were in use throughout the occupational sequence (being found in association with Moche II, Moche III, and Moche IV ceramics).

Platform I of Huaca de la Luna

In the past, based on the analysis of cane-marked adobes (Hastings and Moseley 1975) and ceramics (Topic 1977), scholars have argued that there existed a Gallinazo component inside Huaca de la Luna. However, although cane-marked adobes are often associated with Gallinazo-style ceramics structures, we know today that they were also used in Moche architecture. Furthermore, it is worth mentioning that the ceramics Topic analyzed were essentially Castillo Decorated vessels, which we know occurred throughout the sequence in the urban sector.

More recently, Castillo Decorated ceramics were found on Huaca de la Luna. The second largest structure at Huacas de Moche, Huaca de la Luna is known to have functioned as a major civic-ceremonial center (Figure 7.1). Gallinazo-style ceramics were found in burial contexts in one grave only, as well as within plaza 3C, where evidence of human sacrifices was found. In 1997, an important burial (tomb 18) was uncovered within excavation unit 12a (Tufinio 2004).

This grave, found at the bottom of a looter's pit and therefore badly disturbed, was built inside the adobe fill that sealed structure D of Huaca de la Luna (Figures 7.1, 7.8). Fortunately, some of the offerings were found in areas that remained untouched by the looters. An elaborate textile emblem was found, as well as ceramic vessels of Moche and Gallinazo style. Indeed, two vessels were undeniably of Moche style. However, the third (a grave marker) was typical of Castillo Modeled ceramics from the Virú Valley (Figure 7.9).

In parallel with the previously cited work (during the 2000 and 2001 field seasons), Moisés Tufinio and John Verano conducted excavations inside plaza 3C (Figure 7.1; Tufinio 2002), a space used together with structure C of Huaca de la Luna. Their work revealed that this plaza had served over a long period of time for the performance of rituals related to the sacrifice of prisoners (Tufinio 2002:57). José Armas analyzed a collection of diagnostic sherds from this plaza, nearly all of which were classified as Moche III. These included sherds of utilitarian and ritual vessels (such as bottles and *floreros*) and sculptured vessels representing naked prisoners, adorned with black fugitive paint (Armas 2002: Figs. 232, 233, 246).

However, 19 fragments from the collection were clearly of Castillo Decorated style. These fragments were of small jars and face-neck jars with everted or convex neck and rounded lip (Armas 2002:177, Table 16). None of these vessels was painted. Rather, they were decorated with incisions, excisions, and modeled applications (Figure 7.10). Armas explains the presence of ceramics of Gallinazo style within a Moche III context by arguing that these fragments came from earlier deposits or that "certain Gallinazo forms could have coexisted with Moche III-style ceramics" (Armas 2002:194–195). The fact that such vessels were found in association with the last occupation levels atop Huaca de la Luna shows how persistent this ceramic style was, although the mechanisms that allowed this to happen still need to be understood.

Current evidence shows that Castillo Decorated ceramics are found in different regions along the Peruvian north coast in contexts dating to all subphases of the Early Intermediate period. This style may have originated from Virú, but it is present in other north-coast valleys where local variants developed. These ceramics are essentially utilitarian vessels, although we saw that they were sometimes uncovered in ritual contexts.

FIGURE 7.8. Excavation of tomb 18 on platform I of Huaca de la Luna at Huacas de Moche.

FIGURE 7.9. Decorated utilitarian ceramic vessel from tomb 18
at Huaca de la Luna, Huacas de Moche.

In her dissertation, Fogel noted that there is virtually no difference between ceramic assemblages from the Moche and Virú Valleys (Fogel 1993:106–107). She mentioned that when differences do occur, they are usually related to the nature of the clay used (Fogel 1993:106). We believe this would seem to support the idea that there were various centers of production, rather than a mass production of Castillo Incised and Modeled ceramics in Virú distributed to populations along the coast through long-distance trade.

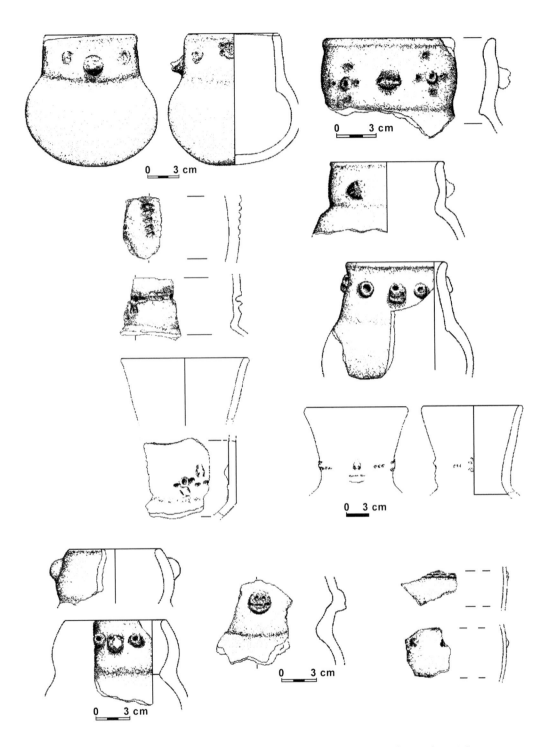

FIGURE 7.10. Decorated utilitarian ceramic fragments from plaza 3C
at Huaca de la Luna, Huacas de Moche.

DISCUSSION

We must now examine the Gallinazo phenomenon with regard to the notions of ethnic identity
and sociopolitical change as expressed through
utilitarian and elite ceramic styles. If Kossinna
was right in arguing that archaeological remains
(material culture) are a reflection of ethnicity, the

wide distribution and continuity observed in north-coast utilitarian ceramic styles suggests that this area was home to a homogeneous ethnic group during the pre-Hispanic period.

As seen previously, cultural continuity clearly extends to the whole of the Early Intermediate period, at least at Huacas de Moche. During this long period, local inhabitants inevitably witnessed periodic changes in the political sphere. These changes certainly influenced their social life and economy, but apparently did not affect the production of utilitarian ceramics. In this context, the Castillo Decorated ceramic type may have formed part of a utilitarian ware tradition (featuring domestic forms such as cooking jars, storage jars, plates, bowls, and miniature jars) shared by various north-coast societies.

The question remains as to why there existed so much continuity. It could be argued that utilitarian vessels remained nearly unchanged through time simply because they were not considered suitable vehicles for ideology and their production was not under political control. This was clearly not the case for artifacts specifically produced for the elites in various north-coast valleys.

Along the north coast, stylistic changes observed by archaeologists in architecture and in the production of fine mortuary ceramics and elite paraphernalia were essentially the reflection of major social and political changes closely associated with the ruling elite. In parallel with Castillo Decorated utilitarian ceramics, a number of elite styles—such as the Gallinazo Negative and Carmelo Negative styles, the Southern Moche style (Moche and Chicama Valleys), the Northern Moche style (Lambayeque and Jequetepeque Valleys), and the Vicús style—were in use along the north coast during the Early Intermediate period. As mentioned previously, each of these styles originated, developed, and eventually disappeared. The negative-resist style associated with the ruling elite in the Virú Valley illustrates how elite styles are essentially historical phenomena.

According to Bennett (1950), in Virú the ceramic types that best emblematized the governing elites were the Gallinazo Negative and Carmelo Negative ceramics. The Gallinazo Neg-

ative and Carmelo Negative ceramic styles are clearly associated with Virú's governing elite, although a few pieces were also found in other coastal valleys, such as Chicama, Moche, Chao, and Santa. Gallinazo Negative ceramics—mainly sculptured vessels, stirrup-spout vessels, double-bodied ceramics, lentil-shaped cancheros, jars with appliqué, and face-neck jars—generally feature a smooth and moderately to highly polished surface. The quintessential feature of the negative-resist style is the use of the negative painting technique (monochrome negative-resist paint) for decorating the surface of ceramic vessels.[5]

Gallinazo Negative and Carmelo Negative ceramics were apparently part of a unique stylistic current in the northern highlands and along the north and central coasts during the Early Intermediate period. According to Strong and Evans, these Gallinazo Negative and Carmelo Negative ceramic types are stylistically related to vessels produced in the northern highlands and Recuay region and to Pachacamac and Chancay ceramics from the central coast (Bennett 1950:111; Strong and Evans 1952:242–244).

As such, these negative-resist types would be part of what Kroeber defined as the "Negative Horizon" (Kroeber 1944). Recent research in Virú demonstrated that negative-resist ceramic types were seldom used in non-ritual contexts (Catalán et al. 1991). Following this idea, it seems acceptable to argue that Gallinazo Negative and Carmelo Negative were ceramic types strongly related with ritual and elite burial contexts.

In Chicama and Moche, this art style (Gallinazo Negative and Carmelo Negative) was soon supplanted by the Moche style, whereas in other areas (such as Virú) it probably maintained its popularity. At one moment in history, however, the Moche style was adopted by all north-coast societies for ideological or political reasons, or was imposed through military conquests. This would seem to challenge Shimada and Maguiña's idea that the "Gallinazo" represented a distinct and persistent ethnic group along the Peruvian north coast that was eventually integrated into a new, multiethnic society dominated by the Moche (Shimada and Maguiña 1994).

CONCLUSIONS

If most archaeologists agree that Moche fine wares—especially stirrup-spout bottles, often decorated with fine-line paintings—are the most effective features available for identifying Moche ruling elites, scholars should logically use Gallinazo Negative and Carmelo Negative ceramics for identifying "Gallinazo" elites and hence the Gallinazo culture (and not use Castillo Incised and Modeled containers which, as we have seen, were part of a utilitarian ceramic tradition spread in time and across space). We believe that a significant error was made in using Castillo Decorated ceramics to identify Gallinazo settlements in Virú or elsewhere along the coast, as has been done in the past.

When discussing the Gallinazo occupation of the Virú Valley, Strong and Evans specifically referred to Gallinazo ceramics as "negative-painted pottery" (Strong and Evans 1952:238). However, these authors mention Heinrich Ubbelohde-Doering's discovery at Pacatnamú of ceramic vessels with "paste, form, and punctate or incised decoration" reminiscent of Gallinazo vessels with "no visible evidences of negatively painted decorations" (Strong and Evans 1952:241). They then tentatively suggest that "a culture related to that of Gallinazo in Virú, but lacking negative painting techniques, formerly existed in the Jequetepeque region and . . . was later incorporated or evolved into a northern aspect of the Mochica culture" (Strong and Evans 1952:241).

A similar error has consisted in assuming, based on the coexistence of Moche elite ceramics and Gallinazo utilitarian wares, that Gallinazo populations were under the control of the Moche ruling elites. Indeed, several investigators have reported the presence of ceramics of Gallinazo style in contexts associated with Early Moche vessels (Larco Hoyle 1945; Topic 1977; Shimada 1994; Shimada and Maguiña 1994; Donnan and Cock 1999; Donnan 2003; Franco, Gálvez, and Vásquez 2003; Gumerman and Briceño 2003) and Middle and Late Moche ceramics (Chapdelaine and Pimentel 2001, 2002; Castillo 2003).

As we saw, this alleged cohabitation is usually inferred based on the presence of Moche fine ware and Castillo Decorated utilitarian containers. According to Gayoso and Gamarra, however, it would be wrong to claim that the presence of Castillo Decorated ceramics within Moche contexts is evidence that a local Gallinazo population was under the control of Moche rulers (Gayoso and Gamarra 2005). According to these authors, the Castillo Decorated style at Huacas de Moche is simply a utilitarian decorative style that was used from the earliest phases and that remained popular until the site was abandoned. They argue that this was due to the fact that utilitarian ceramics remained unchanged through time, adding:

> This type of material was produced without social control because it was not considered to be elements of prestige. . . . [I]t is for this reason that we can find ceramic of [Castillo Decorated] style in Moche contexts without this being evidence of a form of dominion or a form of enslavement of Gallinazo groups. It simply means that the local people continued to decorate utilitarian ceramics as was traditionally done. (Gayoso and Gamarra 2005:403)

It is now essential to reconsider this information. A dominating ethnic group occupied the Moche Valley from as early as the Formative to the Late Intermediate period. This society was the foundation on which the so-called Gallinazo, Moche, and Chimú political entities developed. Throughout a succession of periods of political domination and episodes of foreign rule, this group maintained its tradition of burying the dead with a certain type of ceramic vessel that represented one of the quintessential features of north-coast prehistory.

In light of the results obtained by the Virú Valley Project, it can be argued that Gallinazo Negative and Carmelo Negative are two ceramic types that represent north-coast variants of a more general negative-resist ceramic tradition. Indeed, the negative-resist style was adopted by different societies that developed along the north and central coasts and in the northern sierra. Among those were people who started to manufacture Gallinazo Negative and Carmelo Negative ceramics prior to the emergence of the Moche phenomenon. At one point, some Gallinazo rulers started to adopt a style that today we associate with the Moche, whereas others maintained the Gallinazo style until the end of the Moche II or Moche III period, when it started to disappear.

Based on the evidence presented here, we can therefore argue that Gallinazo is both a culture and a style. Indeed, the only way to study the Gallinazo polities that developed along the north coast of Peru is through a careful study of elite ceramic styles. Only in this way will it be possible to discuss the nature of the political entities that produced and consumed this form of material culture.

ACKNOWLEDGMENTS

The authors would like to thank Jean-François Millaire for the translation of this article from Spanish and for his comments and suggestions throughout the editorial process.

NOTES

[1] In the Virú Valley, these two types were introduced during the Early Gallinazo phase. Gallinazo Negative was the most popular of the two types, although Carmelo Negative became more abundant during the Late Gallinazo phase. Both ceramic types were produced until the Huancaco phase. Vessels generally present a smooth surface (sometimes polished), and the most popular shapes represented are sculptural vessels, stirrup-spout bottles, double-chambered vessels, *cancheros* (dippers), jars decorated with appliqué, and face-neck jars (Bennett 1939:86–89).

[2] This stylistic feature also appears later at Pacatnamú, San José de Moro, and Pampa Grande. Similar ceramic vessels were uncovered by Christopher Donnan and his team at Masanca in the middle Jequetepeque Valley (Donnan, Navarro, and Cordy-Collins 1998; Donnan 2006).

[3] The burial is referred to as tomb A53-1 by Donnan and Cock (1999) and as tomb 2 elsewhere.

[4] Unfortunately, little information is available on the Instituto Nacional de Cultura excavations in published format.

[5] With this technique, the entire surface of the vessel was coated with wax, excluding the areas constituting the design. The vessel was subsequently covered with black pigment and fired. During the firing process, the protective coating burned so that the design appeared in negative. According to Gordon Willey, this decorative method may well be related to metallurgical techniques in that both made use of variants of the lost-wax technique (Willey 1948:12).

REFERENCES

Armas, José
2002 Análisis del material ceramográfico de la Plaza 3C. In Proyecto Arqueológico Huaca de la Luna: Informe técnico 2001, Santiago Uceda and Ricardo Morales (eds.), pp. 177–198. Manuscript on file, Universidad Nacional de Trujillo, Trujillo.

Attarian, Christopher J.
2003 Pre-Hispanic Urbanism and Community Expression in the Chicama Valley, Peru. Unpublished Ph.D. dissertation, University of California, Los Angeles.

Bennett, Wendell C.
1939 *Archaeology of the North Coast of Peru: An Account of Exploration and Excavation in Viru and Lambayeque Valleys*. Anthropological Papers of the American Museum of Natural History Vol. 37, Pt. 1. New York: The American Museum of Natural History.
1950 *The Gallinazo Group: Viru Valley, Peru*. Yale University Publications in Anthropology 43. New Haven: Yale University Press.

Billman, Brian R.
1996 The Evolution of Prehistoric Political Organizations in the Moche Valley, Peru. Unpublished Ph.D. dissertation, University of California, Santa Barbara.
1999 Reconstructing Prehistoric Political Economies and Cycles of Political Power in the Moche Valley, Peru. In *Settlement Pattern Studies in the Americas: Fifty Years Since Virú*, Brian R. Billman and Gary M. Feinman (eds.), pp. 131–159. Washington, D.C.: Smithsonian Institution Press.

Castillo, Luis Jaime
2003 Los últimos Mochicas en Jequetepeque. In *Moche: Hacia el final del milenio*, Santiago Uceda and Elías Mujica (eds.), vol. 2, pp. 65–123. Lima: Universidad Nacional de Trujillo and Fondo Editorial, Pontificia Universidad Católica del Perú.

Catalán, Mary, Nelly Cortéz, Raúl Chunga, Carmen Quispe, and Amelia Ulloa
1991 Análisis de la cerámica Gallinazo en el Castillo de Tomaval: Sector sud oeste. Valle de Virú. Unpublished bachelor's thesis, Universidad Nacional de Trujillo, Trujillo.

Chapdelaine, Claude
2001 The Growing Power of a Moche Urban Class. In *Moche Art and Archaeology in Ancient Peru*, Joanne Pillsbury (ed.), pp. 69–87. Washington, D.C.: National Gallery of Art and Yale University Press.

Chapdelaine, Claude, and Víctor Pimentel
    2001 Informe del Proyecto Arqueológico PSUM
          (Proyecto Santa de la Universidad de Mon-
          tréal): La presencia moche en el valle del
          Santa, costa norte del Perú – 2000. Unpub-
          lished report submitted to the Instituto
          Nacional de Cultura, Lima. (See electronic
          publication at www.mapageweb.umontreal.ca/
          chapdelc)
    2002 Informe del Proyecto Arqueológico PSUM
          (Proyecto Santa de la Universidad de Montre-
          al): La presencia moche en el valle del Santa,
          costa norte del Perú – 2001. Unpublished
          report submitted to the Instituto Nacional de
          Cultura, Lima. (See electronic publication at
          www.mapageweb.umontreal.ca/chapdelc)
Childe, V. Gordon
    1929 *The Danube in Prehistory*. Oxford: Oxford Uni-
          versity Press.
    1936 *Man Makes Himself*. London: Watts.
    1978 *Los orígenes de la civilización*. Madrid: Fondo de
          Cultura Económica.
Donnan, Christopher B.
    1973 *Moche Occupation of the Santa Valley, Peru*.
          Berkeley: University of California Press.
    2001 Moche Burials Uncovered. *National Geographic*
          199(3):58–73.
    2003 Tumbas con entierros en miniatura: Un nuevo
          tipo funerario moche. In *Moche: Hacia el final
          del milenio*, Santiago Uceda and Elías Mujica
          (eds.), vol. 1, pp. 43–78. Lima: Universidad
          Nacional de Trujillo and Fondo Editorial,
          Pontificia Universidad Católica del Perú.
    2006 A Moche Cemetery at Masanca, Jequetepeque
          Valley, Peru. *Ñawpa Pacha* 28:151–193.
Donnan, Christopher B., and Guillermo A. Cock
    1999 Excavaciones en Dos Cabezas, valle de
          Jequetepeque 1998: Quinta temporada de tra-
          bajo de campo, quinto informe parcial.
          Unpublished report submitted to the Institu-
          to Nacional de Cultura, Lima.
Donnan, Christopher B., H. Navarro, and Alana
    Cordy-Collins
    1998 Proyecto Masanca. Unpublished report submit-
          ted to the Instituto Nacional de Cultura, Lima.
Fogel, Heidy
    1993 Settlements in Time: A Study of Social and
          Political Development during the Gallinazo
          Occupation of the North Coast of Perú [sic].
          Unpublished Ph.D. dissertation, Yale Univer-
          sity, New Haven.
Ford, James A.
    1949 Cultural Dating of Prehistoric Sites in Virú
          Valley, Peru. In *Surface Survey of the Virú Val-
          ley, Peru*, James A. Ford and Gordon R. Willey

          (eds.), pp. 29–87. Anthropological Papers of
          the American Museum of Natural History
          Vol. 43, Pt. 1. New York: The American
          Museum of Natural History.
Franco, Régulo, César Gálvez, and Segundo Vásquez
    2003 Modelos, función y cronología de la Huaca
          Cao Viejo, Complejo El Brujo. In *Moche:
          Hacia el final del milenio*, Santiago Uceda and
          Elías Mujica (eds.), vol. 2, pp. 125–177. Lima:
          Universidad Nacional de Trujillo and Fondo
          Editorial, Pontificia Universidad Católica del
          Perú.
Gayoso, Henry, and Nadia Gamarra
    2005 La cerámica doméstica de Huacas de Moche:
          Un intento de tipología y seriación. In Proyec-
          to Arqueológico Huaca de la Luna: Informe
          técnico 2004, Santiago Uceda and Ricardo
          Morales (eds.), pp. 391–404. Manuscript on
          file, Universidad Nacional de Trujillo, Trujillo.
Gumerman, George, and Jesús Briceño
    2003 Santa Rosa–Quirihuac y Ciudad de Dios:
          Asentamientos rurales en la parte media del
          valle de Moche. In *Moche: Hacia el final del
          milenio*, Santiago Uceda and Elías Mujica
          (eds.), vol. 1, pp. 217–243. Lima: Universidad
          Nacional de Trujillo and Fondo Editorial,
          Pontificia Universidad Católica del Perú.
Hastings, C. Mansfield, and M. Edward Moseley
    1975 The Adobes of Huaca del Sol and Huaca de la
          Luna. *American Antiquity* 40(2):196–203.
Hecker, Wolfgang, and Giesela Hecker
    1980 El estilo Jequetepeque I. *Indiana* (Berlin) 6:
          293–306.
Johnson, Matthew
    2000 *Teoría arqueológica: Una introducción*. Barce-
          lona: Editorial Ariel.
Kaulicke, Peter
    1994 La presencia mochica en el Alto Piura: Pro-
          blemática y propuestas. In *Moche: Propuestas y
          perspectivas*, Santiago Uceda and Elías Mujica
          (eds.), pp. 327–358. Travaux de l'Institut
          Français d'Études Andines 79. Lima: Univer-
          sidad Nacional de La Libertad and Instituto
          Francés de Estudios Andinos.
Kroeber, Alfred
    1944 *Peruvian Archeology in 1942*. Viking Fund Pub-
          lications in Anthropology 4. New York: Viking
          Fund.
    1957 *Style and Civilizations*. Ithaca, New York: Cor-
          nell University Press.
Larco Hoyle, Rafael
    1945 *La cultura virú*. Buenos Aires: Sociedad Geo-
          gráfica Americana.
    2001 [1938–1940] *Los Mochicas*. 2 vols. Lima: Museo
          Arqueológico Rafael Larco Herrera.

Muelle, Jorge C.

1960 El concepto de estilo. In *Antiguo Perú: Espacio y tiempo*, pp. 15–28. Lima: Librería Editorial Juan Mejía Baca.

Shimada, Izumi

1994 *Pampa Grande and the Mochica Culture*. Austin: University of Texas Press.

2001 Late Moche Urban Craft Production: A First Approximation. In *Moche Art and Archaeology in Ancient Peru*, Joanne Pillsbury (ed.), pp. 177–205. Washington, D.C.: National Gallery of Art and Yale University Press.

Shimada, Izumi, and Adriana Maguiña

1994 Nueva visión sobre la cultura gallinazo y su relación con la cultura moche. In *Moche: Propuestas y perspectivas*, Santiago Uceda and Elías Mujica (eds.), pp. 31–58. Travaux de l'Institut Français d'Études Andines 79. Lima: Universidad Nacional de La Libertad and Instituto Francés de Estudios Andinos.

Strong, Willliam D., and Clifford Evans

1952 *Cultural Stratigraphy in the Virú Valley, Northern Peru: The Formative and Florescent Epochs*. New York: Columbia University Press.

Tello, Ricardo, Giovanna Agreda, Jorge Chiguala, Giovanna Pinillos, Julia Tufinio, and Olivier Velásquez

2004 Investigaciones iniciales en el Conjunto Arquitectónico 30, área urbana moche. In *Investigaciones en la Huaca de la Luna 1998–1999*, Santiago Uceda, Elías Mujica, and Ricardo Morales (eds.), pp. 261–312. Trujillo: Facultad de Ciencias Sociales, Universidad Nacional de Trujillo.

Tello, Ricardo, Arleny Encomenderos, Magali Gutiérrez, Johnny Siccha, Carmen Mercado, Marco Rodríguez, Fabián García, David González, and Melina Vera

2006 Investigaciones en el Conjunto Arquitectónico 35, centro urbano moche. In *Investigaciones en la Huaca de la Luna 2000*, Santiago Uceda, Elías Mujica, and Ricardo Morales (eds.), pp. 149–183. Trujillo: Facultad de Ciencias Sociales, Universidad Nacional de Trujillo.

Tello, Ricardo, Fanny Mamani, Christian Hidalgo, Sandy Obregón, and Nancy Corrales

2002 La penúltima ocupación del Conjunto Arquitectónico N° 35 de las Huacas del Sol y de la Luna. In Proyecto Arqueológico Huaca de la Luna: Informe técnico 2001, Santiago Uceda and Ricardo Morales (eds.), pp. 95–128. Manuscript on file, Universidad Nacional de Trujillo, Trujillo.

Tello, Ricardo, Francisco Seoane, Krisna Smith, Jorge Meneses, Alonso Barriga, and Jessenia Palomino

2003 El Conjunto Arquitectónico N° 35 de las Huacas del Sol y de la Luna. In Proyecto Arqueológico Huaca de la Luna: Informe técnico 2002, Santiago Uceda and Ricardo Morales (eds.), pp. 83–132. Manuscript on file, Universidad Nacional de Trujillo, Trujillo.

Topic, Theresa L.

1977 Excavations at Moche. Unpublished Ph.D. dissertation, Harvard University, Cambridge, Massachusetts.

1982 The Early Intermediate Period and Its Legacy. In *Chan Chan: Andean Desert City*, Michael E. Moseley and Kent C. Day (eds.), pp. 255–284. Albuquerque: University of New Mexico Press.

Trigger, Bruce G.

1989 *A History of Archaeological Thought*. Cambridge, UK: Cambridge University Press.

Tufinio, Moisés

2002 Plaza 3c. In Proyecto Arqueológico Huaca de la Luna: Informe técnico 2001, Santiago Uceda and Ricardo Morales (eds.), pp. 47–58. Manuscript on file, Universidad Nacional de Trujillo, Trujillo.

2004 Excavaciones en la unidad 12A (ampliación norte), Plataforma 1, Huaca de la Luna. In *Investigaciones en la Huaca de la Luna 1998–1999*, Santiago Uceda, Elías Mujica, and Ricardo Morales (eds.), pp. 20–39. Trujillo: Facultad de Ciencias Sociales, Universidad Nacional de Trujillo.

Tylor, Edward B.

1871 *Primitive Culture*. London: John Murray.

Uceda, Santiago

2005 Los de arriba y los de abajo. In Proyecto Arqueológico Huaca de La Luna: Informe técnico 2004, Santiago Uceda and Ricardo Morales (eds.), pp. 283–317. Manuscript on file, Universidad Nacional de Trujillo, Trujillo.

Willey, Gordon R.

1948 A Functional Analysis of "Horizon Styles" in Peruvian Archaeology. In *A Reappraisal of Peruvian Archaeology*, Wendell C. Bennett (ed.), pp. 8–15. Memoirs of the Society for American Archaeology 4. Menasha, Wisconsin: Society for American Archaeology and Institute of Andean Research.

Wilson, David J.

1988 *Prehispanic Settlement Patterns in the Lower Santa Valley, Peru: A Regional Perspective on the Origins and Development of Complex North Coast Society*. Washington D.C.: Smithsonian Institution Press.

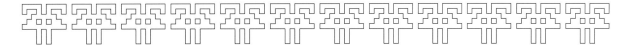

CHAPTER 8

BIOLOGICAL ORIGINS AND RELATIONS AMONG CERRO OREJA AND OTHER PREHISTORIC NORTHERN ANDEAN MORTUARY POPULATIONS USING EPIGENETIC DENTAL TRAITS

Richard C. Sutter

As a number of contributors to this volume point out, the cultural definition of Gallinazo and its relations to other Early Intermediate–period cultures of northern Peru are both unclear and in need of further study. Moreover, although a number of studies have described Gallinazo graves and mortuary practices (Bennett 1939, 1950; Donnan and Mackey 1978; Fogel 1993), we currently know very little about the biological relations among the Gallinazo and other prehistoric populations of northern Peru.

Rosa Cortez's (2000) study of adult remains from the Gallinazo cemetery at Cerro Oreja in the Moche Valley indicated that individuals were of roughly the same stature as members of other prehistoric north-coast populations. On the other hand, Celeste Gagnon's (2004) examination of dental pathologies on remains from the same site suggest that these people lived on a diet low in carbohydrates, as indicated by the low levels of caries and antemortem tooth loss. Richard Sutter and Rosa Cortez's (2005) biodistance study, which addressed the origins of Moche human sacrificial victims from plaza 3A at Huaca de la Luna, included (three temporally) distinct Gallinazo mortuary populations from Cerro Oreja.

Our analyses, based on seven genetically influenced (epigenetic) dental traits, suggested that the populations from the Gallinazo cemetery at Cerro Oreja and the Moche mortuary sample from the urban sector at Huacas de Moche were nearly indistinguishable genetically and were likely part of the same breeding populations (assuming temporal overlap between the samples) or had an ancestral-descendant relationship (if the Gallinazo samples predate the Moche sample).

A program of ancient mitochondrial DNA (mtDNA) analysis on human remains from a number of north-coast cultures is currently underway (Shinoda et al. 2002; Shimada et al. 2005), but only preliminary results of analyses conducted on Gallinazo remains have been reported (Shimada 2004). The mtDNA data suggest that Moche and Sicán populations from archaeological contexts north of the Moche Valley were far more variable than those from the Moche Valley. Indeed, Izumi Shimada and his coauthors noted that all 45 individuals sequenced from the Moche Valley—including individuals from the urban sector, elites from the Huaca de la Luna platforms, and human sacrificial remains from plaza 3A—belong to haplogroup A (Shimada et al. 2005).

Shimada (2004) also reported that all Moche and five Gallinazo individuals sampled from the Virú Valley also belong to haplogroup A, suggesting that south of the Chicama Valley, coastal populations represent a coherent breeding population that may have gone through a genetic bottleneck at some time in their recent past. These general conclusions are supported by an epigenetic dental trait study I conducted on human remains from 44 prehistoric Andean mortuary populations.

Indeed, analyses indicate that the Early Intermediate–period north-coast Andeans represent a fairly cohesive breeding population (Sutter 2008). I also argue that although the Cotton Preceramic mortuary population from Huaca Prieta is descended from the colonizing South American Paleo-Indians, the Early Intermediate–period Moche and Gallinazo mortuary samples were descendants of a second demographic expansion into South America, the impact of which occurred sometime around the beginning of the Initial period on the north coast of Peru.

This chapter provides a preliminary assessment of the phenetic relations between the Gallinazo mortuary samples from the Moche Valley site of Cerro Oreja and other prehistoric northern Andean mortuary samples for which I have collected epigenetic dental trait data. Correspondence analysis (CA) was used to characterize epigenetic dental trait variation among the Gallinazo mortuary samples, and then to estimate genetic relatedness using mean measure of divergence (MMD) analyses calculated from dental trait data.

MORTUARY POPULATIONS SELECTED FOR ANALYSIS

Eleven prehistoric Andean mortuary populations were analyzed for this study. In total, these 11 populations represent the dentitions of 654 individuals from four distinct chronological periods: the Paleo-Indian, Cotton Preceramic, Initial period, and Early Intermediate period. The Early Intermediate–period samples come from three distinct phases: Salinar, Gallinazo, and Moche.

Ten of the 11 populations are from northern Peru (Figure 8.1), whereas the Paleo-Indian mortuary sample consists of 34 individuals whose remains come from throughout the Andes and date to at least 8,000 years ago (Bórmida 1966; Engel 1977, 1987; Chauchat and Dricot 1979; Beynon and Siegel 1981; Vallejos 1982; Bird 1988; Chauchat 1988; Muñoz, Arriaza, and Aufderheide 1993; Standen and Santoro 2004). A detailed description of the Paleo-Indian sample composition can be found elsewhere (Sutter 2008).

Although the wide geographic distribution of remains used for the Paleo-Indian sample is problematic, it is unavoidable because of the small number of individuals available for study. Furthermore, the sample composition for the Andean Paleo-Indians is consistent with how early human remains have been analyzed in other epigenetic biodistance studies (Turner 1983, 1985; Powell 1993, 1995; Powell and Neves 1999).

Two mortuary samples are available for the Cotton Preceramic period (ca. 3100–1800 B.C.). The first consists of 40 individuals excavated by Junius Bird at Huaca Prieta, part of the El Brujo Complex in the lower Chicama Valley (Bird and Hyslop 1985).[1] Graves excavated by Bird include offerings of cotton textiles and pyroengraved gourds. However, at this site 12 individuals were buried with Early Initial–period ceramics, suggesting that these burials date to a later phase (ca. 1800–750 B.C.).

However, when compared using χ^2 analysis, none of the dental traits observed for the Preceramic- and Initial-period remains significantly differed, justifying their treatment as a single sample. The second Cotton Preceramic sample comes from La Galgada in the Callejón de Huaylas, near the Tablachaca River (Grieder 1988).[2] Although La Galgada is a Preceramic site, it provides some of the earliest evidence for social stratification and agriculture in the Andes. This mortuary population gathers the remains of 45 individuals interred within different rooms of the temple complex at the site.

Four of the 11 mortuary samples come from Cerro Oreja, a major settlement located on the south side of the Moche Valley at a distance of 61 km from the coast. Survey and excavation at the site indicated a limited occupation during the Early Horizon Cupisnique phase (Carcelén 1995; Billman

1997, 1999), but this is primarily an Early Intermediate–period settlement (200 B.C.–A.D. 750). Excavations led to the discovery of more than 900 burials, the vast majority of which date to the Salinar phase (ca. 200 B.C.) and subsequent Gallinazo (ca. 100 B.C.–A.D. 200) phases (Carcelén 1995).

According to a survey by Brian Billman, the occupation at Cerro Oreja was limited during the Salinar phase but greatly increased at the beginning of the first century B.C., when it became the principal settlement of the valley (Billman 1997, 1999). According to Billman, this coincided with evidence for abandonment of the middle valley in the face of large-scale incursions by highlanders from the east.

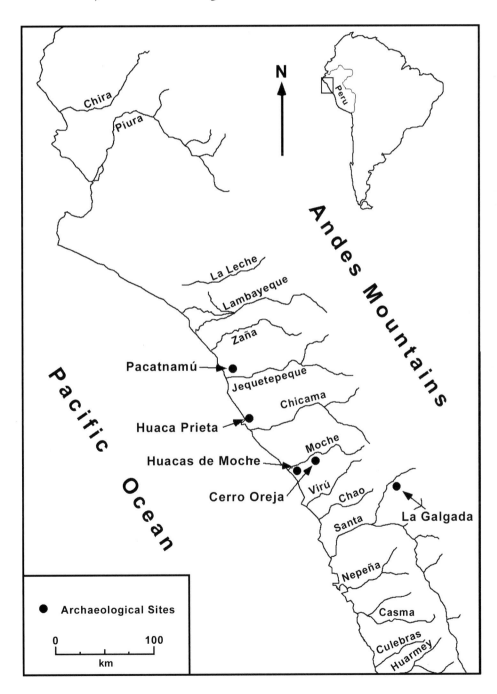

FIGURE 8.1. Map of the north coast of Peru indicating relevant archaeological sites discussed in the text.

While data on the Gallinazo occupation of Cerro Oreja have yet to be published, some information on the graves and associated ceramics is available in the form of a technical report submitted to Peru's Instituto Nacional de Cultura (Carcelén 1995). The earliest graves at the site date to the Cupisnique phase, but they were not analyzed—given their limited number (eight individuals) and because too few observations were made for each dental trait to justify their inclusion as a mortuary sample. Graves from the subsequent Salinar phase at the site consist of individual burials in extended position on their backs. Grave goods often included between three and ten Salinar-style ceramics. Other offerings have not yet been fully reported.

Some of the graves from the Gallinazo phase contained only Castillo Incised and Castillo Modeled ceramics (e.g., grave 784), whereas others (e.g., grave 125) contained Castillo and possibly Gallinazo Negative ceramics. Until these graves are analyzed and radiocarbon dating is available, only a relative temporal placement of the burials is possible. Stratigraphic and formal information on the graves indicate that they date to three successive subphases: Gallinazo Pre-Estructuras, Gallinazo Estructuras, and Gallinazo Pos-Estructuras (Carcelén 1995). Gallinazo Pre-Estructuras burials were placed in simple pits and contained relatively few ceramic offerings. During the Estructuras subphase, more elaborate tombs with formal floors and walls were constructed. On top were less elaborate burials dating to the Pos-Estructuras subphase.[3]

To detect possible trends, such as gene flow into the Moche Valley, individuals associated with Salinar and each of the three relative Gallinazo subphases were treated as temporally distinct mortuary samples. In the present study, I analyzed the remains of 65 individuals from the Salinar phase (Cerro Oreja–Salinar), 128 from the Gallinazo Pre-Estructuras phase (Cerro Oreja–G1), 93 from the Gallinazo Estructuras phase (Cerro Oreja–G2), and 76 from the Gallinazo Pos-Estructuras phase (Cerro Oreja–G3).

Incidentally, a spatially discrete Moche cemetery was also excavated at the site. However, the remains are currently unavailable for study. Although the chronological relation between the Gallinazo and Moche cemeteries is presently unclear, José Carcelén reports the discovery of what could be three intrusive Moche burials in the Gallinazo domestic area (Carcelén 1995).

Three other samples from the Early Intermediate period come from the site of Huacas de Moche in the Moche Valley. This settlement is located 6 km from the coast and features two monumental adobe structures (Huaca del Sol and Huaca de la Luna), a vast residential sector, and a number of cemeteries (Hastings and Moseley 1975; Moseley 1975; Topic 1982; Bawden 1996; Chapdelaine 2001; Larco Hoyle 2001 [1938–1940]). This was the primary Moche site in the valley during the Moche phase, and is thought by some to represent the capital of the southern Moche polity.

Little research has been done on Huaca del Sol, but it has been argued that it was the seat of the local political elite (Hastings and Moseley 1975; Topic 1982). On the other hand, work conducted on Huaca de la Luna under the direction of Santiago Uceda revealed that it consisted of a large ceremonial structure composed of three platforms and adjacent plazas (Uceda 2001). No evidence of residential activity was found in regard to this building. Moreover, the discovery of colorful friezes of Moche deities, elite tombs of Moche priests, and human sacrifices all attest to the importance of this structure as a ceremonial center.

Between the two platform mounds, extensive archaeological work documented a vast urban sector in which ceramic, metal, and textile workshops were identified (Chapdelaine 2001; Uceda 2001). Early studies of burial and architectural evidence suggested some degree of social stratification within this portion of the site (Topic 1982), but recent excavations indicate that the residential area may have been more homogeneous than previously thought, with most of the architecture and house burials representing elite craft-specialist residents (Chapdelaine 2001).

The samples from Huacas de Moche include 37 individuals from the Moche IV (ca. A.D. 500–600) occupation of the urban sector (Tello, Armas, and Chapdelaine 2003), 63 burials from platforms I and II of Huaca de la Luna (Montoya 1997; Tello 1997; Tufinio 2000), and 42 adult male sacrificial victims from plaza 3A of Huaca de la Luna

(Bourget 1997, 2001; Bourget and Millaire 2000; Verano 2001).[4] These mortuary samples are labeled HM–Urban Sector, HLL–Platforms, and HLL–Plaza 3A.

The northernmost mortuary sample is from the site of Pacatnamú, located near the coast in the Jequetepeque Valley. Pacatnamú lies on a natural plateau on the north side of the valley, overlooking the river mouth, and features numerous Late Intermediate–period adobe platform mounds, enclosed walled compounds, and spatially discrete cemeteries (Donnan and Cock 1986). For this study, I examined the dentitions of 31 individuals from Early Intermediate–period cemetery H45 CM1 at Pacatnamú (Donnan and McClelland 1997; Verano 1994).[5] Radiocarbon dates and grave offerings associated with intact burials from this cemetery suggest that it was used by commoners and that it dates to the Middle Moche period (ca. A.D. 500–650).

METHODS

Dental Traits Scoring and Selection

For this study, all individuals' dentitions were visually inspected and scored for 32 morphologic tooth cusp and root traits (Table 8.1) using standardized casts and descriptions (Turner, Nichol, and Scott 1991). Epigenetic tooth traits have been shown to closely reflect biological relations among humans and other nonhuman primates derived from molecular data (Braga 2001) and are highly heritable among living populations (Biggerstaff 1970, 1973; Portin and Alvesalo 1974; Brewer-Carias, Le Blanc, and Neel 1976; Escobar, Melnick, and Conneally 1976; Scott 1977, 1980; Berry 1978; Harris and Bailit 1980; Hassanali 1982; Corruccini and Sharma 1985; Nichol 1989; Lease and Sciulli 2005).

Epigenetic tooth traits have been used to estimate genetic relations among living populations (Sofaer, MacLean, and Bailit 1972, Sofaer, Smith, and Kaye 1986; Wijsman and Neves 1986) and prehistoric populations (Green 1982; Turner 1985, 1987, 1990; Lukacs and Hemphill 1991; Powell 1995; Haydenblit 1996; Rightmire 1999; Higa et al. 2003; Irish 2005). Although some investigators presume discrete dental traits to be quasi-continuous (Turner, Nichol, and Scott 1991), others have found that many of these traits are controlled by major genes with variable expression and show varying degrees of environmental influence (Nichol 1989).

Richard Scott and Christy Turner demonstrated that only a few dental traits' expressions are sexually dimorphic or intercorrelated on a global level (Scott and Turner 1997). Such traits have the advantage of being scoreable for highly fragmented skeletal material. Given that all traits were scored, inter-observer error is not an issue. In a previous study, I reported that my intra-observer errors were well within recommended ranges of acceptability (Sutter 1997:162–167).

Many of the dental traits are scored using an ordinal scale, whereas others are simply recorded as present or absent (see Turner, Nichol, and Scott [1991] and Scott and Turner [1997] for detailed trait descriptions and a discussion of scoring procedures). These ordinally scaled dental traits are then dichotomized for subsequent statistical and biodistance analyses. The dental trait scores for the prehistoric Andean remains reported here are dichotomized using the presence/absence ranges reported by Turner (1985, 1987, 1990). Dental trait frequencies for each mortuary sample are calculated using the individual-count method (Turner and Scott 1977).

In cases where an individual exhibits asymmetry in the expression of a given trait, the greatest level of expression is used. This scoring procedure assumes that a single genotype is responsible for any given trait's expression, and that when asymmetry exists among bilateral traits, the side exhibiting the maximum expression is closest to the true underlying genotype for the trait. The procedure also maximizes sample sizes. In cases where a given trait is observable for one antimere but not the other, the observable side is counted as the maximum expression for that trait.

Traits were eliminated if fewer than 10 observations were made for more than 20% (three or more) of the mortuary samples examined here. The rationale is that the accuracy of biodistance results based on traits with too few observations will be suspect due to potential problems of representativeness. Males and females were combined to retain acceptable sample

Table 8.1. Epigenetic dental traits, dental trait scores, and presence/absence ranges used in this study.

Maxillary Traits	Abbrev.	Teeth Examined for Trait Presence	Range	Presence[*]
Winging	WING	Maxillary central incisors	0–1	1
Shoveling	SHOV	Maxillary incisors and canines	0–7	2–7
Labial convexity	LABC	Maxillary incisors	0–4	1–4
Double shoveling	DSHOV	Maxillary incisors, canine, and first premolar	0–6	2–6
Tuberculum dentale	TD	Maxillary and mandibular canines	0–6	1–6
Interruption groove	INTG	Maxillary incisors	0–1	1–2
Distal accessory ridge	UCDAR	Maxillary and mandibular canines	0–5	2–5
Mesial ridge	UCMR	Maxillary canines	0–3	1–3
Mesial and distal accessory cusps	MDAC	Maxillary premolars	0–1	1
Distosaggital ridge	DSR	Maxillary premolars	0–1	1
Odontome	ODONT	Maxillary premolars	0–1	1
Premolar root number	PMRT	Maxillary premolars	1–3	1
Metacone	META	Maxillary molars	0–6	5–6
Hypocone	HYPO	Maxillary molars	0–6	5–6
Metaconule	CUSP5	Maxillary molars	0–5	1–5
Carabelli's trait	CARA	Maxillary molars	0–7	2–7
Parastyle	PARA	Maxillary molars	0–5	1–5
Enamel extensions	EE	Maxillary molars and premolars	0–3	2–3
Peg/reduced/congenital absence	P/R/CA	Maxillary 3rd molar, maxillary 2nd premolar lateral incisor	0–1	1
Mandibular Traits	Abbrev.	Teeth Examined for Trait Presence	Range	Presence[*]
Shoveling	SHOV	Mandibular incisors	0–3	1–3
Tome's root	TOME	Mandibular first premolar	0–7	4–7
Distal accessory ridge	LDAR	Mandibular canine	0–5	2–5
Canine root number	LCRT	Mandibular canine	1–2	2
Odontome	ODONT	Mandibular premolars	0–1	1
Groove pattern	PATT	Mandibular molars	Y + X	Y
Cusp number	CUSPNO	Mandibular M3 and M2	4–6	4
		Mandibular M1	4–6	6
Protostylid	PROTO	Mandibular molars	0–7	2–7
Hypoconulid (cusp 5)	CUSP5	Mandibular molars	0–5	1–5
Entoconulid (cusp 6)	CUSP6	Mandibular molars	0–5	1–5
Metaconulid (cusp 7)	CUSP7	Mandibular molars	0–4	1–4
Lower molar root number	LMRT	Mandibular M3 and M2	1–3	2
		Mandibular M1	1–3	3
Congenital absence	CA	Mandibular 3rd molar, 1st premolar, and central incisor	0–1	1

* Presence/absence ranges based on those used by Turner (1985, 1987).

sizes ($n > 10$). Although dental traits have been shown to exhibit little sexual dimorphism (Scott and Turner 1997), I conducted χ^2 analysis on the remaining dental traits to determine whether their presence was influenced by sex. None of the 17 retained for analysis are significantly associated with sex. Among the 32 dental traits examined for the mortuary samples under study, only 17 had a sufficient number of observations. The frequencies for the 17 traits used in this study are presented in Table 8.2.

TABLE 8.2. Number present/number of observations for 17 maxillary and mandibular epigenetic dental traits examined in this study.

	MAXILLARY EPIGENETIC TRAITS								
Mortuary Samples	UM3PCA	UM2 META	UM2 HYPO	UM1 CARA	UM1 PARA	UM1EE	UP1RT	UI2PCA	UI1WING
Paleo-Indian	0/13	8/9	4/8	2/9	2/13	2/10	10/10	1/17	2/12
Huaca Prieta	4/30	23/27	13/22	6/18	1/25	11/19	19/26	0/39	9/38
La Galgada	1/11	3/11	4/10	1/5	2/5	0/5	16/17	1/13	10/18
Cerro Oreja–Salinar	0/10	11/14	4/12	7/18	5/16	4/10	9/9	0/19	7/9
Cerro Oreja–G1	1/50	27/42	9/40	27/68	12/67	6/24	35/42	1/68	19/28
Cerro Oreja–G2	4/35	20/34	9/26	10/44	5/41	7/21	32/36	1/45	22/26
Cerro Oreja–G3	2/24	12/21	6/20	9/37	3/37	3/9	19/24	0/47	16/19
HM–Urban Sector	3/22	15/20	7/17	2/13	1/17	9/15	16/20	0/23	17/21
HLL–Platforms	4/25	22/27	5/25	6/28	0/28	10/21	17/17	1/34	13/29
HLL–P3A	6/40	31/33	17/30	3/28	10/33	8/27	29/33	1/40	22/35
Pacatnamú–H45CM1	6/20	13/15	7/12	6/18	2/20	2/12	12/16	2/26	11/22
	MANDIBULAR EPIGENETIC TRAITS								
Mortuary Samples	LM3CA	LM2 PATT	LM2RT	LM1 PROTO	LM1 CUSP7	LM1RT	LP1TOME	ULP12 ODONT	
Paleo-Indian	1/15	2/6	10/10	0/8	0/6	1/11	1/13	0/24	
Huaca Prieta	2/33	0/17	23/26	0/16	4/21	0/28	0/15	0/55	
La Galgada	5/21	2/13	18/25	1/15	2/15	0/22	0/25	0/19	
Cerro Oreja–Salinar	0/13	0/15	7/10	5/17	1/17	0/16	0/10	2/100	
Cerro Oreja–G1	3/60	2/35	26/40	7/47	9/59	1/52	5/50	6/155	
Cerro Oreja–G2	1/46	5/25	18/24	2/38	3/41	2/42	3/40	2/119	
Cerro Oreja–G3	1/38	4/20	18/27	1/35	1/37	1/29	2/24	0/83	
HM–Urban Sector	1/19	4/12	8/14	5/13	0/14	0/16	0/14	0/39	
HLL–Platforms	4/38	5/32	14/54	6/42	6/43	0/35	0/32	2/55	
HLL–P3A	7/41	4/32	23/32	11/34	0/32	0/34	1/36	2/109	
Pacatnamú–H45CM1	1/21	1/12	10/16	6/14	2/14	1/16	2/21	1/42	

Correspondence Analysis

As an initial step, I employ CA to identify the relations among the epigenetic traits considered in the present study and to understand which dental traits vary most among the mortuary samples considered here. CA is also referred to as correspondence factor analysis, dual scaling, or principal components analysis (PCA) of qualitative data, and represents an extension of general PCA procedures for frequency or percentage data.

CA has been employed in previous anthropological studies (Greenacre and Degos 1977), including a number that analyze epigenetic dental traits (Sciulli 1990; Kitawaga et al. 1995; Coppa et al. 1998; Irish 2005). Rather than using a correlation matrix, CA utilizes a χ^2 distance matrix as input for PCA. The benefit of this analysis is that (as in PCA) CA provides visually interpretable plots of the underlying dimensions present in the data. It is also like PCA in that the first dimension accounts for most of the variation present in the χ^2 analysis of frequency data, whereas subsequent dimensions are orthogonal to one another and account for sequentially less variation.

An additional advantage of CA analysis is that it minimizes intra- and inter-row variation (which can be caused when large differences are present in sample sizes) and standardizes data across rows and columns. For the present study, CA was conducted on the dental trait frequencies matrix using the 11 mortuary samples as rows and the 17 epigenetic dental traits as columns. The results from CA analysis provide information on inter-sample and inter-trait variation.

Mean Measure of Divergence Analysis

Although the results of CA analysis provide an indication of relations among the mortuary samples, the biodistances among the samples were also calculated using C.A.B. Smith's MMD. This is because the interpretable dimensions (the first three or four) of CA analysis typically account for a relatively small amount of variation in epigenetic biodistance data, whereas MMD uses all uncorrelated traits and thereby provides a measure that takes into account all variation present in the traits used.

Although a number of alternative biodistance measures exist, I chose MMD because its properties are well understood and because it is widely used and accepted by scholars conducting biodistance studies using epigenetic traits. Furthermore, the MMD biodistance measure is highly correlated with other biodistance measures (Constandse-Westermann 1972; Sneath and Sokal 1973; Finnegan and Cooprider 1978; Bedrick, Lapidus, and Powell 2000; González-José, Dahinten, and Hernández 2001; Edgar 2004; Hallgrímsson et al. 2004; Irish 2005), and in recent comparisons of MMD to other alternative biodistance analyses MMD has been shown to produce more conservative statistical results (Hallgrímsson et al. 2004:265).

Prior to calculation of MMD, I arcsine-transformed the dental trait frequencies for each mortuary sample using the Freeman and Tukey angular transformation, as recommended by Richard Green and Judy Myers Suchey (1976). This transformation stabilizes bivariate variances for extreme frequencies (>0.95, <0.05) even when the sample sizes are relatively small (<10). Importantly, MMD can produce negative values (Sjøvold 1973; Green 1982). This occurs when there is very little or no difference in arcsine-transformed frequencies across the traits for the two samples being compared.

Although negative MMD values are not statistically meaningful, they indicate that the two mortuary samples being compared are statistically indistinguishable. According to recommendations by Edward Harris and Torstein Sjøvold (2004), negative MMD values should be set to zero prior to undertaking subsequent multivariate statistical analyses of the biodistance matrix. I also calculated standard deviations and standardized MMD (stMMD) values; stMMD values are statistically significant at the 0.025 level if their value is greater than 2.00 (Sjøvold 1977; Harris and Sjøvold 2004).

Finally, a measure of uniqueness (MU) was also calculated for each of the 11 mortuary samples (Donlon 2000; Markov 2001). The MU provides a ranked measure of how different a given mortuary sample's biological relatedness is to the other samples being compared: a low MU indicates that a given sample is closely related to all other samples, whereas a larger value indicates that a given sample's biological relatedness to the other samples being compared is more remote.

The matrix of stMMDs was analyzed using hierarchic clustering and nonmetric multidimensional scaling (MDS) procedures. Hierarchic cluster analysis is used to find natural groupings among similarity or dissimilarity data (Aldenderfer and Blashfield 1984; Norusis 1994). Hierarchic cluster analysis produces two-dimensional tree diagrams of nested clusters that often depict visually interpretable results. Nonmetric MDS is also a useful procedure for producing interpretable graphic representations of complex dissimilarity matrices using the number of dimensions specified by the investigator (Kruskal 1964; Kruskal and Wish 1984). Nonmetric MDS procedures were employed because they accurately reflect rank orders of dissimilarity matrices when they are non-Euclidean, as in the case of stMMD values.

RESULTS

Dental Trait Frequencies

Visual inspection of Table 8.2 reveals considerable variation across the 17 epigenetic tooth cusp and root traits and among the 11 mortuary samples under study. Among the three Gallinazo samples, peg and congenitally absent maxillary third molars, second incisors, mandibular third molars (UM3 PCA, UI2PCA, LM3CA), and metacone and hypocone of the second maxillary molar (UM2META and UM2HYPO) are found at relatively low frequencies compared to other populations.

The parastyle and enamel extensions of the first maxillary molar (UM1PARA and UM1EE), first maxillary premolar root number (UP1RT), and the root number of the lower second and first molars (LM2RT and LM1RT) are also at low levels of expression among the Gallinazo samples. For the protostylid of the lower first molar (LM1 PROTO), the frequencies for the Gallinazo samples are relatively low and decrease through time at Cerro Oreja.

On the other hand, Carabelli's trait of the first maxillary molar (UM1CARA), winging of the maxillary first incisors (UI1WING), Y-cusp pattern of mandibular second molars (LM2PATT), and Tome's root (LP1TOME) of the first mandibular premolar are at relatively high levels of expression among the Gallinazo mortuary samples. There are no clear frequency trends among the Gallinazo samples for cusp 7 of the first mandibular molar (LM1CUSP7) or for the odontome expression (ULP12ODONT).

Correspondence Analysis Results

Although a visual inspection of the dental trait frequencies presented in Table 8.2 can provide us with an impression of how each trait varies among the samples, it does not necessarily tell us which traits are most responsible for differences among the 11 northern Andean mortuary populations. The result of the CA for dental trait frequencies allows us to understand the relationships among the 17 dental traits considered.

The overall inertia of the CA, each of the 10 dimensions' inertia (Eigenvalues), and each of the dimensions' corresponding proportion of inertia (proportion of variance accounted for) and cumulative inertia are presented in Table 8.3. Here, the CA accounts for 19.34% of the variation present. Joel Irish (2005) points out that this level may appear low but that it is very common in studies

TABLE 8.3. Eigenvalues and their variances for the correspondence analysis of 17 epigenetic dental traits and 11 prehistoric Andean mortuary samples.

DIMEN-SIONS	EIGEN-VALUE	% OF VARIANCE	CUMULATIVE % OF VARIANCE
1	0.0469	24.27	24.27
2	0.0357	18.45	42.72
3	0.0314	16.21	58.93
4	0.0297	15.36	74.29
5	0.0217	11.24	85.53
6	0.0143	7.28	92.92
7	0.0077	4.00	96.92
8	0.0035	1.80	98.72
9	0.0019	1.00	99.71
10	0.0006	0.29	100.00
Total	0.1934	100.00	100.00

that consider so many variables. Indeed, the total CA inertia value reported in this study is approximately the same as he achieved in his analysis of Nubian populations.

The first two dimensions of the CA analysis account for 24.27% and 18.45%, respectively, of the variation explained by the overall CA results (4.69% and 3.57%, respectively, of the overall variation). Figure 8.2 illustrates the column plot of relative trait contributions to the first two dimensions of the CA. On this figure, we can see UM1EE, LM1PROTO, UM3PCA, and ULP12ODONT on the positive end of the first dimension, whereas UI2PCA, UM1PARA, and LM3CA are the most negative traits along the first dimension. This indicates that the seven traits have the greatest contribution to determining the first dimension. For the second dimension, LM1PROTO and LM1RT are the two most influential traits.

The two-dimensional row plot in Figure 8.3 demonstrates the relationships among the 11 northern Andean samples based on the 17 dental traits. The urban sector sample from Huacas de Moche is the most positive along the first dimension, whereas the Cotton Preceramic La Galgada sample is most negative. Along the second dimension, the Pacatnamú–H45CM1 and HLL–Plaza 3A samples scale most positively, whereas the Paleo-Indian populations are the most negative sample. The three Gallinazo samples from Cerro Oreja are found relatively close to the origins of the first and second dimensions, indicating that these samples are all relatively intermediate with respect to other samples considered.

The Andean Paleo-Indian and Cotton Preceramic La Galgada samples are outliers, found on the left-hand side of the graphic, indicating a more distant relationship to the other northern Andean samples. The Cotton Preceramic Huaca Prieta sample clusters closely with all Early Intermediate–period mortuary samples. Such tight clustering indicates that all north-coast mortuary samples exhibit similar trait frequencies for the 17 tooth and root traits analyzed using CA.

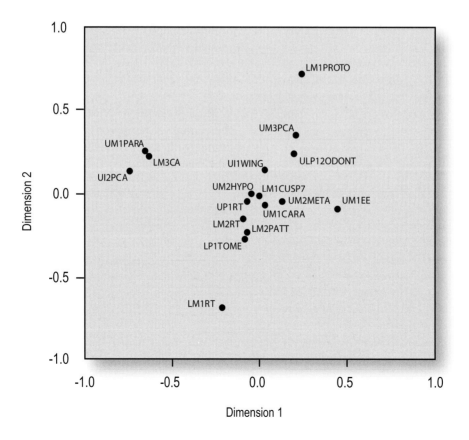

FIGURE 8.2. Two-dimensional column plot from correspondence analysis of 17 epigenetic dental traits.

One of the primary advantages of CA is the ability to produce biplots of column and row variables, in this case with the columns being dental traits and the rows being the mortuary samples. It is important to note, however, that the data points in Figures 8.2 and 8.3 are not on the same scale. Indeed, a biplot allows a more direct comparison of the two plots by placing column and row variables on the same scale within the same plot, thereby allowing us to determine which dental traits are most influential on the relations among the mortuary samples.

Figure 8.4 presents the biplot for the 11 mortuary samples and 17 epigenetic dental traits examined in this study. In the graphic, the Cerro Oreja Gallinazo samples cluster along the first

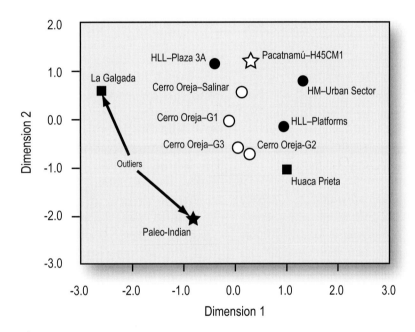

FIGURE 8.3. Two-dimensional row plot from correspondence analysis of 11 northern Andean mortuary samples.

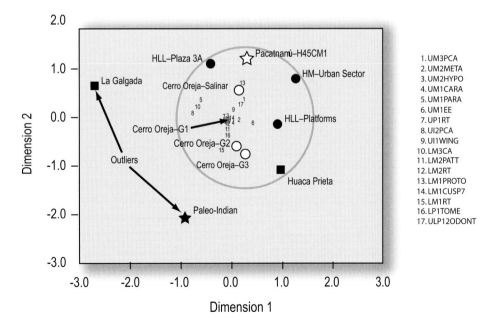

FIGURE 8.4. Two-dimensional biplot from correspondence analysis of 11 northern Andean mortuary samples and 17 epigenetic dental traits.

dimension with maxillary traits such as central incisor winging (UI1WING), metacone and hypocone of the second molar (UM2META and UM2HYPO), Carabelli's trait of the first maxillary molar (UM1CARA), and root number of the first maxillary premolar (UP1RT).

Mandibular traits are such as the protostylid and cusp 7 of the first molar (LM1PROTO and LM1CUSP7), root number for the first and second mandibular molars (LM1RT and LM2RT), cusp pattern of the second molar (LM2PATT), and Tome's root of the first mandibular premolar (LP1TOME). These are the traits most influential in separating the north-coast samples from the Andean Paleo-Indian and Cotton Preceramic La Galgada samples.

Mean Measure of Divergence Analyses

Using the 17 epigenetic dental traits, the CA only accounts for 19.34% of the total variation present among the 11 Andean mortuary samples under study. Furthermore, given that only the first and second dimensions of the CA analysis are displayed in Figures 8.2 through 8.4 (for ease of interpretation), the total amount of variation represented in these figures is even further reduced (to 8.26%; 42.72% of the total inertia).

It is doubtful that this can accurately reflect biodistance relations among the 11 Andean mortuary samples under study. For this reason, MMD values between each sample have been calculated. Although one should ideally try to use as many epigenetic traits as possible to estimate biological distances among samples, a potential problem is that biodistance values can be distorted when traits are intercorrelated. Therefore, following procedures recommended by Irish (2005), the Kendall's tau-b correlation was computed for the 17 traits reported here. Among the 136 correlation coefficients, 16 (11.7%) are significant positive associations.

Nearly all significant correlations are due to six traits that correlate with multiple traits, however. These traits are UM3PCA, UM2HYPO, UM1 CARA, UI2PCA, LM1PROTO, and LM1RT. As Irish (2005) correctly pointed out, there are two alternatives: one can calculate MMD using all traits and risk undue influence by intercorrelated traits, or reduce the number of traits to only those

not intercorrelated and risk estimating biological distances among the samples using too few traits.

To address criticisms by Izumi Shimada and Robert Corruccini (2005) (who suggested that our results were suspect because we used too few traits, and thus recommended that all traits be included) in regard to a previous study (Sutter and Cortez 2005), I conducted MMD analyses using the full complement of 17 traits and using the reduced number of 11 uncorrelated traits.

Following the analysis using all 17 traits, it was determined that the inclusion of the 6 intercorrelated traits differed little from those derived using only 11 uncorrelated traits: the differences in the relationships among the mortuary samples were primarily in magnitude rather than rank order. Therefore, for the sake of brevity, only those results using the remaining 11 uncorrelated traits are discussed here. Further, the results using all 17 traits are suspect because the MMD statistic requires that traits not be intercorrelated (Sjøvold 1977; Harris and Sjøvold 2004).[6]

The MMD values and their related statistics for the 11 samples using only the 11 uncorrelated traits are presented in Table 8.4. We learn from this table that the 11 mortuary samples examined here are all relatively closely related, given the nonsignificant MMD values. The only MMD value that is significant at the 0.025 level is between the Cerro Oreja–G2 and Huaca Prieta samples. None of the inter-sample MMD values among the Early Intermediate–period north-coast mortuary samples is significant.

Regarding the MU values, Huaca Prieta is the most divergent sample (followed by HLL–Platforms), whereas the sample from Pacatnamú is the least divergent. The three Gallinazo samples from Cerro Oreja exhibit roughly intermediate MU values, ranking third (Cerro Oreja–G1), fourth (Cerro Oreja–G3), and fifth (Cerro Oreja– G2).

The resulting hierarchic cluster diagram of the MMD data is presented in Figure 8.5, highlighting that two main clusters exist among the northern Andean mortuary samples. The first cluster gathers the Huaca Prieta sample and the HLL–Platforms sample, whereas the second cluster features the remaining nine mortuary samples analyzed. Two subclusters are present within the second cluster: the first subcluster features the Paleo-Indian and HLL–Plaza 3A sam-

TABLE 8.4. Mean measure of divergence values, their variance, and standardized mean measure of divergence values for 11 prehistoric Andean mortuary samples derived using 11 epigenetic dental traits.

	Paleo-Indian	Huaca Prieta	La Galgada	Cerro Oreja–Salinar	Cerro Oreja–G1	Cerro Oreja–G2	Cerro Oreja–G3	HM–Urban Sector	HLL–Plat-forms	HLL–Plaza 3A	Pacat-namú–H45CM1
Paleo-Indian	— — —										
Huaca Prieta	0.18 0.19 0.93	— — —									
La Galgada	0.21 0.24 0.87	0.33 0.17 1.97	— — —								
Cerro Oreja–Salinar	0.18 0.24 0.77	0.13 0.16 0.79	0.15 0.22 0.70	— — —							
Cerro Oreja–G1	0.19 0.16 1.14	0.13 0.09 1.41	0.04 0.14 0.29	-0.01 0.14 -0.10	— — —						
Cerro Oreja–G2	0.18 0.17 1.06	0.22 0.10 2.25	0.10 0.15 0.64	0.00 0.15 0.02	0.00 0.07 -0.04	— — —					
Cerro Oreja–G3	0.22 0.19 1.16	0.21 0.12 1.81	0.12 0.17 0.73	0.04 0.17 0.23	0.00 0.09 0.03	-0.05 0.10 -0.54	— — —				
HM–Urban Sector	0.24 0.21 1.14	0.19 0.14 1.36	0.24 0.19 1.26	0.07 0.19 0.37	0.08 0.11 0.74	0.00 0.12 0.01	-0.04 0.14 -0.26	— — —			
HLL–Plat-forms	0.14 0.18 0.77	0.08 0.11 0.78	0.26 0.16 1.67	0.08 0.16 0.53	0.11 0.08 1.35	0.12 0.09 1.31	0.13 0.11 1.25	0.08 0.13 0.59	— — —		
HLL–Plaza 3A	0.09 0.17 0.54	0.17 0.10 1.79	0.18 0.15 1.24	0.02 0.15 0.10	0.08 0.07 1.05	0.09 0.08 1.17	0.09 0.10 0.96	0.07 0.12 0.56	0.14 0.09 1.55	— — —	
Pacat-namú H45CM1	0.10 0.21 0.46	0.04 0.14 0.32	0.09 0.19 0.50	0.04 0.19 0.20	-0.03 0.11 -0.31	0.04 0.12 0.33	0.03 0.14 0.21	0.08 0.16 0.49	0.06 0.13 0.50	0.03 0.12 0.23	— — —
Measure of Unique-ness	8.83	13.41	9.86	3.62	5.57	6.20	5.58	6.26	10.30	9.19	2.92

ples, and the second subcluster gathers the remaining seven samples.

Within the latter, the samples appear to be chronologically clustered: the Cotton Preceramic La Galgada sample is the most distantly related, whereas the Early Intermediate–period Cerro Oreja–Salinar, Cerro Oreja–G1, and Pacatnamú–H45CM1 samples are closely related. The same is

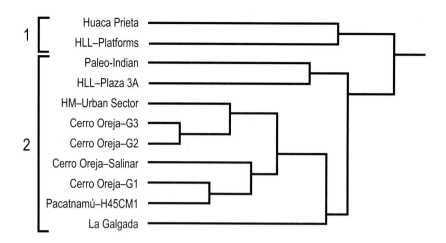

FIGURE 8.5. Hierarchic cluster diagram of MMD data highlighting two main clusters among the northern Andean mortuary samples.

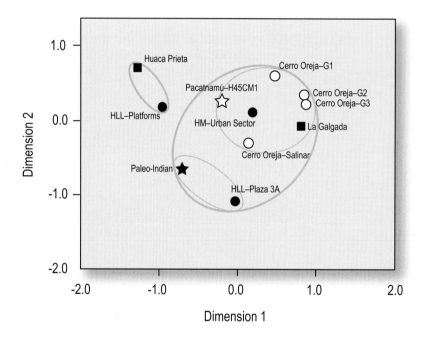

FIGURE 8.6. Two-dimensional MDS solution for the biodistance relations reported in Table 8.4.

true for the Cerro Oreja–G2, Cerro Oreja–G3, and HM–Urban Sector samples.

The two-dimensional MDS solution for the biodistance relations reported in Table 8.4 is presented in Figure 8.6. The two-dimensional solution accounts for 88% of the total variation. To aid in its interpretation, the clusters and subclusters identified in the hierarchic cluster analysis are superimposed on the MDS diagram. Interesting-

ly, Figure 8.6 points to relatively close distances between the samples from Cerro Oreja and the samples from the urban sector at Huacas de Moche, the Pacatnamú sample from the Jequetepeque Valley, and the Cotton Preceramic La Galgada sample from the Callejon de Huaylas.

The proximity of these samples in multidimensional space implies relatively close phenetic relations among these seven mortuary populations and suggests that the urban sector at Huacas de Moche and the four Cerro Oreja samples (all from the Moche Valley) may represent descendants of an earlier influx of peoples from the adjacent highlands to the east.

Conversely, the HLL–Platforms sample is more distantly related to the other Early Intermediate–period north-coast samples, and its relative proximity to the earlier Andean Paleo-Indian and Huaca Prieta mortuary populations suggests that the elites at Huaca de la Luna may represent direct descendants of earlier coastal populations, with little subsequent gene flow from the adjacent highlands. Until additional northern Andean samples have been analyzed, however, this interpretation should be considered tentative.

The sacrificial victims sample from plaza 3A at Huaca de la Luna is an outlier and is more similar to the Andean Paleo-Indian sample than it is to the other Early Intermediate–period samples. Within the context of this study, it is unclear, based on its position, from which population(s) the sacrificial victims sample from plaza 3A at Huaca de la Luna might ultimately derive.

DISCUSSION

Within this study, multiple analyses of epigenetic dental trait data have been presented in hopes of shedding light on genetic affinities of the Gallinazo populations from Cerro Oreja. Importantly, any conclusions I might draw from this study should be considered a first approximation, as these results may be specific to Gallinazo people residing in the Moche Valley and may not apply to Gallinazo populations from other north-coast valleys. Furthermore, results presented here are based on only a few north Andean mortuary samples. The discussion of the results focuses on the MMD analyses using 11 uncorrelated dental traits (Table 8.4; Figure 8.6), as these are the least objectionable on methodological grounds.

The nonsignificant MMD results of this study indicate that the three Cerro Oreja Gallinazo samples and other Early Intermediate–period north-coast mortuary samples reported here belonged to a relatively coherent breeding population. These conclusions agree with those that I (Sutter 2008; Sutter and Cortez 2005) and others

(Shimada 2004; Shimada et al. 2005) have previously reached. In addition, given the close relations among each of the three temporally distinct Cerro Oreja Gallinazo samples and the sample from the urban sector at Huacas de Moche, it is evident that at least within the Moche Valley, the Gallinazo and Moche individuals sampled are very closely related.

Conversely, based on phenetic differences apparent between the Cerro Oreja Gallinazo samples and the HLL–Plaza 3A sample, it is unlikely that the Cerro Oreja Gallinazo were a source of sacrificial victims. Given the absence of radiocarbon dates for the Gallinazo samples from Cerro Oreja, it is not possible to say whether the HM–Urban Sector sample is descended from earlier Moche Valley Gallinazo or if it represents a closely related yet ethnically distinct group from the same breeding population. These interpretations are also in line with those I have presented elsewhere (Sutter and Cortez 2005).

A previous study by Sutter and Cortez (2005) examined only eight Early Intermediate–period samples also analyzed here. A closer examination of those results permits a better understanding of population dynamics among the Early Intermediate–period samples without the influence of other temporally and spatially distant samples. Considering the overall solution, it is apparent that the samples from Cerro Oreja and from the urban sector at Huacas de Moche form one grouping, whereas the HLL–Platforms and Pacatnamú–H45CM1 samples form a second. The HLL–Plaza 3A sample is an outlier relative to the other Early Intermediate–period mortuary populations.

Within the context of comparisons among the Cerro Oreja samples, the close proximity apparent among the Salinar and subsequent three Gallinazo samples strongly suggests that the Gallinazo at Cerro Oreja were directly descended from the earlier Salinar population. The chronological ordering of the Cerro Oreja samples along the first dimension suggests that some (albeit relatively little) gene flow occurred over time at Cerro Oreja. If strictly genetic drift were responsible for relations at the site, a more random ordering would be predicted among the Cerro Oreja samples.

Given the focus of this chapter, perhaps the most intriguing results from the previous study are the close phenetic relations apparent between the Gallinazo and HM–Urban Sector samples. Even when a more limited number of dental characteristics were used, the HM–Urban Sector and Gallinazo samples were found to be statistically indistinguishable from one another. Within the MDS solution, the HM–Urban Sector and Cerro Oreja–Salinar and Gallinazo samples are found in close proximity in the upper right-hand corner of the diagram.

If we assume that only the most recent Cerro Oreja–G3 sample was contemporaneous with the HM–Urban Sector sample, the results from Sutter and Cortez (2005) would suggest that the Moche and Gallinazo represent different ethnic groups within the same breeding population. This is in contrast to the more distant phenetic relations apparent between the Cerro Oreja Gallinazo mortuary populations and the HLL–Platforms sample.

Given that all of the biodistances reported by Sutter and Cortez (2005) for the Gallinazo and HLL–Platforms samples were nonsignificant (ranging from 0.92 standard deviations for the comparison between the HLL–Platforms and Cerro Oreja–G3 samples to 1.62 standard deviations for comparisons between the HLL–Platforms and Cerro Oreja–G1 samples), they likely belong to the same breeding population. However, it is intriguing that all biodistance comparisons between the HM–Urban Sector sample and the Gallinazo samples are more similar than the biodistance comparison between the HM–Urban Sector and HLL–Platforms samples.

Were the residents of the urban sector at Huacas de Moche descended from Moche Valley Gallinazo and members of the priestly elite derived from a different segment of the north-coast breeding population? Did differing marriage patterns result in the detected differences between the HLL–Platforms sample and the Gallinazo mortuary populations? Or, perhaps, are the apparent phenetic differences between the HLL–Platforms and Gallinazo samples partly explainable by temporal differences? Any attempt to understand these differences will require additional samples with good chronological control from the Moche and other nearby valleys.

Much like the HLL–Platforms sample, comparisons between the Pacatnamú and Gallinazo mortuary populations are nonsignificant. The apparent phenetic differences are almost certainly due (in part) to geographic distance between the Pacatnamú–H45CM1 sample from the Jequetepeque Valley and the Gallinazo sample from the Moche Valley. The HLL–Plaza 3A sacrificial victims sample represents an outlier relative to the Gallinazo and all other Early Intermediate–period samples. Sutter and Cortez (2005) report that biodistances between the sacrificial victims sample and the Cerro Oreja Gallinazo sample are all significant at the 0.025 level.

As I have asserted elsewhere in this chapter, these comparisons largely eliminate the Cerro Oreja Gallinazo as a source of the Huaca de la Luna plaza 3A sacrificial victims. In any case, it is important to point out that the general phenetic patterns apparent among the eight Early Intermediate–period samples reported by Sutter and Cortez (2005) are largely confirmed by the additional traits and mortuary samples utilized in this study.

As Santiago Uceda, Henry Gayoso, and Nadia Gamarra's contribution to this volume (Chapter 7) indicates, Moche and utilitarian Gallinazo ceramics are present at every level at Huacas de Moche, suggesting that Moche and Gallinazo ceramic styles were largely contemporaneous. If this characterization applies to the entire Moche Valley, it is tempting to suggest that the Moche and Gallinazo represent two genetically coherent yet ethnically distinct groups within the same polity.

Indeed, until the chronology of Cerro Oreja is more precisely defined, a highly plausible scenario for the Moche presence at Cerro Oreja is that it was contemporaneous with the Gallinazo occupation. It is now increasingly clear that Gallinazo and Moche ceramics co-occur throughout the north-coast region. As some contributors to this volume indicate, there are likely status distinctions between Castillo Incised and Modeled and Gallinazo Negative ceramics. Christopher Donnan's contribution indicates that elite tombs at Dos Cabezas sometimes contain Castillo Incised and Modeled ceramics and Moche-style vessels (see Chapter 2), whereas Jean-François Millaire's contributions (Chapters 1, 9) document that Castillo Incised and Modeled and Gallinazo Negative ceramics co-occur at Huaca Santa Clara in the Virú Valley.

Assuming that the Moche and Gallinazo mortuary samples examined here were contemporaneous, the aforementioned evidence begs the question as to exactly which cultural markers are being used to signify ethnic variation among Early Intermediate–period north-coast populations. In her dissertation, Heidy Fogel (1993) argued that Moche and Gallinazo populations shared mortuary practices, ceremonial architecture, huaca construction, and a number of other cultural traits.

Based on his comparison of textiles from Huaca Santa Clara in the Virú Valley and from Pacatnamú in the Jequetepeque Valley, Millaire argued that both archaeological cultures must have shared a common set of techniques and a unique visual repertoire (Millaire 2005). As I have argued elsewhere (Sutter 2000), biocultural groups may share material culture yet be genetically distinct—or genetically indistinguishable populations may explicitly express cultural distinctions (Sutter 2005a). Indeed, I would suggest that we should avoid asserting that a direct one-to-one correlation between specific classes of artifacts and ethnicity exists. Additional archaeological and biological research on the Gallinazo will be required to tease these relations out.

On a broader level, results of this study are interpretable in light of the pan-Andean patterns I report elsewhere (Sutter 2005a, 2008). Following the initial colonization of South America by Paleo-Indian groups, a subsequent demographic expansion into the continent occurred during the mid-Holocene climatic optimum, driven by food-producing populations. Importantly, this gene flow would have been due to differential fertility between relatively lower-fertility foraging and horticultural populations on the southern side of the front and the higher fertility among those who made the economic shift to food production on the northern side of the front.

This form of demographically driven gene flow (demic expansion) should not be equated with "population replacement." Instead, demic expansion represents a more subtle growth in which the spread of populations (and their genes) —within areas where fluid marriage networks already existed among adjacent regions—would

not have been apparent to the lower-fertility populations on the south side of the demographic wave. I hypothesized that this migratory wave proceeded from the north toward the south via the highlands, and then down into the coastal valleys (Sutter 2005a, 2005b, 2008).

The Gallinazo mortuary populations from Cerro Oreja, the urban sector sample from Huacas de Moche, and those found on the right-hand side of Figure 8.6 are characterized by relatively higher frequencies of dental traits associated with the second migratory event. Relative to the other Early Intermediate–period samples, the HLL–Platforms sample has relatively lower dental trait frequencies associated with the second migratory wave. Within the context of the broader pan-Andean phenetic patterns, the relationship depicted in Figure 8.6 suggests that the Moche elite at Huaca de la Luna may represent a population with a higher degree of genetic continuity with earlier coastal populations, as indicated by its proximity to the Andean Paleo-Indian and Huaca Prieta mortuary samples (relative to the HM–Urban Sector and Cerro Oreja Gallinazo populations).

Given each of the Cerro Oreja mortuary samples' relative position along the first dimension— with the Cerro Oreja–Salinar sample being farthest to the left and the Cerro Oreja–G2 and –G3 samples being farthest to the right—I suggest that gene flow from the adjacent highlands to the east continued through the Early Intermediate period, with relatively less occurring during the Gallinazo Estructuras and Pos-Estructuras occupational phases at Cerro Oreja (Cerro Oreja–G2 and –G3).

A number of conclusions can be reached based on the results of this limited study. First, all Early Intermediate–period populations represented by the mortuary samples examined belonged to a relatively coherent breeding population. Second, the Gallinazo samples from Cerro Oreja shared close phenetic relations with the urban sector population from Huacas de Moche. Third, although additional samples and analyses are needed, it is likely that the Gallinazo population at Cerro Oreja received relatively greater gene flow from highland populations to the east than did other coastal populations. Last, neither the Gallinazo at Cerro Oreja nor the other mortuary populations considered here were likely the source of victims represented by the sacrificial victims sample from plaza 3A at Huaca de la Luna.

ACKNOWLEDGMENTS

This research was funded by NSF Grant 9816958. Key facilities and logistic support for this research were provided by the Museo de Arqueología, Antropología e Historia of the Universidad Nacional de Trujillo and by the Instituto Nacional de Cultura – La Libertad. I am grateful to my many friends and colleagues who granted me permission to examine their collections, including Christopher Donnan, José Carcelén, and Santiago Uceda. Ana María Hoyle, Cesar Gálvez, Jesús Briceño, and John Verano also helped facilitate our research. Rosa Cortez was my lab assistant during my data collection for the Cerro Oreja materials. Her help was greatly appreciated. I would also like to thank Jean-François Millaire for inviting me to contribute to this volume and for his ceramic identifications based on figures from José Carcelén's INC report. Any and all errors in interpretation or fact are my own.

NOTES

[1] The collection from Huaca Prieta is presently held at the American Museum of Natural History, New York.

[2] The collection from La Galgada is presently held at the Museo Nacional de Arqueología, Antropología e Historia del Perú, Lima.

[3] The collections from Cerro Oreja are presently held at the Instituto Nacional de Cultura – La Libertad, Trujillo.

[4] The collections from Huacas de Moche are presently held at the Museo de Arqueología, Antropología e Historia of the Universidad Nacional de Trujillo, Trujillo.

[5] The collection from H45CM1 at Pacatnamú is presently held at the Instituto Nacional de Cultura – La Libertad, Trujillo.

[6] The results using all 17 traits are available upon request.

REFERENCES

Aldenderfer, Mark S., and Roger K. Blashfield
    1984 *Cluster Analysis*. Quantitative Applications in the Social Sciences 44. Beverly Hills, California: Sage Publications.

Bawden, Garth
    1996 *The Moche*. Cambridge, Massachusetts: Blackwell.

Bedrick, Edward J., Jodi Lapidus, and Joseph F. Powell
    2000 Estimating the Mahalanobis Distance from Mixed Continuous and Discrete Data. *Biometrics* 56(2):394–401.

Bennett, Wendell C.
    1939 *Archaeology of the North Coast of Peru: An Account of Exploration and Excavation in Viru and Lambayeque Valleys*. Anthropological Papers of the American Museum of Natural History Vol. 37, Pt. 1. New York: The American Museum of Natural History.
    1950 *The Gallinazo Group: Viru Valley, Peru*. Yale University Publications in Anthropology 43. New Haven: Yale University Press.

Berry, A. Caroline
    1978 Anthropological and Family Studies on Minor Variants of the Dental Crown. In *Development, Function and Evolution of Teeth*, P. M. Butler and Kenneth A. Joysey (eds.), pp. 81–98. London: Academic Press.

Beynon, Diane E., and Michael I. Siegel
    1981 Ancient Human Remains from Central Peru. *American Antiquity* 46(1):167–178.

Biggerstaff, Robert H.
    1970 Morphological Variations for the Permanent Mandibular First Molars in Human Monozygotic and Dizygotic Twins. *Archives of Oral Biology* 15(8):721–730.
    1973 Heritability of the Carabelli Cusp in Twins. *Journal of Dental Research* 52(1):40–44.

Billman, Brian R.
    1997 Population Pressure and the Origins of Warfare in the Moche Valley, Peru. In *Integrating Archaeological Demography: Multidisciplinary Approaches to Prehistoric Population*, Richard R. Paine (ed.), pp. 285–310. Carbondale: Center for Archaeological Investigations, Southern Illinois University at Carbondale.
    1999 Reconstructing Prehistoric Political Economies and Cycles of Political Power in the Moche Valley, Peru. In *Settlement Pattern Studies in the Americas: Fifty Years Since Virú*, Brian R. Billman and Gary M. Feinman (eds.), pp. 131–159. Washington, D.C.: Smithsonian Institution Press.

Bird, Junius B.
    1988 *Travels and Archaeology in South Chile*, John Hyslop (ed.). Iowa City: University of Iowa Press.

Bird, Junius B., and John Hyslop
    1985 *The Preceramic Excavations at the Huaca Prieta, Chicama Valley, Peru*. Anthropological Papers of the American Museum of Natural History

Vol. 62, Pt. 1. New York: The American Museum of Natural History.

Bórmida, Marcelo
1966   Los esqueletos de Lauricocha. *Acta praehistorica* (Buenos Aires) 5(7):1–34.

Bourget, Steve
1997   Las excavaciones en la Plaza 3A de la Huaca de la Luna. In *Investigaciones en la Huaca de la Luna 1995*, Santiago Uceda, Elías Mujica, and Ricardo Morales (eds.), pp. 51–59. Trujillo: Facultad de Ciencias Sociales, Universidad Nacional de La Libertad.
2001   Rituals of Sacrifice: Its Practice at Huaca de la Luna and Its Representation in Moche Iconography. In *Moche Art and Archaeology in Ancient Peru*, Joanne Pillsbury (ed.), pp. 89–109. Washington, D.C.: National Gallery of Art and Yale University Press.

Bourget, Steve, and Jean-François Millaire
2000   Excavaciones en la Plaza 3A y Plataforma II de la Huaca de la Luna. In *Investigaciones en la Huaca de la Luna 1997*, Santiago Uceda, Elías Mujica, and Ricardo Morales (eds.), pp. 47–60. Trujillo: Facultad de Ciencias Sociales, Universidad Nacional de Trujillo.

Braga, José
2001   Cranial Discrete Variation in the Great Apes: New Prospects in Palaeoprimatology. In *Phylogeny of the Neogene Hominoid Primates of Eurasia*, Louis de Bonis, George D. Koufos, and Peter Andrews (eds.), pp. 151–190. Hominoid Evolution and Climate Change in Europe Vol. 2. Cambridge, UK: Cambridge University Press.

Brewer-Carias, Charles A., Steven Le Blanc, and James V. Neel
1976   Genetic Structure of a Tribal Population, the Yanomama Indians. XIII: Dental Microdifferentiation. *American Journal of Physical Anthropology* 44(1):5–14.

Carcelén, José
1995   Proyecto de rescate arqueológico Chavimochic: Informe de entrega de obra, vol. 2(4), Rescate arqueológico flanco norte y arenales al oeste de Cerro Oreja. Canal Madre – II Etapa: Variante Cerro Oreja. Unpublished final report submitted to the Instituto Nacional de Cultura – La Libertad, Trujillo.

Chapdelaine, Claude
2001   The Growing Power of a Moche Urban Class. In *Moche Art and Archaeology in Ancient Peru*, Joanne Pillsbury (ed.), pp. 69–87. Washington, D.C.: National Gallery of Art and Yale University Press.

Chauchat, Claude
1988   Early Hunter-Gatherers on the Peruvian Coast. In *Peruvian Prehistory: An Overview of Pre-Inca and Inca Society*, Richard W. Keatinge (ed.), pp. 41–66. Cambridge, UK: Cambridge University Press.

Chauchat, Claude, and Jean-Marie Dricot
1979   Paléontologie humaine: Un nouveau type humain fossile en Amérique du Sud: L'homme de Paiján (Pérou). *Comptes rendus des séances de l'Académie des sciences, Série D. Sciences naturelles* (Paris) 289:387–389.

Constandse-Westermann, Trinette S.
1972   *Coefficients of Biological Distance: An Introduction to the Various Methods of Assessment of Biological Distances between Populations, with Special Reference to Human Biological Problems.* Oosterhout, Netherlands: Anthropological Publications.

Coppa, Alfredo, Andrea Cucina, Domenico Mancinelli, Rita Vargiu, and James M. Calcagno
1998   Dental Anthropology of Central-Southern Iron Age Italy: The Evidence of Metric versus Nonmetric Traits. *American Journal of Physical Anthropology* 107(4):371–386.

Corruccini, Robert S., and Krishan Sharma
1985   Within- and between-Zygosity Variance in Oral Traits among U.S. and Punjabi Twins. *Human Heredity* 35(5):314–318.

Cortez V., Rosa
2000   Estatura del hombre prehispánico en la costa norte del Perú. Unpublished bachelor's thesis, Universidad Nacional de Trujillo, Trujillo.

Donlon, D. A.
2000   The Value of Infracranial Nonmetric Variation in Studies of Modern *Homo Sapiens*: An Australian Focus. *American Journal of Physical Anthropology* 113(3):349–368.

Donnan, Christopher B., and Guillermo A. Cock (editors)
1986   *The Pacatnamu Papers*, Volume 1. Los Angeles: Museum of Cultural History, University of California.

Donnan, Christopher B., and Carol J. Mackey
1978   *Ancient Burial Patterns of the Moche Valley, Peru.* Austin: University of Texas Press.

Donnan, Christopher B., and Donna McClelland
1997   Moche Burials at Pacatnamu. In *The Pacatnamu Papers*, Volume 2: *The Moche Occupation*, Christopher B. Donnan and Guillermo A. Cock (eds.), pp. 17–187. Los Angeles: Fowler Museum of Cultural History, University of California.

Edgar, Heather J. H.
2004   Dentitions, Distance, and Difficulty: A Comparison of Two Statistical Techniques for

Dental Morphological Data. *Dental Anthropology* 17(2):55–62.

Engel, Frédéric A.
1977 Early Holocene Funeral Bundles from the Central Andes. *Paleopathology Newsletter* 19: 7–8.
1987 *De las begonias al maíz: Vida y producción en el Perú antiguo.* Lima: Centro de Investigación de Zonas Aridas, Universidad Nacional Agraria.

Escobar, Victor, Michael Melnick, and P. Michael Conneally
1976 The Inheritance of Bilateral Rotation of Maxillary Central Incisors. *American Journal of Physical Anthropology* 45(1):109–115.

Finnegan, Michael, and Kevin Cooprider
1978 Empirical Comparison of Distance Equations Using Discrete Traits. *American Journal of Physical Anthropology* 49(1):39–46.

Fogel, Heidy
1993 Settlements in Time: A Study of Social and Political Development during the Gallinazo Occupation of the North Coast of Perú [sic]. Unpublished Ph.D. dissertation, Yale University, New Haven.

Gagnon, Celeste M.
2004 Food and the State: Bioarchaeological Investigations of Diet in the Moche Valley of Perú [sic]. *Dental Anthropology* 17(2):45–54.

González-José, Rolando, Silvia Dahinten, and Miguel Hernández
2001 The Settlement of Patagonia: A Matrix Correlation Study. *Human Biology* 73(2):233–248.

Green, David Lee
1982 Discrete Dental Variations and Biological Distances of Nubian Populations. *American Journal of Physical Anthropology* 58(1):75–79.

Green, Richard F., and Judy Myers Suchey
1976 The Use of Inverse Sine Transformations in the Analysis of Non-Metric Cranial Data. *American Journal of Physical Anthropology* 45 (1):61–68.

Greenacre, M. J., and L. Degos
1977 Correspondence Analysis of HLA Gene Frequency Data from 124 Population Samples. *American Journal of Human Genetics* 29:60–75.

Grieder, Terence
1988 *La Galgada, Peru: A Preceramic Culture in Transition.* Austin: University of Texas Press.

Hallgrímsson, Benedikt, Barra Ó Donnabháin, G. Bragi Walters, David M. L. Cooper, Daníel Gudbjartsson, and Kari Stefánsson
2004 Composition of the Founding Population of Iceland: Biological Distance and Morphological Variation in Early Historic Atlantic Europe. *American Journal of Physical Anthropology* 124(3):257–274.

Harris, Edward F., and Howard L. Bailit
1980 The Metaconule: A Morphologic and Familial Analysis of a Molar Cusp in Humans. *American Journal of Physical Anthropology* 53 (3):349–358.

Harris, Edward F., and Torstein Sjøvold
2004 Calculation of Smith's Mean Measure of Divergence for Intergroup Comparisons Using Nonmetric Data. *Dental Anthropology* 17(3): 83–93.

Hassanali, Jameela
1982 Incidence of Carabelli's Trait in Kenyan Africans and Asians. *American Journal of Physical Anthropology* 59(3):317–319.

Hastings, C. Mansfield, and M. Edward Moseley
1975 The Adobes of Huaca del Sol and Huaca de la Luna. *American Antiquity* 40(2):196–203.

Haydenblit, Rebeca
1996 Dental Variation among Four Prehispanic Mexican Populations. *American Journal of Physical Anthropology* 100(2):225–246.

Higa, Takako, Tsunehiko Hanihara, Hajime Sunakawa, and Hajime Ishida
2003 Dental Variation of Ryukyu Islanders: A Comparative Study among Ryukyu, Ainu, and Other Asian Populations. *American Journal of Human Biology* 15(2):127–143.

Irish, Joel D.
2005 Population Continuity vs. Discontinuity Revisited: Dental Affinities among Late Paleolithic through Christian-Era Nubians. *American Journal of Physical Anthropology* 128(3): 520–535.

Kitawaga, Yoshikazu, Yoshitaka Manabe, Joichi Oyamada, and Atsushi Rokutanda
1995 Deciduous Dental Morphology of the Prehistoric Jomon People of Japan: Comparison of Nonmetric Characters. *American Journal of Physical Anthropology* 97(2):101–111.

Kruskal, Joseph B.
1964 Multidimensional Scaling by Optimizing Goodness of Fit to a Nonmetric Hypothesis. *Psychometrika* 29:1–27.

Kruskal, Joseph B., and Myron Wish
1984 *Multidimensional Scaling.* Quantitative Applications in the Social Sciences 11. Beverly Hills, California: Sage Publications.

Larco Hoyle, Rafael
2001 [1938–1940] *Los Mochicas.* 2 vols. Lima: Museo Arqueológico Rafael Larco Herrera.

Lease, Loren R., and Paul W. Sciulli
2005 Brief Communication: Discrimination between European-American and African-American Children Based on Deciduous Dental Metrics and Morphology. *American Journal of Physical Anthropology* 126(1):56–60.

Lukacs, John R., and Brian E. Hemphill
  1991 The Dental Anthropology of Prehistoric Baluchistan: A Morphometric Approach to the Peopling of South Asia. In *Advances in Dental Anthropology*, Marc A. Kelley and Clark Spencer Larsen (eds.), pp. 77–119. New York: Wiley-Liss.

Markov, G. G.
  2001 Microgeographical Non-Metrical Cranial Diversity of the Fat Dormous (*Glis glis* L.). *Trakya University Journal of Scientific Research* 2(2):115–119.

Millaire, Jean-François
  2005 Woven Identities in Gallinazo Textiles from Huaca Santa Clara, Virú Valley. Paper presented at the 45th Annual Meeting of the Institute of Andean Studies, University of California, Berkeley.

Montoya, María
  1997 Excavaciones en la unidad 11 de la Plataforma I de la Huaca de la Luna. In *Investigaciones en la Huaca de la Luna 1995*, Santiago Uceda, Elías Mujica, and Ricardo Morales (eds.), pp. 23–28. Trujillo: Facultad de Ciencias Sociales, Universidad Nacional de La Libertad.

Moseley, M. Edward
  1975 Prehistoric Principles of Labor Organization in the Moche Valley, Peru. *American Antiquity* 40(2):191–196.

Muñoz Ovalle, Iván, Bernardo Arriaza Torres, and Arthur C. Aufderheide (editors)
  1993 *Acha-2 y los orígenes del poblamiento humano en Arica.* Arica: Ediciones Universidad de Tarapaca.

Nichol, Christian R.
  1989 Complex Segregation Analysis of Dental Morphological Variants. *American Journal of Physical Anthropology* 78(1):37–59.

Norusis, Marija J.
  1994 *SPSS Professional Statistics 6.1.* Chicago: SPSS.

Portin, Petter, and Lassi Alvesalo
  1974 The Inheritance of Shovel Shape in Maxillary Central Incisors. *American Journal of Physical Anthropology* 41(1):59–62.

Powell, Joseph F.
  1993 Dental Evidence for the Peopling of the New World: Some Methodological Considerations. *Human Biology* 65(5):799–819.

  1995 Dental Variation and Biological Affinity among Middle Holocene Human Populations in North America. Unpublished Ph.D. dissertation, Texas A&M University, College Station.

Powell, Joseph F., and Walter A. Neves
  1999 Craniofacial Morphology of the First Americans: Patterns and Process in the Peopling of the New World. *Yearbook of Physical Anthropology* 42:153–188.

Rightmire, G. Philip
  1999 Dental Variation and Human History. *Review of Archaeology* 20(2):1–3.

Sciulli, Paul W.
  1990 Deciduous Dentition of a Late Archaic Population of Ohio. *Human Biology* 62(2):221–245.

Scott, G. Richard
  1977 Classification, Sex Dimorphism, Association, and Population Variation of the Canine Distal Accessory Ridge. *Human Biology* 49(3):453–469.

  1980 Population Variation of Carabelli's Trait. *Human Biology* 52(1):63–78.

Scott, G. Richard, and Christy G. Turner
  1997 *The Anthropology of Modern Human Teeth: Dental Morphology and Its Variation in Recent Human Populations.* Cambridge, UK: Cambridge University Press.

Shimada, Izumi
  2004 Comments on the "Southern Moche: Understanding the First Expansionist State on the North Coast of Peru." Paper presented at the 69th Annual Meeting of the Society for American Archaeology, Montreal. (See electronic publication at *www.anthro.umontreal.ca/colloques/2004/SAA04/index.html*)

Shimada, Izumi, and Robert Corruccini
  2005 Comments on "The Nature of Moche Human Sacrifice" by Richard C. Sutter and Rosa J. Cortez. *Current Anthropology* 46(4): 540–541.

Shimada, Izumi, Ken-ichi Shinoda, Steve Bourget, Walter Alva, and Santiago Uceda
  2005 MtDNA Analysis of Mochica and Sicán Populations of Pre-Hispanic Peru. In *Biomolecular Archaeology: Genetic Approaches to the Past*, David M. Reed (ed.), pp. 61–92. Carbondale: Center for Archaeological Investigations, Southern Illinois University.

Shinoda, Ken-ichi, Izumi Shimada, Walter Alva, and Santiago Uceda
  2002 DNA Analysis of Moche and Sican Populations: Results and Implications. Paper presented at the 67th Annual Meeting of the Society for American Archaeology, Denver.

Sjøvold, Torstein
  1973 The Occurrence of Minor Non-Metrical Variants in the Skeleton and Their Quantitative Treatment for Population Comparisons. *Homo* 24:204–233.

  1977 Non-Metrical Divergence between Skeletal Populations: The Theoretical Foundation and Biological Importance of C.A.B. Smith's Mean Measure of Divergence. *OSSA* [*International Journal of Skeletal Research*] 4 (Supplement 1).

Sneath, Peter H. A., and Robert R. Sokal
  1973 *Numerical Taxonomy: The Principles and Practice of Numerical Classification.* San Fransisco: W. H. Freeman.

Sofaer, Jeffrey A., C. J. MacLean, and Howard L. Bailit
  1972 Heredity and Morphological Variation in Early and Late Developing Human Teeth of the Same Morphological Class. *Archives of Oral Biology* 17:811–816.

Sofaer, Jeffrey A., Patricia Smith, and Edith Kaye
  1986 Affinities between Contemporary and Skeletal Jewish and Non-Jewish Groups Based on Tooth Morphology. *American Journal of Physical Anthropology* 70(2):265–275.

Standen, Vivien G., and Calogero M. Santoro
  2004 Patrón funerario arcaico temprano del sitio Acha-3 y su relación con Chinchorro: Cazadores, pescadores, y recolectores de la costa norte de Chile. *Latin American Antiquity* 15 (1): 89–109.

Sutter, Richard C.
  1997 Dental Variation and Biocultural Affinities among Prehistoric Populations from the Coastal Valleys of Moquegua, Peru, and Azapa, Chile. Unpublished Ph.D. dissertation, University of Missouri, Columbia.
  2000 Prehistoric Genetic and Culture Change: A Bioarchaeological Search for Pre-Inka Altiplano Colonies in the Coastal Valleys of Moquegua, Peru, and Azapa, Chile. *Latin American Antiquity* 11(1):43–70.
  2005a A Bioarchaeological Assessment of Prehistoric Ethnicity among Early Late Intermediate Period Populations of the Azapa Valley, Chile. In *Us and Them: Archaeology and Ethnicity in the Andes*, Richard M. Reycraft (ed.), pp. 183–205. Los Angeles: Cotsen Institute of Archaeology, University of California.
  2005b The Prehistoric Peopling of South America as Inferred from Epigenetic Dental Traits. *Andean Past* 7:183–217.
  2008 Prehistoric Population Dynamics in the Peruvian Andes. In *Andean Civilization: A Tribute to Michael E. Moseley*, Joyce Marcus and Patrick R. Williams (eds.), pp. 9–38. Los Angeles: Cotsen Institute of Archaeology, University of California.

Sutter, Richard C., and Rosa J. Cortez
  2005 The Nature of Moche Human Sacrifice: A Bio-Archaeological Perspective. *Current Anthropology* 46(4):521–549.

Tello, Ricardo
  1997 Excavaciones en la unidad 12 de la Plataforma I de la Huaca de la Luna. In *Investigaciones en la Huaca de la Luna 1995*, Santiago Uceda, Elías Mujica, and Ricardo Morales (eds.), pp.

29–37. Trujillo: Facultad de Ciencias Sociales, Universidad Nacional de La Libertad.

Tello, Ricardo, José Armas, and Claude Chapdelaine
  2003 Prácticas funerarias moche en el complejo arqueológico Huacas del Sol y de la Luna. In *Moche: Hacia el final del milenio*, Santiago Uceda and Elías Mujica (eds.), vol. 1, pp. 151–187. Lima: Universidad Nacional de Trujillo and Fondo Editorial, Pontificia Universidad Católica del Perú.

Topic, Theresa L.
  1982 The Early Intermediate Period and Its Legacy. In *Chan Chan: Andean Desert City*, Michael E. Moseley and Kent C. Day (eds.), pp. 255–284. Albuquerque: University of New Mexico Press.

Tufinio, Moisés
  2000 Excavaciones en la unidad 13, frontis norte de la Plataforma I de la Huaca de la Luna. In *Investigaciones en la Huaca de la Luna 1997*, Santiago Uceda, Elías Mujica, and Ricardo Morales (eds.), pp. 33–39. Trujillo: Facultad de Ciencias Sociales, Universidad Nacional de Trujillo.

Turner, Christy G.
  1983 Dental Evidence for the Peopling of the Americas. In *Early Man in the New World*, Richard Shutler (ed.), pp. 147–157. Berverly Hills, California: Sage Publications.
  1985 The Dental Search for Native American Origins. In *Out of Asia: Peopling the Americas and the Pacific*, Robert Kirk and Emöke Szathmary (eds.), pp. 31–78. Canberra, Australia: Journal of Pacific History.
  1987 Late Pleistocene and Holocene Population History of East Asia Based on Dental Variation. *American Journal of Physical Anthropology* 73(3):305–321.
  1990 Major Features of Sundadonty and Sinodonty, Including Suggestions about East Asian Microevolution, Population History, and Late Pleistocene Relationships with Australian Aboriginals. *American Journal of Physical Anthropology* 82(3):295–317.

Turner, Christy G., and G. Richard Scott
  1977 Dentition of Easter Islanders. In *Orofacial Growth and Development*, Albert A. Dahlberg and Thomas M. Graber (eds.), pp. 229–249. The Hague: Mouton Publishers.

Turner, Christy G., Christian R. Nichol, and G. Richard Scott
  1991 Scoring Procedures for Key Morphological Traits of the Permanent Dentition: The Arizona State University Dental Anthropology System. In *Advances in Dental Anthropology*, Marc A. Kelley and Clark Spencer Larsen (eds.), pp. 13–31. New York: Wiley-Liss.

Uceda, Santiago
  2001 Investigations at Huaca de la Luna, Moche
        Valley: An Example of Moche Religious
        Architecture. In *Moche Art and Archaeology in
        Ancient Peru*, Joanne Pillsbury (ed.), pp. 47–67.
        Washington, D.C.: National Gallery of Art
        and Yale University Press.
Vallejos, Miriam
  1982 El hombre preagricola de las cuevas Tres Ven-
        tanas de Chilca, Perú: Textilería. *Zonas aridas*
        (Lima) 2:21–32.
Verano, John W.
  1994 Características físicas y biología osteológica
        de los Moche. In *Moche: Propuestas y pers-
        pectivas*, Santiago Uceda and Elías Mujica
        (eds.), pp. 307–326. Travaux de l'Institut

Français d'Études Andines 79. Lima: Univer-
        sidad Nacional de La Libertad and Instituto
        Francés de Estudios Andinos.
  2001 War and Death in the Moche World: Osteo-
        logical Evidence and Visual Discourse. In
        Moche Art and Archaeology in Ancient Peru,
        Joanne Pillsbury (ed.), pp. 111–125. Wash-
        ington, D.C.: National Gallery of Art and
        Yale University Press.
Wijsman, Ellen M., and Walter A. Neves
  1986 The Use of Nonmetric Variation in Estimat-
        ing Human Population Admixture: A Test
        Case with Brazilian Blacks, Whites, and
        Mulattos. *American Journal of Physical Anthro-
        pology* 70(3):395–405.

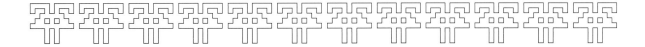

CHAPTER 9

WOVEN IDENTITIES IN THE VIRÚ VALLEY

Jean-François Millaire

What we wear transforms our appearance. We speak silently, signaling layers of meaning through our clothing.

Margot Blum Schevill (1991:3)

In the Americas, the ancient past is usually explored through the concept of archaeological cultures (defined by recurring assemblages of artifacts in time and across space) generally assumed to be representative of groups of people who lived in a given area during a certain period. The term *culture* is therefore understood as the material manifestation of the producers and users of artifacts, and archaeologists usually tacitly agree that a careful study of *material culture* is adequate for defining the social characteristics of their creators.

This view has led to the persistent suggestion that *style* is a reflection of *identity*, and to the more challenging submission that "identity genealogies" can be reconstructed through the careful mapping of styles across time and space. Over the last 50 years, however, basic conceptions of the relation between patterns in material culture and ethnic identity have been challenged (Binford and

Binford 1966; Hodder 1982; Conkey and Hastorf 1990), and today a majority of scholars recognize the complexity of research into ancient identity. As a result, most archaeologists are now aware of the fact that material culture does not simply *reflect* identity but can *structure* and *be structured by* aspects of individual and communal identities (Emberling 1997; S. Jones 1997; Díaz-Andreu et al. 2005; Reycraft 2005; Insoll 2007).

In the Andean region, most archaeological cultures were originally defined on the basis of ceramic styles alone (Willey 1945), although subsequent research in each area usually led to finer-grained characterizations of local cultural history (with research on settlement patterns, architecture, funerary practices, and so forth). That being said, ceramics are still widely regarded as the primary source of information for reconstructing local and regional cultural sequences.

While doing so, Andeanists presume that each culture expressed its identity (at least to some extent) through the production and use of specific types of containers with particular forms and decoration. Yet, in most cases it is impossible to

149

know to what extent identity was expressed through this channel. As a result, it is only fair to say that Andeanists are extremely ill equipped to study ancient identity if they limit their inquiry to the production and use of clay pots.

This chapter stresses the importance of combining the study of ceramics with a wider array of material manifestations in order to assess ancient identities through multivariate lines of evidence. More specifically, I argue that textiles (in conjunction with ceramics, architecture, and other material evidence) hold great potential for reconstructing ancient identities in the Andes, a thesis that will sound like a truism to most Andean textile specialists.

Indeed, throughout the Andes, textiles appear to have been a very important channel for expressing ethnic affiliation (Schevill 1991; Schevill, Berlo, and Dwyer 1991; Oakland 1992). As Amy Oakland noted, more than any other category of artifacts, textiles are the ethnic markers *par excellence* throughout the Andean region, providing archaeologists with a powerful tool for identifying distinct groups in prehistoric contexts (Oakland 1992:318). The present research therefore partly relies on the premise that textiles have served (and still serve) as identity markers in the Andean region.

In this regard, recent archaeological fieldwork in the Virú Valley has produced interesting data on some discrepancies that can exist between ceramics and textiles as sources of information. This chapter presents preliminary results from excavations carried out at Huaca Santa Clara, a medium-size administrative center in the middle Virú Valley.

The discovery of an exceptional collection of textiles led me to reexamine the cultural characterization of three "archaeological cultures" from the Peruvian north coast: Gallinazo, Virú, and Moche. Indeed, Huaca Santa Clara offered an incomparable opportunity to study collections of utilitarian and fine-ware ceramics in conjunction with textiles from the very same contexts and hence most likely manufactured and used by the same people. These collections therefore offer great potential for studying ancient identities as expressed through various channels of materiality.

GALLINAZO AS A CULTURAL SUBSTRATE

As I argued in the introductory chapter of this volume, I believe we Andeanists have made two important mistakes in studying what is commonly known as the Gallinazo culture. First, archaeologists have compounded two ceramic ensembles under the label "Gallinazo": incised and appliquéd pottery (mainly domestic in nature and originally classified as Castillo Incised and Castillo Modeled types by members of the Virú Valley Project) and negative-painted, fancy ceramic vessels defined as Gallinazo Negative ware (Ford and Willey 1949; Bennett 1950; Strong and Evans 1952; Willey 1953; Collier 1955).

Prior to the roundtable in Trujillo, it had become clear to me that incised and appliquéd pottery—the typical "Gallinazo" face-neck jars (Figure 9.1)—types were found in every valley of the Peruvian north coast. On the other hand, based on my own research I understood Gallinazo Negative ceramics (Figure 9.2) to represent a corporate ware, the production of which was largely restricted to the Virú Valley. The Trujillo roundtable was therefore partly aimed at testing this hypothesis and at refining our understanding of what I preferred to call the "Gallinazo phenomenon."

From what we heard at this meeting and from the written contributions included in this volume, those two ceramic ensembles indeed should never have been compounded under the same label, as they represent two very different material manifestations. The first corresponds to a pan–north-coast tradition of utilitarian ceramics, often decorated with coarse incised and modeled designs. I believe these containers and their style should be simply referred to as "Gallinazo." The second (Gallinazo Negative) clearly corresponds to corporate-style ceramics produced by Virú artisans. The term "Virú ceramic" therefore seems to represent the best label for this earthenware ensemble.

It now becomes interesting to reexamine north-coast cultural history including other forms of material manifestation. For example, it is clear that societies that produced and used ceramics of Vicús, Moche, and Virú styles shared a common

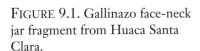

FIGURE 9.1. Gallinazo face-neck jar fragment from Huaca Santa Clara.

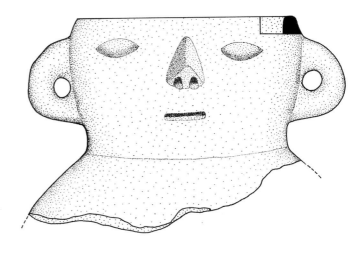

FIGURE 9.2. Gallinazo Negative *canchero* from Huaca Santa Clara.

architectural tradition—although regionalisms obviously existed. In parallel with monumental buildings, domestic architecture would seem to be a promising research avenue, but it is still scantily known outside the Moche Valley (Brennan 1980; Bawden 1982, 1990; Moore 1992; Billman 1999; van Gijseghem 2001; Chapdelaine 2002; Makowski 2002).

Similarly, metallurgy might offer an interesting angle for studying the nature of this pan–north-coast tradition and documenting regionalisms (J. Jones 1979; Schorsch 1998; Centeno and Schorsch 2000; Kaulicke 2006). Funerary practices—because they are inevitably deeply

rooted in tradition but can nevertheless be subject to political manipulations (Kroeber 1927; Cannon 1989; Millaire 2002)—are also a promising field of study, although here again our sample is heavily skewed toward Moche.

Since recent fieldwork at the site of Huaca Santa Clara, a collection of textiles associated with fine Virú and utilitarian Gallinazo ceramics has become available for study, providing us with an unprecedented corpus of material from other-than-Moche contexts. The results from preliminary analyses of these fabrics discussed in this chapter will hopefully contribute to this inquiry into ancient identities along the Peruvian littoral.

Huaca Santa Clara

The Virú polity developed between approximately 200 B.C. and A.D. 700, a period marked by major social, economic, and political developments along the north coast of Peru, the most important being the development of Moche. Indeed, evidence indicates that one or several Moche centers undertook a hegemonic policy in about the fourth century A.D., imposing some form of control over the valleys south of Moche.

To document the nature of the mechanisms used to foster the integration of populations from diverse cultural backgrounds within the Moche political and religious sphere, between 2001 and 2005 I conducted a research project at Huaca Santa Clara in Virú, a settlement assumed by members of the Virú Valley Project to have fallen under Moche rule (Willey 1953). Soon this project became a full-fledged investigation of the Virú polity through the study of one of its satellite administrative centers. Huaca Santa Clara is located in the middle valley, south of the Virú River (Figure 9.3). The settlement consists of a series of adobe platforms built on the flanks of a small hill that dominates the landscape near the present-day village of Virú.

Huaca Santa Clara was one of several settlements that formed part of the Virú city-state system. These sites can easily be classified into three broad categories. The first corresponds to the Gallinazo Group, a site believed to have been Virú's capital city (Bennett 1950; Fogel 1993). The distribution of the Gallinazo Group platforms is interesting in that rather than a *group*, it really represents a *string* of buildings laid out along an axis that follows the natural path hikers would take when traveling south along the coastal plain.

The second category of sites includes a number of medium-size administrative settlements often described as citadels (*castillos*). Six of these centers (Castillo de Tomaval, Castillo de San Juan, Sarraque, Virú Viejo, Castillo de Napo, and Huaca Santa Clara) were strategically perched on hilltops. The third category of settlements corresponds to small platforms and hamlets scattered throughout the valley floor. According to

FIGURE 9.3. Map of Virú Valley. *Illustration courtesy of NASA Landsat Program 2000, Landsat ETM+ scene ELP009R066_7T20000602, SLC-Off, USGS, Sioux Falls.*

Gordon Willey, the citadels, together with the Gallinazo Group, formed the backbone of the valley's political infrastructure: a hierarchical system of settlements in which the population was drawn to major administrative sites, each controlling part of the valley floor (Willey 1953: 378–382).

At Huaca Santa Clara, we first mapped all pre-Hispanic structures still visible at the surface. Excavations were then carried out in various sectors to document Virú architecture (Millaire 2004). Residential architecture was uncovered at the top of the settlement, accessible only through a complex system of steps and baffled entrances. The administrative nature of the settlement was confirmed after the discovery of large-scale storage

facilities for agricultural products on the three lower natural terraces of the hill.

Throughout the excavation process, typical Virú ceramics (Gallinazo Negative, Carmelo Negative, Gallinazo Broad-Line Incised, Callejón, Queneto Polished) were recovered from undisturbed contexts, providing solid data for assessing the cultural affiliation of the site. Six samples of organic material from excavations in open areas and deep stratified deposits were analyzed using the radiometric dating method. As can be seen in Figure 9.4, when calibrated using two standard deviations,[1] these dates indicate that the Virú occupation of the site lasted for a long period, as all intercepts of radiocarbon age are enclosed between 10 B.C. and A.D. 670.

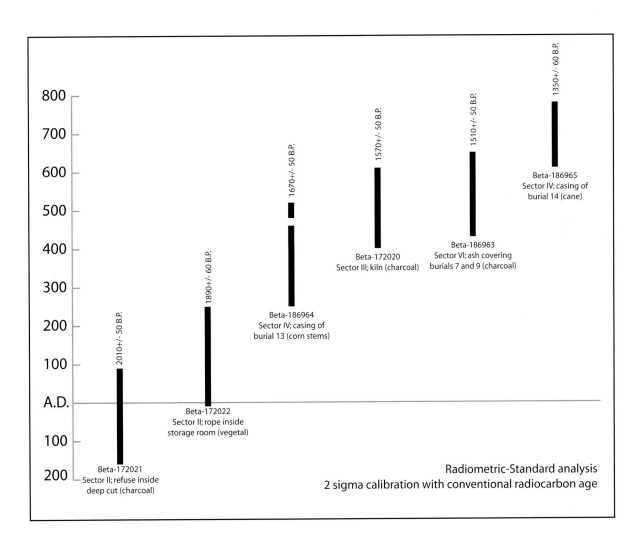

FIGURE 9.4. Radiocarbon dates from the Virú occupation at Huaca Santa Clara.

VIRÚ TEXTILES

During the excavation process, more than 700 textile fragments were uncovered from superficial levels, living areas, storage facilities, and burials. This collection is unique in that it represents the first systematic data set of Virú textiles from a secure archaeological context. Fortunately, these fragments were unusually well preserved, thanks to the elevation of the settlement in relation to the valley floor.

Most of these textiles were found on the eastern flank of the hill, an area protected from the salty winds of the Pacific Ocean. The textile fragments under study were made using a variety of techniques. After analysis, the material was classified into three broad categories: fabrics with continuous warps and wefts, tapestries, and compound weaves.

Fabrics with Continuous Warps and Wefts

More than 70% of all fragments from Huaca Santa Clara were plain weaves. Of all plain-weave fragments analyzed, more than 99% were made entirely of cotton. Most yarns were S-spun and unplied. Seventy-five fragments were made of basket weave, obtained by combining two threads of warp, of weft, or of both in a plain-weave pattern. The fabrics were therefore manufactured by

crossing systems of threads rather than by individual threads (Seiler-Baldinger 1994:88).

Most of these fabrics were undecorated, but some were made with pairs of threads of different color; others were decorated with warp or weft stripes of varying colors. One fabric was decorated with stylized catfish motifs (Figure 9.5). This fabric was also unusual in being made with yarns of Z-spun and S-plied camelid fibers re-plied in Z. Other fragments of plain weave were decorated with circular designs made with the tie-dye technique, whereas a few fabrics were decorated with simple embroidered designs.

Twill weaves were less common. Only 27 fragments were identified. The main feature of twill weaves is that weft threads are passed over one warp thread and then under two or more warps, over one and under two or more warps, and so forth, producing characteristic diagonal ribs (O'Neale 1946). Most of the fragments recovered were made entirely of undyed S-spun cotton yarns, but four fragments were made of red-colored camelid fibers.

Our excavations also led to the discovery of a collection of warp-faced fabrics, produced by a technique that creates fabrics in which only one system of threads is visible (Figure 9.6). Most of these textiles were adorned with stripes in shades of cream and brown. In the Andean region,

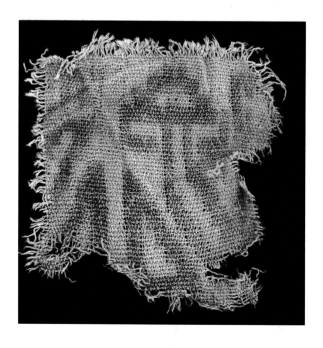

FIGURE 9.5. Photograph and drawing of plain weave with catfish motifs from Huaca Santa Clara.

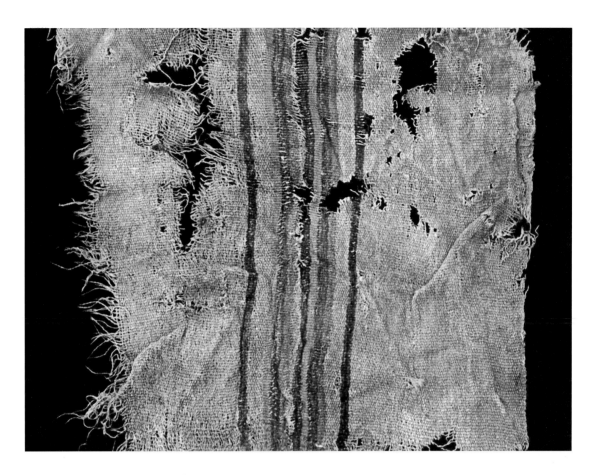

FIGURE 9.6. Warp-faced fabric from Huaca Santa Clara.

warp-patterned weaves are traditionally associated with the highland and with the southern portion of the coastal plain (Rowe 1977; Oakland 1992).

The discovery of 53 fragments of warp-faced fabrics in association with utilitarian Gallinazo and fine-ware Virú ceramics was therefore a surprise to us. Even stranger was the fact that nearly all of these fabrics were made of camelid hair and that the threads were systematically Z-spun and S-plied. All of these structural characteristics seem foreign to the north coast. Based on preliminary evidence, it could be argued that these textiles were products of exchange.

Tapestry Weaves

A large proportion of the fabrics recovered consisted of tapestry weaves. Tapestries from Huaca Santa Clara fall into two broad categories: tapestries with discontinuous and interlocking warps and wefts, and tapestries with continuous warps.

Our collection includes 17 tapestry weaves made with discontinuous and interlocking warps and wefts (Figure 9.7). Each consisted of a series of sections of fabric of distinct color, visually reminiscent of patchwork (O'Neale 1933). Unlike patchwork, however, the various portions of the fabric were not sewn but interlocked.

The majority of tapestries uncovered were made of continuous warps and discontinuous weft, however. All of these but two were made with unplied S-spun cotton warps. Wefts were of cotton or camelid hair. Cotton wefts were generally S-spun and unplied, whereas most camelid hair wefts were S-spun and Z-plied. Unlike the warp-faced fabrics cited previously, these colorful yarns were spun according to the coastal spinning technique. In most cases, the wefts changed direction without an interlock, creating vertical slits between the colored areas (a feature typical of coastal textiles).

This type of tapestry comprises some of the most impressive fabrics uncovered at Huaca Santa

FIGURE 9.7. Tapestry with discontinuous and interlocking warps and wefts from Huaca Santa Clara.

Clara. All textiles except one were made with colored wefts, and they present the most elaborate designs. Some specimens display geometric or curvilinear motifs, whereas others show figurative designs. Animals are represented in a few cases. For example, one tapestry fragment is adorned with at least two rows of fish executed in four distinct colors (Figure 9.8).

Another presents a fringe decorated with a series of felines, and others are adorned with stylized catfish motifs (Figure 9.9). Two tapestry fragments are adorned with human characters. The first fragment shows a series of human heads,

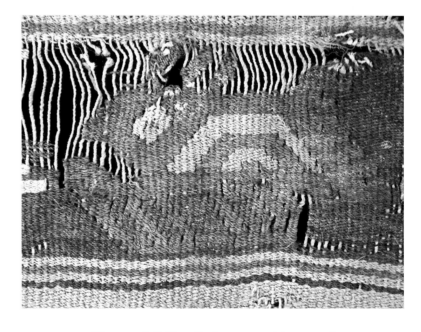

FIGURE 9.8. Detail of tapestry with rows of fish from Huaca Santa Clara.

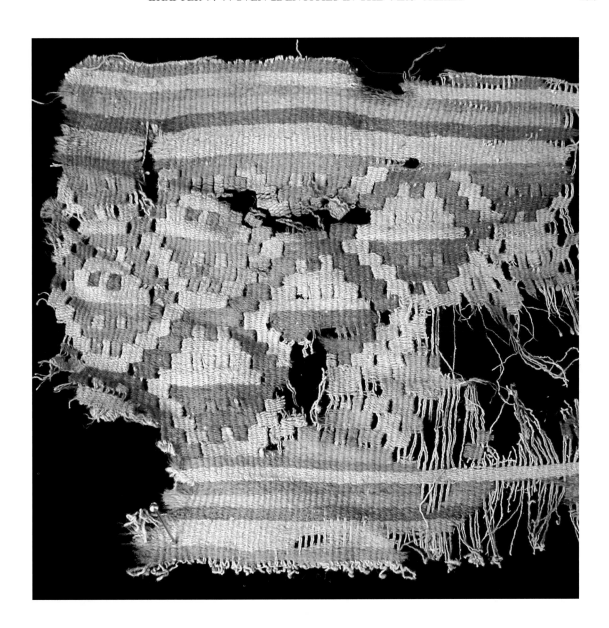

FIGURE 9.9. Tapestry with interlocked catfish motifs from Huaca Santa Clara.

as well as a war mace and a round shield. The other tapestry (Figure 9.10)—one of the most elaborate textiles recovered at Huaca Santa Clara—depicts a series of human figures, with elaborated headdresses, standing next to what appear to be clubs and rectangular shields.

Finally, two tapestry fragments are decorated with highly complex motifs. The first (Figure 9.11) shows a series of crested animals, sometimes referred to as the "Lunar Animal" or "Moon Animal" (Mackey and Vogel 2003). These animals have clawed legs, a crested head, and elongated appendages on their backs and below their lower

jaws. This textile is decorated with squared patterns with distinct background colors. The squares are organized to form a stepped motif. Within each square is a crested animal, whose body contrasts with the background.

A textile uncovered by Wendell Bennett at the Gallinazo Group is adorned with similar figures (Bennett 1939:Fig. 15a). The second textile is a very large mantle originally decorated with four double-headed fox-serpents. This theme is also highly common in north-coast art, but it is the first example known from a secure Virú context.

FIGURE 9.10. Elaborate tapestry with human characters from Huaca Santa Clara.

FIGURE 9.11. Elaborate tapestry with crested animal motifs from Huaca Santa Clara.

Compound Weaves

Another type of fabric uncovered at Huaca Santa Clara corresponds to what Irene Emery defines as "compound weaves" (Emery 1966:140). It includes examples of supplemental-weft weaves and double-weave fabrics. The collection comprises seven textiles with discontinuous supplemental wefts (in all but two cases the wefts were made of camelid hair).

Only two examples of double weaves were uncovered at Huaca Santa Clara. With this technique, two fabrics were produced, one over the other, by means of four sets of elements. The first double cloth uncovered appears to have been a cushion of some sort, prepared from a single, long band of fabric folded and sewn closed. The fabric was made of two layers of beige cotton basket weave, one of which was of a slightly lighter tone than the other.

The pattern obtained through the double-weave process consists of a series of stylized catfish motifs. Catfish motifs were also found on a second double-weave fabric (Figure 9.12), which has two layers of cotton plain weaves, one made with blue yarn and the other with cream threads. In this case, note that the stylized catfish heads are set in rhombuses and that their eyes are highlighted on one side with embroidered squares.

Fabric Quality

Most of the fragments were too small to permit identification of the original woven works, but from the better-preserved fragments we were able to identify a variety of garments and accessories that were likely worn by the local residents or brought to the site as part of a local tribute payment system. The corpus includes several examples of loincloths, shirts, waistbands, and mantles. Based on the techniques and materials used, and on the overall aesthetic quality of the fabrics, Virú textiles can be classified into three broad categories: plain clothes, decorated garments, and fabrics of exceptional quality.

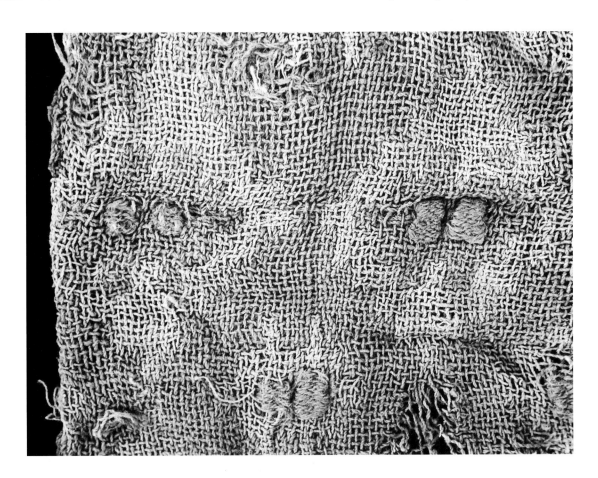

FIGURE 9.12. Double-weave fabric with catfish motifs from Huaca Santa Clara.

Numerous plain clothes were uncovered at Huaca Santa Clara. These correspond to undecorated plain-weave cotton textiles in shades of beige and brown. Such textiles were produced everywhere along the coastal plain prior to the Spanish conquest and therefore provide very little information on ancient group identities.

The second group of textiles is much more interesting in the context of the present study: it comprises garments produced with more elaborate weaving techniques (e.g., Figures 9.5, 9.7–9.9, 9.12) and usually adorned with some form of decoration. These fabrics were likely woven by the wearers or by members of the individual's household (Millaire 2008), although contextual information is still missing on local textile production. It could be argued that the designs woven into these fabrics correspond in one way or another to their owner's identity—reflecting or claiming it, or contributing to its construction (Oakland 1992). Current evidence suggests that these textiles were not the best-quality fabric produced in Virú, however.

At Huaca Santa Clara, only a few textile fragments of exceptional quality were uncovered: fabrics that were probably worn by or destined to be used by the valley rulers or members of their court (e.g., Figures 9.10, 9.11). These fabrics are extraordinary in structural complexity and aesthetic achievement, and were clearly made by outstanding artisans. As such, they likely conveyed imagery that "branded" local rulers relative to other coastal leaders, in a manner similar to the way fine-ware ceramics appear to have emphasized localness within the larger north-coast ceramic tradition. In other words, these fabrics might have been the textile equivalent of Vicús, Moche, or Virú wares: a material manifestation that underscored the identity of the locals (*us*) in relation to others (*them*).

VIRÚ TEXTILES AND THE *TRADICIÓN NORCOSTEÑA*

Until now, relatively few textiles were available for defining Virú textile style. As seen here, the most salient characteristic of elaborate Virú fabrics was the use of undyed cotton in plain weaves and the use of camelid hair dyed in bright colors for creating sophisticated designs on slit tapestries and fabrics with supplemental wefts. This largely confirms William Conklin's insight that one of the most salient features of textile production in Virú was the use of camelid fibers in a region where until then only cotton was apparently used (Conklin 1975:18; 1978:300).

However, as more than one north-coast specialist said when examining this collection, one is struck not by Virú textiles' artistic and technical idiosyncrasy, but by their belonging to the wider north-coast textile tradition. Indeed, on the basis of the techniques used, the internal structure of the fabrics, and the motifs represented, most textiles from this collection are typically *norcosteños*.

Huaca Santa Clara textiles are structurally closely related to fabrics produced elsewhere in the valley and by neighboring groups who produced and used Moche-style ceramics. In Virú, Junius Bird published preliminary notes from his analysis of some of the textiles recovered by members of the Virú Valley Project (Bird 1952). The fabrics examined were found in contexts originally defined as "Gallinazo" or as "Mochica" (succeeding periods) based on ceramic association, but these cultural ascriptions would of course need to be revised based on the advances made during the Trujillo roundtable. Interestingly, Bird found that textiles from his "Gallinazo" and "Mochica" contexts were constructed using the same types of yarn and exhibited minor variation between the two groups of fabrics (Bird 1952: 357–360).

A similar pattern emerges from a stylistic analysis of the fabrics. At Huaca Santa Clara, one of the most common motifs was the stepped pattern (Figure 9.7), a design found throughout the Andes. Another pan-Andean theme was the feline, represented on a tapestry fragment from our collection. Other motifs were essentially norcosteños. This is clearly the case of the stylized catfish, recurrent throughout this collection, a theme also widely represented on Moche fabrics and found on other media from this neighboring society. For example, it represents the second most important design on Huaca de la Luna sculpted friezes (Bourget 1994; Uceda 2001:Figs. 10, 11) and is widely represented on Salinar and Moche ceramics (Larco Hoyle 2001 [1938–1940]).

Incidentally, the stylized catfish is also found on a painted mural from the site of Huancaco (in Virú), a settlement occupied during the terminal Early Intermediate period (Bourget 2001:Fig. 71). Another *norteño* design used to adorn Virú fabrics is the crested animal, a motif also found on pyro-engraved gourds and ceramics at Huaca Santa Clara and widely represented in Moche, Recuay, and Chimú art.

Beyond Virú, in the Santa Valley, a collection of textiles from residential contexts excavated and analyzed by Christopher Donnan featured weaves, decoration, and patterning comparable to those of textiles documented at Huaca Santa Clara (Donnan 1973; Conklin 1978). More recently, a collection of textiles from the site of El Castillo was excavated by Claude Chapdelaine and his team. Again, preliminary analyses suggest that the locals produced fabrics that were extremely close structurally and stylistically to Virú textiles, although regionalisms were also noted (Chapdelaine and Pimentel 2003; Claude Chapdelaine, personal communication, 2008).

Regrettably, the Moche Valley provides a poor environment for textile preservation, and only a relatively small number of textiles have been recovered and analyzed in some detail. Based on a collection recovered by Max Uhle at Huacas de Moche, Lila O'Neale published the earliest study of Early Intermediate–period textiles, noting the prominence of undecorated cotton plain weaves and the importance of brocaded cloths (supplementary wool weft) featuring geometric designs (O'Neale 1947:244–245; Conklin 1978).

William Conklin and Eduardo Versteylen later analyzed textiles from a Moche III burial from Huaca del Sol (Conklin and Versteylen 1978), highlighting the importance of twill as a weaving technique and describing two elaborate artifacts uncovered during the excavation. The first is a pouch made of double cloth, decorated with a scene divided into two panels (Conklin and Versteylen 1978:Fig. 4). The top panel depicts a human–snail being (a common theme in Moche art), whereas the lower panel shows a row of fish, a motif extremely similar to a pattern seen on a Virú tapestry from Huaca Santa Clara (Figure 9.8). The second artifact is a comb that features a crested animal, a theme popular in Virú (Figure

9.11) and Moche art. The textiles from this grave are also structurally similar to those from Huaca Santa Clara.

Farther north, textiles from the Moche occupation of Pacatnamú provide one of the best published data sets to which our data can be compared. Early Intermediate–period fabrics were first uncovered in 1938 by Heinrich Ubbelohde-Doering (1967, 1983; Conklin 1978). One tomb (tomb E1)—associated with Gallinazo incised and appliquéd pottery as well as with Moche-style ware—contained two exceptional slit tapestries decorated with a series of composite human–strobe-shell (*Strombus galeatus*) figures (Hecker and Hecker 1983:Fig. 35).

A large quantity of textiles was also later uncovered during excavations conducted at the Pacatnamú site, and analyzed by Christopher and Sharon Donnan. This collection comprises a wide range of fabrics, a few of which were probably elite objects. However, most clearly belonged to common people (Donnan and Donnan 1997: 231–232). At Pacatnamú, most textiles were of plain weave, although several examples of twills were identified. This collection also included elaborate fabrics, such as tapestries and double weaves. Several textiles were decorated with stripes, whereas others were decorated with stepped motifs.

The most salient design appears to have been the stylized catfish motif, however. Interestingly, on one fabric (Donnan and Donnan 1997:Fig. 2), the motifs were arranged in an interlocking pattern similar to that found at Huaca Santa Clara, and a head cloth was adorned with a pair of stylized catfish heads. Some of the most elaborate designs were found on double cloths, however. One piece uncovered was a bag adorned with an elaborately dressed warrior (Donnan and Donnan 1997:Fig. 13). This recalls a pattern on a textile from Huaca Santa Clara (Figure 9.10), which was uncovered some 130 km to the south.

Discovered still farther north, textiles from the tombs of Sipán are currently being analyzed by Heiko Prümers, whose initial analyses confirm that the fabrics buried with important individuals were manufactured by weavers who had technical skills and a symbolic repertoire in common with other coastal groups (Prümers 1995a, 1995b, 2000). For example, one of the fabrics examined by Prümers features a network of stylized catfish designs with square eyes (Prümers 1995a:Fig. 13) highly reminiscent of those found on the double weave shown in Figure 9.12.

Although Donnan and Donnan conclude their analysis of the Pacatnamú collection by describing what they see as the structuring principle of the "Moche textile tradition," the characteristics they mention describe equally well the Virú fabrics from Huaca Santa Clara. Interestingly, a similar trend is observed when our collection is compared with textiles from the neighboring site of Huaca Dos Cabezas, a collection studied by María Jesús Jiménez (2000).

Again, although Jiménez defines the fabrics as typifying a "Moche textile style," I would argue that the collection can better be described as falling within a more inclusive norcosteña tradition. A cursory examination of textiles from contexts associated with Moche-style ceramics (largely from Pacatnamú) by Luis Jaime Castillo and Flora Ugaz (1999) seems to face the same predicament. In other words, textiles from contexts associated with Moche and Virú ceramics are much more closely related in terms of structure and visual art than scholars initially assumed.

These similarities hold true to the extent that it seems they were the product of a unique tradition, incorporating technical skills and artistic tastes drawn from the same cultural background. This is not what might be expected, considering the major differences these two societies show in terms of fine-ware ceramic art. The fact that these contemporaneous groups shared the same textile technology and wore cloths adorned with extremely similar designs should serve as a cautionary tale for all archaeologists presently working on the concept of identity using ceramic data alone.

As I am currently studying relations between Moche and Virú societies in the context of state formation on the north coast, how should I interpret this collection of textiles? I have argued elsewhere (Millaire 2004) that the Virú Valley residents apparently did not fall under the *direct* rule of war leaders from Huacas de Moche and that the local elites remained in control of the land and people until at least the terminal Early Intermediate period. The region was nevertheless probably affected by endemic competition between hegemonic city-states.

In this context, the north coast would have hosted not two opposing ethnic groups, but several polities of common cultural origin. Current evidence on utilitarian ceramics seems to indicate that Moche and Virú societies were closely related—occupying adjacent lands and engaged in constant economic and political interaction throughout the Early Intermediate period. These neighboring city-states probably shared part of their religious beliefs, artistic conventions, and symbolism. The data presented here also suggest that these societies shared much more than was previously thought in terms of technology, artistic expression, and dress code. As Amy Oakland argued, ethnicity:

> conforms to the view that different cultures can live side by side and do the same things, interacting yet maintaining their distinctiveness, or conversely members of one culture can live far apart and maintain their similarity. (Oakland 1992:318–319)

According to this view of culture, the variability related to the material record can be seen as a consequence of that distinctiveness in views and behavior within and between cultural groups (Pyszczyk 1989). If Oakland is right in arguing that textiles were the main channel through which ethnicity was visually expressed in the ancient Andes, similarities observed between Virú and Moche textiles in terms of structure and style are certainly meaningful and should be explored by all archaeologists interested in reconstructing north-coast cultural history.

ACKNOWLEDGMENTS

I wish to thank my wife, colleague, and editor, Magali Morlion, for her precious help in processing and analyzing the textile collection from Huaca Santa Clara. If she had not spent her time, talent, care, and patience on these fabrics, I can't see how they could have been studied so promptly. Without her, this and so many other enthralling projects would simply not have been possible.

NOTE

[1] All dates are calibrated using INTCAL 98 (Stuiver et al. 1998).

REFERENCES

Bawden, Garth
1982 Community Organization Reflected by the Household: A Study of Pre-Columbian Social Dynamics. *Journal of Field Archaeology* 9(2): 165–181.
1990 Domestic Space and Social Structure in Pre-Columbian Northern Peru. In *Domestic Architecture and the Use of Space: An Interdisciplinary Cross-Cultural Study*, Susan Kent (ed.), pp. 153–171. Cambridge, UK: Cambridge University Press.

Bennett, Wendell C.
1939 *Archaeology of the North Coast of Peru: An Account of Exploration and Excavation in Viru and Lambayeque Valleys.* Anthropological Papers of the American Museum of Natural History Vol. 37, Pt. 1. New York: The American Museum of Natural History.
1950 *The Gallinazo Group: Viru Valley, Peru.* Yale University Publications in Anthropology 43. New Haven: Yale University Press.

Billman, Brian R.
1999 Reconstructing Prehistoric Political Economies and Cycles of Political Power in the Moche Valley, Peru. In *Settlement Pattern Studies in the Americas: Fifty Years Since Virú*, Brian R. Billman and Gary M. Feinman (eds.), pp. 131–159. Washington, D.C.: Smithsonian Institution Press.

Binford, Lewis R., and Sally R. Binford
1966 A Preliminary Analysis of Functional Variability in the Mousterian of Levallois Facies. *American Anthropologist* 68(2):238–295.

Bird, Junius
1952 Appendix 3: Textile Notes. In *Cultural Stratigraphy in the Virú Valley, Northern Peru: The Formative and Florescent Epochs*, William D. Strong and Clifford Evans (eds.), pp. 357–360. New York: Columbia University Press.

Bourget, Steve
1994 El mar y la muerte en la iconografía moche. In *Moche: Propuestas y perspectivas*, Santiago Uceda and Elías Mujica (eds.), pp. 425–447. Travaux de l'Institut Français d'Études Andines 79. Lima: Universidad Nacional de La Libertad and Instituto Francés de Estudios Andinos.
2001 Proyecto Huancaco: Investigaciones arqueológicas del periodo Intermedio Temprano del valle de Virú, costa norte del Perú. Informe: Cuarta temporada. Unpublished report submitted to the Instituto Nacional de Cultura, Lima.

Brennan, Curtiss T.
1980 Cerro Arena: Early Cultural Complexity and Nucleation in North Coastal Peru. *Journal of Field Archaeology* 7(1):1–22.

Cannon, Aubrey
1989 The Historical Dimension in Mortuary Expressions of Status and Sentiment. *Current Anthropology* 30(4):437–458.

Castillo, Luis Jaime, and Flora Ugaz
1999 The Context and Technology of Mochica Textiles. In *Tejidos milenarios del Perú/Ancient Peruvian Textiles*, José Antonio de Lavalle and Rosario de Lavalle de Cárdenas (eds.), pp. 235–250. Lima: Integra AFP.

Centeno, Silvia A., and Deborah Schorsch
2000 The Characterisation of Gold Layers on Copper Artifacts from the Piura Valley (Peru) in the Early Intermediate Period. In *Gilded Metals: History, Technology and Conservation*, Terry Drayman-Weisser (ed.), pp. 223–240. London: Archetype Publications.

Chapdelaine, Claude
2002 Out in the Streets of Moche: Urbanism and Sociopolitical Organization at a Moche IV Urban Center. In *Andean Archaeology I: Variations in Sociopolitical Organization*, William H. Isbell and Helaine Silverman (eds.), pp. 53–88. New York: Kluwer Academic/Plenum Publishers.

Chapdelaine, Claude, and Víctor Pimentel
2003 Un tejido único Moche III del sitio Castillo de Santa: Una escena de cosecha de yuca. *Bulletin de l'Institut Français d'Études Andines* (Lima) 32(1):23–50.

Collier, Donald
1955 *Cultural Chronology and Change as Reflected in the Ceramics of the Virú Valley, Peru.* Chicago: Chicago Natural History Museum.

Conkey, Margaret W., and Christine A. Hastorf (editors)
1990 *The Uses of Style in Archaeology.* Cambridge, UK: Cambridge University Press.

Conklin, William J.
1975 An Introduction to South American Archaeological Textiles with Emphasis on Materials and Techniques of Peruvian Tapestry. In *Archaeological Textiles: Irene Emery Roundtable on Museum Textiles, 1974 Proceedings*, Patricia L. Fiske (ed.), pp. 17–30. Washington, D.C.: Textile Museum.
1978 Estructura de los tejidos moche. In *Tecnología andina*, Rogger Ravines (ed.), pp. 299–332. Lima: Instituto de Estudios Peruanos.

Conklin, William J., and Eduardo Versteylen
1978 Appendix 1: Textiles from a Pyramid of the Sun Burial. In *Ancient Burial Patterns of the*

Moche Valley, Peru, Christopher B. Donnan and Carol J. Mackey (eds.), pp. 384–398. Austin: University of Texas Press.

Díaz-Andreu, Margarita, Sam Lucy, Stasa Babic, and David N. Edwards
2005 *Archaeology of Identity: Approaches to Gender, Age, Status, Ethnicity and Religion*. London: Routledge.

Donnan, Christopher B.
1973 *Moche Occupation of the Santa Valley, Peru*. Berkeley: University of California Press.

Donnan, Christopher B., and Sharon G. Donnan
1997 Moche Textiles from Pacatnamu. In *The Pacatnamu Papers*, Volume 2: *The Moche Occupation*, Christopher B. Donnan and Guillermo A. Cock (eds.), pp. 215–242. Los Angeles: Fowler Museum of Cultural History, University of California.

Emberling, Geoff
1997 Ethnicity in Complex Societies: Archaeological Perspectives. *Journal of Archaeological Research* 5(4):295–344.

Emery, Irene
1966 *The Primary Structures of Fabrics*. Washington, D.C.: Textile Museum.

Fogel, Heidy
1993 Settlements in Time: A Study of Social and Political Development during the Gallinazo Occupation of the North Coast of Perú [sic]. Unpublished Ph.D. dissertation, Yale University, New Haven.

Ford, James A., and Gordon R. Willey (editors)
1949 *Surface Survey of the Virú Valley, Peru*. Anthropological Papers of the American Museum of Natural History Vol. 43, Pt. 1. New York: The American Museum of Natural History.

Hecker, Giesela, and Wolfgang Hecker
1983 Gräberbeschreibung. In *Vorspanische Gräber von Pacatnamú, Nordperu*, by Heinrich Ubbelohde-Doering, pp. 39–131. Materialien zur Allgemeinen und Vergleichenden Archäologie 26. Munich: C. H. Beck.

Hodder, Ian
1982 *Symbols in Action: Ethnoarchaeological Studies of Material Culture*. Cambridge, UK: Cambridge University Press.

Insoll, Timothy (editor)
2007 *The Archaeology of Identities: A Reader*. London: Routledge.

Jiménez, María Jesús
2000 Los tejidos moche de Dos Cabezas (valle de Jequetepeque): Hacia una definición del estilo textil mochica. In *Actas de la I Jornada internacional sobre textiles precolombinos*, Victòria Solanilla Demestre (ed.), pp. 76–96. Barcelona:

Departament d'Art, Universitat Autònoma de Barcelona and Institut Català de Cooperació Iberoamericana.

Jones, Julie
1979 Mochica Works of Art in Metal: A Review. In *Pre-Columbian Metallurgy of South America*, Elizabeth P. Benson (ed.), pp. 53–104. Washington, D.C.: Dumbarton Oaks Research Library and Collections.

Jones, Siân
1997 *The Archaeology of Ethnicity: Constructing Identities in the Past and Present*. London: Routledge.

Kaulicke, Peter
2006 The Vicús-Mochica Relationship. In *Andean Archaeology III: North and South*, William H. Isbell and Helaine Silverman (eds.), pp. 85–111. New York: Springer.

Kroeber, Alfred
1927 Disposal of the Dead. *American Anthropologist* 29:308–315.

Larco Hoyle, Rafael
2001 [1938–1940] *Los Mochicas*. 2 vols. Lima: Museo Arqueológico Rafael Larco Herrera.

Mackey, Carol, and Melissa Vogel
2003 La luna sobre los Andes: Una revisión del animal lunar. In *Moche: Hacia el final del milenio*, Santiago Uceda and Elías Mujica (eds.), vol. 1, pp. 325–342. Lima: Universidad Nacional de Trujillo and Fondo Editorial, Pontificia Universidad Católica del Perú.

Makowski, Krzysztof
2002 Arquitectura, estilo e identidad en el Horizonte Tardío: El sitio de Pueblo Viejo-Pucará, valle de Lurín. *Boletín de arqueología PUCP* (Lima) 6:137–170.

Millaire, Jean-François
2002 *Moche Burial Patterns: An Investigation into Prehispanic Social Structure*. BAR International Series 1066. Oxford: BAR.
2004 Moche Political Expansionism as Viewed from Virú: Recent Archaeological Work in the Close Periphery of a Hegemonic City-State System. In New Perspectives on the Moche Political Organization, Jeffrey Quilter, Luis Jaime Castillo, and Joanne Pillsbury (eds.), manuscript accepted for publication. Washington, D.C.: Dumbarton Oaks Research Library and Collection.
2008 Moche Textile Production on the Peruvian North Coast: A Contextual Analysis. In *The Art and Archaeology of the Moche: An Ancient Andean Society of the Peruvian North Coast*, Steve Bourget and Kimberly L. Jones (eds.), pp. 229–245. Austin: University of Texas Press.

Moore, Jerry D.

1992   Pattern and Meaning in Prehispanic Peruvian Architecture: The Architecture of Social Control in the Chimu State. *Latin American Antiquity* 3(2):95–113.

Oakland Rodman, Amy

1992   Textiles and Ethnicity: Tiwanaku in San Pedro de Atacama, North Chile. *Latin American Antiquity* 3(4):316–340.

O'Neale, Lila M.

1933   A Peruvian Multicolored Patchwork. *American Anthropologist* 35(1):87–94.

1946   Mochica (Early Chimu) and Other Peruvian Twill Fabrics. *Southwestern Journal of Anthropology* 2(3):269–294.

1947   A Note on Certain Mochica (Early Chimu) Textiles. *American Antiquity* 12(4):239–245.

Prümers, Heiko

1995a   Ein ungewöhnliches Moche-Gewebe aus dem Grab des "Fürsten von Sipán" (Lambayeque-Tal, Nordperu). *Beiträge zur Allgemeinen und Vergleichenden Archäologie* (Munich) 15:309–337.

1995b   Un tejido moche excepcional de la tumba del "Señor de Sipán" (Valle de Lambayeque, Perú). *Beiträge zur Allgemeinen und Vergleichenden Archäologie* (Munich) 15:338–369.

2000   Apuntes sobre los tejidos de la tumba del "Señor de Sipán," Perú. In *Actas de la I Jornada internacional sobre textiles precolombinos*, Victòria Solanilla Demestre (ed.), pp. 97–109. Barcelona: Departament d'Art, Universitat Autònoma de Barcelona and Institut Català de Cooperació Iberoamericana.

Pyszczyk, Heinz W.

1989   Consumption and Ethnicity: An Example for the Fur Trade in Western Canada. *Journal of Anthropological Archaeology* 8:213–249.

Reycraft, Richard Martin (editor)

2005   *Us and Them: Archaeology and Ethnicity in the Andes*. Los Angeles: Cotsen Institute of Archaeology, University of California.

Rowe, Ann P.

1977   *Warp-Patterned Weaves of the Andes*. Washington, D.C.: Textile Museum.

Schevill, Margot Blum

1991   The Communicative Power of Cloth and Its Creation. In *Textile Traditions of Mesoamerica and the Andes: An Anthology*, Margot Blum Schevill, Janet Catherine Berlo, and Edward B. Dwyer (eds.), pp. 3–15. New York: Garland.

Schevill, Margot Blum, Janet Catherine Berlo, and Edward B. Dwyer (editors)

1991   *Textile Traditions of Mesoamerica and the Andes: An Anthology*. New York: Garland.

Schorsch, Deborah

1998   Silver-and-Gold Moche Artifacts from Loma Negra, Peru. *Metropolitan Museum Journal* 33:109–136.

Seiler-Baldinger, Annemarie

1994   *Textiles: A Classification of Techniques*. Washington, D.C.: Smithsonian Institution Press.

Strong, William D., and Clifford Evans

1952   *Cultural Stratigraphy in the Virú Valley, Northern Peru: The Formative and Florescent Epochs*. New York: Columbia University Press.

Stuiver, Minze, Paula J. Reimer, Edouard Bard, J. Warren Beck, G. S. Burr, Konrad A. Hughen, Bernd Kromer, Gerry McCormac, Johannes Van Der Plicht, and Marco Spurk

1998   INTCAL 98 Radiocarbon Age Calibration. *Radiocarbon* 40(3):1041–1083.

Ubbelohde-Doering, Heinrich

1967   *On the Royal Highways of the Inca: Archaeological Treasures of Ancient Peru*. New York: Frederick A. Praeger Publisher.

1983   *Vorspanische Gräber von Pacatnamú, Nordperu*. Materialien zur Allgemeinen und Vergleichenden Archäologie 26. Munich: C. H. Beck.

Uceda, Santiago

2001   Investigations at Huaca de la Luna, Moche Valley: An Example of Moche Religious Architecture. In *Moche Art and Archaeology in Ancient Peru*, Joanne Pillsbury (ed.), pp. 47–67. Washington, D.C.: National Gallery of Art and Yale University Press.

van Gijseghem, Hendrik

2001   Household and Family at Moche, Peru: An Analysis of Building and Residence Patterns in a Prehispanic Urban Center. *Latin American Antiquity* 12(3):257–273.

Willey, Gordon R.

1945   Horizon Styles and Pottery Traditions in Peruvian Archaeology. *American Antiquity* 1:49–56.

1953   *Prehistoric Settlement Patterns in the Virú Valley, Perú* [sic]. Smithsonian Institution, Bureau of American Ethnology Bulletin 155. Washington, D.C.: Government Printing Office.

CHAPTER 10

GALLINAZO AND MOCHE AT THE SANTA RITA B ARCHAEOLOGICAL COMPLEX, MIDDLE CHAO VALLEY

Jonathan D. Kent, Teresa Rosales Tham, Víctor Vásquez Sánchez, Richard A. Busch, and Catherine M. Gaither

This chapter explores new data regarding the occurrence of materials traditionally referred to as "Gallinazo" at the site of Santa Rita B in the middle Chao Valley. Following a description of the site and relevant aspects of our investigations, we discuss the nature of the materials present. We offer some preliminary inferences regarding the significance of these remains for the site and the valley, and then a broader perspective that includes a consideration of the possible interactions among the producers of Gallinazo, Moche, and Recuay material culture.

The site of Santa Rita B is situated in the lower portion of the middle Chao Valley, near the town of Santa Rita at a mean elevation of 384 m a.s.l. (Figure 10.1). The principal drainage of the Chao Valley, the Chao River, is formed primarily by two major affluent streams: the Huamanzaña River to the south (the largest contributor of water to the lower parts of the valley) and the Tutumo River to the north. These converge roughly 10 km to the west of Santa Rita B. Minor rivers (the Chorobal and Cerro Blanco Rivers)

are found farther north, and these streams also contribute water to the Chao River (ONERN 1973).

Santa Rita B is located on an alluvial outwash fan, the surface of which is covered with aeolian, alluvial, and colluvial soils. The surface shows the effects of numerous past episodes of flooding and rock-and-mud slides (*huaycos*) and is strewn with rounded boulders varying in diameter from 0.3 to more than 2 m. These boulders provided building materials for the occupants of many portions of the site.

The settlement lies in a strategic position. It is on the northern side of the Huamanzaña River, and our survey indicates that it extends all the way across the floodplain formed by this river. It also sits at the point of emergence of the Huamanzaña River from the Andean Precordillera. To move from the highlands to the coast within the Chao Valley, a traveler would likely have to pass through Santa Rita B.

One of our project's working hypotheses is that this position in the constricted valley neck

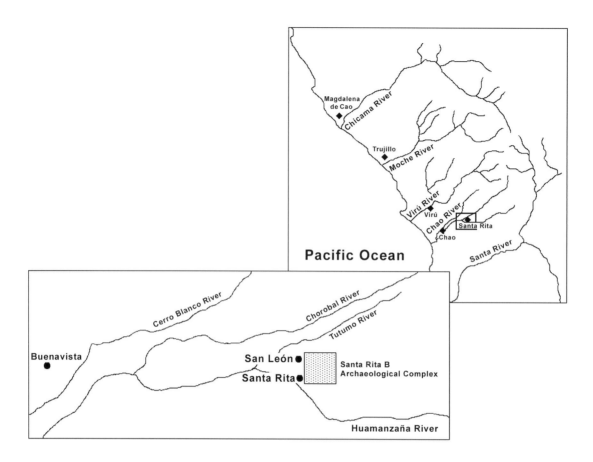

FIGURE 10.1. Location of Santa Rita B Archaeological Complex.

would have permitted virtually complete control over the movement of people, animals, and goods between the highlands and coast in this region. Based on our dates for the settlement, this control may have been an important factor in the continual (and possibly continuous) occupation of the site for more than 3,000 years.

The site was initially registered in 1976 by an archaeological team under the direction of Mercedes Cárdenas Martín as part of an investigation of the Chao and adjacent coastal valleys, funded by the Volkswagen Foundation (Cárdenas 1976, 1977–1978). Using a combination of aerial photographs and pedestrian surveys, researchers described the site of Santa Rita B as comprising an architectural complex primarily of stone (read, *pirca*) construction (Figure 10.2). Four hundred meters to the north, another architectural complex was identified and originally designated as the San León site. Some 500 m to the west, a

third site was identified on a natural hill and designated Cerro Santa Rita.

This Peruvian team identified ceramic sherds dating to the Early Intermediate period (Salinar and Moche) and possibly to the Middle Horizon—the material having been classified "tiahuanacoide" during the survey (Cárdenas 1976). Unspecified Early Intermediate–period and Middle Horizon materials were also noted at Cerro Santa Rita and San León. The Santa Rita B site was also noted to include variously sized enclosed corrals that contained camelid coprolites (Cárdenas and Milla 1976). An extensive wall, which traversed the entire eastern portion of the site and reached the adjacent foothills to the north (designated *muralla pircada*), was also recorded (Cárdenas 1976:53).

Following this initial set of observations, no other archaeological work occurred until we undertook fieldwork in 1998 (Rosales 1999).

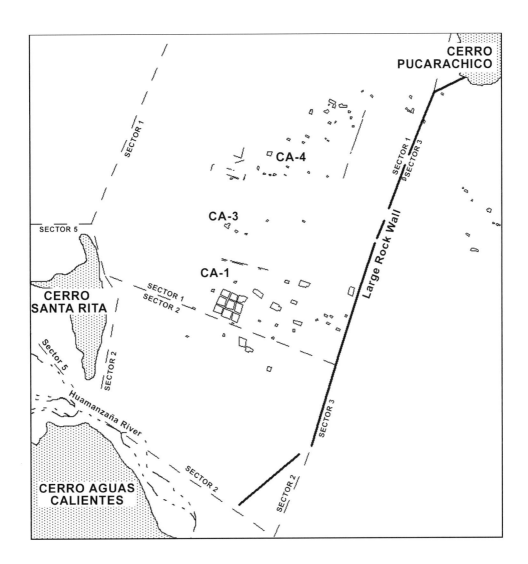

FIGURE 10.2. Plan of Santa Rita B Archaeological Complex
showing topographic features, sectors, and architectural complexes (CA).

Beginning that year and continuing until the present, archaeological investigations have been codirected by Jonathan Kent and Teresa Rosales and have involved three principal institutions: California Institute for Peruvian Studies (CIPS), Centro de Investigaciones Arqueobiológicas y Paleoecológicas Andinas (ARQUEOBIOS), and Metropolitan State College of Denver.

In trying to delimit site boundaries, we recognized almost immediately that the distribution of architecture and surface material culture was practically continuous among the three separate sites previously cited. This being the case, we decided it was more appropriate to incorporate Cerro Santa Rita, San León, and Santa Rita B into a single entity: the Santa Rita B Archaeological Complex.

San León (originally designated by Cárdenas as 17f-14M-7) was renamed architectural complex 4 (CA-4), whereas Cerro Santa Rita (originally denominated 17f-14M-5) is now referred to as sector 5. The site originally defined as Santa Rita B (17g-14M-8) was subdivided into sectors 1 and 2 of the larger archaeological complex. Sector 3 was assigned to a newly discovered area of architectural complexes and petroglyphs located east of the large rock wall. These new designations are shown in Figure 10.2.

EARLY INTERMEDIATE–PERIOD OCCUPATION AT SANTA RITA B

Surveys and excavations in various sectors led to the discovery of ceramic sherds dating to the Middle Horizon, Late Intermediate, Late Horizon, and Colonial periods—confirming that the site was in use over a long period (Cárdenas 1976; Kent, Rosales, and Vásquez 2003; Kent et al. 2005). The site also features an extensive Early Intermediate–period occupation, even though most of the structures are now buried beneath later occupation levels.

During our investigations at Santa Rita B, we noticed the presence of Gallinazo-style ceramics. In identifying these materials, we used a set of characteristics defined by Wendell Bennett (1950), Donald Collier (1955), and William Strong and Clifford Evans (Strong and Evans 1952), as well as criteria appearing in Heidy Fogel's dissertation (Fogel 1993). The most commonly observed ceramic attributes of Gallinazo-style ceramics from Santa Rita B coincide with the types defined as Castillo Modeled and Castillo Incised in the Virú Valley (Strong and Evans 1952:309–316). The most important of these attributes are:

- Brick-red, dark reddish-orange, or reddish-brown paste color

- Oxidized firing

- Medium temper (varying from 0.25 to 0.5 mm)

- Frequently eroded or only occasionally smoothed on exterior surfaces

- Use of triangular punctates in zones on the exterior

- Use of modeled adornments (especially of those representing the human head, with a modeled nose or button-like eyes with a low-relief central point as a pupil). Also frequent are modeled animal heads, such as monkey- or bat-like figures (Figure 10.3). At Santa Rita B, ceramics with these attributes were found only in sectors 1 (architectural complex 3) and 5 (Cerro Santa Rita).[1]

Sector 1 (Architectural Complex 3)

Architectural complex 3, measuring 27 × 28 m, features nearly a dozen pirca-like walled enclosures (Figure 10.4). Pirca is defined here as stacked-rock construction (usually rounded river cobbles easily obtainable from the surface of this outwash alluvial fan), occasionally with mud mortar. The individual enclosures share common walls within the complex and are of varying sizes and shapes. Thicknesses of the walls vary from 0.4 to 1 m, and the thicker walls are frequently made in a core-and-veneer masonry style. Using the dimensions of rocks fallen from the walls, we were able to estimate that the original wall heights ranged from 0.7 m for interior walls to 1.5 m for exterior walls. Two low benches (at least 0.6 m high) are also present.

Surface ceramics include sherds from various periods and styles. Some fragments featured fine to very fine paste (oxidized-fired to an orange color) and decoration with a yellow or cream slip. Some of these were painted with red or black lines of medium width in a style typical of Middle to Late Moche ceramics. Other sherds were undecorated but featured the same paste. Some fragments came from sculptural (anthropomorphic, zoomorphic, or phytomorphic) vessels, whereas others are from bowls (straight rimmed and flaring rimmed) and globular vessels possibly used as cooking pots (*ollas*).

These vessels possibly indicate the presence of Moche utilitarian ware at Santa Rita B. Typical Castillo Modeled and Castillo Incised ceramic fragments were also found (decorated sherds and undecorated fragments), featuring medium, coarse, or very coarse temper with evenly fired paste (to a reddish-orange color) or unevenly fired paste (to the same reddish-orange color but with a gray core). As is common in the Castillo wares, zoomorphic modeled adornments and zonal decorations with punctations were observed.[2]

Excavations began in 2002 in order to clarify the use of interior space in the complex, to define activity areas, and to try to detect changes in use over time. A series of trenches and square test units were excavated within two enclosures (Fig-

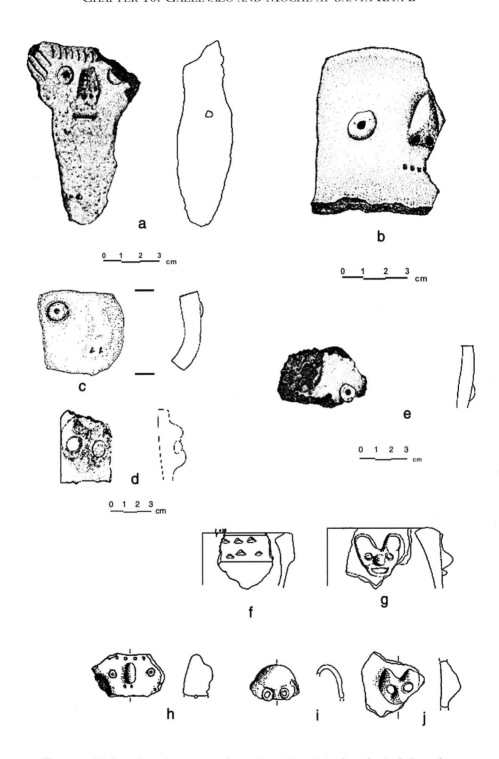

FIGURE 10.3. Selected ceramics from Santa Rita B Archaeological Complex.

ure 10.4): enclosure 1 (R-1) and enclosure 6 (R-6). Additional units were excavated in enclosure 10 (R-10) and to the east of the complex, an area we designated architectural area 11 (AA-11).

Of most importance here are the results of excavations in enclosure 1. In the northeast corner of this enclosure, a 2 × 2 m test unit (unit 2) was excavated to a depth of almost 2 m below

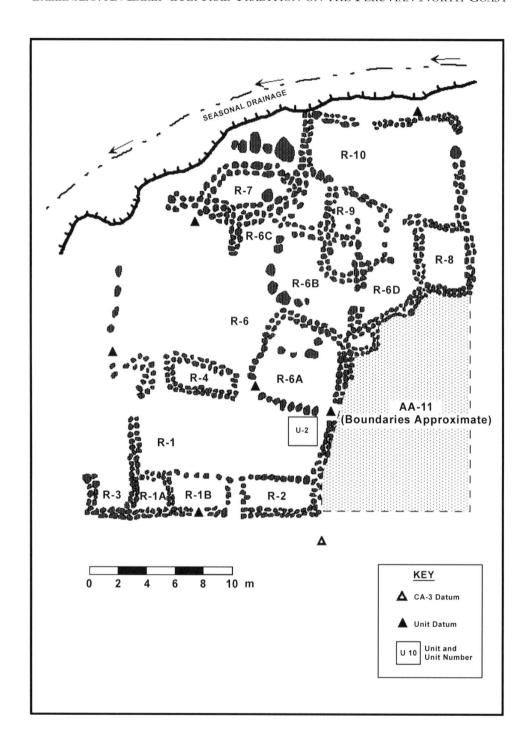

FIGURE 10.4. Plan of architectural complex 3 showing enclosures
(R-1 through R-10) and architectural area 11 (AA-11).

datum—roughly 1.5 m below the present surface
(Figure 10.5). At 148 cm below datum, a rock wall
was identified. This wall differed in construction
from the walls visible on the surface of architectural complex 3. The former comprised rounded,
sub-rounded, and angular rocks (20 to 30 cm in

diameter) set into a mud mortar. The corner of
this wall was rounded, an unusual characteristic
for this time period (Bawden 1999:81).

At a depth of 197 cm below datum, an almost
perfectly flat and well-preserved floor of compacted mud was uncovered within the area delim-

ited by the walls. On and immediately above this floor, there was a mixture of undecorated ceramic fragments, possibly from Moche utilitarian pottery and Castillo-style vessels. Also immediately above the floor, a concentration of carbon and ash provided material for radiocarbon dating. This produced a conventional radiocarbon age of 1470 ± 80 B.P. (cal A.D. 420–690, 2 sigma calibration; Beta-198387).[3]

Immediately to the west of unit 2, in enclosure 1, we encountered a series of human skeletons, some partial and others more or less complete (Figure 10.6). We have interpreted these as human sacrifices associated with at least one principal personage (burial 4): a young individual showing occipital cranial deformation. This individual was buried with a young camelid, laid in the same burial position at its side (Gaither et al., in press).

A Middle Moche (Moche III or Moche IV) mold-made bowl was placed next to burial 2, and a sample of organic material uncovered between burial 2 and burial 3 was analyzed using the radiometric method. This

produced a conventional radiocarbon age of 1290 ± 50 B.P. (cal A.D. 650– 870, 2 sigma calibration; Beta-198388). Because of the stratigraphic position of the burials and associated materials, we regard these as postdating the floor associated

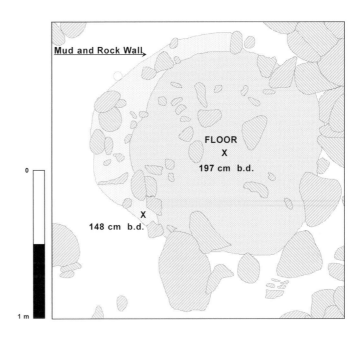

FIGURE 10.5. Plan of unit 2 in enclosure 1 (R-1) showing excavated mud-and-rock wall and well-preserved compacted mud floor.

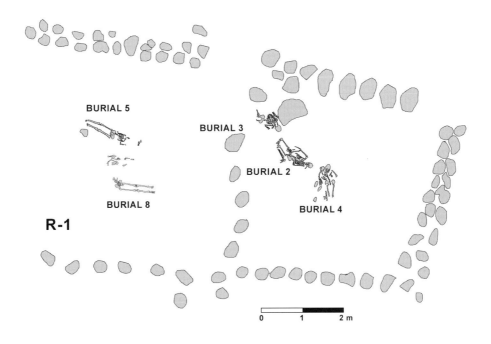

FIGURE 10.6. Burials and sacrifice victims in enclosure 1 (R-1).

with ceramics of Gallinazo and Moche styles. Radiocarbon determinations seem to support this inference.

Of the estimated 6,000 pottery sherds recovered during the excavation in CA-3, only 190 diagnostic fragments dated to the Early Intermediate–period occupation of the site. The vast majority were Moche-style fragments (186), whereas two sherds were of Gallinazo style and two of Recuay style. Analysis by Jorge Chiguala Azabache indicated that the Gallinazo-style sherds came from a jar with appliquéd decoration and from a thick-walled storage vessel (Kent, Rosales, and Vásquez 2003:43–47; Kent et al. 2005:35–37). The evidence is in no way indicative of a strong Gallinazo presence at Santa Rita B, but the presence of this material in architectural complex 3 and elsewhere at the site must be accounted for.

Sector 5 (Cerro Santa Rita)

Gallinazo-style ceramics were slightly more abundant in sector 5, on the flanks of Cerro Santa Rita (Figure 10.2). Investigations in this sector began in 1998 with a reconnaissance and a small surface collection. Geologically, the hill is an intrusive volcanic feature, the upper portion of which is roughly 80 m higher than the surrounding landscape. The igneous rocks making up the hill include gneiss, andesite, and potassium feldspar with occasional quartz veins. This rock fractures easily and naturally into large fragments with flat faces and is an ideal building material.

In Cárdenas's (1976) report, the site was described as a cemetery. Our investigations revealed the existence of numerous rectangular structures and other rock features on the hill, however, along with food remains and utilitarian pottery, indicating that more than just burials were present. We observed numerous stone enclosures of various sizes made of diverse types of stone (although most were made of the naturally occurring igneous rock). Some of the largest enclosures are found near the hilltop and may have functioned as platforms. On some of the steeper slopes, retaining walls were built with river cobbles.

Surface ceramics in this sector were again dominated by predominantly undecorated oxidized-fired sherds. A small number of Castillo-type

fragments were also found, including modeled figurines. Moche-style ceramics—some of which were decorated but many simply utilitarian in nature (Figure 10.3a)—were present, along with small amounts of kaolinite white-slipped or red- or black-on-cream decorated sherds. These resemble ceramics from the Recuay highlands area (Grieder 1978:65–68; Wegner 1981; Lau 2005:83) and from the middle-upper Moche Valley (Billman, Fiestas, and Ringberg 2004:176, Fig. D.III.7).

In sector 5, excavations were carried out within four zones (Figure 10.7). In 2002, excavations were conducted in zones 1, 2, and 4 (Kent, Rosales, and Vásquez 2003; Van Heukelem 2004), and in 2005 work was carried out in zone 3. No Gallinazo-style pottery was found within zone 1, although four sherds were found on the surface (Kent, Rosales, and Vásquez 2003:58).

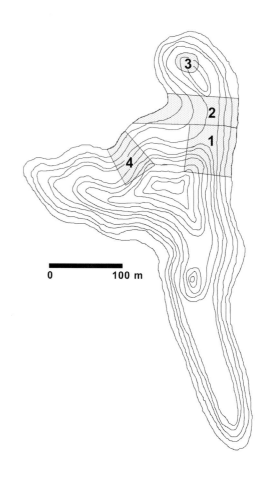

FIGURE 10.7. Plan of sector 5 (Cerro Santa Rita) showing the four architectural and topographical excavation zones. *Illustration after Van Heukelem (2004).*

Fine-ware sherds (possibly from Moche utilitarian vessels) were found in the excavated contexts, along with a smaller number of Recuay-like painted fragments. In zone 2, out of the 32 diagnostic fragments, 4 were of Gallinazo style, including fragments from two jars, one olla, and a figurine (Figure 10.3f, h, i; Kent, Rosales, and Vásquez 2003:53). In zone 4, 7 of the 97 diagnostic fragments were of Gallinazo style, including parts of ollas, a handle, and 4 fragments with modeled adornments.[4]

In zone 3, the remains of three platform walls were exposed (Figure 10.8). Between two of those

walls (CM-2 and CM-3) are the remains of three floors of compacted yellowish-brown mud. One of these floors is associated with Moche-style and Gallinazo-style ceramics, possibly including a fragment of a decorative-war mace made of baked clay. If future excavations confirm that these were indeed platforms, it would suggest that some type of ceremonial activities were carried out side by side with domestic activities.

A ceramic analysis by Jorge Chiguala Azabache showed that the vast majority (69.3%) of diagnostic sherds from this zone came from Moche-style ceramic vessels. The sample also

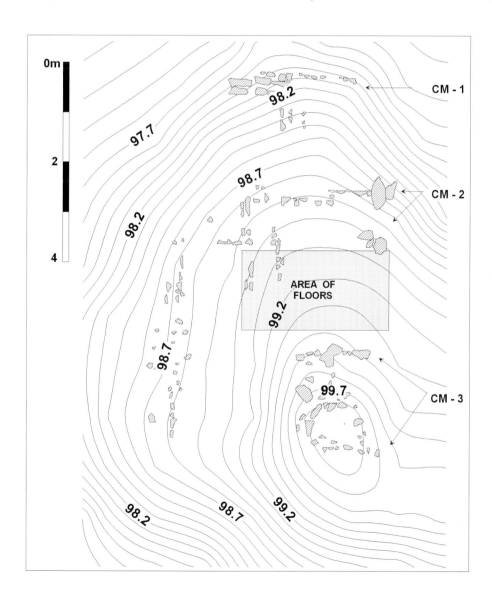

FIGURE 10.8. Plan of wall complexes of zone 3 in sector 5 (Cerro Santa Rita)
indicating the location of floors and walled compounds (CM).

contained 11 Gallinazo-style fragments (4.9%), stylistically similar to ceramics from the Virú and Santa Valleys. Forms include constricted-neck and expanding-rim jars—similar to those described by David Wilson (1988:401, Fig. 4a) for the Suchimancillo phase in Santa—as well as a figurine and ceramics in Virú's Castillo Modeled style. Interestingly, this sample also comprised a surprisingly high percentage of Recuay-like painted sherds (25.8%).

Finally, as mentioned previously, the Santa Rita B site is also known to include variously sized enclosed corrals that contained camelid coprolites (Cárdenas and Milla 1976). At least seven major corrals (measuring on average 24 × 18 m) have been identified so far (Rosales 2000:Plano P-1). No other site in the Chao Valley has been reported to have corrals. Corrals have generally been poorly reported in the archaeological literature of the north coast of Peru, however, and therefore we cannot yet make inter-valley comparisons.

Also of interest is the fact that our excavations in various Early Intermediate–period contexts at the site demonstrated the presence of very young camelids (newborn to three months old), which suggests local breeding of these animals (Rosales, Kent, and Vásquez 2003:16). Together, these data most likely reflect the great importance of camelid keeping and breeding at the site.

DISCUSSION

The Castillo-type ceramics uncovered at Santa Rita B are viewed as principally related to domestic activities because they were found in habitation contexts. This conclusion seems to correlate well with Christopher Donnan's suggestion that what has come to be recognized as Gallinazo ceramics (coarse containers decorated with incised designs and modeled appliqué) were not the product of a distinct cultural entity, but rather represent a utilitarian ceramic tradition used by commoners all along the northern coast of Peru (Donnan 2005; see also Chapter 2).

Donnan suggests that the indicator of a distinct Gallinazo culture would be the negative-painted wares in use by the elite members of that society, rather than the Castillo types mentioned. The fact that two distinct domestic ceramic traditions are represented in our sample leads us to question this scenario, however. As previously mentioned, at

Santa Rita B, ceramic sherds from utilitarian contexts fall within two distinct types: fragments whose paste and temper are typical of Castillo Modeled and Castillo Incised ceramics, and sherds with temper and paste typical of Moche ceramics.

This confirms that two utilitarian ceramic traditions coexisted at this site, but one wonders how these two traditions came to be used in the same contexts. Did Moche "commoners" live in this area, producing vessels according to their own tradition? Alternatively, could in-traded Moche-type containers have been used by the local population when conducting specific activities? If this were the case, it would restore the Castillo-type vessels to being the products of an ethnic group distinct from the makers of Moche domestic pottery.

Another aspect of the problem is that its solution depends somewhat on what our archaeological goals are. If our goal is to find temporally diagnostic material culture assignable to a limited time frame in order to improve our material cultural chronology, Donnan's suggestion is heuristically valuable. If our goal is to identify ethnic groups and movement of people throughout the northern coast of Peru, perhaps utilitarian wares hold an underutilized potential for approaching the problem. If our goal is to determine functional variations in material culture that can be interpreted as reflecting choices among various wares, much more precise contextual data on the occurrence of utilitarian ware throughout the north coast are needed.

With regard to the discovery of Recuay-style ceramics in contexts also associated with Moche-style and Castillo-type ceramics, it is worth noting that a similar situation was documented by Donald Proulx in the Nepeña Valley (Proulx 1982). According to Proulx, the makers of Recuay ceramics had come down from the highlands (at a time when Salinar ceramics were being produced on the coast) and peacefully occupied the upper parts of the Santa, Nepeña, and Casma Valleys. It now seems reasonable to add the Chao Valley to the list of those affected by the migration of Recuay pottery makers.

Thus far, however, we have no data suggesting that this movement predates the occupation of Santa Rita B by the users of Moche-style and Castillo-type pottery. The presence of Recuay artifacts in these valleys could also have been the result of trade between highland and coastal populations. In this context, it is unfortunate that so little emphasis has been placed on the possible role played by pastoralists. This is partly understandable, however, given that Proulx did not find Recuay ceramics in Early Intermediate–period contexts from the lower Nepeña Valley (Proulx 1982), and given that the surveys of the lower and middle Chao Valley (first carried out by Cárdenas [1977–1978] and later as part of the Proyecto Especial CHAVIMOCHIC [Uceda 1988; Carcelén and Angulo 1999]) also failed to produce Recuay-style ceramics.

Given the strategic position of Santa Rita B in the lower part of the middle valley, the presence of Recuay ceramics is a key to understanding the nature of this settlement. If these vessels were brought to the site by traveling highlanders, it is likely that those people also carried other products to exchange for coastal products. With whom were they trading? The ceramic data seem to indicate that their trading partners may have been the users of Moche and Castillo Modeled and Castillo Incised pottery. The imposing presence of numerous corrals at Santa Rita B allows us to suggest that camelid caravans were the means of transport used in exchange. The site of Santa Rita B would thus be viewed as an important node in the economies of the region.

If, as hypothesized previously, the coast was inhabited by two ethnic groups (represented by Moche- and Castillo-style materials), we might well ask if they were exactly contemporaneous or if Castillo-type containers predated Moche ceramics. This temporal dimension has been central to the traditional view of the relation between Gallinazo and Moche phenomena (Fogel 1993; Bawden 1999).

As Garth Bawden and others have pointed out, the situation is more complex than was originally thought, as Gallinazo and Moche ceramics appear in coeval contexts in many parts of the coast. Bawden does, however, see the emergence and spread of Moche as largely the result of an ideological hegemony exercised by an elite stratum of Moche people over preexisting polities (including a Gallinazo polity), especially during the Middle Moche period (Bawden 1999:237–244).

In demonstrating the overwhelmingly high percentages of Moche ceramics in most contexts, the data from our excavations suggest that Moche authorities likely assumed control over Santa Rita B at some point in history, probably by A.D. 500. The dominant presence of Moche authorities in strategically situated sites (such as Santa Rita B) would have been an indispensable economic element in controlling the movement of goods between highlands and coast, and in controlling the means of transportation involved. It was just such control that may have formed the basis of wealth of the Moche elite.

ACKNOWLEDGMENTS

We would like to express our appreciation for the financial and moral support provided by the following institutions: Metropolitan State College of Denver, California Institute for Peruvian Studies, Centro de Investigaciones Arqueobiológicas y Paleoecológicas Andinas (ARQUEOBIOS), University of Denver, and Instituto Nacional de Cultura – La Libertad. Certain people who have been key members of our research team and whom we would like to thank include Jorge Chiguala Azabache, Francisco Cruz Aguirre, Stacy Greenwood, Michelle Lappgaard, Oswaldo Rebaza Gutiérrez, and Percy Vicherrez Mendoza. We would like to thank Jean-François Millaire for inviting us to participate in the roundtable and for serving as editor of the published papers. We wish to acknowledge Larry Conyers, who has made valuable contributions to our perceptions of the site. Our thinking on the issues discussed in this chapter also benefited greatly from informal discussions and comments during the roundtable with Christopher Donnan, Jean-François Millaire, Richard Burger, Luis Jaime Castillo, and Krzysztof Makowski. The authors, of course, assume complete responsibility for the data and ideas presented herein.

NOTES

[1] These attributes are considered Middle and Late Gallinazo characteristics by Heidy Fogel (1993).

[2] We also uncovered ceramic sherds (with medium to coarse temper) from globular jars and straight- and everted-rim bowls, decorated with modeled serpentine lines, raised triangles, nested spirals, and raised dots (with a tendency to zonal placement of the

motifs). These sherds are reminiscent of Early Chimú vessels from Middle Horizon and Late Intermediate-period contexts (dating to about A.D. 900) in the Moche Valley (Donnan and Mackey 1978:275). Upon excavation, it was determined that these fragments were only found in the upper stratum of architectural complex 3 in association with skeletal materials dating to about A.D. 1100 (Gaither et al., in press).

3 All dates are calibrated using INTCAL 98 (Stuiver et al. 1998).

4 The handle is similar to a vessel from the Late Suchimancillo phase defined by David Wilson (1988: Fig. 223).

REFERENCES

Bawden, Garth
1999 *The Moche*. Malden, Massachusetts: Blackwell.

Bennett, Wendell C.
1950 *The Gallinazo Group: Viru Valley, Peru*. Yale University Publications in Anthropology 43. New Haven: Yale University Press.

Billman, Brian, Miguel Fiestas Chunga, and Jennifer Ringberg
2004 Investigaciones arqueológicas en el sitio Cerro León en el valle medio de Moche. Temporadas de campo 2002 y 2004, vol. 1, métodos y resultados. Unpublished report submitted to the Instituto Nacional de Cultura, Lima.

Carcelén Silva, José, and Orlando Angulo Zavaleta
1999 *Catastro de los sitios arqueológicos del área de influencia del canal de irrigación Chavimochic: Valle viejo de Chao*. Trujillo: Instituto Nacional de Cultura – La Libertad, Proyecto Especial Chavimochic.

Cárdenas Martín, Mercedes
1976 *Informe preliminar del trabajo de campo en el valle de Chao (Departamento de La Libertad)*. Lima: Instituto Riva Agüero, Seminario de Arqueología, Pontificia Universidad Católica del Perú.
1977–1978 Obtención de una cronología del uso de los recursos marinos en el antiguo Perú. *Arqueología PUC* (Lima) 19–20:3–26.

Cárdenas Martín, Mercedes, and Carlos Milla
1976 Catastro del valle de Chao: Obtención de una cronología del uso de los recursos marinos en el antiguo Perú, 1975–1978. Unpublished site forms in possession of author.

Collier, Donald
1955 *Cultural Chronology and Change as Reflected in the Ceramics of the Virú Valley, Peru*. Chicago: Chicago Natural History Museum.

Donnan, Christopher B.
2005 Moche-Gallinazo en el valle bajo de Jequetepeque. Paper presented at the roundtable: "Gallinazo: Una tradición cultural temprana en la costa norte del Perú," Trujillo.

Donnan, Christopher B., and Carol J. Mackey
1978 *Ancient Burial Patterns of the Moche Valley, Peru*. Austin: University of Texas Press.

Fogel, Heidy
1993 Settlements in Time: A Study of Social and Political Development during the Gallinazo Occupation of the North Coast of Perú [sic]. Unpublished Ph.D. dissertation, Yale University, New Haven.

Gaither, Catherine M., Jonathan D. Kent, Víctor Vásquez Sánchez, and Teresa Rosales Tham
In press Ritual Continuity in Burial and Sacrifice on the Northern Peruvian Coast. *Latin American Antiquity*.

Grieder, Terence
1978 *The Art and Archaeology of Pashash*. Austin: University of Texas Press.

Kent, Jonathan D., Teresa E. Rosales Tham, and Víctor F. Vásquez Sánchez
2003 Informe final (temporada 2002): Manejo ecosustentable y desarrollo cultural del Complejo Arqueológico Santa Rita "B." Unpublished final report submitted to the Instituto Nacional de Cultura, Lima.

Kent, Jonathan D., Teresa E. Rosales Tham, Víctor F. Vásquez Sánchez, and Catherine M. Gaither
2005 Informe final (temporada 2004): Manejo ecosustentable y desarrollo cultural del Complejo Arqueológico Santa Rita "B." Unpublished final report presented to the Instituto Nacional de Cultura, Lima.

Lau, George F.
2005 Core-Periphery Relations in the Recuay Hinterlands: Economic Interaction at Chinchawas, Peru. *Antiquity* 79(303):78–99.

ONERN (Oficina Nacional de Evaluación de Recursos Naturales)
1973 *Inventario, evaluación y uso natural de la costa: Cuencas de los ríos Moche, Virú y Chao*. Lima: ONERN.

Proulx, Donald A.
1982 Territoriality in the Early Intermediate Period: The Case of Moche and Recuay. *Ñawpa Pacha* 20:83–96.

Rosales Tham, Teresa E.
1999 Informe final (temporada 1998): Manejo ecosustentable y desarrollo cultural del Complejo Arqueológico Santa Rita "B." Unpublished final report submitted to the Instituto Nacional de Cultura, Lima.

2000 Informe final (temporada 1999): Manejo eco-sustentable y desarrollo cultural del Complejo Arqueológico Santa Rita "B." Unpublished final report submitted to the Instituto Nacional de Cultura, Lima.

Rosales Tham, Teresa, Jonathan D. Kent, and Víctor Vásquez Sánchez
2003 Complejo arqueológico Santa Rita "B," valle de Chao. *Revista arqueológica SIAN* (Trujillo) 8(14):13–17.

Strong, William D., and Clifford Evans
1952 *Cultural Stratigraphy in the Virú Valley, Northern Peru: The Formative and Florescent Epochs.* New York: Columbia University Press.

Stuiver, Minze, Paula J. Reimer, Edouard Bard, J. Warren Beck, G. S. Burr, Konrad A. Hughen, Bernd Kromer, Gerry McCormac, Johannes Van Der Plicht, and Marco Spurk
1998 INTCAL 98 Radiocarbon Age Calibration. *Radiocarbon* 40(3):1041–1083.

Uceda, Santiago
1988 *Catastro de los sitios arqueológicos del área de influencia del canal de irrigación Chavimochic: Valles de Santa y Chao.* Trujillo: Instituto Departamental de Cultura – La Libertad.

Van Heukelem, Michelle
2004 Archaeology of Northern Peru: Cerro Santa Rita. Unpublished master's thesis, University of Denver, Denver.

Wegner, Steven A.
1981 Identifying Recuaydom: An Expanded Ceramic Inventory for Identifying Recuay Settlement Sites. Paper presented at the 46th Annual Meeting of the Society for American Archaeology, San Diego.

Wilson, David
1988 *Prehispanic Settlement Patterns in the Lower Santa Valley, Peru: A Regional Perspective on the Origins and Development of Complex North Coast Society.* Washington, D.C.: Smithsonian Institution Press.

CHAPTER 11

GALLINAZO CULTURAL IDENTITY IN THE LOWER SANTA VALLEY: Ceramics, Architecture, Burial Patterns, and Sociopolitical Organization

Claude Chapdelaine, Víctor Pimentel, and Jorge Gamboa

The main objective of the Santa Project of the Université de Montréal was to document the Moche presence in the Santa Valley and to study the incorporation of this southern valley into the southern Moche expansionist state. To achieve these goals, a closer look at the local population was essential. Following an intensive survey of the valley during the 1980s, David Wilson identified a large number of sites that dated to the Suchimancillo period (ca. A.D. 0–400), which he attributed to the Gallinazo culture (Wilson 1988: 151–198).

In this chapter, Suchimancillo-period sites are described as "Gallinazo de Santa" settlements to stress local idiosyncrasies while emphasizing general similarities with cultural manifestations identified in other north-coast valleys (Bennett 1950; Strong and Evans 1952; Willey 1953; Donnan and Mackey 1978; Fogel 1993; Shimada and Maguiña 1994; Bawden 1996; Millaire 2004). The Gallinazo de Santa is thus defined as the local culture that was confronted with the arrival of Moche intruders, probably about A.D. 300. In this chapter, we present new data from the site of El Castillo, identified by Wilson (1988:551) as a small Late Suchimancillo hamlet (LSUCH-143) but now considered to represent a civic-ceremonial center.

This will bring us to discuss the Gallinazo de Santa cultural identity through ceramics, architecture, and burial patterns. This discussion will also enable us to highlight the geopolitical importance of this site in the Santa Valley. Excavations carried out during four seasons at this key site (Chapdelaine and Pimentel 2001, 2002, 2003; Chapdelaine, Pimentel, and Bernier 2003; Chapdelaine et al. 2004; Chapdelaine, Pimentel, and Gamboa 2005) will help us discuss the complex relation between the local population and the Moche intruders, their cohabitation, and the eventual demise of the Gallinazo polity as a result of Moche expansion and colonization of newly irrigated lands of the lower Santa Valley (Figure 11.1).

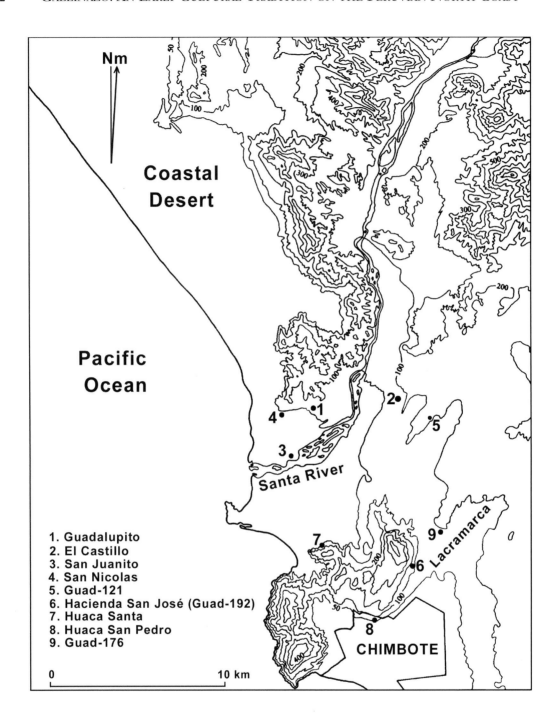

FIGURE 11.1. Location of major sites in the Santa Valley.

THE GALLINAZO DE SANTA OCCUPATION AT EL CASTILLO

Toward the beginning of this project in 2000, El Castillo was considered to represent a Moche site with a very small Gallinazo occupation. Working on the Northern Terrace (Figure 11.2), where Christopher Donnan had identified a dense Moche III–phase occupation (Donnan 1973), we found little evidence of a Gallinazo component. The 2001 field season included work on the hilltop sector to verify the nature of the occupation. While excavating various units in the Central and Eastern Plazas—and within an elongated monu-

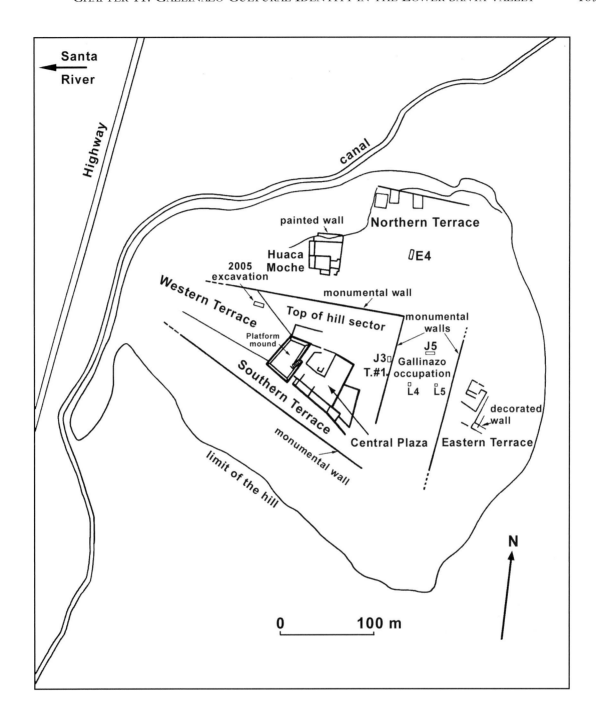

FIGURE 11.2. General plan of El Castillo.

ment marking the southern limit of the public area, east of the major platform (Figure 11.3)— we encountered no ceramics of Moche style. Most artifacts were typical of the Gallinazo de Santa style.

This result prompted us to reconsider the cultural affiliation of the hilltop platform. After considering its architecture—which is similar to that of Castillo de Tomaval in Virú based on its location, its monumentality, the type of adobes used, and a similar construction technique with stone foundations and stone-faced walls—we concluded that Gallinazo de Santa authorities were responsible for the massive construction and

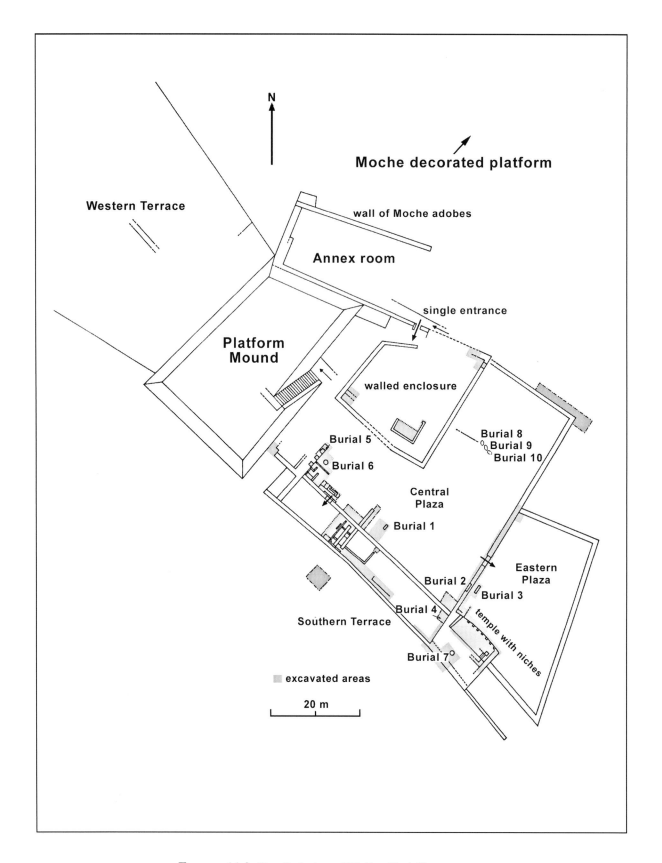

FIGURE 11.3. Detailed plan of El Castillo hilltop sector.

landscape organization found on the hilltop. These preliminary results led us to undertake a major reevaluation of this civic-ceremonial center, starting with a study of its architecture.

Gallinazo de Santa Architecture at El Castillo

The human occupation at El Castillo covers the entire surface of this natural hill, from the lower slopes to the hilltop (Figure 11.2), but it probably also extended over the cultivated fields that surround the site today. This settlement was therefore located above the valley floor, on a prominent topographic feature of the lower valley, like most other settlements of this period in Santa (e.g., LSUCH-145, LSUCH-149, LSUCH-121, LSUCH-103, and LSUCH-25; see also Wilson 1988:179–182). Common houses were built with selected fieldstones and mortar, whereas elite residences and public architecture were often constructed with adobes. From the outset, it is thus important to distinguish public from domestic buildings.

Public Architecture
The hilltop is the only sector that could be considered a built landscape for public rituals. The natural summit has been completely transformed: it now features an impressive platform mound (accessed via a stairway) and a number of plazas (Figure 11.3). It is argued here that the Gallinazo de Santa were responsible for the construction of most buildings in this sector.

The platform, which measures 48 m long × 28 m wide × 10 m high, is made of cane-marked adobes (see also Wilson 1988:207). The west-central portion of the platform is totally destroyed, possibly the result of Colonial-period looting. Access to the hilltop sector was likely limited to a single entrance located on the north side of the hill (Figure 11.3). The Central Plaza (52 m long × 49 m wide) features in its northwest corner a walled enclosure (24 m long × 21 m wide) made of cane-marked adobes, with a small room in its southeast corner. The Eastern Plaza is smaller, extending north–south to a maximum of 40 m and averaging 20 m in width, offering an open area of about 720 m^2. This plaza features a

small temple with seven niches and is bordered by a perimeter wall to the east, made of cyclopean-type stones.

Donnan (1973) and Wilson (1988) considered these archaeological features part of a Moche platform mound, although they expressed doubts about its cultural affiliation. Describing his finds from test pits and on the surface around the monument, Donnan (1973:40) stated, "None, however, yielded any sherds of Moche style nor were there any Moche style sherds on the surface of this area. The surface sherds, as well as those in the habitation refuse, were generally plainware and were not of a known style."

Donnan (1973:40) also identified some Gallinazo-style pottery in the lowest levels of test pits in the northern sector, arguing that "[t]he sherds from the lowest level in the two pits were generally nondiagnostic, but a few modeled pieces showed resemblances to the Gallinazo style of the Virú Valley." Discussing the nature of this site, which he argued had been occupied during the Moche III phase, Donnan noted that El Castillo:

> was first occupied prior to Moche occupation of the Santa Valley. This early occupation is indicated by the refuse forming the lowest levels of pits 1 and 4 on the north side of the hill. It may be that the large solid mound at the summit of the hill, as well as part of the adjacent structures to the north and east was begun at this time. This suggestion is put forward because of the similarity between the large, thin, cane-marked adobes in the refuse and those forming the interior of the mound. (Donnan 1973:41)

Wilson had similar doubts when describing the large platform built of cane-marked adobes (which he judged to be a good Late Suchimancillo diagnostic), but finally decided to associate its construction date with the Guadalupito (or Moche) period on the basis of the rarity of Gallinazo-style ceramics on the surface (Wilson 1985:742). Clearly, excavations were needed to understand the nature of the hilltop complex and the cultural affiliation of its builders. Based on current evidence, we now consider the large adobe platform located on the hilltop of El Castillo to be a Gallinazo de Santa structure for the following reasons.

- *The size, shape, and mode of production (cane-marked) of the adobes.* Cane-marked adobes have traditionally been considered a Gallinazo-specific feature (Bennett 1950; Strong and Evans 1952; Donnan 1973; Wilson 1988; Moseley 1992; Shimada 1994; Shimada and Maguiña 1994; compare Chapter 2).

- *The construction method.* This involves the use of large foundation stones visible on the northern facade (a feature also found at Castillo de Tomaval in Virú) and its related wall delimiting the Central Plaza to the north. At the northern limit of the hilltop, a monumental wall made with cane-marked adobes also features large foundation stones in certain sections (Figure 11.2).

- *The presence of stairs for accessing the top structures.* This is an unusual feature of Moche architecture. The work of Steve Bourget at Huancaco is interesting in this regard: 13 stairs were uncovered during the excavation of the platform mound (Bourget 2003, 2004). Moreover, this site featured ceramics that were distinct from classical Moche ware.

- *The general layout of the hilltop public architecture.* This features large walls made of cane-marked adobes and massive stone walls to delimit the Eastern Plaza and the flattened area on the hilltop. The construction method and layout are strikingly similar to those of Castillo de Tomaval in Virú, which is considered a Gallinazo site later occupied by Moche settlers (Santiago Uceda and Víctor Pimentel, personal communication, 2005).

- *An offering of four complete typical Gallinazo-style ceramic vessels.* This also included three lids and one bone tool (Figure 11.4) found close to the present surface of the elongated monument marking the southern limit of the public area (Chapdelaine and Pimentel 2002). A small Gallinazo-style gilded-copper plaque featuring a warrior (Figure 11.5) was found nearby, and a similar figure made of wood was uncovered in the lowest level of the Eastern Terrace, together with several domestic Gallinazo rim sherds. Various decorated vessels (Figures 11.6, 11.7), domestic containers (Figure 11.8), Salinar-style polished stone tools, and decorated textiles also suggest a possible Gallinazo cultural identity.

Natural *Spondylus* shells were found within the smaller room of the walled enclosure in the Central Plaza, as well as beads made of the same material. *Spondylus* shells have been found on a single occasion within a Moche context in Santa (Guad-176), and we concur with Wilson's argument that it is during the Late Suchimancillo period that we find the greatest number of sites with this exotic good (Wilson 1988:197).

From the previously cited archaeological and architectural evidence, the logical conclusion is that the major platform mound at El Castillo was indeed built by members of the Gallinazo de Santa society prior to the arrival of the Moche (compare Chamorro 1999). It is not yet possible to define a sequence for the Gallinazo de Santa occupation, but distinct construction phases suggest a long history marked by a series of modifications of the civic-ceremonial area.

Residential Architecture

Fieldwork has revealed a Gallinazo presence on all terraces and apparently the highest occupation density in areas near the hilltop. It is difficult to assess the size of the population that originally lived on the hilltop sector, but it is definitely higher than Wilson's (1988:551) estimate.

During our fieldwork, small-scale excavations were carried out in residential sectors on the upper section of the Eastern Terrace and on the Western Terrace. On the Eastern Terrace, habitations were built on various levels between two parallel, massive stone walls. This area, which covers approximately 1 hectare (ha), may have been occupied by a population of about 100 to 200. No complete house has yet been exposed, but from our excavations it is clear that adobes and stones were used for building walls. One

FIGURE 11.4. Four Gallinazo vessels found in a cache.

FIGURE 11.5. Gallinazo-style gilded-copper plaque featuring a warrior.

FIGURE 11.6. Gallinazo decorated ceramics.

FIGURE 11.7. Gallinazo vessels of the Castillo Modeled type.

hearth made with cane-marked adobes (38 × 16 × 10 cm) was excavated in the Eastern Terrace sector.

The Western Terrace was explored during the 2005 field season, and excavations in a large unit (5 × 15 m) revealed a very complex architectural layout. The Western Terrace is an area located west of the main platform. This terrace is relatively small (less than 1 ha), and we argue that it was home to a group of about 100 privileged members of Gallinazo de Santa society.

One large room we uncovered featured a ramp. This could be an influence of the Moche colonists over the local residents toward the end of the Gallinazo de Santa occupation of the Western Terrace, an additional datum that suggests the cohabitation of the two cultures at the same site. A small percentage of Moche ceramics was also found in that room. In an earlier context, a well-made stairway descending along the northern edge of the leveled terrain is reminiscent of the stairs associated with the hilltop platform.

The El Castillo site was clearly not a large habitation center, but more probably a civic center featuring a modified hilltop for the performance of large-scale ceremonies and residential sectors reserved for elites. It is thus probable that only the latter were allowed to settle on the slopes of the Eastern and Western Terraces, close to the ceremonial sector. Although little is known about the surrounding habitation sectors at El Castillo, it is likely that commoners inhabited nearby villages.

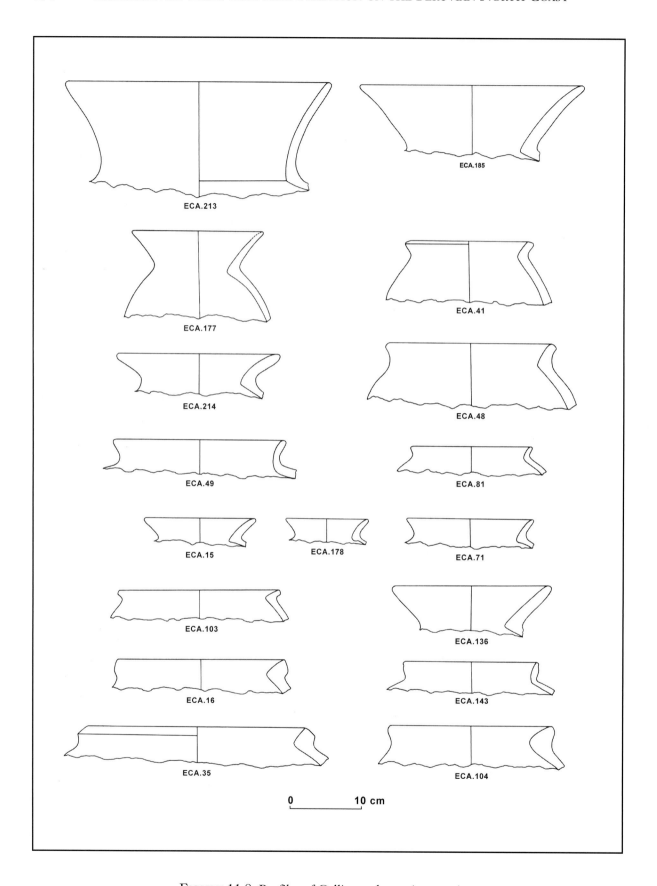

FIGURE 11.8. Profiles of Gallinazo domestic ceramics.

Gallinazo de Santa Burials

Human remains associated with the Gallinazo de Santa occupation of the site were uncovered in two distinct areas: within the hilltop complex and on the eastern flank of this architectural ensemble. Not a single burial conforms to the common north-coast funerary pattern—that is, an individual buried in extended dorsal position with ceramic offerings. As a result, although these burials are associated with the Gallinazo de Santa occupation of the site, the identity of the deceased is still unclear.

The remains of 10 individuals were uncovered within the hilltop architectural complex. A stillborn child (burial 6) wrapped in a plain textile was found near the surface. It was probably originally deposited in a shallow pit. The other skeletons were unusual. Based on contextual and bioarchaeological data, we argue that these represent human offerings dedicated to the architectural complex. Three skeletons were largely incomplete (burials 4, 5, and 7), whereas the other six (burials 1, 2, 3, 8, 9, and 10) were better preserved, lying in extended position, close to the present surface of the site.

Even these skeletons were partly disturbed, however (except burial 10, which was only partially excavated). Burial 1 was facedown, with its right leg upside down, alongside the left leg. Burials 2 and 3 both lacked bones from one leg. The skull of burial 9 was missing (a possible case of decapitation), whereas burial 8 was missing both legs (for a detailed presentation of the bioarchaeology of these burials, see Chapter 12).

Seven burials were found within a 4 × 5 m trench excavated in 2005 on the Eastern Terrace (see Chapter 12). Below an eroded clay floor we found the remains of a young female aged between 18 and 20 (burial 24), buried with a decorated spindle whorl with rounded extremities (of Gallinazo style). This skeleton happened to have been placed immediately above a large wall made of cane-marked adobes. This individual had received a severe blow to the head, which may have been lethal.

The other skeletons uncovered inside this trench were found in a thick layer of organic material that featured Gallinazo-style domestic ceramic sherds and Moche-style decorated ceramics (in the first centimeters below the current surface). Burial 25 was a woman (aged between 16 and 20) buried alone. Burial 26 was a young individual, possibly female, aged between 11 and 13. Burial 27, which corresponds to an old woman more than 50 years of age, is a second clear example of decapitation. Her head and the first three cervical vertebrae were missing, and cut marks were visible on the fourth and fifth cervical vertebrae. Burial 28 corresponds to the remains of a young individual, aged between 11 and 13, placed directly under the old woman and wrapped in several plain textiles. Burial 29 was a woman, aged between 35 and 45, placed on top of another woman aged between 45 and 55 (burial 30).

All the skeletons found within this 4 × 5 m trench seem to correspond to female individuals of different ages. Body treatment and corpse position are unusual, but it is likely that these individuals were part of a ritual linked to the rebuilding of a terrace immediately below the hilltop.

The archaeological context of the burials uncovered within the hilltop complex and on the upper terrace of its eastern flank is a complicated issue, considering earlier interpretation of the site's cultural affiliation. Our excavations revealed that this architectural ensemble had been built and remodeled not by the Moche, but by the local population: the Gallinazo de Santa. The burials lying near the surface of the hilltop plaza must therefore correspond to the terminal occupation of the sector.

In regard to the burials of the upper Eastern Terrace, the proximity to the hilltop, the presence of a large retention wall made of huge stones, the cane-marked adobe wall, and the spindle whorl mentioned previously all indicate a Gallinazo occupation of this sector. Moreover, the majority of the ceramic fragments found within the 4 × 5 m excavation unit are of Gallinazo style. Taking all of these architectural, stratigraphic, and cultural material data into consideration, it seems logical to ascribe these burials to the Gallinazo de Santa occupation of the site.

As a general interpretation for these two sets of burials, it is important to note that none of these individuals had received a proper burial. Indeed, the corpses had been laid in various positions, and not a single ceramic vessel was found as offering. Moreover, based on the bioarchaeological analysis of those remains, it seems clear that at least some of these individuals had been sacrificed, whereas other skeletons may have been manipulated some time after death occurred. This reinforces our argument that these individuals correspond to human offerings dedicated to the architectural complex by the Castillo de Santa builders.

Gallinazo de Santa Ceramics

During the excavation process, 2,344 diagnostic fragments (such as rim sherds and decorated pieces) were recovered and analyzed, helping us understand the occupational sequence of the site. Indeed, ceramics are often the key to identifying the cultural affiliation of archaeological sites. In this regard, the El Castillo site was challenging because it was occupied by the Gallinazo de Santa and subsequently by the Moche and Tanguche cultures, each leaving its mark on the hill.

The ceramic assemblage recovered from the eastern flank of the site is dominated by undecorated domestic ceramics. As outlined in Table 11.1, the lower terraces featured large percentages of Moche and Tanguche ceramics. On the other hand, based on the material recovered from our excavations, the upper terraces were undoubtedly occupied by the Gallinazo de Santa, with a minor Moche presence.

Gallinazo de Santa domestic ceramics were identified on the basis of characteristic paste, color, decoration, and rim shape, which set these apart from Moche domestic ceramics, sometimes found in the same context. The paste of Gallinazo de Santa domestic ceramics varied from a very

high density of temper visible on the sherds' surfaces to a fine-grained temper associated with a well-made paste. These ceramics are generally maroon in color, and their firing process is always oxidation. We have recognized three distinct qualities of paste:

- ▣ A coarse paste, predominantly maroon in color

- ▣ A maroon to pinkish paste with medium-grained temper

- ▣ A high-quality and well-fired paste varying between maroon and pink in color with fine-grained temper

Moche domestic pottery (which is almost never decorated) shows a tighter control over the paste (which is reddish), the firing process, and the overall quality. The morphology of Gallinazo domestic ceramics is also different from that of Moche domestic ceramics. The neck jars (*cántaros*) and cooking pots (*ollas*) have a longer neck, with a section profile more divergent to the outside, especially for the cooking pots and a variant of the neck jars (Figure 11.8).

Regarding Gallinazo decorated ceramics, our sample comprises several fragments of the Castillo Modeled type (Figure 11.7), which are very similar to those defined by Wendell Bennett and colleagues from work in the Virú Valley (Bennett 1950; Strong and Evans 1952). The neck jars with this type of molded or modeled impressions are surprisingly rarely associated with high-quality and fine-grained temper paste. They are regularly made of medium to coarse paste. This suggests that Castillo Modeled ceramics were associated with domestic activities.

Table 11.1. Distribution of ceramic sherds by culture on the eastern flank of El Castillo.*

Sector/ Culture	Gallinazo		Moche		Tanguche		Total	
	N	%	N	%	N	%	N	%
Lower terraces	122	6.3	874	45.5	927	48.2	1,923	82.0
Upper terraces	382	90.7	39	9.3	0	0.0	421	18.0
Total	504	21.5	913	39.0	927	39.5	2,344	100.0

* Domestic and decorated ceramic fragments were not segregated for this table, but for the Gallinazo sample, the majority is undecorated pottery (see Bélisle 2003 for a detailed description of the Tanguche sample).

The number of fine Gallinazo pottery sherds with negative painting is still small at El Castillo (fewer than 20 fragments). Some stirrup-spout fragments decorated with horizontal bands of black pigment were identified, and at least one or two could be part of a whistling vessel (Figure 11.6). Other rim fragments pertain to neckless jars. We also found part of a container with a broken handle (which might be conical in shape) as well as kaolinite ceramic fragments (decorated with black geometric motifs) that suggest contact with highland cultures. Incidentally, although Gallinazo-style domestic ceramics were found in all areas excavated so far, the negative black-painted vessels are limited to the hilltop and the Western Terrace.

One important difference between Gallinazo de Santa and Moche ceramic production relates to standardization. Indeed, although there seems to be only one standard quality in Moche domestic ceramics (Figure 11.9), Gallinazo de Santa containers showed much more diversity. As mentioned previously, there were at least three qualities of Gallinazo vessels based on type of paste

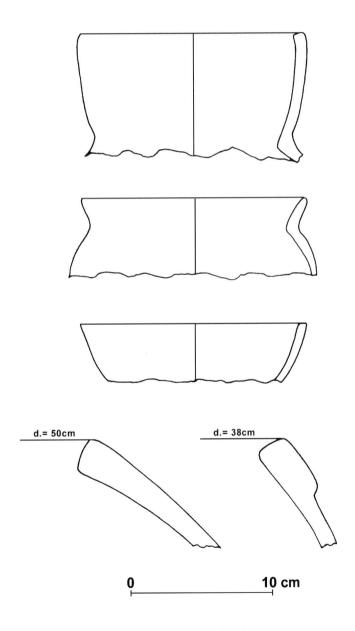

d.= 50cm   d.= 38cm

0   10 cm

FIGURE 11.9. Profiles of Moche domestic ceramics.

used, and these vessels feature a high diversity of rim profiles on cooking jars (ollas with or without a neck), jars, bowls, and storage jars (with or without a collar). This contrasts with standardized Moche domestic ceramics (see Wilson [1988] and Fogel [1993] for examples of rim profiles).

Gallinazo dippers (*cancheros*) have not been identified at El Castillo (some small fragments classified as neckless ollas might be cancheros). Moreover, decorative elements—although not complex or covering a significant portion of the exterior surface—are more frequent on the Gallinazo pottery. The frequency of decoration on domestic vessels (in particular, on Castillo Modeled ceramics) is more common on the medium-quality vessels than on fine ware.

Gallinazo de Santa Radiocarbon Dates

Eight samples of organic material were analyzed using the accelerator mass spectrometry (AMS) method. Four samples are from the hilltop sector, and four others are from the Eastern Terrace (Table 11.2). One of these samples (ECE-1) is from a fill between two plastered clay floors (3a and 3b) below what we identified as a Moche plaza. Few cane-marked adobes were found, but the fact that about 22% of all ceramic fragments were of Gallinazo style strongly suggests that the Gallinazo de Santa were still living nearby to pro-vide garbage or construction material to fill the area prior to the creation of a new floor.

The context is thus not Gallinazo but Moche, with a mixed assemblage. The uncalibrated date of 1560 ± 50 B.P. is strikingly close to a date obtained from the deepest level within a Gallinazo room on the upper level of the Eastern Terrace, and to a second date of 1580 ± 50 B.P. from an adjacent Gallinazo compound. These three dates are also coherent with a radiocarbon date of 1650 ± 50 B.P. from a Gallinazo hearth from the upper terrace. Incidentally, these four dates are also roughly contemporaneous with the Moche date from the lower level of the same terrace.

The situation is more complex with the four samples from the hilltop sector. Two dates obtained on corncobs are much older than expected: 2410 ± 100 B.P. and 3000 ± 80 B.P. Although there was no external sign of it, it is likely that contamination occurred. The best result is a date of 1540 ± 50 B.P., from a fill below floor 2 of the Central Plaza (a few meters away from the southern building). This date is similar to the dates obtained from a secure context on the upper level of the Eastern Terrace.

Four dates therefore allow us to posit a strong Gallinazo de Santa presence at El Castillo between 1650 ± 50 B.P. and 1540 ± 50 B.P. (all dates remain uncalibrated). The last sample was taken from a small hearth which cut through the

TABLE 11.2. Radiocarbon dates associated with the Gallinazo de Santa occupation of El Castillo.

SAMPLE	MATERIAL	CONTEXT	LAB NUMBER	RADIOCARBON DATE (B.P.)
ECA-1	Corncobs	Central Plaza, fill below floor 2	TO-9739	1540 ± 50
ECA-2	Corncobs	Central Plaza, fill between floors 1 and 2	TO-9740	2410 ± 100
ECA-3	Corncobs	Central Plaza, small hearth feature intruding into floor 1	TO-9741	1410 ± 50
ECA-4	Corncobs	Central Plaza, fill between plastered clay floor and bedrock	TO-10586	3000 ± 80
ECE-1	Corncobs	Eastern Terrace, low terrace, between floors 3a and 3b	TO-10587	1560 ± 50
ECE-2	Corncobs	Eastern Terrace, fill between floors 3 and 4	TO-10588	1560 ± 50
ECE-3	Corncobs	Eastern Terrace, Gallinazo hearth	TO-10589	1650 ± 50
ECE-4	Corncobs	Eastern Terrace, fill between floors 2 and 3	TO-10590	1580 ± 50

ultimate floor at the base of a large niche flanking the western extremity of the southern building on the hilltop. This hearth may have been the product of a ritual linked to the abandonment of the ceremonial area, but no diagnostic ceramics were found within or near this feature.

We thus assumed that this hearth was part of a Gallinazo occupation, even though the date for it seems late. Indeed, dates of about 1410 ± 50 B.P. are usually associated with Moche IV–phase material culture. In the context of El Castillo, it could be the youngest date for the Moche III phase. It is also possible that this feature was associated with the last ritual act carried out at the site by the departing Gallinazo population who were being moved inland by the new Moche IV–phase rulers based at Guadalupito.

El Castillo in the Gallinazo de Santa Sociopolitical System

Based on new data collected since 2000 at El Castillo, Wilson's (1988) earlier assumption that the site was a small Gallinazo hamlet needs to be revised. It is now clear that this settlement represented a larger settlement with impressive public architecture. El Castillo could have been a local political center (the seat of a polity at the chiefdom level) or a civic-ceremonial center. Although data are limited for assessing the political importance of El Castillo in the lower Santa Valley political network, the size of the platform and the associated plazas and buildings on the hilltop suggest that it represented a key settlement.

Based on the small habitation sectors identified so far at El Castillo and the small number of habitation sites located nearby (Wilson 1988: 182), we are tempted to argue that this site was a ceremonial center. The available radiocarbon dates for the Gallinazo occupation indicate that it was occupied during the later phase of Gallinazo development (see Fogel [1993] for her comments on Wilson's chronology of Early and Late Gallinazo sites in Santa). How long that later Gallinazo phase lasted is unknown, but El Castillo certainly remained a key site within the lower Santa Valley political network.

According to Wilson, the Gallinazo de Santa society was originally prosperous, and was divided into three polities (Figure 11.10), each being organized as a complex chiefdom (1988:307, 322–323). In this context, Wilson (1988:160–161, 183) also argued that Huaca Santa was the most important settlement in the lower Santa Valley during the Early and Late Suchimancillo periods. This major site is linked to El Castillo by an important canal. The two sites were probably co-eval and may have been complementary within the same lower Santa Valley polity. El Castillo had a high platform and associated plazas for conducting religious functions, and Huaca Santa featured large walled enclosures and habitation terraces covering an estimated 70 ha and had the highest demographic concentration of the area.

Alternatively, these settlements may have been the seats of smaller competing polities. The hypothesis is unlikely for two reasons, however. First, we know very little of the Huaca Santa site apart from the fact that it features a series of large walled enclosures (Wilson 1988:160–161, 183). Incidentally, these enclosures could have been built in later times (Tanguche, Tambo Real). The Early Intermediate–period occupation is difficult to assess without excavations, but a visit to the site confirmed the presence of an extensive occupation.

Second, the low density of Gallinazo habitation sites in the lower Santa Valley limits the likelihood of there having been two distinct polities. However, in our sample the number of Gallinazo sites identified is definitely underrepresented due to the impact of Moche agricultural development. Indeed, the intensive irrigation of the lower Santa Valley by the Moche may have destroyed several Gallinazo sites.

No excavations have been carried out at other major Gallinazo sites in the valley, and very few items typically identified with the elite have been found. Several ceramic types were documented by Wilson through his surface collections, but undecorated domestic wares prevailed. Of significance were the presence of kaolinite ceramic fragments in good numbers, the scarcity of negative black painting, and the limited number of bottles (Wilson 1988:393–442).

El Castillo was undoubtedly an important settlement, but based on current evidence it remains difficult to assess whether it was the center of an independent polity (a local chiefdom) or a civic-

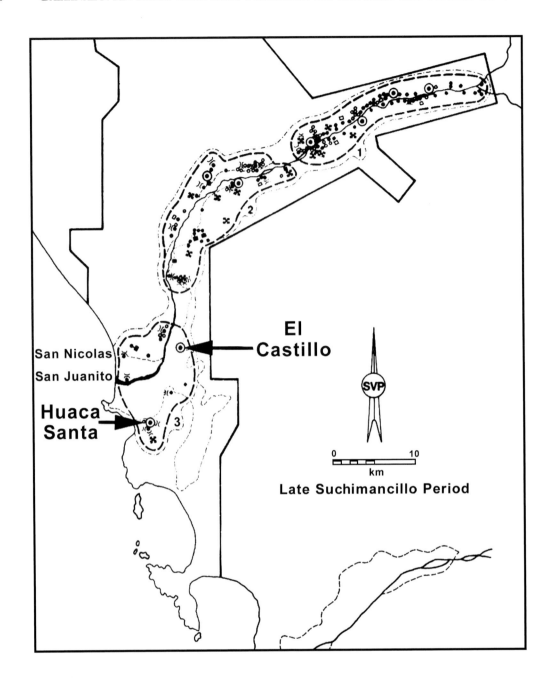

FIGURE 11.10. Gallinazo site clusters of the Santa Valley. *Illustration after Wilson (1988).*

ceremonial center related to Huaca Santa and part of a wider lower Santa chiefdom. Nevertheless, we should stress the fact that El Castillo was at some point ruled by powerful elites capable of centralizing human energy to build an impressive ceremonial landscape on a hilltop that could be seen from all directions within the lower Santa Valley.

MOCHE PRESENCE AT EL CASTILLO

The first intensive survey of the Santa Valley, carried out by Donnan (1973), led to the identification of a large number of Moche sites. This work was complemented later by Wilson's (1988) work, which identified more Moche settlements. Two hundred and five Moche sites had been identified prior to our fieldwork—including hamlets, small and large habitation sites, cemeteries, civic-ceremonial centers, local centers, and a regional capital (Donnan 1973; Wilson 1988).

We were able to identify more Moche sites during our fieldwork. As part of the Santa Project of the Université de Montréal, El Castillo (and especially the Northern Terrace) became a key context for documenting the Moche presence in the valley. Architectural, mortuary, and artifactual evidence all confirm the presence of Moche populations in the Santa Valley.

Moche Architecture

A platform located on the upper level of the Northern Terrace immediately below the Gallinazo platform on the hilltop was likely built by the Moche (Figures 11.2, 11.11). This is evidenced by the presence of a mural, which features a club-and-shield polychrome design executed in the typical Moche style (Wilson 1988:207, 211). The size, shape, construction technique, and overall quality of the adobes also strongly suggest that this structure was constructed by the Moche. Indeed, none of the adobes are cane-marked, all faces being smooth except for a single vertical mark visible on several adobes (which could be the result of the rope used to transport the bricks). The adobes are standardized, with dimensions averaging 32 × 20 × 15 cm, which contrasts with some cane-marked adobes (which average 38 × 28 × 9 cm).

To date, four compounds have been defined in the large-scale excavations carried out in the lower portion of the Northern Terrace. The architecture is of high quality, with well-plastered clay floors associated with dividing walls, benches, niches, and patios linked to one another by small ramps. The adobes are similar to those used to build the decorated platform. The layout of this complex system of terraces has been identified as an administrative sector (Figure 11.11). In compounds 1 and 4, the floors were clean and there were no formal hearths, leading us to conclude that these were nonresidential areas. Compounds 2 and 3 were likely used for a wider variety of activities, including domestic ones. Indeed, here more refuse

was found, one room featured niches, and the construction technique was of low quality.

On the lower level of the Eastern Terrace (Figure 11.2), we found an architectural complex comprising a small platform located in the southwest corner of a large plaza measuring about 80 × 20 m. The adobes, the ramp system, the long lateral bench, and the elevated platform with a small bench are associated with Moche occupation of the site. Burials with decorated Moche textiles—especially one representing a scene of yucca harvest (Chapdelaine and Pimentel 2003)—were found below the plaza.

The discovery of a decorated wall in the southeastern corner of the elevated platform pertaining to the last Moche III–phase occupation was reminiscent of decorated walls found at the Gallinazo Group (Bennett 1950). If this cross-motif is indeed a Moche construction made under Gallinazo influence, it could be possible to infer that the Gallinazo de Santa were still living in the area and that they maintained their influence. The decorated wall was erected when the plaza was still in use (floor 1), and the only date available for this sector (1560 ± 50 B.P.) comes from an earlier floor (floor 3). The decorated wall was therefore built relatively late in the Moche occupation of the site.

The last architectural element that could be associated with the Moche is located on the hilltop. Based on the type of adobes and on the change in orientation, the Moche built a wall attached to the northwestern corner of the principal platform to delimit a large annex room immediately above the Moche platform located on the upper level of the Northern Terrace (Figure 11.3). The Moche occupation of this area was probably not intensive, because no Moche ceramics were found on the surface of this large annex room. This wall is the only visible Moche intrusion on the hilltop, and we could not dismiss the possibility that it was constructed by the original residents of the site using Moche bricks.

Moche Burials

Several Moche burials have been found on the Northern Terrace (Chapdelaine, Pimentel, and Gamboa 2005), and others were identified in the lower level of the Eastern Terrace (Chapdelaine,

Pimentel, and Bernier 2003). Two looted burials from compound 2 contained the remains of high-status individuals—likely Moche leaders of the Northern Terrace. A young individual was interred at the base of the northern perimeter wall.

The unusual nature of the burial leads us to believe that it was part of a ritual marking the reconstruction of this sector. The ceramic offerings comprise two stirrup-spout bottles of high quality, seven domestic vessels, four neck jars, and five ollas. Incidentally, at Huacas de Moche it was unusual for the Moche to bury an individual with both decorated and domestic vessels. This situation is not uncommon in the Santa Valley, however (Donnan 1973).

Moche Ceramics

The lasting conviction that the Moche had conquered the Santa Valley—based on an overwhelming quantity of Moche ceramic artifacts (Wilson 1988)—has been challenged lately (Quilter 2002). Our work has for the first time provided solid contextual data from extensive excavations to help document the Moche presence in the Santa Valley. Indeed, examples of all goods known to the repertoire of skilled Moche artisans was recovered at El Castillo: decorated and domestic ceramic vessels, figurines, spoons, musical instruments (trumpets, whistles, ocarinas, pan pipes, rattles, and so on), club-shaped roof ornaments, masks, spindle whorls, beads, pendants, and so forth.

A large collection of Moche III–phase ceramic has been recorded at El Castillo. Domestic vessels are slightly more common, but decorated vessels (painted, molded, or modeled) are well represented. Flaring bowls are the most popular type, followed by neck jars, bottles, and long-neck jars (see Chapdelaine [2008] for an overview of Moche ceramics of Santa).

Moche Radiocarbon Dates

Several radiocarbon dates were obtained from secure Moche contexts. One date that came from the lower level of the Eastern Terrace (sample ECE-1) was presented in Table 11.2. The other nine samples came from the Northern Terrace (Table 11.3). Two were obtained from the platform decorated with a club-and-shield polychrome mural (ECHM), whereas the other samples come from compounds 1 through 3 (Figure 11.11).

The results from these AMS dates are in agreement with the idea that two cultural groups inhabited the site at the same time. The oldest Moche date (1670 ± 50 B.P.) is equivalent to the oldest available Gallinazo date. Two dates are much older and must be rejected. Sample ECN-3 came from an ash layer mixed with charcoal

TABLE 11.3. Radiocarbon dates associated with the Moche occupation of El Castillo.

SAMPLE	MATERIAL	CONTEXT	LAB NUMBER	RADIOCARBON DATE (B.P.)
ECN-1	Charcoal	Northern Terrace, C1, room 6, below floor 11	TO-8967	2000 ± 90
ECN-2	Maguey wood	Northern Terrace, C1, room 1, below floor 4	TO-8968	1240 ± 50
ECN-3	Charcoal	Northern Terrace, C3, room 7, below floor 7	TO-8969	2310 ± 140
ECN-4	Reeds	Northern Terrace, C3, room 2, niche below floor 4	TO-8970	1540 ± 50
ECN-5	Charcoal	Northern Terrace, C2, room 5, below floor 8	TO-9742	1480 ± 50
ECN-6	Corncobs	Northern Terrace, C2, room 5, below floor 11	TO-9743	1600 ± 50
ECN-7	Corncobs	Northern Terrace, C2, room 5, below floor 1	TO-9744	1420 ± 50
ECHM-1	Corncobs	Northern Terrace, N-E corner, room 5, below floor 1	TO-10591	1530 ± 50
ECHM-2	Corncobs	Northern Terrace, East Platform, below floor 2	TO-10592	1670 ± 50

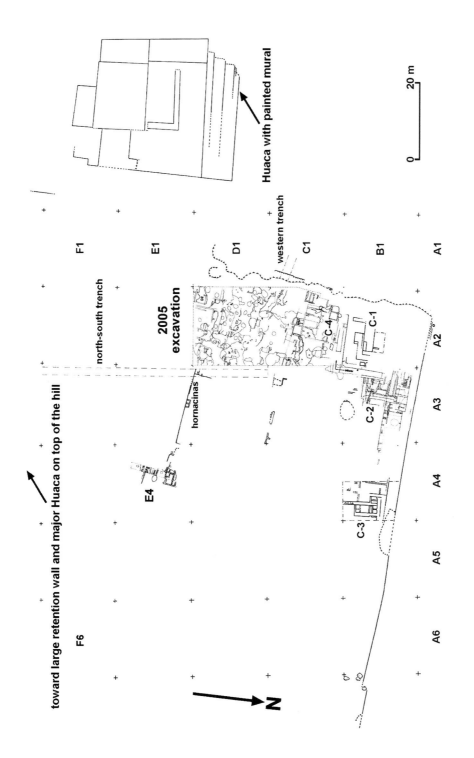

FIGURE 11.11. Detailed plan of Northern Terrace at El Castillo.

below the last plastered clay floor associated with the Moche occupation.

The date is good, but the result is linked to an older occupation, possibly related to Wilson's Vinzos period. Sample ECN-1 was taken from a secure Moche context, which contained diagnostic Moche III artifacts, but the result is at least 250 to 300 years older than is acceptable. This sample was likely contaminated by the presence of algarrobo charcoal, which could have produced an old-wood effect on the date. The other sample from compound 1 (ECN-2) also came from a secure context: a buried post still in place beside a ramp. The date is too young, however—probably because of contamination of the unburned maguey wood by termites.

The three dates from compound 2 (ECN-5, -6, and -7) offered results coherent with their relative positions in the stratigraphic sequence. The oldest date came from a context very similar to that of sample ECN-1 (a deep floor close to the sterile sand), and the date obtained from the corn-cob is 400 years younger. Regarding the other two dates from compound 2, the youngest cannot be accepted as a Moche III–phase date.

Samples ECN-4 and ECHM-1 are equivalent and suggest that the Moche occupied compound 3 and the northeastern corner of the platform mound at the same time. The other date from the platform area (ECHM-2) was obtained from a deep context within the eastern side of the massive monument, and if our reconstruction of the building events is right, the sample dates the first modification of the platform core. The result of 1670 ± 50 B.P. is thus satisfying, and it is for the moment the oldest Moche date at El Castillo.

The calibration of this date at 95% confidence gives us a time interval of A.D. 240 to 470 (at 68%: A.D. 335–425).[1] It is thus safe to propose a Moche arrival at El Castillo in about A.D. 300. It is more difficult to establish the end of the Moche occupation, however. On the basis of several dates and their precise stratigraphic position, an average of 1520 ± 50 B.P. was obtained from three samples (ECN-4, ECN-5, and ECHM-1). The calibration of this average date at 95% confidence gives us a time interval between A.D. 450 and 640 (at 68%: A.D. 465–610).

We propose that the Moche occupation at El Castillo lasted until about A.D. 500, although it could be as late as A.D. 550. About A.D. 500, Moche power shifted from El Castillo to Guadalupito—a time that also witnessed an increase in the absolute number of sites associated with Moche IV–phase material culture in the lower Santa Valley. The Moche occupation at El Castillo during phase IV was limited, and the site had lost all its splendor and political power.

Cohabitation of the Gallinazo and Moche at El Castillo

The identification in various sectors of El Castillo of two distinct cultural groups that lived in close proximity is definitely one of the most interesting conclusions of our work so far. The general horizontal distribution of diagnostic Gallinazo and Moche evidence at the site supports the assumption that both groups occupied different parts of the hill at the same time: the Gallinazo de Santa kept the hilltop and the upper terraces, with the exception of the Northern Terrace, which was occupied by the Moche.

This cohabitation is dated and is associated with the Moche intrusion in the lower Santa Valley during the Moche III phase (between ca. A.D. 300 and 450–500). Radiocarbon dates support the idea that during this period the Gallinazo occupied the upper portion of the hill, whereas the Moche occupied the lower portion of the Northern and Eastern Terraces. Most intriguing is the fact that the Gallinazo maintained their ritual activities on the hilltop, whereas the Moche erected their own platform mound on the northern slope, overlooking an extensive system of leveled terraces likely used for administrative operations.

This cohabitation hypothesis makes the interpretation of the site more complex and forces us to investigate the notion of cultural identity. Cultural interactions would have been constant, and the effects could eventually be detected on both participating cultures. Detailed analysis of material culture is needed before attempting to measure the impact of one culture on the other. Of course, ceramic production is the prime subject to look for, but we must admit that our general analysis of the Santa ceramic data was not oriented toward the fine-grained analysis of several attributes needed in order to tackle this task. The identification of a ceramic cultural tradition through the study of selected attributes is common practice, but attributing ceramic fragments to a specific ethnic group is more challenging.

We are inclined to believe that the cohabitation had tangible effects on both Gallinazo and Moche ceramic production. That being said, we are tempted to give more weight to the Moche, according them the role of donor and viewing the Gallinazo as benefactors. According to this scenario, Gallinazo ceramists would have been influenced by Moche ceramists in their production of domestic ware. In this regard, we believe there was some overlap in the shape (but largely in the paste and surface finish) of Gallinazo and Moche domestic ceramic production.

The partial blending of these two domestic-ware traditions, if recognized, could be called "Gallimoche." The basic description could be a distinctive Gallinazo paste (color, temper, finish, and firing) with a typical Moche shape; or vice versa, a distinctive Moche paste (color, temper, finish, and firing) with a typical Gallinazo shape. In our limited analysis of more than 5,000 ceramic fragments from El Castillo, the Gallinazo imitation of a Moche shape is most often recognized. Only a fine-grained analysis of these ceramic collections will confirm or reject this hypothesis. Finally, it should be noted that cohabitation and the expected exchanges and influences lasted several generations in the lower Santa Valley—enough time to experiment, to innovate, and to modify certain cultural and technological habits.

CHANGES IN MOCHE STRATEGY

The fact that in this region the local population (Gallinazo de Santa) was not displaced after the Moche immigrated makes us question the conquest theory, in which the Moche are presented as conquerors. The use of armed forces is not visible in the archaeological record, and it seems incompatible with the data from El Castillo. Instead, we can imagine this intrusion as a quest by Moche "entrepreneurs" (motivated more by economic factors) to participate in the agricultural development of the lower Santa Valley.

This first stage of Moche intrusion may have lasted about 150 years, and is associated with the Moche III phase. During this time, a relatively small Moche population was engaged in diplomatic alliances with local elites to allow the northerners to settle peacefully under the protection of El Castillo leaders. Economic improvements over time and growing production of stable goods were strong incentives for the Moche to take more interest in their investments. Their presence became more important for the Moche rulers from the capital city of Huacas de Moche, and a change of strategy was initiated.

Several interrelated events occurred in a short period in the lower Santa Valley that had severe impacts on the local population. Radiocarbon dating is not precise enough to pinpoint these events in time, but we consider that they took place during the Moche IV phase (ca. A.D. 500–600). Four events are discussed here briefly:

- ▣ The construction of a new irrigation canal to open new lands for Moche colonists in the southwestern portion of the lower Santa Valley, known as Lacramarca

- ▣ The establishment of new colonies in Lacramarca and, most importantly, a new local center, Huaca San Pedro, overlooking the irrigation canal

- ▣ The construction of a new regional center at Guadalupito (formerly known as Pampa de los Incas), with two massive platform mounds, large adjacent plazas, an extensive urban sector, connecting roads, several cemeteries, and smaller habitation sites in its periphery

- ▣ The decline of El Castillo and relocation of the Gallinazo de Santa population to the middle and upper Santa Valley

New Lands for Moche Colonists

The Moche conquest of the Santa Valley is difficult to explain with archaeological data alone. The impressive number of Moche sites distributed over the middle and lower Santa Valley was (for awhile) enough evidence to propose a military conquest, especially considering the number of battle scenes and weapons represented in Moche iconography. Land appropriation is one way of complementing the scenario and of gaining better insight into what pushed the Moche to change their strategy.

During phase III, they were apparently happy to share the benefits with their local allies—working to improve agricultural production and to have their resources grow steadily year after year. The Moche must have initiated a new design for the irrigation network to expand significantly into the lower valley. Small extensions are visible east of the former canal, above and below El Castillo, and most sites associated with these expansions are Moche sites. The radical change was the construction of a 14-km-long canal, which passed behind El Castillo, running toward the south-southeast and divided into two branches at the neck of the area known as Lacramarca.

These two canals run, respectively, 11 km to the east and 13 km to the west. The western branch is the major canal that brings water to the archaeological sites of Hacienda San José and Huaca San Pedro. One well-preserved section of this canal is visible south of Hacienda San José (Guad-192), and its size is truly monumental. Previous research and our own fieldwork in the Lacramarca area confirm the total absence of Gallinazo de Santa sites in this area.

The presence of 34 Moche sites (including 10 cemeteries, 19 villages, 2 local centers, and possibly 3 civic-ceremonial centers) indicates that the new irrigation canal was intended for Moche colonists (for the location of most of these sites, see Wilson [1988:204]). Moche leaders were definitely the owners of these new irrigated fields. Land property was probably at stake here, and we argue that their ownership could only have been achieved through military or political conquest.

Colonization of the Lacramarca Area

Excavations carried out at Hacienda San José and surface collections at other Moche sites of the Lacramarca area allow us to conclude that the area was occupied largely by Moche immigrants. This population influx is dated to the Moche IV phase. The ceramic assemblage is quite similar to the collection from Guadalupito (Chapdelaine 2008), and the same diversity in ceramic produc-

tion is observed. Two Moche burials have been documented: one of the individuals was associated with a typical decorated vessel (Chapdelaine and Pimentel 2003), whereas the other had pieces of copper inside the mouth and in one hand (a copper spatula was found nearby).

All of these sites are located along the irrigation canal, and the area seems to have been extensively populated—reaching Huaca San Pedro. This site, linked to all other Lacramarca sites by the canal, is characterized by the construction of a large platform (the second largest Moche platform in the Santa Valley). A medium-size village was located nearby, and this area (fronting the ocean) may have been a key local center for the Moche polity of Santa in their interaction with the inhabitants of the Nepeña Valley to the south.

A New Regional Capital Center

Guadalupito is considered to represent the Santa Valley's regional center during the Moche IV phase because of its size, architectural layout, and strategic position in the landscape. Very few ceramics of the Moche III phase have been found on this settlement, and only a limited number of Gallinazo-style ceramics (largely Castillo Modeled) were uncovered. The urban sector was therefore apparently occupied by a homogeneous group. Guadalupito should thus be considered a Moche site and the capital of the Santa Province within the southern Moche state (Chapdelaine 2004a, 2004b).

The Decline of El Castillo

As mentioned previously, the construction of Guadalupito is linked to the decline of El Castillo. If during the Moche III phase cohabitation had stimulated interactions between the local population and Moche immigrants, the new strategy implemented by the Moche during phase IV (gaining control over irrigated lands, old and new, in the lower portion of the valley) provided less room for maintaining these relations. Because the majority of the known sites of the lower valley during this phase are Moche, one has the impression that there was no room left for the Gallinazo and so the Moche rulers decided to move them inland.

This possible Gallinazo population displacement appears to be supported by the large number of Gallinazo sites recorded by Wilson in the middle and upper Santa Valley. Indeed, this is an area with limited agricultural productivity, which could hardly have supported such a large population density under normal conditions. In the future, it is thus our intention to conduct limited excavations at several Gallinazo sites in the middle Santa Valley (and to obtain radiocarbon dates) to verify the hypothesis that some settlements were contemporaneous with Guadalupito and Hacienda San José.

Radiocarbon dates of comparable age could support our hypothesis that a Gallinazo population was displaced into remote areas where Moche sites are rare. It is difficult to propose the collapse of the Gallinazo de Santa society and of its elites before exploring some sites to date them with some precision. Could local leaders have become Moche vassals, losing their military and economic powers and their capacity to control large population segments?

The series of events discussed previously and the radical changes occurring between Moche phases III and IV may shed some light on the burials recovered at El Castillo in what we considered a Gallinazo context. From that perspective, it seems possible to link these burials to a very late phenomenon in the history of the Gallinazo occupation. Some external pressure on the Gallinazo elite could have stimulated the unusual burial practices previously described. The Moche living on the Northern and Eastern Terraces may have had a role in this development.

DISCUSSION

The Santa Valley is a key area for understanding the southern expansion of the Moche, but this also rests on a better comprehension of the Gallinazo culture and its cultural characteristics. New excavations are needed to document three aspects of this Gallinazo cultural history of the lower Santa Valley. First, we have to confirm the presence of the Gallinazo prior to the arrival of the Moche. Uncalibrated radiocarbon dates ranging between

1800 and 1700 B.P. are expected in the lowest levels of occupation, at sites such as El Castillo, San Juanito, and San Nicolas (Figure 11.1).

Second, we should determine whether or not the San Juanito and San Nicolas Gallinazo populations are contemporaneous with the Moche and Gallinazo groups that cohabited at El Castillo. If this is the case, we should obtain similar uncalibrated dates ranging between 1600 and 1500 B.P. Third, we must find evidence of the abandonment of the San Juanito and San Nicolas sites when the Moche administration moved to Guadalupito during phase IV. We have hypothesized that at that time the local population was displaced and moved toward the middle and upper sections of the valley, whereas Moche colonists occupied the lands closer to the sea.

To improve our understanding of the demographic consequences of the Moche takeover (during phase IV) of the entire lower Santa Valley and the proposed displacement of the local Gallinazo population upriver, at least two Gallinazo sites in the middle valley should be examined. The goals would be to establish their respective occupational sequence and to date the major features. Uncalibrated radiocarbon dates between 1500 and 1400 B.P. are expected in order to support our hypothetical reconstruction of a population movement and the maintenance of Gallinazo settlements throughout the Moche occupation of the Santa Valley.

Regarding the Gallinazo sociopolitical organization at a larger scale, we are not ready yet to agree with the conclusion of Heidy Fogel, who argues that the Gallinazo polity was an expansionist multi-valley state with its capital at the Gallinazo Group in the Virú Valley (Fogel 1993:164, 295–297). Much more work should be done, but each Gallinazo polity in the northern valleys certainly reached the political level of highly developed chiefdom.

By comparing material culture and architecture from several valleys, we find sufficient similarities between what we consider Gallinazo in Santa (Suchimancillo in Wilson's terminology) with contemporaneous Gallinazo or Virú groups inhabiting other valleys (Figure 11.12) to suggest the existence of some form of interaction network. These polities probably interacted and participated in an exchange system (a type of confederation). These links are a basis for explaining the cultural similarities.

Within the perspective of interacting hierarchic societies, Colin Renfrew's (1996) Peer Polity Interaction model is worth exploring as a system in which the competing elites lacked sufficient power to conquer the adjacent valleys. The geopolitical situation of this Gallinazo peer polity interaction network was thus characterized by decentralized political power, and it is precisely during this time that the Moche came into action

in Santa, becoming economic partners with Gallinazo elites and, in particular, with the leaders at El Castillo.

At the local level, one major problem is how to define Gallinazo phases similar to those defined for the Virú Valley (Fogel 1993). The Gallinazo ceramic sequence should be eventually challenged by new ceramic data. Commenting on Wilson's Gallinazo sequence, Fogel stated that "the Suchimancillo sequence for the Santa Valley needed to be totally revised. . . . Needless to say, this makes the published Gallinazo settlement

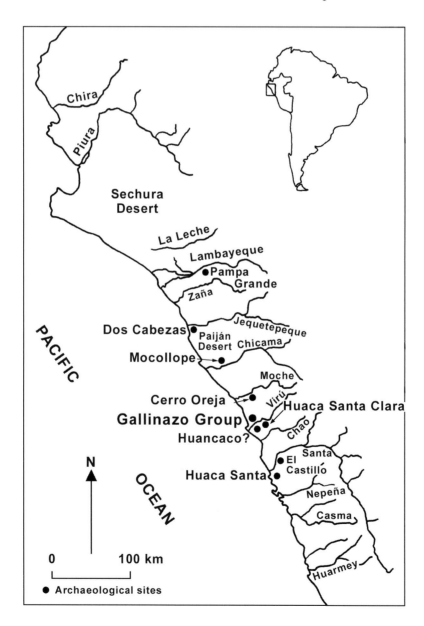

FIGURE 11.12. Location of major Gallinazo sites on the north coast of Peru.

pattern data from the Santa Valley extremely problematic" (Fogel 1993:16).

The recognition of El Castillo as a powerful center that possibly displaced communities in the middle and upper valley between A.D. 500 and 800 is a new challenge to the development of a comprehensive Gallinazo settlement pattern. The importance of El Castillo is vital in understanding the cluster identified by Wilson with Huaca Santa as the primary center (Figure 11.10). The monumental platform mound on El Castillo hilltop has no counterpart at Huaca Santa. It is thus tempting to propose that Huaca Santa may have been an administrative center and El Castillo a religious center within a single complex chiefdom.

NOTE

1 All dates are calibrated using INTCAL 98 (Stuiver et al. 1998).

REFERENCES

Bawden, Garth
  1996 *The Moche*. Cambridge, Massachusetts: Blackwell.
Bélisle, Véronique
  2003 L'occupation tanguche de l'Horizon Moyen du site El Castillo, vallée de Santa, côte nord du Pérou. Unpublished master's thesis, Université de Montréal, Montreal.
Bennett, Wendell C.
  1950 *The Gallinazo Group: Viru Valley, Peru*. Yale University Publications in Anthropology 43. New Haven: Yale University Press.
Bourget, Steve
  2003 Somos diferentes: Dinámica ocupacional del sitio Castillo de Huancaco, valle de Virú. In *Moche: Hacia el final del milenio*, Santiago Uceda and Elías Mujica (eds.), vol. 1, pp. 245–267. Lima: Universidad Nacional de Trujillo and Fondo Editorial, Pontificia Universidad Católica del Perú.
  2004 A Case of Mistaken Identity? The Moche Presence in the Viru Valley. Paper presented at the 69th Annual Meeting of the Society for American Archaeology, Montreal. (See electronic publication at *www.anthro.umontreal.ca/colloques/ 2004/SAA04/index.html*)

Chamorro, Víctor
  1999 Cronología y función de la Huaca San Pedro, Chimbote, valle de Santa. Unpublished licentiate thesis, Universidad Nacional de Trujillo, Trujillo.
Chapdelaine, Claude
  2004a The Moche Occupation of the Lower Santa Valley and the Nature of the Southern Moche State. Paper presented at the 69th Annual Meeting of the Society for American Archaeology, Montreal. (See electronic publication at *www.anthro.umontreal.ca/colloques/2004/SAA04 /index.html*)
  2004b Moche Political Organization in the Santa Valley: A Case of Direct Rule through Gradual Control of the Local Population. In New Perspectives on the Moche Political Organization, Jeffrey Quilter, Luis Jaime Castillo, and Joanne Pillsbury (eds). Manuscript accepted for publication. Washington, D.C.: Dumbarton Oaks Research Library and Collection.
  2008 Moche Art Style in the Santa Valley: Between Being "à la Mode" and Developing a Provincial Identity. In *The Art and Archaeology of the Moche: An Ancient Andean Society of the Peruvian North Coast*, Steve Bourget and Kimberly L. Jones (eds.), pp. 129–152. Austin: University of Texas Press.
Chapdelaine, Claude, and Víctor Pimentel
  2001 Informe del Proyecto Arqueológico PSUM (Proyecto Santa de la Universidad de Montréal): La presencia moche en el valle del Santa, costa norte del Perú – 2000. Unpublished report submitted to the Instituto Nacional de Cultura, Lima. (See electronic publication at *www.mapageweb.umontreal.ca/chapdelc*)
  2002 Informe del Proyecto Arqueológico PSUM (Proyecto Santa de la Universidad de Montreal): La presencia moche en el valle del Santa, costa norte del Perú – 2001. Unpublished report submitted to the Instituto Nacional de Cultura, Lima. (See electronic publication at *www.mapageweb.umontreal.ca/chapdelc*)
  2003 Un tejido único Moche III del sitio Castillo de Santa: Una escena de cosecha de yuca. *Bulletin de l'Institut Français d'Études Andines* (Lima) 32(1):23–50.
Chapdelaine, Claude, Víctor Pimentel, and Hélène Bernier
  2003 Informe del Proyecto Arqueológico PSUM (Proyecto Santa de la Universidad de Montreal): La presencia moche en el valle del Santa, costa norte del Perú – 2002. Unpublished report submitted to the Instituto Nacional de

Cultura, Lima. (See electronic publication at *www.mapageweb.umontreal.ca/chapdelc*)

Chapdelaine, Claude, Víctor Pimentel, and Jorge Gamboa
    2005 Contextos funerarios moche del sitio El Castillo de Santa: Una primera aproximación. *Corriente arqueológica* (Lima) 1:13–41.

Chapdelaine, Claude, Víctor Pimentel, Gérard Gagné, Jorge Gamboa, Delicia Regalado, and David Chicoine
    2004 Nuevos datos sobre Huaca China, valle de Santa, Perú. *Bulletin de l'Institut Français d'Études Andines* (Lima) 33(1):55–80.

Donnan, Christopher B.
    1973 *Moche Occupation of the Santa Valley, Peru.* Berkeley: University of California Press.

Donnan, Christopher B., and Carol J. Mackey
    1978 *Ancient Burial Patterns of the Moche Valley, Peru.* Austin: University of Texas Press.

Fogel, Heidy
    1993 Settlements in Time: A Study of Social and Political Development during the Gallinazo Occupation of the North Coast of Perú [sic]. Unpublished Ph.D. dissertation, Yale University, New Haven.

Millaire, Jean-François
    2004 Gallinazo-Moche Interactions at Huaca Santa Clara, Virú Valley (North Coast of Peru). Paper presented at the 69th Annual Meeting of the Society for American Archaeology, Montreal. (See electronic publication at *www. anthro. umontreal. ca/colloques/2004/SAA04/index. html*)

Moseley, Michael E.
    1992 *The Incas and Their Ancestors: The Archaeology of Peru.* London: Thames and Hudson.

Quilter, Jeffrey
    2002 Moche Politics, Religion, and Warfare. *Journal of World Prehistory* 16(2):145–195.

Renfrew, Collin
    1996 Peer Polity Interaction and Socio-Political Change. In *Contemporary Archaeology in Theory,*
R. Preucel and Ian Hodder (eds.), pp. 114–142. Cambridge, Massachusetts: Blackwell.

Shimada, Izumi
    1994 *Pampa Grande and the Mochica Culture.* Austin: University of Texas Press.

Shimada, Izumi, and Adriana Maguiña
    1994 Nueva visión sobre la cultura gallinazo y su relación con la cultura moche. In *Moche: Propuestas y perspectivas*, Santiago Uceda and Elías Mujica (eds.), pp. 31–58. Travaux de l'Institut Français d'Études Andines 79. Lima: Universidad Nacional de La Libertad and Instituto Francés de Estudios Andinos.

Strong, William D., and Clifford Evans
    1952 *Cultural Stratigraphy in the Virú Valley, Northern Peru: The Formative and Florescent Epochs.* New York: Columbia University Press.

Stuiver, Minze, Paula J. Reimer, Edouard Bard, J. Warren Beck, G. S. Burr, Konrad A. Hughen, Bernd Kromer, Gerry McCormac, Johannes Van Der Plicht, and Marco Spurk
    1998 INTCAL 98 Radiocarbon Age Calibration. *Radiocarbon* 40(3):1041–1083.

Willey, Gordon R.
    1953 *Prehistoric Settlement Patterns in the Virú Valley, Perú* [sic]. Smithsonian Institution, Bureau of American Ethnology Bulletin 155. Washington, D.C.: Government Printing Office.

Wilson, David J.
    1985 Prehispanic Settlement Patterns in the Lower Santa Valley, North Coast of Peru: A Regional Perspective on the Origins and Development of Complex Society. Unpublished Ph.D. dissertation, University of Michigan, Ann Arbor.
    1988 *Prehispanic Settlement Patterns in the Lower Santa Valley, Peru: A Regional Perspective on the Origins and Development of Complex North Coast Society.* Washington, D.C.: Smithsonian Institution Press.

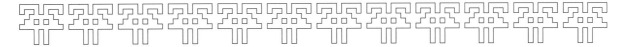

CHAPTER 12

GALLINAZO DISPOSAL OF THE DEAD AND MANIPULATION OF HUMAN REMAINS AT EL CASTILLO DE SANTA

Gérard Gagné

The El Castillo site is located in the Santa Valley on the north coast of Peru. Archaeological investigations under the supervision of Claude Chapdelaine (2004) documented the Gallinazo de Santa occupation of this site through a careful analysis of construction techniques, artifacts, and a program of radiocarbon dating. During the excavation process, several burials were uncovered in two different sectors of the site: inside an area defined as the Central Plaza (located near the hilltop) and on the Eastern Terrace, the highest terrace on the east side of the hill (Figure 12.1).

A bioarchaeological analysis of these remains reveals that the Gallinazo de Santa shared a number of mortuary practices with other north-coast societies. Among other patterns identified, careful examination of the skeletons shows that this people engaged in various types of manipulation of human remains.

HUMAN REMAINS FROM EL CASTILLO

Of the 18 individuals identified during the excavation process, 10 were uncovered within or near the Central Plaza and 8 on the Eastern Terrace (Figures 12.2, 12.3).[1] Some of the burials consisted of only a few bone fragments, whereas others were almost complete. Bone preservation was generally good, but some contexts had been affected by looting. Six burials were badly disturbed and could not be analyzed. Appendix A contains information on the 12 burials that could be analyzed.

At El Castillo, body orientation and position varied greatly. Some individuals were buried in extended supine position, but a few were buried facedown. Other individuals were buried on their backs, with legs folded to the chest or toward the side of the body (lying on their side). Orientation of the head was also variable. On the Central Plaza and Eastern Terrace, corpses were buried along a north–south axis (with the head located toward the north or south), but some skeletons on the Eastern Terrace were also lying on an east–west axis.

There is no apparent difference in burial orientations according to gender or age. Only two burials featured fragments of cane casings, but several burials contained textiles that were apparently used as shrouds. Only a few of these burials contained artifacts.

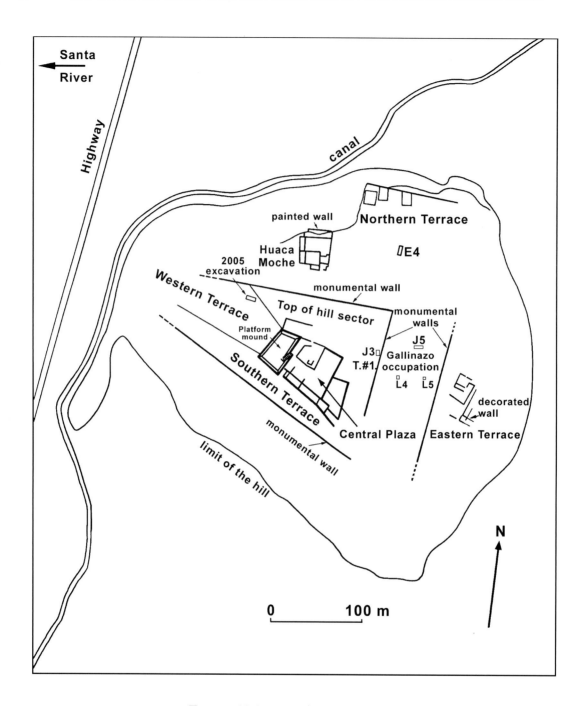

FIGURE 12.1. General plan of El Castillo.

DISPOSAL OF THE DEAD AND MANIPULATION OF HUMAN REMAINS

Bioarchaeological analyses revealed that half of the individuals under study showed signs of having been sacrificed or having been mutilated just before or shortly after death occurred. Evidence of mutilation was identified by the presence of trauma on the skeleton. These traumas were classified into four categories: perimortem trauma, postmortem decapitation, postmortem fractures, and postmortem removal of human remains.

Perimortem Trauma

Analyses revealed that two individuals were probably killed by blows to the head (burials 1 and

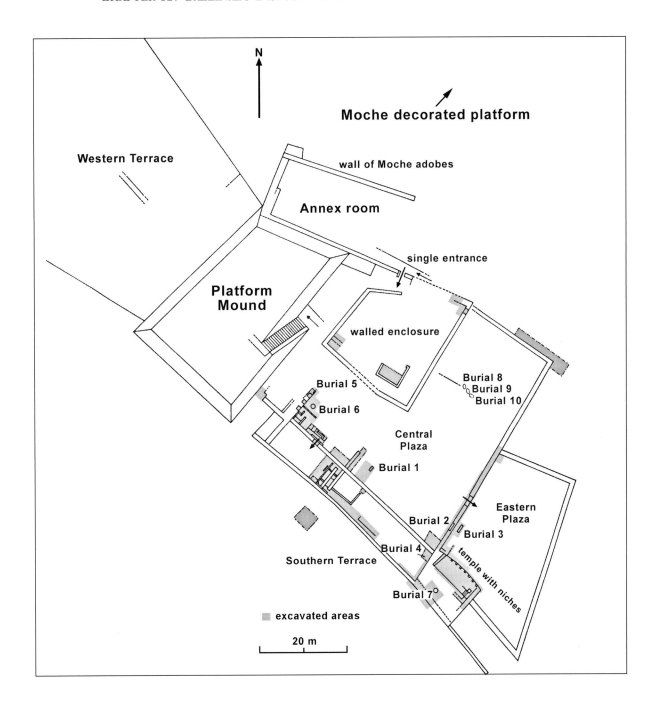

FIGURE 12.2. Location of burials on the hilltop sector.

24), and a third (burial 8) may have been strangled. All three potential victims were young individuals: two were aged between 18 and 20 and one between 14 and 16.

Burial 1

The first case of perimortem trauma is burial 1. It was found near the southwestern wall of the Central Plaza. It contained the almost-complete skeleton of a male, aged between 18 and 20 (based on pelvis morphology). The corpse had been buried facedown in extended position, with the head toward the northeast. The skeletal remains were in anatomical position, except for the lower extremities, which present evidence of postmortem disturbance. No grave offering, textile, or evidence of a coffin was found, except for a wooden ear tube on the left side of the skull.

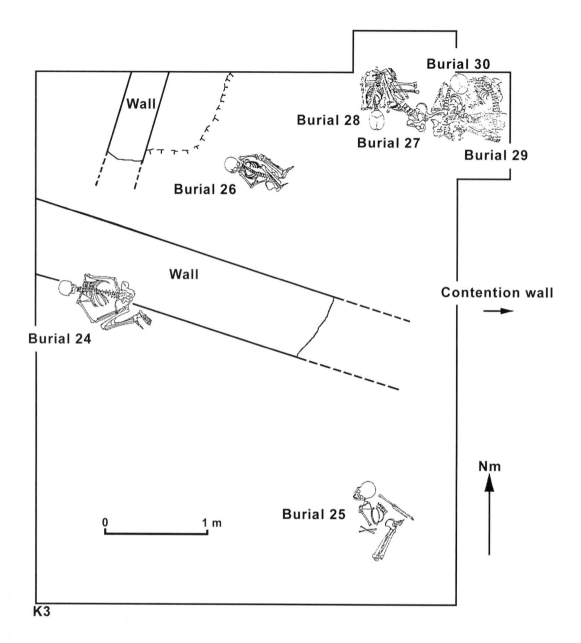

FIGURE 12.3. Location of burials within 4 × 5 m trench on the Eastern Terrace.

The skeleton presents a perimortem fracture on the frontal bone, extending to the right orbit cavity. The pattern of bone cracking, with fragments of bone bent inward, is characteristic of a blunt-force injury, possibly a direct blow to the head (Burns 1999). The fracture was unhealed and was probably the cause of the death, or at least was made at the time of death. This is reminiscent of Moche rituals documented by Steve

Bourget and John Verano at Huaca de la Luna in which victims of human sacrifice were often killed by a blow to the head with a wooden mace (Verano 1995:195; Bourget 2001:110).

A healed depressed fracture was also present on the right side of the skull, at the meeting point of the coronal and sagittal sutures. The fracture presents a depressed elliptic area with smooth edges. This type of fracture was also documented among the Moche by Verano (2001:178), who argues that it is related to manual combat techniques.

Burial 24

The second case of perimortem trauma is burial 24. It was found inside a pit excavated on top of a wall running east–west on the Eastern Terrace. This burial contained the almost-complete skeleton of a female, aged between 18 and 20, with mummified hands and feet. This was a primary burial in a very good state of preservation. The corpse was placed parallel to the wall, with the head toward the west. The corpse was buried facedown, with both knees drawn up to the chest on the left side of the body. Fragments of cane, reed, textile, and animal bones (some cremated) were uncovered inside the burial pit, and a spindle whorl was found near the left shoulder of the deceased.

The skull of this individual presents a perimortem fracture on the left parietal bone. It is a depressed elliptic area with cracks radiated in periphery, revealing the perimortem nature of the fracture. This blow could have been the cause of death.

Burial 8

A third case of perimortem trauma is burial 8. It was found on the Central Plaza and contained the remains of an immature individual, aged between 14 and 16. Based on its robustness, the skeleton probably belongs to a male. The body was on its back, on a north–south axis, with the head toward the north and the face looking east. The lower part of the skeleton was missing, but the remaining bones were in anatomical connection.

No grave offering was found inside the burial pit, but a rope was found around the neck of the deceased, possibly indicating a case of strangulation. There was no direct evidence of perimortem trauma, however, and the hyoid was intact. Strangulation victims often present a broken hyoid bone, but strangulation with a rope does not always leave traces on the skeleton. Therefore, absence of fracture does not automatically disprove the strangulation hypothesis. Based on Moche iconography, Elizabeth Benson (1975:108) has argued that ropes might be a generic symbol for

the funerary process, whereas Verano (2001:165) associates the presence of a rope around the neck of some mummies with sacrifice by strangulation.

Postmortem Decapitation

Two cases of decapitation were documented at El Castillo (burials 9 and 27). In both burials, the skull was missing and cut marks were identified on the cervical vertebrae. Analyses suggest that this evidence does not represent human sacrifice by decapitation but rather examples of postmortem mutilation.

Burial 9

The first case, burial 9, was found on the Central Plaza and contained the incomplete skeleton of a young male, aged between 25 and 30. The corpse was buried on a north–south axis, with the feet toward the south. The body was buried facedown in an extended position, with knees lightly flexed. The bones were in perfect anatomical connection, indicating that the body was buried shortly after death occurred. The pit contained no grave offering.

The skull was missing, along with the first five cervical vertebrae. Three ropes were tied around the ankles, and cut marks were found on the sixth and seventh vertebrae and left clavicle. The cuts are parallel shallow incisions, approximately 0.15 mm wide × 2.4 mm in length. On the vertebrae (Figure 12.4a), the cut marks are obliquely oriented, running from the right superior side to the left inferior side of the body. The sixth cervical vertebra has four incisions on the anterior face of the body. They are close to the transverse process, and one of them even runs to the anterior and posterior surfaces of the transverse process on the right side. The seventh cervical vertebra shows two incisions on the anterior surface of the body. They run in parallel and can be associated with incisions on the sixth vertebra.

On the clavicle (Figure 12.4c, d), incisions were found on the anterior surface of the acromial extremity, whereas some cut marks extend to the anterior part of the right transverse process. The cut marks are obliquely oriented from the lateral and superior side of the body to the medial and

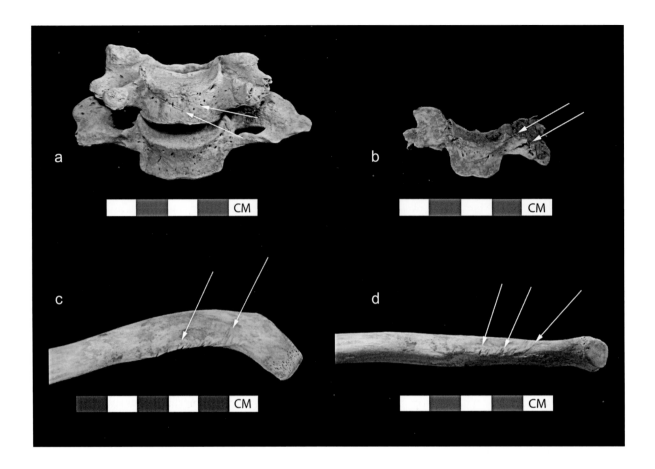

FIGURE 12.4. Cut marks on vertebrae (*a*) and clavicle
(*c* and *d*) from burial 9 and on vertebra (*b*) from burial 27.

inferior side of the body. Tim White (1992:231) argued that in some cases cut marks on the superior and anterior clavicular surfaces are related to the "removal of the platysma and sternocleidomastoid muscles, possibly during decapitation."

These cut marks are more likely related to the dismemberment of the arm from the shoulder, however. Indeed, the caraco-clavicular ligament and the trapezoid and deltoid muscles were likely sectioned in an effort to separate the clavicle from the shoulder blade and to remove the arm (humerus). This suggests that the manipulations were aimed at severing two parts of the body at the same time: the head and the left arm.

Burial 27
The second case of decapitation is burial 27. This individual was found inside a pit located near the edge of the Eastern Terrace, in close association with burials 28 through 30. Burial 27 was found immediately on top of burial 28 and could repre-

sent a double burial. It corresponds to a gracile female, aged over 50. Based on the presence of grooves of pregnancy on the pubis, it is argued that this individual had had children. The corpse was placed on its left side, with the head toward the northwest. Many textile fragments were found inside the pit, with a small concentration near the stomach. Camelid wool and numerous camelid bones were also associated with the skeleton.

Most bones were in anatomical connection, but the skull and the first cervical vertebrae of this individual were missing. In addition, the fourth and fifth cervical vertebrae each featured a single perimortem cut mark. These are small oblique incisions on the anterior surface of the body of the vertebra (Figure 12.4b). Unlike burial 9, however, the cut marks on burial 27 run from the upper left to the lower right of the body. The absence of the skull and the presence of cut marks suggest that this is a second case of decapitation.

Decapitation Process

The two decapitated individuals mentioned previously present cut marks either on the fourth and fifth vertebrae for the female or on the sixth and seventh for the male. A similar pattern was documented by Alana Cordy-Collins (2001) at the Moche site of Dos Cabezas, but it contrasts with other cases discussed by Verano (2001), where the head of the victims was severed at the base of the neck, probably by pulling it back to expose this region. Mary Frame (2001:63) described a ceramic vessel from the Paracas culture that features a scene of human sacrifice with a backward-bent figure. Other Peruvian cultures might have used a similar technique for decapitating victims. Cordy-Collins (2001:29) discussed another example in which the victim lies on its back and the head is pulled up.

The cut marks on the victims from El Castillo were made with the extremity of a sharp knife used in a repeated movement to cut through muscles and tendons. This is not the pattern typically associated with sacrifice. Indeed, death by direct decapitation results in more pronounced damage to the vertebra. Usually, the body and the pedicle are broken (Verano 1986). No such damage was seen on the bones of individuals from El Castillo. Discussing the relation between cut marks and ritual activity, David Frayer noted how cut marks on the cervical vertebrae usually relate to:

> the final disposition of the corpses in preparation for burial. The cutmarks are located in regions where the deep vertebral muscles and ligaments would need to be severed to disarticulate the head from the spinal column. Since the most frequent and deepest cutmarks occur on the ventral surface, it is clear that the decapitation began by cutting the throat. . . . (Frayer 1997:205)

The dimension, number, and the location of cut marks from the two cases mentioned previously confirm that they represent cases of postmortem mutilation rather than killing by decapitation.

Postmortem Fractures

In some instances, we were able to identify physical traumas associated with the wrapping of the corpse. The corpses were so tightly bound that some bones presented postmortem fractures.

Fractures are usually localized at the extremity of the leg bones. It is difficult to link such traumas with human sacrifice without any traces of ante-mortem physical violence. These individuals were bound with ropes, textile, or shrouds and were buried quickly after death occurred.

Whatever the technique used, the goal was clearly to immobilize the body. Five skeletons (all buried on the Eastern Terrace) present such fractures: burials 25, 26, and 28–30. Three individuals are adult females, and the other two are children aged between 11 and 13. Four out of five skeletons were wrapped in a shroud.

Burial 25

The first case of postmortem fracture was identified in burial 25, a young female aged between 16 and 20. The burial was found approximately 2.5 m southeast of burial 24. The corpse, which was disarticulated, had originally been placed on its right side, in a flexed position, with both legs folded up to the pelvis. The skull was lying on its base, without any anatomical connection with the vertebral column.

The third cervical vertebra presents a postmortem fracture of the pedicle, as if the head and neck had been pried back to allow an inhumation inside too small a burial pit. The tibia and fibula were forcibly folded up so that they touched the femur. The legs were thus perpendicular to the chest and were probably tied at the moment of burial to achieve such an anatomical posture. On the other hand, this position suggests that the corpse was quickly covered up and that decomposition occurred in situ.

Burial 26

The second case of postmortem trauma identified is burial 26, a young person aged between 11 and 13. The skeleton was uncovered on the north side of the east–west wall (near burials 27–30). In this area, the soil was filled with debris, and it was impossible to document the grave architecture. The corpse was oriented east–west, with the head toward the west. The skeleton was in a very good state of preservation.

The corpse was placed on its back, the legs folded on the chest. The feet were just over the pelvis, the knees touching the ribs. Bones were gracile, and measurements on the skeleton and tooth suggest that it is a female—even if sex determination at this age is uncertain. Many textile fragments were found in association with the burial, and they may represent the remains of a shroud. A spindle whorl was also found, near the right elbow.

The body was forcibly tied, as evidenced by the fact that the extremities of many of the long bones show perimortem or postmortem fractures. For example, the ischium was broken at the pubis joint. The left humerus was also higher than the normal anatomical position, and it looks as if the arm and shoulder were lifted at the time of the burial. All of these anatomical connections are in accordance with a decomposing corpse in a relatively tight environment.

Burial 28

The third case of postmortem trauma is burial 28, an immature individual aged between 11 and 13 (buried together with burial 27). Burial 28 was placed on a north–south axis, with the head toward the south. Skeletal analyses suggest that this was also a young girl. The body was placed on its back, legs folded toward the chin. The knees touched the shoulders, whereas the feet were placed over the pelvis (facing inward). Textile fragments were found in association with the burial, and some were still over the head and the right leg. The corpse was wrapped in a shroud.

The skull was lying on its base and shows *Cribra orbitalia* on both orbits. The humeri were found under the legs (femur, tibia, and fibula), the forearms were folded, and the hands were placed below the chin. Perimortem fractures were present on the extremity of the long bones and on the pelvic bones. Even when such a force is applied, joints are generally in good anatomical connection. This posture and fractures suggest a forcibly tied corpse.

Burials 29 and 30

Burial 29 was possibly originally buried with burial 30. A reed mat separated the two corpses. Based on contextual information, it was difficult to confirm that this was a double burial, however. Burial 29 was oriented on a north–south axis, with the head toward the north. The individual was a woman aged between 35 and 45. Grooves of pregnancy on the pubis suggest that she had

had children. Squatting facets are present on the tibias, indicating a regular kneeling position, possibly for domestic activity. The skull has a slight occipital bun and an *Os incae*.[2] Arthritis is present between the third cuneiform and the third metatarsal joint. One toe shows fusion of its distal and medial phalanxes.

The corpse was placed in a flexed position on its right side. The upper part of the body was flexed, and the neck was bent toward the knees. The corpse was definitely tied and buried quickly. Although pressure was forcibly applied to the corpse, the joints kept their anatomical connection. Pressure to retain the corpse in that position was so great that the extremities of the long bones show perimortem breakage.

Burial 30 was partly beneath burial 29. This was the body of a female aged between 45 and 55, buried on a south–north axis, with the head toward the north. Joints were in anatomical connection, except for the skull, found on its base. The skeleton is almost complete and in a very good state of preservation (hair was preserved). The skull was originally covered with a gourd bowl. This individual presents characteristics reminiscent of burial 29. Both were of medium stature, their noses are projected, and they have a small bun on the occipital bone. Both had had children, as suggested by the presence of grooves of pregnancy on the pubis.

The corpse was placed on its back, and the legs were folded with great force up to the head. The legs were so tightly pressed on the chest that the extremity of the long bones and the pelvis show postmortem fractures. Similar force was applied to the head, resulting in a twisted neck. After decomposition, the atlas rolled over and stayed upside down in the interior of the mandible. From this, we can conclude that the corpse was buried soon after death occurred, after it was tightly bound.

Postmortem Removal of Human Remains

Due to the large number of factors that can be involved, it is extremely difficult to know why certain human remains are missing from burial contexts (Verano 2001). Body parts were sometimes removed accidentally, but north-coast societies are known to have performed rituals that involved the removal of body parts and desiccated remains from old burials and for reburying the latter in new mortuary contexts (Nelson 1998; Millaire 2004). Such rituals are well documented, but their meaning is not yet clearly understood, although it has been suggested that body parts could have helped the dead in their journey to the afterlife (Millaire 2004).

At El Castillo, some burials were missing a few bones. In some cases, it was unclear whether the bones had been removed intentionally or accidentally. For example, six burials (burials 4, 5, 6, 7, 10, and 18) were so severely disturbed they could not be properly analyzed. Nevertheless, we are confident in the identification of rituals that involved the removal of body parts during grave reopening events.

Burial 1

The young sacrificed male from burial 1 was missing both feet, and the legs show evidence of postmortem manipulation: the tibia and fibula were removed and placed beside the left femur. Moreover, although the right hand was found under the pelvis, the long bones of the right arm are missing. The disturbance of the legs and removal of the right arm without disturbance of the other bone connections was only possible if the body was completely skeletonized. It is therefore argued that this is a case of ritual grave reopening.

Burial 2

A similar pattern was documented in burial 2. It was found on top of a wall dividing the Central Plaza from the Eastern Plaza. Adobe bricks had been removed to provide room for the burial. The individual, a robust male aged between 35 and 55, was buried on a north–south axis, with his head to the south (facing west). The body was probably wrapped in a shroud and placed in a rudimentary coffin, as suggested by remains of a reed mat and textile fragments.

No grave offering was found. The skeleton was in a very good state of preservation: all bones were present and in anatomical position, except for the right femur and innominate. That being said, the lower part of the right leg (tibia and fibula) and the foot were in place and in anatomical connection, indicating that the femur was removed once the soft tissue had decomposed.

Burial 3

Close to burial 2 was another individual, burial 3. Analyses suggest that it was a young female in her twenties. The body was placed on its left side, with the legs slightly folded in an incomplete fetal position. The head was oriented toward south, facing west. The position of the body suggests that the grave was too small for the corpse. The corpse was originally wrapped in a textile shroud, and a gourd bowl had been placed over the head.

Fragments of reed mat were found in the burial pit, and a spindle whorl was uncovered near the head. The skeleton was in anatomical connection, but almost every bone of the right side of the body was missing. From the degree of anatomical connection, it is suggested that the missing bones were removed when the body was completely skeletonized. The fact that the other anatomical connections remained intact indicates that care was taken when removing the bones.

Burial 8

This burial was a possible case of strangulation. The upper part of the skeleton was in anatomical connection, but the legs and feet were missing from the burial pit. Close examination of this context suggests that the grave was also reopened in pre-Columbian times and that the lower body was removed from the grave.

Burial 9

Burial 9, discussed previously as a case of postmortem decapitation, was also missing its right forearm. It is argued that these bones may have been removed during another reopening event.

Burial 27

As mentioned previously, burial 27 is a possible case of decapitation: the skull had been severed with a sharp object, leaving cut marks on the cervical vertebrae. Interestingly, most bones of the legs were also missing. These bones could only have been removed from the burial once the corpse was in an advanced stage of decomposition, however. Indeed, body parts could hardly have been removed at the time of the burial without leaving traces on the bones or without disturbing the anatomical connections. This evidence suggests yet another case of grave reopening.

DISCUSSION

A comparison of the two sectors in which burials were found reveals interesting patterns. Several burials were uncovered on the Eastern Terrace (Figure 12.3), and contextual evidence indicates that they were interred during successive burial events. Four individuals (burials 27–30) were uncovered inside a large burial pit excavated through an area filled with refuse on the north side of the east–west wall.[3] Close examination of the burial context reveals that these four individuals were buried at the same time.

The biological composition of the sample is interesting: there are three adult females, all older than 35, and one child aged between 11 and 13. A fifth individual found near this multiple grave (burial 26) is also a child aged between 11 and 13. Based on the bone morphology, both subadults could be females. Two more skeletons were found in this area: one on top of the east–west wall (burial 24) and the other south of the wall (burial 25). These were two young adult females, aged between 16 and 20.

As mentioned previously, the skeletons from this terrace presented postmortem traumas caused by the tight binding of the corpses with ropes. These burials may therefore represent a particular funerary pattern that involved a group of persons (or victims) buried in a restricted location. No particular biological traits could help establish if these individuals were genetically or socially related.[4]

On the hilltop sector, the pattern is different. Radiocarbon dating suggests that this area witnessed the last period of Gallinazo construction at the site (see Chapter 11). Here, all burials were found inside shallow graves excavated within or near the Central Plaza (Figure 12.2). The distribution of burials by age and sex is significant: in this sector, males, females, and children are all represented. The same holds true for burial orientation: on the Eastern Terrace, individuals were buried on a north–south or east–west axis, whereas on the hilltop sector the deceased were systematically buried on a north–south axis. Finally, in this sector none of the corpses were buried in a contracted position (as was the case on the Eastern Terrace).

Another interesting pattern documented at El Castillo has to do with body position: three corpses were buried facedown (burials 1, 9, and 24). Culturally, placement of the dead in an extended supine position refers to a state of sleep, whereas placement of the dead in a sitting position conveys the idea of a person awakened (Rowe 1995:28). A corpse buried facedown is more difficult to explain. In different cultures from around the world, the facedown burial position is typically used in cases of "bad death" (Thomas 1975; Barber 1988).

It could therefore be argued that the individuals buried facedown were feared and that the community wished that they would quickly reach the world of the dead. The fact that these individuals were nevertheless given a "proper" burial treatment suggests a certain degree of ambivalence, as these burials also denote a certain respect for the dead. A similar pattern may explain why some corpses were tightly bound before they were buried on the Eastern Terrace: the ropes may have actually been used to symbolically "immobilize" the soul of the dead.

The evidence presented previously also indicates that two adults had been decapitated after they were dead—another pattern worth discussion. One was further dismembered: his left arm was severed, as judged by the presence of cut marks on the clavicle. Our analyses also indicated six cases of grave reopening that involved the removal of human remains from the burial. Because information on Gallinazo mortuary practice is scarce or unpublished, however, it is almost impossible to assess whether the patterns identified represent the "burial norm" or what could be described as "deviant mortuary behaviors."

Research on the burial practices of the coeval Moche society has shown that burials were placed in various contexts (below house floors, inside cemeteries, or within platform mounds) and present a wide range of variation with regard to body position, grave organization, and associated offerings (Donnan 1995; Millaire 2002).[5] Some Moche funerary contexts did feature sacrificed individuals, and several cases of postmortem manipulation of human remains have also been documented (Verano 1986, 1995, 2001; Millaire

2004). As such, it can be argued that the Gallinazo de Santa shared with the Moche an interest in the manipulation of human remains.

Some archaeologists believe that both groups actually shared many cultural traits, and Jean-François Millaire has even suggested that they may have come from a single breeding population (2005; see also Chapters 1, 9). The similarities between Gallinazo and Moche manipulations of human remains could also be explained by the fact that members of both cultures actually lived side by side at the site during a certain period. Indeed, there is clear evidence that the Moche colonized the area. However, Chapdelaine and his team showed how the valley witnessed a period of cohabitation before it fell under Moche rule (Chapdelaine and Pimentel 2001, 2002; Chapdelaine, Pimentel, and Bernier 2003; see also Chapter 11).

Finally, two cases of perimortem skull fracture were recorded at El Castillo, representing the first documented cases of Gallinazo human sacrifice. Why these individuals were sacrificed and buried in the hilltop sector is a difficult question to answer, however. Discussing the sacrificial victims from Huaca de la Luna, Bourget (2001) argued that they had been killed during a period of extreme stress caused by the climatic disruption associated with an El Niño event.

Commenting on the nature of this site, Garth Bawden noted that it could, in fact, represent an aberrant form of funerary behavior because Moche sacrificial victims are usually found in or adjacent to the tombs of rulers (Bawden 2005: 534). Neither of these patterns seems to fit the evidence available from El Castillo. These were no retainers, and although some individuals were sacrificed, they were nevertheless provided with a proper burial.

Chapdelaine and colleagues (see Chapter 11) have argued that the Moche immigration and domination of the valley had exerted important social stresses on the Gallinazo de Santa population. Under these circumstances, in response to such cultural stresses it is possible that the local Gallinazo de Santa elite performed rituals that involved human sacrifice, a pattern that has been documented elsewhere (Taylor 2002).

Recent archaeological work in the Santa Valley has therefore provided important insights into the Gallinazo de Santa culture. Research on several settlements has shown that the Gallinazo were well established in the area and that the El Castillo site represented the core of the local political system prior to Moche colonization (Chapdelaine 2004; see also Chapter 11).

The discovery of human burials at this site was an unprecedented opportunity to document Gallinazo de Santa funerary customs. Some of the most stimulating results of the present bioarchaeological analysis have to do with the identification of rituals that involved the burial of victims of human sacrifice, the decapitation of recently deceased individuals and subsequent interment, the process of tight-binding dead individuals to a degree that sometimes led to postmortem fractures, and grave reopening events associated with the removal of certain body parts.

As mentioned previously, because information on Gallinazo mortuary practice is scarce in the literature, it is difficult to know whether the burial patterns identified at El Castillo represent a "burial norm" in Gallinazo de Santa mortuary practices or "deviant mortuary behaviors." What is clear is that Gallinazo burial customs show similarities with Moche funerary practice, especially with regard to postmortem dismemberment and grave reopening (Millaire 2004). Gallinazo de Santa burials are unique, however, in that some of their dead were buried tightly bound in a contracted position. Future research in Santa will certainly help us document further the mortuary practices of members of the Gallinazo de Santa culture.

ACKNOWLEDGMENTS

I would first like to express my gratitude to Claude Chapdelaine for having given me the opportunity to take part in this wonderful field project. I would also like to thank him for his helpful comments on earlier drafts of this text. I am also grateful to Jean-François Millaire for his invaluable assistance throughout the editing process. Finally, a special thanks to Hélène Bernier for her work in the field, excavating many of the burials presented in this chapter.

NOTES

1   The position of burial 18 is not indicated in the figures.

2   The skull had been disturbed by modern looting and was found nearby (not shown in drawing).

3   The fact that these individuals were buried without offering (within a midden) is not necessarily a sign of infamy because the very act of burying someone usually confers sacredness to the burial ground (Delattre 2003).

4   At El Castillo, family ties are suggested in two other cases. In a burial, two individuals in their early teens (13–15 years old) who showed artificial cranial deformations were found together (burial 18), a feature that may be indicative of a family tie. Another possible case is suggested by the presence of upper winged incisors in a burial (burial 7): one was from a child aged between 8 and 10 and the other was from a young adult female aged between 20 and 25.

5   Individuals were usually buried on their backs, in an extended position, although some corpses were lying on one side, and were generally wrapped in a shroud. Ceramic vessels were usually buried with the deceased, and copper items were placed in the hands or inside the mouth.

REFERENCES

Barber, Paul
    1988   *Vampires, Burial, and Death: Folklore and Reality.* New Haven: Yale University Press.

Bawden, Garth
    2005   Comments on "The Nature of Moche Human Sacrifice" by Richard C. Sutter and Rosa J. Cortez. *Current Anthropology* 46(4):534.

Benson, Elizabeth P.
    1975   Death-Associated Figures on Mochica Pottery. In *Death and the Afterlife in Pre-Columbian America*, Elizabeth P. Benson (ed.), pp. 105–141. Washington, D.C.: Dumbarton Oaks Research Library and Collections.

Bourget, Steve
    2001   Children and Ancestors: Ritual Practices at the Moche Site of Huaca de la Luna, North Coast of Peru. In *Ritual Sacrifice in Ancient Peru*, Elizabeth P. Benson and Anita G. Cook (eds.), pp. 93–118. Austin: University of Texas Press.

Burns, Karen R.
    1999   *Forensic Anthropology Training Manual.* Upper Saddle River, New Jersey: Prentice Hall.

Chapdelaine, Claude
    2004   Gallinazo and Moche at El Castillo of Santa: An Interlocking History. Paper presented at the 23rd Annual Meeting of the Northeast Conference on Andean Archaeology and Ethnohistory, Yale University.

Chapdelaine, Claude, and Víctor Pimentel
    2001   Informe del Proyecto Arqueológico PSUM (Proyecto Santa de la Universidad de Montreal): La presencia moche en el valle del Santa, costa norte del Perú – 2000. Unpublished report submitted to the Instituto Nacional de Cultura, Lima. (See electronic publication at *www.mapageweb.umontreal.ca/chapdelc*)
    2002   Informe del Proyecto Arqueológico PSUM (Proyecto Santa de la Universidad de Montreal): La presencia moche en el valle del Santa, costa norte del Perú – 2001. Unpublished report submitted to the Instituto Nacional de Cultura, Lima. (See electronic publication at *www.mapageweb.umontreal.ca/chapdelc*)

Chapdelaine, Claude, Víctor Pimentel, and Hélène Bernier
    2003   Informe del Proyecto Arqueológico PSUM (Proyecto Santa de la Universidad de Montreal): La presencia moche en el valle del Santa, costa norte del Perú – 2002. Unpublished report submitted to the Instituto Nacional de Cultura, Lima. (See electronic publication at *www.mapageweb.umontreal.ca/chapdelc*)

Cordy-Collins, Alana
    2001   Decapitation in Cupisnique and Early Moche Societies. In *Ritual Sacrifice in Ancient Peru*, Elizabeth P. Benson and Anita G. Cook (eds.), pp. 21–33. Austin: University of Texas Press.

Delattre, Valérie
    2003   Pratiques culturelles celtiques. *Histoire antique* (Dijon) 7:36–41.

Donnan, Christopher B.
    1995   Moche Funerary Practice. In *Tombs for the Living: Andean Mortuary Practices*, Tom D. Dillehay (ed.), pp. 111–159. Washington, D.C.: Dumbarton Oaks Research Library and Collection.

Frame, Mary
    2001   Blood, Fertility, and Transformation: Interwoven Themes in the Paracas Necropolis Embroideries. In *Ritual Sacrifice in Ancient Peru*, Elizabeth P. Benson and Anita G. Cook (eds.), pp. 55–92. Austin: University of Texas Press.

Frayer, David W.
    1997   Ofnet: Evidence for a Mesolithic Massacre. In *Troubled Times: Violence and Warfare in the Past*, Debra L. Martin and David W. Frayer (eds.), pp. 181–216. Amsterdam: Gordon and Breach.

Millaire, Jean-François
2002 *Moche Burial Patterns: An Investigation into Prehispanic Social Structure*. BAR International Series 1066. Oxford: BAR.
2004 The Manipulation of Human Remains in Moche Society: Delayed Burials, Grave Reopening, and Secondary Offerings of Human Bones on the Peruvian North Coast. *Latin American Antiquity* 15(4):371–388.
2005 Gallinazo y la tradición nor-costeña. Paper presented at the roundtable "Gallinazo: Una tradición cultural temprana en la costa norte del Perú," Trujillo.

Nelson, Andrew J.
1998 Wandering Bones: Archaeology, Forensic Science and Moche Burial Practices. *International Journal of Osteoarchaeology* 8:192–212.

Rowe, John
1995 Behavior and Belief in Ancient Peruvian Mortuary Practice. In *Tombs for the Living: Andean Mortuary Practices*, Tom D. Dillehay (ed.), pp. 27–41. Washington, D.C.: Dumbarton Oaks Research Library and Collection.

Taylor, Timothy
2002 *The Buried Soul: How Humans Invented Death*. Boston: Beacon Press.

Thomas, Louis-Vincent
1975 *Anthropologie de la mort*. Paris: Payot.

Verano, John W.
1986 A Mass Burial of Mutilated Individuals at Pacatnamu. In *The Pacatnamu Papers*, Volume 1, Christopher B. Donnan and Guillermo A. Cock (eds.), pp. 117–138. Los Angeles: Museum of Cultural History, University of California.
1995 Where Do They Rest? The Treatment of Human Offerings and Trophies in Ancient Peru. In *Tombs for the Living: Andean Mortuary Practices*, Tom D. Dillehay (ed.), pp. 189–227. Washington, D.C.: Dumbarton Oaks Research Library and Collection.
2001 The Physical Evidence of Human Sacrifice in Ancient Peru. In *Ritual Sacrifice in Ancient Peru*, Elizabeth P. Benson and Anita G. Cook (eds.), pp. 165–184. Austin: University of Texas Press.

White, Tim D.
1992 *Prehistoric Cannibalism at Mancos 5MTUMR-2346*. Princeton: Princeton University Press.

Burials at El Castillo

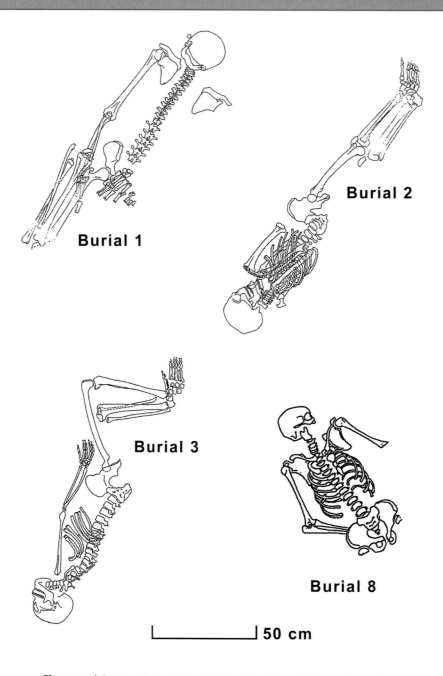

Burial 1

Burial 2

Burial 3

Burial 8

50 cm

FIGURE A1. Burials 1–3, 8 at El Castillo. Note: Magnetic north at top.

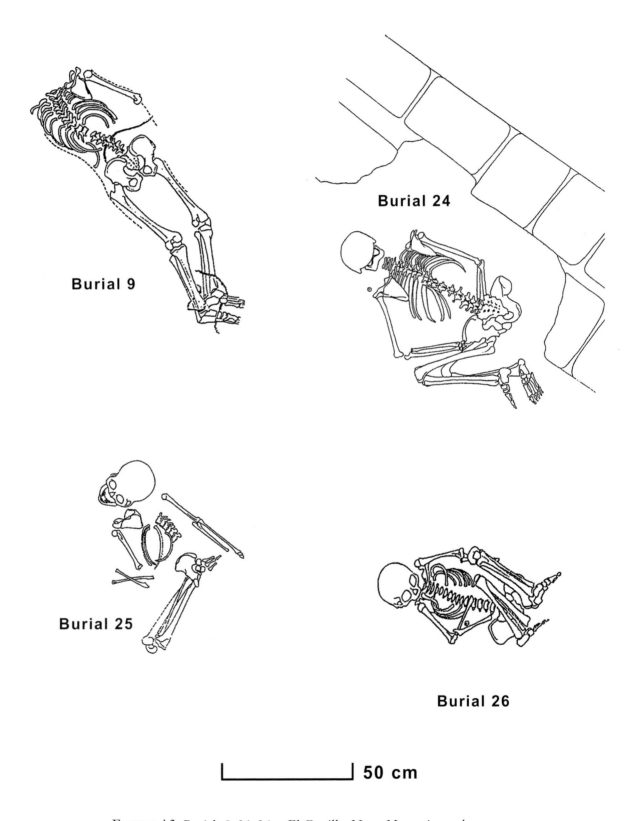

FIGURE A2. Burials 9, 24–26 at El Castillo. Note: Magnetic north at top.

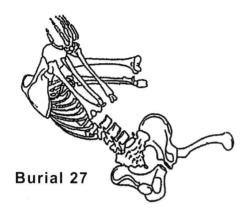

Burial 27

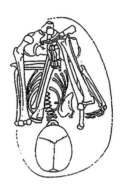

Burial 28

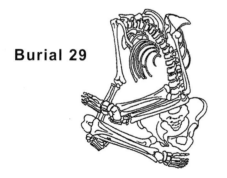

Burial 29

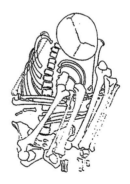

Burial 30

50 cm

FIGURE A3. Burials 27–30 at El Castillo. Note: Magnetic north at top.

CHAPTER 13

GALLINAZO, VICÚS, AND MOCHE IN THE DEVELOPMENT OF COMPLEX SOCIETIES ALONG THE NORTH COAST OF PERU

Luis Jaime Castillo Butters

Without having agreed to do so in advance, the majority of the participants in the present symposium arrived at the same general conclusions regarding the nature of the Gallinazo (or Virú; Larco Hoyle [1945, 1948]) phenomenon and its relation to the Moche. Christopher Donnan (see Chapter 2), probably the most emphatic of all, argues that what we call Gallinazo is nothing more than the popular material culture produced on the north coast before, during, and even after the development of Moche states. Only negative-painted vessels, in the form of Gallinazo Negative and Carmelo Negative ceramic types (Ford 1949), would represent distinct elite styles —easily differentiated from artifacts used by the popular substratum.

All participants of this symposium, at least to some extent, were in agreement with this interpretation, contributing evidence to support the idea that Gallinazo material culture did not disappear with the irruption of the Moche phenomenon, having coexisted and even in some cases surviving its collapse. In the better-documented studies—as in Dos Cabezas and Masanca (see Chapter 2) and in La Leche Valley (Shimada and Maguiña 1994)—the preexistence of Gallinazo materiality as a crucible in which the Moche identity was forged is indisputable.

It seems that with this agreement we can at last explain the strange, yet not so rare, presence of Gallinazo ceramics in Moche burials and other contexts. Until now, the only plausible explanation for such occurrences was that Gallinazo objects were ancient ceramics reused by the Moche, or that they were Moche copies of Gallinazo ware. Now we can assume that the presence of Gallinazo ceramics within rich Moche graves simply corresponds to offering items of somewhat lower status.

Because there is near unanimity on this crucial point, it seems that we have a consensus and that we can all go home satisfied with the results of this magnificent roundtable. There are still loose ends in this formulation, however: some things are left unexplained, and new hypotheses will need to be explored in light of the new paradigm. This chapter explores those aspects I believe still need to be addressed. Ultimately, I would like to argue that there was more continuity between the Gallinazo and Moche cultures than we had originally believed.

THE GALLINAZO PHENOMENON

One peculiar thing about Gallinazo is that many archaeologists working on the north coast feel uncomfortable defining it as a culture, a society, or a style. As a result (and until we find a better term), it is usually simply described as a cultural "phenomenon" that developed in multiple regions along the coast during the first millennia of the present era, manifesting itself in the form of artifacts (particularly ceramics) that shared forms and decorative techniques. But how was this homogeneity achieved? Was there some form of coordination among the various entities that produced Gallinazo objects?

Although Heidy Fogel (1993) argued several years ago (albeit without much evidence) that there existed a multi-valley Gallinazo state, most scholars have been reluctant to accept that the state level of sociopolitical organization was achieved before the Moche (Castillo 1999), and it is traditionally assumed that the Gallinazo phenomenon had no strong internal cohesion. Nevertheless, it is clear from the contributions to this volume that the Gallinazo phenomenon occurred throughout the north coast of Peru, thus achieving important conditions of complex societies: a far-reaching extension and a large population.

But what about the organizational nature of this phenomenon? What about its level of complexity and its institutions? Was Gallinazo a number of complex chiefdoms (*cacicazgos*) that were independent and isolated from one another? Were they articulated through some form of still-uncertain cultural mechanism, process, or institution? A comparison with the Moche will help address these questions.

One critical point to acknowledge is that recent breakthroughs in the study of the Moche were heralded by a better understanding of its political and social organization. The recognition that the Moche had been organized in multiple interacting polities—each developing through distinct historical processes (Quilter 2002; Castillo and Uceda 2008)—has had two main effects. First, it has refocused the study of the Moche on its regional expressions: the diverse political entities, each with its own historical development.

Second, this new perspective has highlighted the fact that a centralized and hierarchic model of Moche political organization is inconsistent and full of contradictions (Castillo and Donnan 1994; Shimada 1994; Bawden 2001, 2004; Dillehay 2001; Millaire 2004). Indeed, if Moche was a unique centralized state, it could hardly have been embodied regionally by the presence of totally different ceramics styles. Similarly, it is difficult to see how the "state styles" (e.g., Moche IV fine-line ceramics and portrait jars) could have been ubiquitous in some regions but not in others. Finally, it is difficult to understand how the development processes, expressed in the speed and direction of formal and stylistic changes, could have been so different from one region to another.

One important aspect of the intellectual process that led to the new and complex theoretical conception of the Moche—a complex of independent states that had followed different developments—was that it was formulated while we still lacked the empirical data to support it. We therefore went on searching for evidence to test the model. As a better understanding of social and political organization has arisen, it is quite interesting to see how everything else seems to fall into place, producing a more coherent and diversified vision of the Moche.

When trying to establish the political and social nature of Gallinazo, it is essential to question its origin and cultural homogeneity. Alternatively, perhaps we should first try to determine if such homogeneity existed—if there is a universe of forms and designs that would correspond to a grand Gallinazo tradition. Now that we are certain of the multiple incarnations of the phenomenon, a detailed comparative study of its forms, techniques, and decorations is in order.

The ceramics we usually call Gallinazo are surprisingly similar all along the north coast for almost a millennium, particularly so with regard to medium-quality ceramic objects. But agreeing that Gallinazo was a popular style (in the sense of the "style of the people") along the north coast for a large part of the Early Intermediate period does not explain the reason for this formal and stylistic homogeneity. In other words, it does not explain why and how the material products of a large number of people along the coast over several centuries could have become harmonized and why and how they came to share so many common traits.

The most popular ceramics considered under the Gallinazo banner (the Castillo Plain, Castillo Incised, and Castillo Modeled types) are so coherent stylistically across the regions in which they are found that it could hardly have been the result of chance or the product of cultural convergence. We should expect that over a thousand years, many production units (for example, ceramic workshops) would have "drifted" into differentiated styles.

The existence of homogeneity among the multiple incarnations of Gallinazo compels us to consider the existence of harmonizing mechanisms. If there exist similarities between artifacts that we call Gallinazo over 400 km of coastal landscape between the Piura and Santa Valleys, it is necessarily because there existed some form of connection or channels of communication between the different human groups that inhabited these regions. It seems acceptable to me to assume that this connection was the result of some form of political, economic, or ideological affinity (Millaire 2004). These mechanisms were likely articulated through a set of norms that harmonized the production: most likely, mechanisms of social interaction such as regional commercial exchanges and ceremonial activities or exogamous marriage and bridal exchanges.

Taking into account that the subject matter of Gallinazo ceramic art is generally not divinities, supernatural beings, priests, or members of the elites but rather ordinary men and women without sumptuous attire, it would seem that there was no need to represent the characters of their religious cosmos. The absence of characters more directly connected with the realms of ideology or

politics suggests that objects produced in this style were not instruments of ideology or of control and manipulation. The somewhat "low profile" of Gallinazo iconography reinforces what Donnan (see Chapter 2) described as the "popular character of this ceramic." From this perspective, Gallinazo objects would express the identity of the commoners.

The economic articulation and interdependence of Gallinazo political entities, and the production and distribution of goods among them, would seem to have been the least important factor leading to the harmonization of material culture. It is likely that autarkic models were the norm among Gallinazo communities and that the most important economic complementarities were developed vertically with the highlands.

Jean-François Millaire (see Chapter 1) stresses the political, ideological, and economic fragmentation of Gallinazo society, arguing that the political configuration of these societies could have corresponded to "city-state systems": political entities that were internally strongly articulated but essentially independent from one another, each evolving within a limited sphere and possibly engaging in confrontation and competition with its neighbors.

It is also improbable that there would have been a political or economic integration among the various regions where this phenomenon appeared, whereby individuals would be in such constant contact that homogenization of their ceramic styles would result. Thus, the Gallinazo style may not have been the result of political action or the effect of the coordination from a leader or from a supra-community entity.

If the Gallinazo style was not the materialization of an organized religion, nor forged by north-coast–wide politics or economics, one remaining explanation for the homogeneity among the multiple regional expressions of the phenomenon is that it was the result of "social interactions." By social interactions I mean opportunities in which individuals coming from more or less isolated communities were in contact with neighboring groups, having the opportunity to experience the ways of life of the others: their traditions, products, technologies, and aesthetics.

If these interactions were of a more permanent nature—for example, when an individual born and raised in a community moved into another—the interactions between local "cultures," their reciprocal influences, and continuous and more frequent contacts should have had a stronger effect. For instance, activities involving a regional gathering (such as exchange markets, traditional festivals, or religious ceremonies sponsored by the state or regional authority—which are still quite frequent in the central Andes) could have had a cultural harmonization effect for those involved.

On the other hand (and equally plausible as an effect), participation in these events could have reinforced local identities and their expressions: for instance, distinctions in clothing (see Chapter 9). Even today, such events bring together people from different villages and are usually attended by traders and producers from remote places. For a ceramist or a weaver, these events would provide ideal opportunities to observe and compare what other artisans were producing—the techniques and motives that went into their creation and decoration of pots and garments.

If exchanges were possible, products obtained in these settings later served as sources of inspiration. Late Moche artisans, for example, were producing copies of polychrome Wari vessels shortly after these objects started to appear in their communities. Although the copies were not as good as the originals, it is interesting to note how much experimentation went on and how fast it occurred.

Even more important than the exchange of objects, regional gatherings have always been *loci* for social interactions and contacts leading to mobility, particularly for the younger members of society, assuming that exogamy was the rule. It therefore seems likely that the most important source of stylistic influence comes from individual women and men incorporated into a new community through matrimony or migration, contributing and "syncretizing" their own knowledge, iconography, techniques, manufacturing processes, understanding of materials, and aesthetics. The stylistic and formal homogeneity of

Gallinazo domestic ceramics could have been one effect of such social interactions among various coastal communities.

Until recently, an assumption has gone unchallenged: that there existed a high stylistic homogeneity among Gallinazo-style artifacts from different parts of the north coast. This assumption has yet to be empirically proven, as it is essentially based on observed similarities between the most conspicuous artifacts in the archaeological record. We still need to define empirically if there was formal and stylistic homogeneity in the ceramic production from different regions, and if co-variations occurred.

Perhaps the similarities are more pronounced between certain regions and less so between others. If at the end of this exercise we come to the conclusion that there existed a large degree of homogeneity, looking for the causes and mechanisms will become imperative. Yet, stylistic homogeneity does not necessarily imply political integration. In Moche archaeology, it took us nearly a hundred years to realize that the stylistic differences reflected in reality a highly complex political map composed of independent polities (Dillehay 2001; Castillo and Uceda 2008).

FROM GALLINAZO TO MOCHE

The presence of Gallinazo ceramics in Moche contexts at Huaca de la Luna (Uceda 2001), Pampa Grande (Shimada 1994), Sipán (Alva 2004), and San José de Moro (Castillo 2001, 2003; Castillo et al. 2008; see also Chapter 4) leaves no doubt that the Moche tradition was founded on a Gallinazo substratum (see Chapter 1) and that the two ceramic traditions coexisted at least until the end of the Moche rule.

In all of these cases, however, Gallinazo-style material is more frequent in the earlier phases, suggesting that the Moche culture evolved from the Gallinazo. But when and how did this evolution occur? And more importantly, what were the conditions under which (and the reasons why) this process took place? Considering that the Moche represented multiple polities, however, it is evident that the processes that led from Gallinazo to Moche were multiple and highly distinct from one region to another.

Searching for the precise location or region where the Moche first appeared—that is to say, where the Gallinazo materiality first transformed into Moche—does not seem to be a very productive path. Subjective criteria (such as the apparent primitiveness of Moche artifacts from Piura) have been used as indicators of the original motherland of the Moche (Klein 1967; Kaulicke 1992). It is now evident, however, that the transformation was a long process and that it happened simultaneously in many valleys of the north coast.

As a result, each process needs to be investigated independently. The Lambayeque, Jequetepeque, Chicama, and Moche Valleys seem to be the most likely candidates for the origin of the Moche, and it is quite possible that these valleys "cross-pollinated" one another in a real co-evolution. The time frame for these processes is quite long, with dates that range the entire A.D. 200 to 500 period (Castillo and Uceda 2008).

Arguing too much about the time and location for this transformation could end up in an irrelevant competition that misses the most important question: why did the Gallinazo transform into the Moche? In my opinion, the window of opportunity that created the conditions for the development of the Moche from the oldest Gallinazo substratum was a sudden growth and development of Gallinazo groups between the first and second centuries before the present era—a growth associated with the rise to power of a new (Moche) elite defined by a new and distinct aesthetic.

The only material basis that could have supported this type of sudden development must have been an increase in resource availability due to better agricultural practices. This suggests that either productivity was increased (i.e., that yields per hectare grew) or that there was an expansion in the total extent of the available arable land. However, yields per hectare were probably at their maximum, considering the technology available at the time, so an expansion of arable lands seems more likely.

There are several reasons to believe that (at least in the Jequetepeque Valley) this period coincides with the extension of agricultural lands due to the development of larger and more efficient irrigation systems. In the first half of the first millennium A.D., the largest irrigation programs were started and completed in the Jequetepeque Valley with the incorporation of the northern Chamán area (Castillo 2004). This process implied the construction of at least four large canals and the necessary infrastructure for water distribution.

Access to new lands, control of waters and irrigation systems, and development of strategies of control and administration of natural resources created the opportunity and conditions for increasingly more acute social, political, and economic differentiation (Castillo 2004). A new social class, which benefited from this new source of wealth, seems to have emerged: the Moche. At first, this new social class would have been a segment of Gallinazo—but slowly transforming the entire Gallinazo society into a new cultural phenomenon. New social classes and unequal economic relationships between social segments required an ideological superstructure to justify and legitimize the new social order.

At the same time the Moche were evolving from their ancestors, a revolution was happening in the realm of ritual, performance, and the production of the necessary materializations of these new ideas. Again, the transition between Gallinazo and Moche was a time of extreme creativity and productivity that influenced the production of both portable objects of unparalleled quality and craftsmanship as well as monumental architecture to support new rituals. The material expressions of this ideology served to differentiate the Gallinazo commoners from the Moche elites and to legitimize the elites' control over the new source of wealth (see DeMarrais, Castillo, and Earle 1996).

We need to examine what is currently known of the formal and stylistic processes that led to the emergence of Moche ceramics in some key regions. In Piura, the Gallinazo substratum evolved into an elaborate Early Moche style we associate with the Loma Negra tombs and with Moche-Vicús ceramics. During the middle phase, stemming from Moche style, artisans developed a style of their own (including forms, techniques, and singular decorative motifs [Makowski 1994]).

It is clear that Gallinazo political entities coexisted with Moche polities in the Lambayeque region during the Early and Middle periods. Izumi Shimada and Adriana Maguiña (1994) proposed a division of this region into two, with the Gallinazo population in control of La Leche Valley and the Moche focusing on the Chancay-Reque Valley. During the Late Moche period, late Gallinazo and Moche V ceramics are found together at Pampa Grande (Shimada 1994). This is quite odd, considering that Moche V was essentially confined to the Chicama Valley (Castillo and Uceda 2008).

In Jequetepeque, work by Donnan (2001) has shown that the Moche style derived in its early stage from a solid and well-established Gallinazo style. During the Middle Moche period, the Gallinazo style declines to the advantage of Moche-style ceramics, which by then started to include utilitarian forms (see Chapter 4). By Late Moche times, the Gallinazo style had nearly disappeared in this region.

In the Chicama and Moche Valleys, evidence indicates the coexistence of Gallinazo and Moche ceramic traditions during the Early and Middle Moche periods, but we still lack data to argue that one tradition derived from the other or that they simply coexisted side by side. Santiago Uceda, Henry Gayoso, and Nadia Gamarra (see Chapter 7) and Gabriel Prieto (Prieto 2004) have demonstrated the coexistence of both ceramic styles at Huaca de la Luna. The fact that Moche ceramics (ceremonial and decorative wares) and Gallinazo (utilitarian containers) pottery were present throughout the sequence led these researchers to believe that these wares were the product of two distinct ceramic manufacture processes used by the same people.

South of Moche, in the Virú and Santa Valleys, a vigorous Gallinazo style existed, probably reflecting the existence of a more complex political formation than those that existed to the north. This was a true state, with its capital at the Gallinazo Group (Bennett 1950; Strong and Evans 1952; Fogel 1993). The latter may have been incorporated into the Moche state based in the Moche and Chicama Valleys through a process of military conquest (Strong and Evans 1952; Willey 1953, 1974; compare Chapter 1).

A reconstruction of the processes that led from Moche to Gallinazo, or that permitted the coexistence of both traditions, does not necessarily imply an understanding of the factors that produced those changes, however. It is common in Andean archaeology to describe a phenomenon yet fail to understand its causes and conditions. In the case of the transition from Gallinazo to Moche, and the survival of Gallinazo as a popular component of Moche, the conditions remain unclear but the processes are clearly different in every region.

Gallinazo expression in domestic ceramics survived all processes that led to the emergence of the Moche. Does it mean that the populations who produced those objects we call Gallinazo survived the transformations that led to the creation of the Moche with fairly little change? Or that those persons who were already fully incorporated into the Moche culture maintained a few characteristics of their former tradition, particularly the production of domestic ceramics in the fashion of their Gallinazo ancestors?

These issues bring us back to question the nature of the Gallinazo phenomenon. Was Gallinazo an ethnic identity, or simply a way of manufacturing ceramics shared by ethnically distinct populations? Was the observed stylistic homogeneity a result of cultural affinity? We have ruled out that the high degree of stylistic homogeneity could have been the outcome of political integration, or the product of conscious decisions taken by the elites. In fact, Gallinazo appears to have been a popular substratum that was not controlled by political institutions or influenced by the dominant ideology. And if this was the case, how did the communication channels that allowed this homogeneity survive all orders of political and economic transformation?

It seems that beneath the formal practices and relations sanctioned by the state there were networks of contact and communication between popular segments of the populations across the north coast of Peru and through an extended period. If we can confirm the existence of such an odd process (which defies the logic of our notion of political integration)—a popular culture that acts as a river that runs through and under the Moche state—we will still need to clarify (among other things) its nature, its units of action, its spheres of interaction, and its mechanisms of harmonization.

INVESTIGATION AND RECONSTRUCTION OF THE GALLINAZO PHENOMENON

One of the limitations we face in reconstructing the Gallinazo phenomenon is the limited quantity of empirical information available from controlled conditions of investigation. So far, only a few projects have specifically focused on Gallinazo. A majority of archaeologists have come to study this phenomenon in the process of conducting salvage projects or as part of wider investigations on north-coast cultural history.

After Wendell Bennett's investigations at the Gallinazo Group (Bennett 1950) more than 50 years ago, no excavations have been undertaken at this site, even though its importance for understanding this phenomenon is unquestionable. A new study of the Gallinazo Group is urgent, but this needs to be done as part of a long-term and large-scale project in order to gain access to the details of the site's occupational history, to its ceramic sequence, and to the activities and rituals performed there.

Regrettably, a large part of north-coast archaeology was based on surface surveys involving few or no systematic excavations (Millaire 2004). Even though Gordon Willey (1953) demonstrated the importance and validity of settlement pattern studies precisely through his original work in the Virú Valley, this type of research by itself does not solve all problems or answer all questions, and it is particularly ill equipped to deal with occupational and functional matters or with social relations and activities.

Although this method usually offers a broad picture, the quantity of information associated with each component is usually very small and lacks proper context. Long-term excavation programs, on the other hand, offer detailed images with an abundance of material but are limited to sites under study. This dichotomy brings us to the academic conundrum in which it is unclear whether it is better to know a lot about a few things or a little about a larger number of things.

Studies based exclusively on surface surveys, surface collections, and mapping (whatever the methods used) usually present a distorted image of the past. They are essentially based on what appears on the surface and what has not been reclaimed by later occupants of the site. On the other hand, research focusing exclusively on a site (whether typical or exceptional) without a broad understanding of regional patterns of site distribution, their relations, and interactions with the environment—as in the case of the excavations conducted in Sipán since 1987—is also not desirable.

Consider, for example, what we would know of Huacas de Moche if this site had been investigated using only "superficial" methods or through a small-scale excavation project. In fact, we know the answer to this question because the site was studied in this way during the 1970s—with results that were frankly deficient, particularly in light of the work conducted there by Santiago Uceda and Ricardo Morales since 1991 (Uceda 2001).

It is clear that scale of investigation and duration of the project are two factors that strongly influence our capacity to understand the phenomena we study. The scale of the excavations at Huacas de Moche, the El Brujo Complex, and San José de Moro provide archaeologists with complex images of the past, rather than a collection of its most salient and "superficial" features.

It is imperative that more research projects be undertaken on Gallinazo sites. These should be multidisciplinary projects dedicated to studying large parts of these settlements and of long enough duration that the investigators' ideas and interpretations can mature and be confronted during subsequent field seasons. With regard to Gallinazo, much still needs to be done in terms of field archaeology, including excavations of domestic and ceremonial settlements, tombs, temples, workshops, and storage facilities. This type of investigation should produce the necessary data for attempting to reconstruct the "Gallinazo world." Clearly, efforts such as those that brought us to this roundtable (and this volume) are steps in the right direction.

REFERENCES

Alva, Walter
  2004 *Sipán: Descubrimiento e investigación*. Lima: Quebecor World Perú.
Bawden, Garth
  2001 The Symbols of Late Moche Social Transformation. In *Moche Art and Archaeology in Ancient Peru*, Joanne Pillsbury (ed.), pp. 285–305. Washington, D.C.: National Gallery of Art and Yale University Press.
  2004 The Art of Moche Politics. In *Andean Archaeology*, Helaine Silverman (ed.), pp. 116–129. Oxford: Blackwell Publishing.
Bennett, Wendell C.
  1950 *The Gallinazo Group: Viru Valley, Peru*. Yale University Publications in Anthropology 43. New Haven: Yale University Press.
Castillo, Luis Jaime
  1999 Los Mochicas y sus antecesores: Las primeras civilizaciones estatales de la costa del Perú. In *Tesoros del Perú antiguo*, Krzysztof Makowski, Paloma Carcedo de Mufarech, Jorge E. Silva, Luis Jaime Castillo, Ulla Holmquist, et al. (eds.), pp. 141–176. [Exhibition catalogue, Museo Arqueológico Rafael Larco Herrera] Córdoba: Publicaciones Obra Social y Cultural CajaSur.
  2001 The Last of the Mochicas: A View from the Jequetepeque Valley. In *Moche Art and Archaeology in Ancient Peru*, Joanne Pillsbury (ed.), pp. 307–332. Washington, D.C.: National Gallery of Art and Yale University Press.
  2003 Los últimos Mochicas en Jequetepeque. In *Moche: Hacia el final del milenio*, Santiago Uceda and Elías Mujica (eds.), vol. 2, pp. 65–123. Lima: Universidad Nacional de Trujillo and Fondo Editorial, Pontificia Universidad Católica del Perú.
  2004 Moche Politics in the Jequetepeque Valley: A Case for Political Opportunism. In New Perspectives on the Moche Political Organization, Jeffrey Quilter, Luis Jaime Castillo, and Joanne Pillsbury (eds.). Manuscript accepted for publication. Washington, D.C.: Dumbarton Oaks Research Library and Collection.
Castillo, Luis Jaime, and Christopher B. Donnan
  1994 Los Mochica del norte y los Mochica del sur. In *Vicús*, Krzysztof Makowski, Christopher B. Donnan, Iván Amaro Bullon, Luis Jaime Castillo, Magdalena Díez Canseco, et al. (eds.), pp. 143–181. Colección Arte y Tesoros del Perú. Lima: Banco de Crédito del Perú.
Castillo, Luis Jaime, and Santiago Uceda
  2008 The Mochicas. In *The Handbook of South American Archaeology*, Helaine Silverman and William H. Isbell (eds.), pp. 707–729. New York: Springer.
Castillo, Luis Jaime, Julio Rucabado Yong, Martín del Carpio, Katiuska Bernuy Quiroga, Karim Ruiz Rosell, Carlos Rengifo Chunga, Gabriel Prieto Burmester, and Carole Fraresso
  2008 Ideología y poder en la consolidación, colapso y reconstitución del estado mochica del Jequetepeque: El Proyecto Arqueológico San José de Moro (1991–2006). *Ñawpa Pacha* 29: 1–86.
DeMarrais, Elizabeth, Luis Jaime Castillo, and Timothy Earle
  1996 Ideology, Materialization, and Power Strategies. *Current Anthropology* 37(1):15–31.
Dillehay, Tom D.
  2001 Town and Country in Late Moche Times: A View from Two Northern Valleys. In *Moche Art and Archaeology in Ancient Peru*, Joanne Pillsbury (ed.), pp. 259–283. Washington, D.C.: National Gallery of Art and Yale University Press.
Donnan, Christopher B.
  2001 Moche Burials Uncovered. *National Geographic* 199(3):58–73.
Fogel, Heidy
  1993 Settlements in Time: A Study of Social and Political Development during the Gallinazo Occupation of the North Coast of Perú [sic]. Unpublished Ph.D. dissertation, Yale University, New Haven.
Ford, James A.
  1949 Cultural Dating of Prehistoric Sites in Virú Valley, Peru. In *Surface Survey of the Virú Valley, Peru*, James A. Ford and Gordon R. Willey (eds.), pp. 29–87. Anthropological Papers of the American Museum of Natural History Vol. 43, Pt. 1. New York: The American Museum of Natural History.
Kaulicke, Peter
  1992 Moche, Vicús Moche y el Mochica Temprano. *Bulletin de l'Institut Français d'Études Andines* 21(3):853–903.
Klein, Otto
  1967 La cerámica mochica: Caracteres estilísticos y conceptos. *Scientia* (Valparaíso) 131.
Larco Hoyle, Rafael
  1945 *La cultura virú*. Buenos Aires: Sociedad Geográfica Americana.
  1948 *Cronología arqueológica del norte del Perú*. Buenos Aires: Sociedad Geográfica Americana.
Makowski, Krzysztof
  1994 Los señores de Loma Negra. In *Vicús*, Krzysztof Makowski, Christopher B. Donnan, Iván Amaro Bullon, Luis Jaime Castillo, Magdalena Díez Canseco, et al. (eds.), pp. 83–141. Colec-

ción Arte y Tesoros del Perú. Lima: Banco de Crédito del Perú.

Millaire, Jean-François
  2004 Moche Political Expansionism as Viewed from Virú: Recent Archaeological Work in the Close Periphery of a Hegemonic City-State System. In New Perspectives on the Moche Political Organization, Jeffrey Quilter, Luis Jaime Castillo, and Joanne Pillsbury (eds.). Manuscript accepted for publication. Washington, D.C.: Dumbarton Oaks Research Library and Collection.

Prieto, Gabriel
  2004 La poza de Huanchaco: Una aldea de pescadores durante el colapso del estado moche, valle de Moche. Unpublished licentiate thesis, Universidad Nacional de Trujillo, Trujillo.

Quilter, Jeffrey
  2002 Moche Politics, Religion, and Warfare. *Journal of World Prehistory* 16(2):145–195.

Shimada, Izumi
  1994 *Pampa Grande and the Mochica Culture*. Austin: University of Texas Press.

Shimada, Izumi, and Adriana Maguiña
  1994 Nueva visión sobre la cultura gallinazo y su relación con la cultura moche. In *Moche: Pro-puestas y perspectivas*, Santiago Uceda and Elías Mujica (eds.), pp. 31–58. Travaux de l'Institut Français d'Études Andines 79. Lima: Universidad Nacional de La Libertad and Instituto Francés de Estudios Andinos.

Strong, William D., and Clifford Evans
  1952 *Cultural Stratigraphy in the Virú Valley, Northern Peru: The Formative and Florescent Epoch*. New York: Columbia University Press.

Uceda, Santiago
  2001 Investigations at Huaca de la Luna, Moche Valley: An Example of Moche Religious Architecture. In *Moche Art and Archaeology in Ancient Peru*, Joanne Pillsbury (ed.), pp. 47–67. Washington, D.C.: National Gallery of Art and Yale University Press.

Willey, Gordon R.
  1953 *Prehistoric Settlement Patterns in the Virú Valley, Perú* [sic]. Smithsonian Institution, Bureau of American Ethnology Bulletin 155. Washington, D.C.: Government Printing Office.
  1974 The Virú Valley Settlement Pattern Study. In *Archaeological Researches in Retrospect*, Gordon R. Willey (ed.), pp. 149–176. Cambridge, Massachusetts: Winthrop Publishers.

CHAPTER 14

CONCLUDING REMARKS

Peter Kaulicke

The majority of the authors who contributed to this volume are "mochicologists," their main concern being the study of the Mochica style or culture.[1] Accordingly, their confrontation with non-Mochica evidence during fieldwork has usually been a largely unforeseen by-product of their original research program. The chronological position of the Gallinazo style, culture, or tradition (all of these qualifications are used in this volume) became disputed shortly after Rafael Larco Hoyle's (1945) original definition of the Virú culture.

Despite Larco Hoyle's argument for the coeval nature of Virú and Mochica, North American archaeologists generally preferred to consider these cultures sequentially (Kaulicke 1992: 857). In this context, Virú was presented as a pre-Mochica phenomenon (Donnan and Mackey 1978:Chart 1; Moseley and Day 1982:Table 1.1), followed by the Mochica—described as a largely "undisturbed" chronological block.

The obvious coexistence of Mochica and Gallinazo (as evidenced in the case studies presented here, and in others cited) calls for an explanation, however. It is becoming increasingly clear that the

Gallinazo and Salinar were not local or regional short-lived phenomena or somewhat ephemeral and faltering cultural or social expressions doomed to give way to the powerful and splendrous Mochica state. Rather, they shared the total area covered by the latter.

As for definitions of what is to be understood as the "Gallinazo style" (in particular, in regard to ceramics), many contributors present a historical background following Larco Hoyle's and William Strong and Clifford Evans's propositions. Thus, types such as Castillo Modeled and Castillo Incised (Strong, Evans, and Lilien 1952:309–325) are accepted as such and recognized in recent excavated materials outside the Virú Valley. Although the views expressed in this volume depart from this common base, interpretations differ widely.

In his introductory chapter in this volume, Jean-François Millaire proposes that north-coast societies lived in city-state–like polities: the region would therefore have hosted not two opposing social formations (Gallinazo and Mochica), but several polities of common cultural origin with different situations from one valley to another. He proposes the term *tradición norcosteña* to account for this phenomenon. In Chapter 9, Millaire also stresses the similarities between Virú textiles (Early Intermediate period) from Huaca Santa Clara (Virú Valley) and Mochica fabrics from other regions.

The chapter by Christopher Donnan (Chapter 2) differs to some extent by proposing that Gallinazo is an "illusion." He makes a strict distinction between the fine ware with negative decoration (not discussed in his chapter) defined by Larco Hoyle and the domestic types defined by Wendell Bennett (1939). The latter ceramics are simply defined as Mochica domestic ware lacking negative decoration, or simply as:

> the common domestic pottery widely used on the north coast of Peru from about 200 B.C. until A.D. 800. During that time, distinct styles of fine ware were in use at different locations and at different time periods. One of these was Gallinazo-style fine ware (Gallinazo Negative), and another was Moche-style fine ware.

Krzysztof Makowski, after a lengthy and complicated discussion, comes to a rather surprising but similar conclusion at the end of Chapter 3. He envisions warrior people (the "Virú-Gallinazo culture") conquering the Peruvian north coast during the second century A.D. Their identity was maintained as:

> the axis of political identity of the Moche elites. Even so, the rise and consolidation of powerful territorial states and the subsequent and indispensable negotiation with the conquered Vicús peoples . . . soon brought about a rapid and profound transformation of the Virú-Gallinazo culture.

Martín del Carpio's Chapter 4 presents burial contexts from excavations at San José de Moro, which he compares with other material in the Jequetepeque Valley. From the beginning, the author concurs with Donnan's interpretation that Gallinazo is a domestic ware in Mochica contexts, but he considers the possibility of changes in domestic wares during the occupation of San José de Moro and other sites. He also discusses the presence of various Mochica fine wares in the

same region, considering the possibility of coevality and mutual exclusivity.

The following two chapters concentrate on major centers in the Chicama Valley: Mocollope and the El Brujo Complex. The chapter by Christopher Attarian (Chapter 5) is decidedly theoretical and concerned with problems related to urbanism, identity, and ethnogenesis. The author states that in Mocollope and the entire Chicama Valley, Gallinazo evidence is earlier than Mochica: "Centralized control is evident at Mocollope in the elaborate elite architecture and the presence of Gallinazo Negative pottery."

The domestic Gallinazo wares in village communities tend to share a common identity that is challenged by involvement in the new urban environment. The author tries to show this change through an analysis of Castillo Incised pottery and comes to the conclusion that "Mocollope was a society composed of distinct communities," developing a new community identity.

The other complex in the Chicama Valley is presented by Régulo Franco and César Gálvez (Chapter 6), who present results from their long-term project at the El Brujo Complex and (to a minor extent) evidence from other sites in the same valley. They stress the coevality of Early Mochica (basically, Mochica I) and Gallinazo. The absence of wear on Gallinazo utilitarian vessels leads the authors to argue that these wares were funerary offerings. Local elites originally controlled the production of Gallinazo-style ceramics, but started to adopt new artistic canons, which the authors describe as Early Mochica (albeit seeming to incorporate Cupisnique elements). The reasons for theses changes, however, are not envisioned.

Santiago Uceda and his collaborators (Chapter 7) wholeheartedly support Donnan's vision of a general domestic ware characterized by the Castillo types, which they describe as an unchanging pottery unrelated to the elite ware of the time. They differentiate two groups of styles, however:

> [T]here were elite styles essentially associated with sumptuous and ritual objects . . . [as well as] styles related to the commoners, usually associated with utilitarian or domestic artifacts. . . . Whereas the evidence suggests that elite styles tended to change and were influenced by sociopolitical develop-

ments, utilitarian styles could remain practically unchanged for long periods—at least during the Early Horizon, Early Intermediate period, and Middle Horizon. One mistake was obviously to lump both groups of styles under the label "Gallinazo" and to use Castillo-style ceramics as evidence of a Gallinazo culture.

The observed "continuity" is explained by the fact that "they were not considered suitable vehicles for ideology and their production was not under political control." This interpretation somehow denies the potential of utilitarian wares as chronological and identity markers.

Through a bioarchaeological approach, Richard Sutter (Chapter 8) comes to the conclusion that "all Early Intermediate-period populations represented by the mortuary samples examined belonged to a relatively coherent breeding population," that "the Gallinazo samples from Cerro Oreja shared close phenetic relations with the urban sector population from Huacas de Moche," and that the Gallinazo population at Cerro Oreja likely "received relatively greater gene flow from highland populations to the east than did other coastal populations."

Jonathan Kent and his collaborators (Chapter 10) present a case study from the middle Chao Valley. In contrast to the majority of sites with monumental architecture presented thus far, the occupation of the Santa Rita B Archaeological Complex is seemingly entirely domestic. The authors sympathize with Donnan's "illusion" hypothesis, but in addition to Gallinazo wares they seem to accept Mochica and Recuay ceramics as ethnic markers.

Chapters 11 and 12 are products of the Santa Project of the Université de Montréal, directed by Claude Chapdelaine. His contribution (written with Víctor Pimentel and Jorge Gamboa) is notable for its more strictly archaeological reasoning and its clear structure—in the sense that Gallinazo and Mochica evidence (architecture, burials, ceramics, radiocarbon dates) is discussed in the context of the same site (El Castillo), erroneously attributed entirely to Mochica by earlier researchers.

This type of presentation allows us to judge statements directly, instead of being forced to accept or refuse given arguments. The authors concur that there is a definite Mochica domestic ware, although it is not described in this text. Chapdelaine, however, should know the problem well, as he worked at Huacas de Moche for several years. The presented data, therefore, speak in favor of "two distinct cultural groups that lived in close proximity" during the Mochica III phase (between about A.D. 300 and 450–500). This "proximity" demands a search for data specifying interactions between the cultural groups.

One aim should be the definition of the "partial blending of these two domestic-ware traditions" (Chapter 11). The authors even present a possible historical narrative of the Mochica occupation in Santa, as an alternative to the improbable conquest hypothesis favored until now, but they are aware that further research is badly needed to confirm their suggestions. Gérard Gagné's detailed bioarchaeological analysis of burial contexts excavated in the same site follows (Chapter 12). Although his observations are interesting, they do not add significantly to possible or probable differentiation with much better-known Mochica burial practices.

ASPECTS OF CONSENSUS

Many of the authors of this volume seem to support Donnan's rather categorical "solution" to the Gallinazo "problem": the Gallinazo style as a type of "mega-domestic ware," omnipresent and unchanged in hundreds of years in a vast space. According to this viewpoint, fine ware automatically indicates the presence of elites, whereas domestic wares represent the "commoners" (see Chapter 7). Thus, the presence of domestic wares (Castillo Modeled and Incised) in basically non-domestic contexts—as in most of the cases presented in this volume—does not seem to bother the authors who maintain this position.

Neither does the fact that relatively coarse vessels with Gallinazo features occur even in the "richest" Mochica burial chambers—such as those at Sipán (Alva 1994:Plates 294, 295) and Dos Cabezas (Donnan 2003, 2007)—seem to call for major attention. On the other hand, the few known Mochica or Gallinazo domestic contexts cannot serve as unequivocal arguments in favor of this "commoner culture." The problem, therefore, seems to lie in a basic terminology that mixes description and material analysis with social or cultural historical interpretations.

This methodological confusion has to be unraveled before coming back to the interpretations offered for the "solution" to the Gallinazo "problem." As many of the projects presented here deal with nondomestic contexts, it is difficult to discern clearly between domestic and nondomestic material evidence—something that in some of the chapters leads to an "elite" point of view. Therefore, it would be wise to separate precise contexts from general interpretations. One of the aspects to be dealt with is the general chronology of the area shared by the Gallinazo and Mochica styles.

The first step consists of providing a chronological background for the entire area wherein these ceramic styles are observed in their various settings. The often-stated coevality, but also non-coevality (relation to successive occurrence), is basically a local observation that cannot be generalized without controlled recurrence and that should be sustained by a consistent series of radiocarbon dates. Unfortunately, the 700 years or so between the Final Formative and evidence of Wari influence in the north coast represent a neglected space only highlighted by an almost exclusive concern with certain aspects of the Mochica culture. The following discussion is based on a number of published reflections (Kaulicke 1991, 1992, 1993, 1994, 1998, 2000, 2006) over the past 16 years.

WORK IN THE UPPER PIURA AREA

The Piura Valley (in particular, the upper Piura area) is one of the most important areas, but it is unfortunately largely unrecognized by the authors of this volume. Material from surface surveys and extensive excavations during 1987 and 1990 led to a sequence that covers the Middle Formative (Early Horizon) to Wari (Middle Horizon) in seven phases, with subphases: Ñañañique 1, Ñañañique 2, Panecillo 1, Panecillo 2, La Encantada, Chapica, Vicús Tamarindo A (VTA), Vicús Tamarindo B (VTB), and Vicús Tamarindo C1 (VTC1) and C2 (VTC2). Of these phases, only the Chapica is exclusively based on surface material (Bats 1991; Guffroy 1994; Kaulicke 2006).

In all phases, monumental structures are associated with particular architectural and ceramic styles, domestic and residential structures, and plazas. The building sequence is characterized by the extensive use of wattle-and-daub walls on platforms from the Formative to the VTA, followed by the use of *tapia* (puddled adobe) platforms during the VTB, by adobe walls (with niches) and platforms with staircases during the VTC1, and finally by the construction of ramps during the VTC2. Changes in domestic and residential architecture are also evident.

Thus, it comes as no surprise that the ceramics are following these changes. However, according to their contexts, the ceramics are often multifunctional (e.g., large vessels for *chicha* production reused as burial recipients [*pithoi*]). There are various VTA pastes and colors associated with burnished surfaces on jars, short-necked *ollas*, and bowls. Decoration includes white paint in simple patterns and modeling (although most fragments are undecorated). Their wall thicknesses range between less than 3 mm to more than 11 mm. The entire complex can be related to Sechura B, Huacapongo Polished, and Puerto Moorin White-on-Red, as well as to Salinar and Gallinazo.

The VTB is characterized by red, pink, or white slips and inferior burnishing in a more varied range of sizes in jars, open bowls, and small bowls. There is more modeled decoration (primarily on face-neck jars), more figurines, and a wider range of white-painted and negative-painted motifs associated with the VTB. Beginning with the VTB, much of this material is used in ritual feasts, the remains of which were deliberately buried. VTC ceramics employ brick-red to orange pastes, but other colors are present: dark brown, pink, and gray.

Fine ceramics feature polished black, burnished black, burnished red, brown, gray, and white (kaolinite), with wall thicknesses between 3 mm and more than 12 mm, although some vessels are extremely thin (less than 1 mm thick). Coarseware containers are often associated with the production of chicha, and medium-ware containers with chicha storage and serving, whereas fineware vessels represent serving vessels. Medium- and fine-ware vessels are often found together in pits: the vessels were likely smashed during the ceremonial burial of feasting remnants.

Some fine-ware (and sometimes medium-ware) containers show evidence of foreign origin (Guayas, Tolita, Cajamarca, and Recuay). Similarities with Virú Valley ceramic types are not limited to Castillo Modeled and (to a lesser extent) Castillo Incised. Similarities are also found with Gallinazo Negative, Carmelo Negative, Sarraque Cream, and Castillo Plain. Negative decoration sometimes occurs on ceramics with otherwise Mochica characteristics, hinting at northern Ecuadorian and highland (Recuay) origins.

Mochica wares are largely associated with monumental or residential architecture, but they do not follow the "classic" style pattern known from the Moche and Chicama Valleys. Although some pieces of Mochica I vessel fragments were found in the excavations, these seem to characterize other types of contexts (probably burials). As such, contexts are not yet known from controlled excavations and the associated material remains to be defined. A chronological position of the VTC1, however, is probable (Kaulicke 1991:Figs. 12–22; 1994:Figs. 10.9–10.16; 2000:Figs. III.7–III.14).

During post-Formative times, the Vicús occupation of the Piura Valley extended from the open north to the forested south (or the western margin of the Piura River), apparently thanks to a technology that enabled the felling of the dense *algarrobo* forests (creating open areas and affording construction material). Thus, a small but expanding center was established between Cerros Vicús and Loma Negra during the VTA and VTB (about A.D. 0–300). In the VTB, a large number of tapia platforms were built, sometimes forming the base for later monumental structures.

The presence of specialized workshops for the production of metal objects, pottery, and textiles in contexts related to monumental and non-monumental architecture suggests social differentiation and the presence of elites. This does not mean that the earlier periods and phases were those of egalitarian societies. In fact, architectural evidence from Ñañañique (Middle to Late Formative) and Chulucanas (Guffroy 1994) points to the opposite. The entire area was affected by one or more El Niño-Southern Oscillation (ENSO) events. Afterward, a fundamental reorganization of the constructed space took place. The complex

grew in dimension, and monumental architecture was built with adobes instead of tapia.

The main structures of VTC are orientated toward the lowest part of Cerros Vicús and Loma Negra. The huge Yécala cemetery, which features a number of mounds, forms the center of this built landscape. While few of the burials were excavated in a controlled way, both Vicús and Mochica styles were present. Thus, it seems that this landscape was sacred, accepted as such by people living and being buried there, but also by people from outside of the Vicús pocket.

In the adjacent highlands, evidence of Mochica and Vicús elements are scarce. The famous (but unfortunately poorly known) Callingará site near Frias could have been a port of trade for the Tolita people. To the north, near Ayabaca, Mario Polia (1995) excavated burial contexts with relatively large amounts of Mochica and Vicús pieces (imported or imitated) in an otherwise completely different cultural setting, a phenomenon that could be understood as processes of acculturation at the elite level.

Finally, the site of Chusís in the lower Piura Valley is a small urban settlement with cemeteries to the east and west of the square city wall. Here, some individuals stood out as a result of their association with Mochica-style, Sechura, and Vicús ceramics, as well as with metal objects. All of the foregoing examples date to the VTC phase, most of them pertaining to the VTC2.

THE LAMBAYEQUE VALLEY

In the Lambayeque Valley, information is available for Huaca La Merced and Sipán. The first was presented during the roundtable in Trujillo by its excavator, Adriana Maguiña, who unfortunately could not deliver her paper for publication. Thus, information is limited to the often-cited paper (Shimada and Maguiña 1994) critiqued by some of the authors of this volume. In general, the architecture and associated ceramics show many parallels with the Vicús area, although the presentation does not allow readers to form a clear idea of the sequence, as it is often compared to material from other sites in the valley (with little stratigraphically controlled data). In any case, it seems that most of the material from Huaca La Merced basically corresponds to the VTC1 and VTC2, with some possible antecedents of the VTB.

The evidence from Sipán is different because all contexts are related to burials, offerings, and other activities connected with ancestor worship. Most importantly, the site consists of a sequence of six overlying architectural structures and associated burial chambers with complex contents and repositories that allow detailed description and comparison (Kaulicke 2000:146–161)—even though the detailed catalogues for each burial are still unavailable. In general, however, differences in metal objects and ceramics suggest a close relation among tomb 1, tomb 2, and the "looted tomb"—the latter featuring vessels produced with the same molds as for those found in tomb 1.

A large number of simple Gallinazo-like vessels date from this phase (Alva 1994:Plates 294, 295). Tomb 2 also seems to have many undecorated jars (and perhaps other vessels) with Gallinazo-like decoration, but these materials remain unpublished. Differing forms and decoration make comparison with the Larco Hoyle phases difficult, but substantial evidence confirms a basic coevality with Mochica IV or the VTC2. Tomb 3 (the "Old Lord") shows a rather uncommon ceramic set, with few traits in common with the usual pottery from Sipán. However, metal objects here are similar to those from other graves. A comparison between the metal objects from Sipán and Loma Negra also hints at tomb 3's coevality with the VTC1 and VTC2, with more pieces related to the VTC2.

We seem to lack evidence on phases earlier than those related to Mochica-like styles in the Lambayeque Valley (the same is true for the Jequetepeque Valley to the south). This is unfortunate because styles such as Gallinazo, Salinar, and perhaps even Mochica probably appeared at this time. Formative styles also could have survived much later than the conventional date of 200 B.C., a phenomenon I call Epi-Formative. On the positive side, it becomes clear that simple ceramics (including those classified as Gallinazo) are common in elite burials in valleys between Piura and Jequetepeque.

This situation also obliges us to consider the presence of various Mochica styles in these val-

leys: the only fine ware classified as Mochica I is believed to have come from "rich" burials, but most of this material comes from uncontrolled contexts. Therefore, its presence in "poorer" funerary contexts is not unexpected. Moreover, it should be noted that sometimes the "pureness" of Mochica style is related to materials other than ceramics. In Loma Negra, metal objects of Mochica style seem to be associated with vessels whose style is at best "Mochicoid," whereas at Pacatnamú textiles are more "Mochica" than the associated ceramic vessels.

CHICAMA, MOCHE, AND THE SOUTHERN VALLEYS

The Chicama and Moche Valleys share much of their material culture, but a lack of systematic correlation obscures the chronological panorama. Two sequences of monumental architecture in the Chicama Valley (Mocollope and Huaca Cao Viejo) reflect different patterns—one considered basically Gallinazo and pre-Mochica (Mocollope), and the other Mochica (with some Gallinazo elements). Although Huaca Cao Viejo shows evidence for practically all of Larco Hoyle's phases (I to IV), their occurrence does not seem to follow the conventional order. Only buildings A through E are defined by contexts and architectural characteristics, including their murals.

Buildings A through C are closely related and are associated with Mochica IV ceramics. However, Mochica I pottery seems to be present in contexts of buildings C and D, whereas the lower buildings are scarcely known. This lack of information does not exclude the possibility that earlier Gallinazo-style ceramics could be more common in (or even exclusive to) the earlier architectural phases, and thus comparable to the situation at Mocollope. Attarian (see Chapter 5) presents some early radiocarbon dates for Mocollope that predate those from Huaca Cao Viejo considerably. The presence of tapia constructions would compare to the VTB in Piura, whereas the sequence at Huaca Cao Viejo should be basically coeval with the Sipán sequence (the VTC1 and VTC2).

At Huacas de Moche, the Huaca de la Luna sequence (buildings A through F) correlates well with Huaca Cao Viejo. A Mochica IV presence is neatly limited to the latter part of the sequence, whereas pre-Mochica evidence is present but poorly associated with the earlier construction phases (the same seems to be true for the urban zone). The large number of burials is not analyzed in a way that offers the reader a clear chronological sequence, and the treatment of Gallinazo elements is too general to be of much chronological use. Finally, the 900 or so burials from Cerro Oreja (most of which are attributed to Gallinazo) remain unpublished. The importance of Cerro Arena, a large Salinar urban site in the same area, seems to be almost forgotten.

I will close this discussion by highlighting a problem: the fact that archaeologists have tended to use early chronological sequences uncritically, without recognizing that they were defined according to (sometimes) outdated analytical procedures. For example, the Virú Valley Project's chronological chart (produced during the 1940s) is still considered useful by some scholars (Wilson 1988).

This reflects a certain disdain for chronology or an incapacity to produce local sequences in order to prove or reject older proposals based on equivocal evidence. Instead of reanalyzing Bennett's materials from the Gallinazo Group or other related sites, it would be more useful to excavate there again with the benefit of better excavation, documentation, and dating techniques and material analyses. The "Gallinazo problem" must not be treated in isolation but assessed with all Mochica and non-Mochica coeval and immediately earlier evidence from the valley.

DISCUSSION

To sum up this part, it should be clear by now that clear-cut separations of stereotype styles (Mochica) and "nonstyles" ("domestic" Gallinazo) are not confirmed by contextual data. The Mochica style(s) should be envisaged as a multitude of fine and not-so-fine vessels, with different distribution patterns—even in the same valley. This diversification alone does not encourage large-scale conquest theories. By concentrating on contexts and architectural sequences, the entire area in question can be divided into basically three phases.

- *First century B.C. to end of second century A.D.* This is practically an unknown phase in many valleys of the Peruvian north coast. It is defined by a number of cultures (the total of shared materiality) on a diversified Formative background, with clear evidence of social complexity. Therefore, the ethnogenesis (see Chapter 5) of Gallinazo, Salinar, and highland societies (Layzón, Huaraz) should be defined on the basis of material evidence from this phase. The Vicús area is of particular importance for the definition of Gallinazo, as many of the constituent elements of the Vicús culture (architecture, burial practices, and fine and coarse wares) were shared with the Virú area during the VTA and VTB.

- *Beginning of third to middle of fourth century A.D.* This phase is better defined by a series of sites with monumental building sequences (usually using adobes differentiated by form and size) and architectural forms (Nima, Huaca La Merced, Sipán, Huaca Cao Viejo, Mocollope, Huaca de la Luna, Gallinazo Group, and so forth). Associated are the early manifestations of the Mochica culture. Although Mochica I–style ceramics are the most spectacular components, other manifestations are also present. Noteworthy is the fact that although Gallinazo Negative ceramics were found in only a few contexts outside Virú, in the Vicús area, they are conspicuous.

- *The latter part of these sequences is better defined and seems to be limited to about a century (mid-fourth to mid-fifth century A.D.).* In Vicús, it represents a cultural climax. The same seems to be true for other valleys. The Gallinazo culture in its ceramic variants still exists, but perhaps somewhat weakened, as is the case with some of the Mochica styles in several valleys. Hybridization seems to occur frequently in this phase, along with imported wares. This still rather crude chronological framework must, of course, be refined by better definitions of the building sequences.

If we come back to the role of ceramics, it seems that their distributions often correspond to feasting events in monumental architectural spaces or to burial contexts. If we envisage the constructed space as a place for interacting individuals, ceramics are only part of the material that was handled in such contexts. They are entangled in actions related to production, consumption, negotiations, and discard (ritualized or not). Different people handle different objects, and value them in different ways.

The production and circulation of liquids seem to have been especially important on the north coast, so that sets of pots of different forms were likely involved in this chain of activities carried out in different places by different persons. Often these activities seem to have depended on the necessities of clients who promoted the production of ceramics and other items. Artisans who depended on these clients lived and worked near the more "elite" space, as is evidenced by archaeological work in the upper Piura and in other regions.

Another issue worth mentioning here has to do with *identity* and *ethnicity*, as some of the authors in this volume use these concepts. These terms should be applied according to their inherent complexity. In the first place, identity is aimed at "the other" and is often visualized via concepts of corporeality. Therefore, textiles, metal, semiprecious stone, and shell paraphernalia are better transmitters of identity than ceramics. This is evident in "rich" burial contexts (Sipán), where ceramics are not placed near the dead but form a type of "social background" (made up of musicians, attendants, warriors, and so forth) inside and outside the burial chamber (repository). In the words of John Janusek:

> Identities are forged in particular social conditions and historical realities. . . . Each type of identification will correspond with a different range of people, memories, practices, places, symbols, and materials. . . . [A]ny complex society consists of social groups that maintain corporate functions, or shared political, economic, and ritual activities. (Janusek 2004:17)

This, of course, includes identifications at the household level (including domestic vessels) with a range of memories, and so forth. Whereas *iden-*

tity is a term related to social personae and their immediate social setting, *ethnicity* is a less precise notion related to a communal cohesion as a somewhat forced, artificial, and stereotyped unity seen from the outside. In this sense, it does not seem to me to be a particularly useful term as a synonym for *ceramic style*.

All in all, the definition of Gallinazo (strictly limited to a usually incomplete ceramic repertoire) cannot be the solution to the existence or nonexistence of societies or polities and their materiality. Face-neck mold-made jars in the Mochica style are "identity markers" in much the same way Gallinazo handmade face-neck jars are (or Recuay and Salinar vessels with these characteristics). Finer or coarser versions do not affect this message. Even the simplified facial features of the Gallinazo coarse ware do seem to change in time, and are not domestic wares in the sense some of the authors in this volume would like to propose.

On the other hand, incomplete information about the distribution, size, internal organization, economic specialization, and long-distance relations between centers within valley oases, whole valleys, or interconnected valleys turn political interpretations into a most hazardous enterprise. Political power is not directly expressed in impressive art styles boasting violence, such as in the Mochica styles. As I pointed out elsewhere:

> [The] Mochica world should be envisaged as a complex and dynamic history in a changing interaction sphere wherein the actors constantly mold and transform their identities and ethnicities as well as their ideology and power relations. These interactions involve other non-Mochica political systems, usually highland polities concentrated in the critical bottle-necks of the upper river valleys, which affected the valley polities in differing but still poorly understood ways. (Kaulicke 2006:91)

Perhaps we should try to envisage this connected world from a Gallinazo perspective. I am quite aware of some rather critical comments contained in this chapter. These were due to my concern with an approach restricted to only one group of material evidence (the coarse ware known as Castillo Modeled and Incised), which does not take into account the richness of the related non-Mochica materiality documented at particular sites or in specific valleys.

In the hundreds of years of its existence, this materiality changed in different ways, originating and disappearing through a variety of circumstances. By "Gallinazo perspective," I mean the development of new, more complex approaches to this material evidence. It should be rewarding to accept the challenge. Authors such as Chapdelaine, Pimentel, and Gamboa see this necessity in concentrating on the particular problems posed by the Gallinazo de Santa. All in all, these constructive case studies had to be published before scholars could draw a more complex and inclusive picture, taking into account the entire extension of this phenomenon.

ACKNOWLEDGMENTS

I would like to thank Jean-François Millaire for his invitation to the roundtable and for his enthusiasm in facing a problem that seems to have been ignored until now.

NOTE

1 I prefer the term "Mochica" as it was coined by Julio Tello and Rafael Larco Hoyle—before Wendell Bennett (1939:124–147) used the term "Moche"— in a sense different from how it is currently used (Kaulicke 1992:857–858).

REFERENCES

Alva, Walter
1994 *Sipán*. Lima: Cervecería Backus & Johnston.
Bats, Jean-Christophe
1991 Ruptures et continuité culturelles dans la basse vallée du Yapatera: Approche typologique formalisée d'un matériel céramique récolté en prospection. *Bulletin de l'Institut Français d'Études Andines* 20(2): 349–380.
Bennett, Wendell C.
1939 *Archaeology of the North Coast of Peru: An Account of Exploration and Excavation in Viru and Lambayeque Valleys*. Anthropological Papers of the American Museum of Natural History Vol. 37, Pt. 1. New York: The American Museum of Natural History.
Donnan, Christopher B.
2003 Tumbas con entierros en miniatura: Un nuevo tipo funerario moche. In *Moche: Hacia el final del milenio*, Santiago Uceda and Elías Mujica (eds.), vol. 1, pp. 43–78. Lima: Universidad Nacional de Trujillo and Fondo Editorial, Pontificia Universidad Católica del Perú.
2007 *Moche Tombs at Dos Cabezas*. Los Angeles: Cotsen Institute of Archaeology at UCLA.
Donnan, Christopher B., and Carol J. Mackey
1978 *Ancient Burial Patterns of the Moche Valley, Peru*. Austin: University of Texas Press.
Guffroy, Jean (editor)
1994 *Cerro Ñañañique: Un établissement monumental de la période formative, en limite de désert (Haut Piura, Pérou)*. Paris: ORSTOM.
Janusek, John W.
2004 *Identity and Power in the Ancient Andes: Tiwanaku Cities through Time*. New York: Routledge.
Kaulicke, Peter
1991 El período intermedio temprano en el Alto Piura: Avances del proyecto arqueológico "Alto Piura" (1987–1990). *Bulletin de l'Institut Français d'Études Andines* 20(2):381–422.
1992 Moche, Vicús Moche y el Mochica Temprano. *Bulletin de l'Institut Français d'Études Andines* 21(3):853–903.
1993 Evidencias paleoclimáticas en asentamientos del alto Piura durante el período Intermedio Temprano. *Bulletin de l'Institut Français d'Études Andines* 22(1):283–311.
1994 La presencia mochica en el Alto Piura: Problemática y propuestas. In *Moche: Propuestas y perspectivas*, Santiago Uceda and Elías Mujica (eds.), pp. 327–358. Travaux de l'Institut Français d'Études Andines 79. Lima: Universidad Nacional de La Libertad and Instituto Francés de Estudios Andinos.
1998 Algunas reflexiones sobre la cronología mochica. In *50 años de estudios americanistas en la Universidad de Bonn: Nuevas contribuciones a la arqueología, etnohistoria, etnolingüística y etnográfica de las Americas*, Sabine Dedenbach-Salazar Sáenz (ed.), pp. 105–128. Estudios Americanistas de Bonn 30. Markt Schwaben, Germany: A. Saurwein.
2000 *Memoria y muerte en el Perú antiguo*. Lima: Fondo Editorial, Pontificia Universidad Católica del Perú.
2006 The Vicús-Mochica Relationship. In *Andean Archaeology III: North and South*, William H. Isbell and Helaine Silverman (eds.), pp. 85–111. New York: Springer.
Larco Hoyle, Rafael
1945 *La cultura virú*. Buenos Aires: Sociedad Geográfica Americana.
Moseley, Michael E., and Kent C. Day (editors)
1982 *Chan Chan: Andean Desert City*. Albuquerque: University of New Mexico Press.

Polia, Mario
    1995 *Los Guayacundos Ayahuacas: Una arqueología desconocida*. Lima: Concejo Municipal de Ayabaca and Fondo Editorial, Pontificia Universidad Católica del Perú.

Shimada, Izumi, and Adriana Maguiña
    1994 Nueva visión sobre la cultura gallinazo y su relación con la cultura moche. In *Moche: Propuestas y perspectivas*, Santiago Uceda and Elías Mujica (eds.), pp. 31–58. Travaux de l'Institut Français d'Études Andines 79. Lima: Universidad Nacional de La Libertad and Instituto Francés de Estudios Andinos.

Strong, William D., Clifford Evans, and Rose Lilien
    1952 Appendix I: Description of Pottery Types. In *Cultural Stratigraphy in the Virú Valley, Northern Peru: The Formative and Florescent Epochs*, William D. Strong and Clifford Evans (eds.), pp. 253–351. New York: Columbia University Press.

Wilson, David J.
    1988 *Prehispanic Settlement Patterns in the Lower Santa Valley, Peru: A Regional Perspective on the Origins and Development of Complex North Coast Society*. Washington, D.C.: Smithsonian Institution Press.

INDEX